HAYNES MAX POWER VW

golf

The definitive guide to **modifying**
by **Bob Jex**

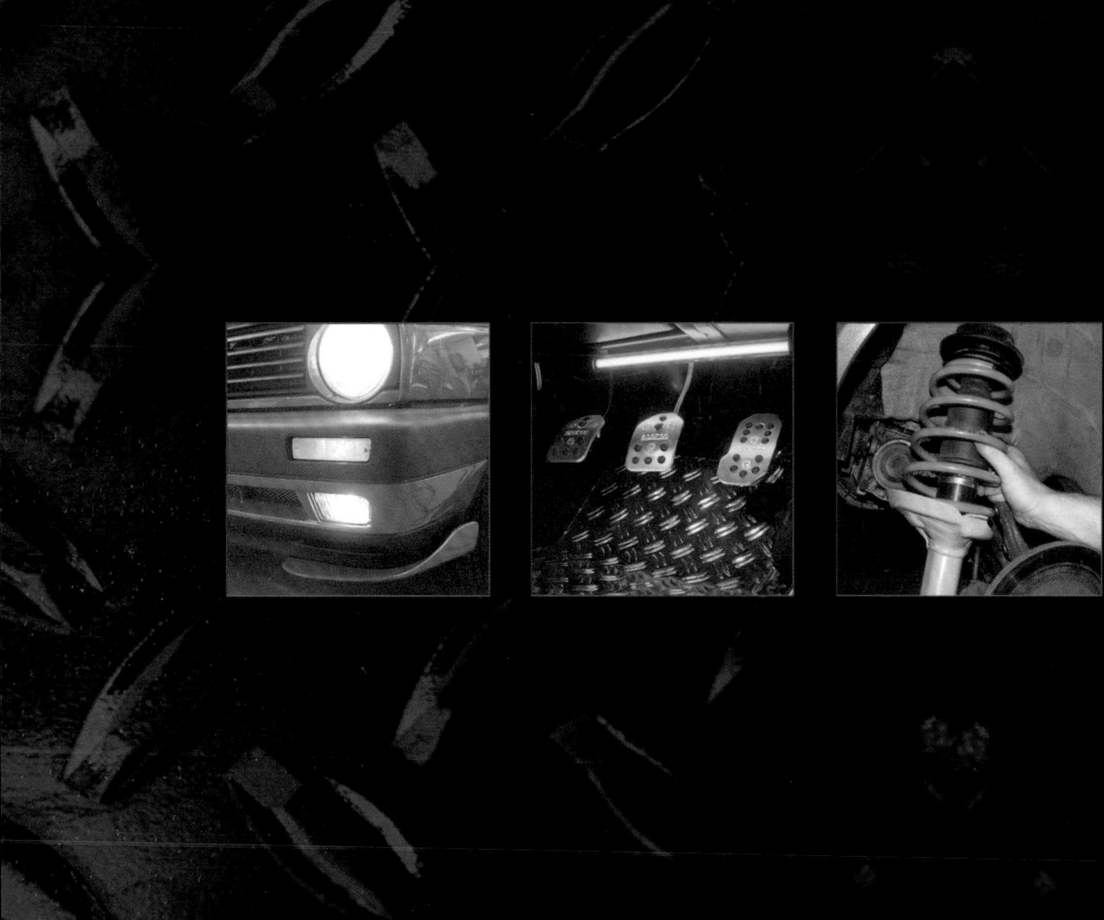

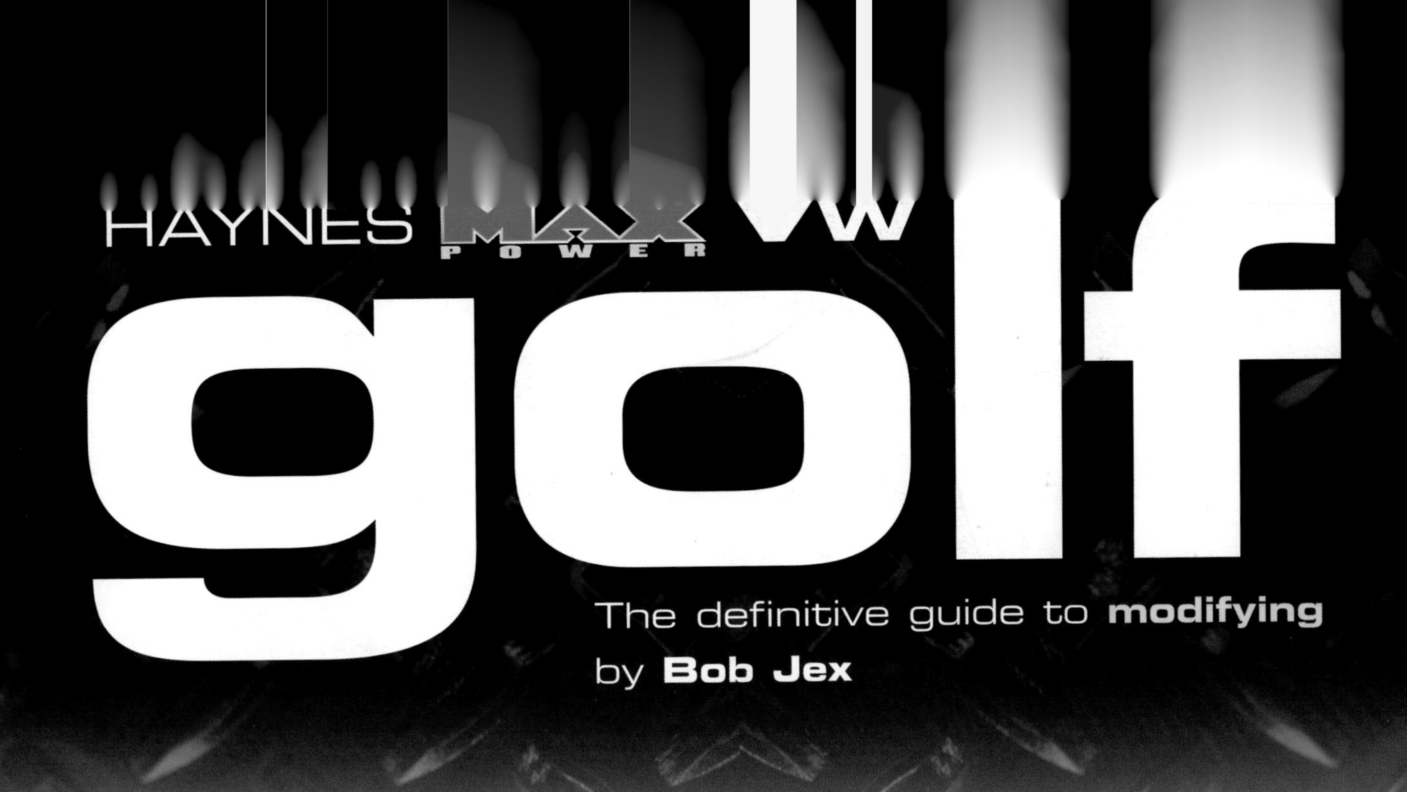

golf

The definitive guide to **modifying**

by **Bob Jex**

Haynes Publishing

© Haynes Publishing 2004

All rights reserved. No part of this book may be reproduced or transmitted in any form or by any means, electronic or mechanical, including photocopying, recording or by any information storage or retrieval system, without permission in writing from the copyright holder.

ISBN 1 84425 185 3

Printed by **J H Haynes & Co Ltd,**
Sparkford, Yeovil, Somerset BA22 7JJ, England.

First published in 2002
Reprinted in 2002
Updated and reprinted in 2004

Tel: 01963 442030 Fax: 01963 440001
Int. tel: +44 1963 442030 Fax: +44 1963 440001
E-mail: sales@haynes.co.uk
Web site: www.haynes.co.uk

Haynes North America, Inc
861 Lawrence Drive, Newbury Park, California 91320, USA

Editions Haynes
4, Rue de l'Abreuvoir
92415 COURBEVOIE CEDEX, France

Haynes Publishing Nordiska AB
Box 1504, 751 45 UPPSALA, Sweden

(3907–9AH3)

It **wasn't my idea** guv'nor!

1 Advice on safety procedures and precautions is contained throughout this manual, and more specifically on page 194. You are strongly recommended to note these comments, and to pay close attention to any instructions that may be given by the parts supplier.

2 J H Haynes recommends that vehicle customisation should only be undertaken by individuals with experience of vehicle mechanics; if you are unsure as to how to go about the customisation, advice should be sought from a competent and experienced individual. Any queries regarding customisation should be addressed to the product manufacturer concerned, and not to J H Haynes, nor the vehicle manufacturer.

3 The instructions in this manual are followed at the risk of the reader who remains fully and solely responsible for the safety, roadworthiness and legality of his/her vehicle. Thus J H Haynes are giving only non-specific advice in this respect.

4 When modifying a car it is important to bear in mind the legal responsibilities placed on the owners, driver and modifiers of cars, including, but not limited to, the Road Traffic Act 1988. IN PARTICULAR, IT IS AN OFFENCE TO DRIVE ON A PUBLIC ROAD A VEHICLE WHICH IS NOT INSURED OR WHICH DOES NOT COMPLY WITH THE CONSTRUCTION AND USE REGULATIONS, OR WHICH IS DANGEROUS AND MAY CAUSE INJURY TO ANY PERSON, OR WHICH DOES NOT HOLD A CURRENT MOT CERTIFICATE OR DISPLAY A VALID TAX DISC.

5 The safety of any alteration and its compliance with construction and use regulations should be checked before a modified vehicle is sold as it may be an offence to sell a vehicle which is not roadworthy.

6 Any advice provided is correct to the best of our knowledge at the time of publication, but the reader should pay particular attention to any changes of specification to the vehicles, or parts, which can occur without notice.

7 Alterations to vehicles should be disclosed to insurers and licensing authorities, and legal advice taken from the police, vehicle testing centres, or appropriate regulatory bodies.

8 The vehicle has been chosen for this project as it is one of those most widely customised by its owners, and readers should not assume that the vehicle manufacturers have given their approval to the modifications.

9 Neither J H Haynes nor the manufacturers give any warranty as to the safety of a vehicle after alterations, such as those contained in this book, have been made. J H Haynes will not accept liability for any economic loss, damage to property or death and personal injury arising from use of this manual other than in respect of injury or death resulting directly from J H Haynes' negligence.

Contents

Haynes Max Power

Buyer's guide

Insurance & The Law

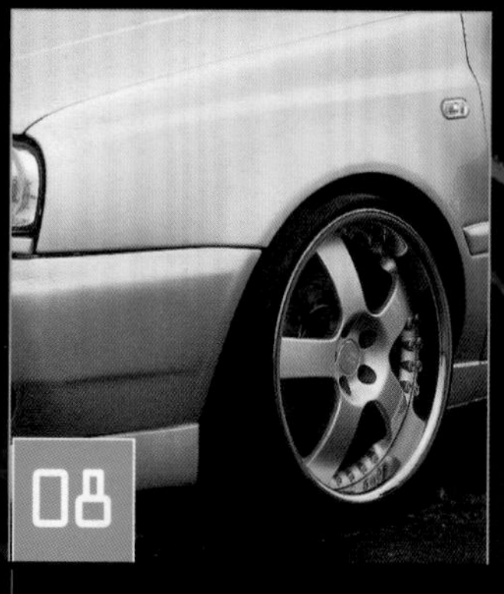

Suspension

Brakes

Interiors

Security

04

Body styling

05

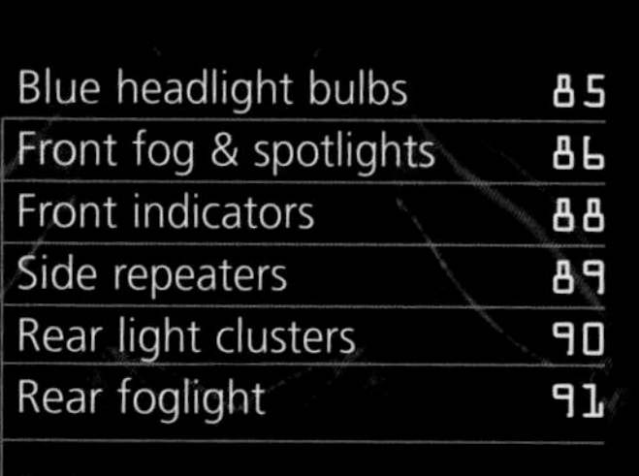

Lights & bulbs

06

Wheels & tyres

07

11

ICE

12

Engines

13

Exhausts

14

Reference

Haynes Max Power

What's that then?

Haynes Publishing have, for the last forty years, been helping people keep their cars on the roads in countries all over the world by publishing maintenance manuals. Chances are you've either got one of them yourself or you know somebody who has.

"Lights & bulbs" includes fitting high-power blue headlight bulbs, coloured rear light clusters.

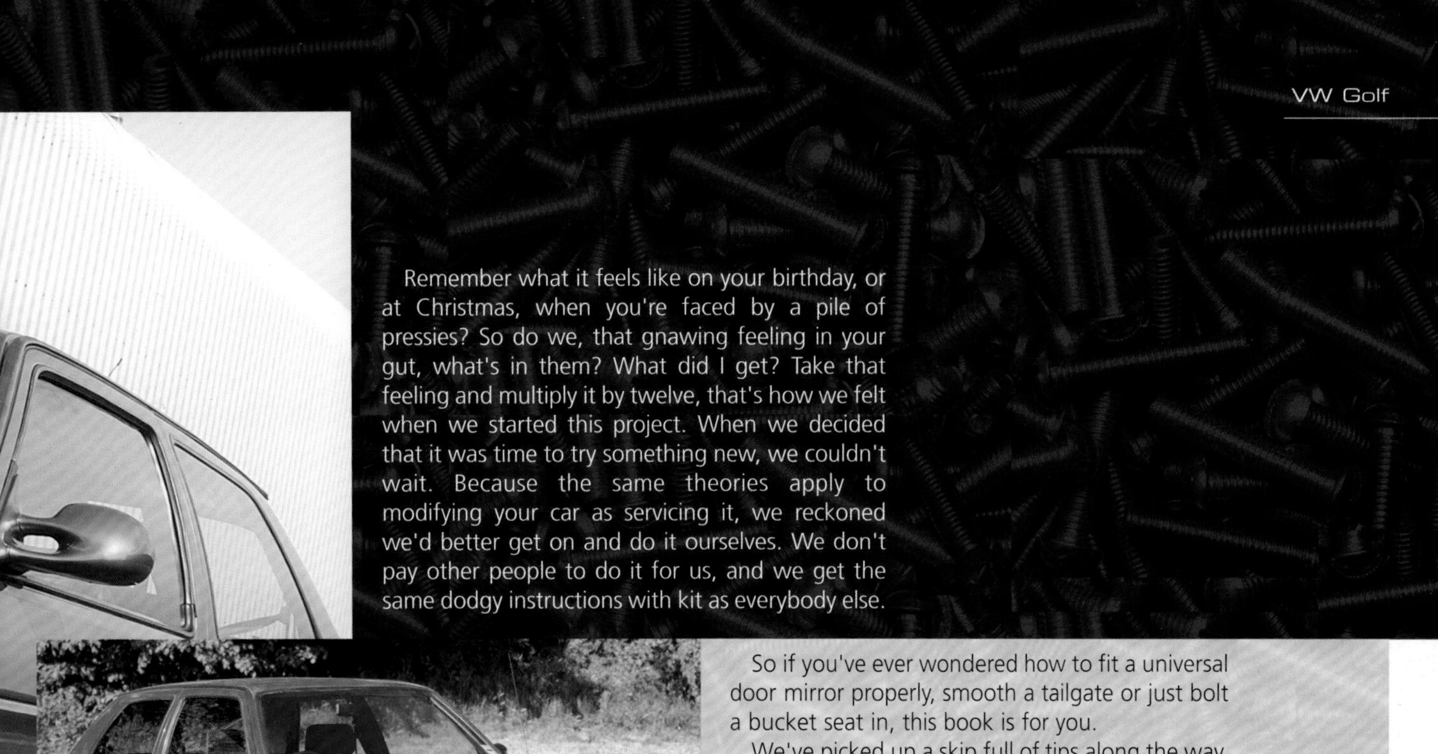

Remember what it feels like on your birthday, or at Christmas, when you're faced by a pile of pressies? So do we, that gnawing feeling in your gut, what's in them? What did I get? Take that feeling and multiply it by twelve, that's how we felt when we started this project. When we decided that it was time to try something new, we couldn't wait. Because the same theories apply to modifying your car as servicing it, we reckoned we'd better get on and do it ourselves. We don't pay other people to do it for us, and we get the same dodgy instructions with kit as everybody else.

Before

After

So if you've ever wondered how to fit a universal door mirror properly, smooth a tailgate or just bolt a bucket seat in, this book is for you.

We've picked up a skip full of tips along the way, and they're all here for you to use. We haven't tried to set any trends, but we've covered every possible process we think you'll need. So where we've tinted a side window, the same rules apply to a rear one, job done.

If you look in the magazines and want some of that, join us, 'cos so do we, and we'll show you how to get it.

We bought a J-plate Mk 2, 1.6 litre Driver, and we've done all the work to that. So whether you've got a GTI or a base CL, we've designed and built this book for us all. So what are you waiting for? Get modding...

"Wheels & tyres" takes a detailed look at all the options.

"Body styling" shows you how to fit universal mirrors to full body kits.

"Interiors" includes seats, painting trim, gear knobs and loads more.

Buyer's guide

Don't buy a dog

The Golf is a top choice if you're looking to modify and there are hundreds of potential bargains out there. The Mk 2 Golf (1984 to 1992) has been around for some time, so you've got to be careful when buying one. The Mk 3 models (1992 to 1998) won't be suffering so much from old age, but obviously they'll also cost more.

The Golf in general has very few weak points, and will only suffer any major problems if it's been abused, or servicing has been neglected. A sign of neglect is a tatty interior - frayed seats, ripped gear lever gaiters and grotty carpets.

At this level, it's far better to buy privately, as long as you know what you're doing - dealers often charge over the odds, but all you'll get for the extra money is a full valet and some degree of comeback if the car's a dog. Whenever you go to look at a car make sure you take someone who 'knows about cars' along with you. If you don't you're asking for trouble.

Is there any service history? If so, this is good, but study the service book carefully - maybe the car's had a history of problems, or maybe it's just had some nice expensive new parts fitted (like a clutch, starter motor or alternator, for instance).

Check the chassis number (VIN number) and engine number on the registration document and on the car. Any sign of welding near one of these numbers should be treated with suspicion. The VIN number appears on a plate at the front or side of the engine

compartment; is there any sign that this plate has been tampered with? The chassis number on this plate should match the one stamped into the rear of the engine compartment (sometimes under a plastic cover) - if the numbers don't match, or if they're not in a straight line, leave the car well alone.

The engine number is stamped into the front face of the engine. It's difficult to spot, but keep looking until you find it - if the number's been ground off, or if there's anything suspicious about it, you could be buying trouble.

A known Golf strong point is that they resist rust well, but that doesn't mean they're immune. Check around the blanking grommet for the "spare" wiper arm, and the inside rear edges of the rear doors on 5-door models. At the rear, check for rust in the vertical seams below the rear lights, which might indicate that the rear panel has been replaced due to an accident. Underneath, the front subframe can rust at the mounting points, and there may be rust at the base of the bulkhead. The only other common area for rust is the tailgate - check especially around the holes for the rear, number plate lights, and (with the tailgate open) at the top round the wiring harness grommets.

Models after August 1985 (C reg onwards) have engines with hydraulic tappets - on these, the engines may rattle slightly when they're first started from cold. Any rattling from earlier engines either means the valve clearances need adjusting, or that the camshaft is worn.

Early Golfs can suffer from worn valve guides, and all models may suffer from hardened/perished valve stem oil seals, giving rise to blue oil smoke from the exhaust. At start-up from cold, check the exhaust for blue smoke; on the test-drive, try lifting off the throttle for a few seconds, then accelerate while watching in the mirror for smoke.

On models with a five-speed gearbox get the car up to 60 mph in 5th, cruise along, then accelerate sharply and immediately lift off the throttle. Repeat this several times - what you're checking for is whether the car jumps out of fifth gear, which indicates that the gearbox is badly worn. On Driver models and GTIs, check that second gear engages cleanly - repeated 'crunched' shifts indicates that the synchros have worn, suggesting the car's had a hard life.

Some Mk 2 GTI models have rear disc brakes, and the handbrake on these can give trouble - check whether there is excess free travel (like two or three inches) felt in the handbrake lever before resistance is felt, as this indicates that the operating lever on the rear calipers may have seized.

On 3-door models, check the seat-tipping knobs on the front seats actually work (operating cables are known to fail). The trip computers on GTIs can fail, and often do so together with the rev counter - the parts to fix this can be expensive.

Whatever you buy, make sure it's got a long MoT (or that you know what it will cost to get one). For added peace of mind, an HPI check will tell you if the car has outstanding finance, has been reported stolen or has been an insurance write-off. Could be money well spent.

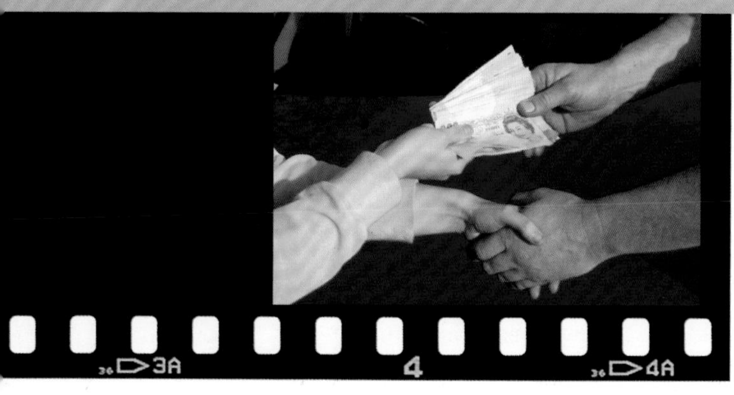

The Mk2 Golf is a top choice if you're looking to modify and there are hundreds of potential bargains out there.

what's what?

Basic 1.05, 1.3 and **1.6 litre** models

The smaller engines are particularly unimpressive, performance-wise, and there ain't much scope for easy improvement - the only argument for one of these is the insurance (group 6/7), which is a good two or three groups lower than a 1.6, and as much as eight groups lower than a GTI.

Mechanically, the smaller engines (1.05 and 1.3 litre) are seen as being less well able to take large mileages than the bigger-block units, with oil leaks, head gasket problems and general internal wear all being reported over 100,000 miles - evidence of proper servicing makes all the difference here. The auto-choke Pierburg carburettor can become troublesome, and is often replaced with a manual-choke Weber unit.

If the engine oil pressure warning light comes on at idle, this is not a good sign - one reason for this is the oil pick-up strainer in the sump having become partially blocked. If this is the only reason for it, it's easy enough to sort, but what damage has been done to the engine in the meantime?

1.6 and **1.8 litre Driver** models

Decent performance, GTI suspension and most of the interior/exterior GTI features, without GTI insurance premiums (hopefully) - in group 11/12, it's three groups lower than a typical GTI. Has it been treated well, or driven in GTI-style? Decent equipment level makes it a better starting point for a trick car than a base model, and it'll be more fun to drive around in while you're saving up for all the changes you want to make.

1.8 litre 8- and **16-valve GTI** models

The early Mk2 GTIs have come right down in price, but that's because they're more than 15 years old. If you want a GTI, remember that there's even more to look out for than on a lesser model.

More so than any other model, check for signs of accident damage, especially at the front end. Ask if it's ever been in a shunt - if the seller says no, but there's paint overspray under the bonnet, what's going on? Also check for paint overspray on the window rubbers, light units and bumpers/trim. With the bonnet open, check that the headlight rear shells are the same colour - new-looking ones merit an explanation from the seller.

You will see later Mk 2 GTI models described as being "big bumper" versions - about the only styling change worth mentioning happened in August 1989, when the (rather puny-looking) old bumpers were replaced with large body-coloured bumpers, front and rear. These later models are more desirable, but if you find a straight earlier example without the big bumpers, one of the German car parts specialists can supply them for sensible money, and we show you how to fit 'em.

Model history

The Mk1 Golf was the original hot hatch, but by the time the Mk4 came along it had turned into a bit of a slug. Luckily for us the Mk2 looked more like the Mk1 - than the Mk3.

February 1984 Mk 2 Golf introduced. Choice of 1.05, 1.3, 1.6 and 1.8 litre petrol engines, and 1.6 litre diesel.
January 1985 5-door GTI introduced. All GTIs have twin-pipe rear exhaust, striped seats, sunroof.
June 1985 Golf 1.3 Match introduced. All-white exterior, white carpets(!) and twin-headlight grille.
September 1985 (C reg) 1.3 litre models now have electronic ignition.
October 1986 (D reg) GTI 16V models now officially imported to UK. 139 bhp 1.8 litre engine, central locking, electric windows, sunroof.
April 1987 Golf Driver models first available, as a special edition. 1.6 litre engine, twin-headlight grille, wheelarch spats and lowered (GTI) suspension. Uprated interior trim and GTI steering wheel.

Rallyes and late GTIs are the most popular. If you can find a low mileage, well looked after one with FSH, buy it...

August 1987 (E reg) 5-bar radiator grille, right-hand-drive windscreen wipers, one-piece front windows with door mirrors moved to front. GTI 8-valve models switch from K-Jetronic fuel injection to electronic "Digifant" system.
October 1988 (F reg) Synchro four-wheel-drive model introduced. 1.8 litre carb engine, 5-door only.
April 1989 Golf Driver models re-launched in 3- and 5-door form.
July 1989 Rallye models officially imported. 5000 produced in Belgium for homologation. Left-hand-drive, 160 bhp 1763 cc G60 supercharged engine with catalyst, flared wheelarches, rectangular headlights, Synchro four-wheel-drive and ABS.
August 1989 (G reg) "Big bumpers" fitted to GL and GTI models (not Drivers). GTI 16V models gain BBS alloys, lose electric windows.
February 1990 (G reg) G60 models imported. A toned-down version of the original Rallye, the G60 was front-drive only, with a 1781 cc supercharged engine (still 160 bhp) and without the flared arches (bigger wheelarch extensions were fitted instead). Round headlights. Available in 3-door and 5-door form.
October 1990 (H reg) Driver models gain sunroof and central locking. GTI 8V models now have power steering (PAS) as standard, also tinted glass and central locking. GTI 16V regains electric windows.
February 1991 Golf Ryder 1.3 litre models introduced, with sunroof and twin-headlight grille. Driver models have rev counter, improved seats.
October 1991 (J reg) Driver models now have 1.8 litre carburettor engine; Ryder models have 1.6 litre engine. GTI 8V models now have BBS alloys, smoked rear lights, electric windows.
February 1992 (J reg) - Mk 3 Golf introduced. Choice of 1.4, 1.6, 1.8 , 2.0 GTI and 2.8 VR6 engines, or 1.9 Umvelt turbo-diesel. Larger and heavier than Mk 2, with fully-galvanised body for improved corrsion protection.

April 1992 (J reg) – Equipment improved on all models – tints and rev counter on most, GL and GTI gain electric windows and sunroof.
September 1993 (L reg) – 2.0 GTI 16-valve launched, with 150 bhp engine. 1.8 Driver added to range, similar to GTI but with 90 bhp 1.8 engine. 1.4 CL gains power steering.
January 1994 (L reg) – Cabriolet models launched, with 1.8 or 2.0 litre engines, twin headlights. Avantgarde has electric windows, alloys, electric hood.
March 1994 (L reg) – Estate models introduced. 1.9 TDi 90 bhp turbo-diesel engine also available.
December 1994 (M reg) – All models gain airbag, immobiliser. GTI models gain ABS, but GTI 16V loses standard sunroof. "Pink Floyd" Cabriolet special edition available.
June 1995 (M reg) – "Rolling Stones" (twin headlights, alloys, silver dials, CD player) and "Match" (alloys, CD player) special editions launched. New GTI "Colour Concept" limited editions introduced, with colour-coded leather interior and trim. VR6 "Highline" introduced with heated leather seats and walnut gear knob.
October 1995 (N reg) – 1.4 and 1.6 litre models gain multi-point injection, with small power increase.
May 1996 (N reg) – SE models added to range (alloys, tinted rear clusters, twin headlights, white dials). Equipment levels improved – L models gain central locking, CL models gain electric windows. "Anniversary" GTI special editions, to celebrate 20 years of the Golf GTI – red alloys, chequered flag design upholstery, red bumper stripes.
December 1996 (P reg) – 1.6 litre models gain 100 bhp engine (previously 75 bhp).
May 1998 (R reg) – Mk 4 Golf models introduced, replacing all Mk 3s apart from the Cabriolet.
June 1998 (R reg) – Cabriolet models have improved equipment levels. New "Colour Concept" limited edition Cabrio models introduced, with colour-coded leather interior and trim.

Performance figures

Mk 2 models	0-60 (mph)	Top speed (mph)
1.05	Pretty darn slow. Let's leave it at that.	
1.3 CL	15.1	93
1.6 diesel	20.9	88
1.6 petrol	11.1	102
1.8 Driver	10.1	108
1.8 GTI 8-valve (up to 1988)	8.4	118
1.8 GTI 8-valve (1988-on)	9.2	118
1.8 GTI 16-valve	7.5	129
Mk 3 models		
1.4	15.4	97
1.6	11.9	104
1.8	12.8	107
2.0 8-valve	9.5	119
2.0 16-valve	8.3	134
2.8 VR6	7.1	138
1.9 TDi	11.2	112

Insurance & The Law

Insurance - a necessary evil

The way the insurance companies work out premiums and assess risks is a mystery to most of us. In general, the smaller the engine you have in your Golf, the less you'll pay for insurance, so a Golf 1.3 CL should be less to insure than a GTI. However, different companies can give wildly different quotes so it's vital to shop around. Always ring as many brokers and get as many quotes as you possibly can. A few extra minutes spent on the phone once a year may result in an extra few hundred quid in your back pocket.

When ringing for quotes, watch your language. Arguing with the bloke/girl on the other end will always get you a higher quote. Also, don't say anything if you get put on hold. Some companies will put you on speaker – to see if you're trying to pull a fast one.

With modified cars, insurance becomes even more of a problem. By modifying a car, you're making it more of a target for thieves (yes, ok, I know you know this). The point is, the insurance companies know this too, and they don't want to be paying out for the car, plus all the money you've spent on it, should it go missing. There is a temptation 'not to tell the insurance' about the mods you've made. Let's deal with this right now. Our experience has been that, while it can be painful, honesty is best. If they find out (and if you have a claim, they may well come and inspect the car) they won't pay out a penny. And if you do make a claim, very few insurers pay out for the modifications, so you get paid out, but based on a standard car. There are many specialist insurers who are more friendly towards fully-loaded cars, but even they won't actually cover the cost of replacement goodies.

What type of cover?

Third Party only

The most basic cover you can get. Basically covers you for damage to other people's cars or property, and for personal injury claims. Virtually no cover for your own stuff, beyond what you get if you take the optional "legal protection" cover.

Third Party, Fire and Theft

As above, with cover for fire and theft, better, but not much better. This is really only cover in the event of a "total loss", if your car goes missing or goes up in smoke. Still no cover for your car if you stack it into a tree, or if someone breaks in and pinches your stereo.

Fully-comprehensive

In theory, covers you for any loss or damage. Will cover the cost of repairing or replacing your car regardless of whether it was your fault or not. With a fully-comp policy, you can "protect" your no-claims bonus for a small fee so you don't automatically lose those hard-earned years' worth of discount if you prang it.

All this extra cover costs more, but is often a better bet in the long run.

Ways to limit your premium

When you phone for a quote your fate is pretty much sealed, but there are a few things you can do to help lower the premium.

1 *Make yourself the only driver.* Pretty self-explanatory. The more people who drive your car, the greater the risk to the company. If you've built up 2 years' worth of no-claims, but your girlfriend/wife hasn't, putting her on your insurance will bump it up, due to her relative inexperience.

2 *Use a garage.* If you have access to a garage use it, insurers love a car to be locked away safe and sound at night.

3 *Fit an approved alarm or immobiliser.* In general, any alarm or immobiliser with a Thatcham rating should be recognised by any insurance company, but it pays to check before fitting. In some cases, the discounts offered are not that great any more - but an alarm still a nice way to get peace of mind.

4 *Build up your no-claims bonus.* You'll only do this by owning and insuring a car in your own name, and then not making any claims. Simple really. Each claim free year you have will aid lowering how much you pay out.

5 *Hang onto your no-claims bonus.* Obviously, the less you claim, the less your insurance will cost. If something happens to your car, don't be in too big a hurry to make a claim before you've thought it all through. How much will it cost to fix? How much is your excess? If you can afford not to claim, then don't do it.

6 *Avoid speed cameras and The Law.* Yes, okay, easier said than done! One SP30 isn't usually too bad, but much more and you'll pay for it, so go easy.

Insurance-friendly mods?

So - what do insurance companies like and dislike, as far as mods go? What do you need to declare, and what can you get away with?

Golden Rule Number One

If in doubt, declare everything. Insurance companies are legally entitled to dispute any claim if the car is found to be non-standard in any way.

Some mods will affect your insurance more than others and no two companies will have the same outlook. Your own circumstances will play a big part too.

Golden Rule Number Two

Before modifying the car, ring your insurers, and ask them how it will affect things

1 Body mods Even a tiny rear spoiler can be classed as a "bodykit" (yes, it's daft, but that's how it is). Anything which alters the exterior appearance should be declared. As long as the mods aren't too radical, the jump in premium should be fairly small. If anything at all.

2 Brakes Uprating standard sized discs, maybe with grooved or drilled discs, seldom affects the insurance, but some get a bit twitchy when you start fitting bigger discs and replacement calipers.

3 Engine mods "Mild" mods such as induction kits and exhausts don't often change premiums, but just the merest mention of "chipping" can make many companies load the premium, or even completely refuse to offer cover. With complete engine transplants, you'll be required to give an engineer's report on the mods before they'll grant cover.

4 Interior mods As with bodykits, unless you go absolutely mental it really shouldn't make a difference, but make sure you tell your insurers all the same.

5 Lights As they're safety-related, you'll probably get asked for lots of details, but as long as you've kept it sensible (and legal, as far as possible) you'll be fine.

6 Security Make sure you mention all security stuff - alarms, immobilisers (including mechanical devices), and locking wheel nuts. Don't tell them you've got a Cat 1 Clifford if your alarm really came from Argos, and don't tell them you garage the car at night if it's stuck out in the road, if they find out, you're on your own.

7 Suspension Average suspension drops of 30-40mm are fine, go much lower and they may charge you more.

8 Wheels The specialist insurers won't mind you having a nice set of alloys, but just about every other insurer will load the premium, sadly.

Your car? or your Dad's?

Don't pretend your Golf belongs to your Dad, and get him to insure it, with you as a named driver. Insurance companies are not stupid. They know that your Dad isn't likely to be running around in a modified car, and they treat any "named driver" application with great suspicion in these cases. This dubious practice also does you no favours in future years. All the time you're living the lie, you're not building up any no-claims bonus of your own.

And **finally**

Not telling the insurance company the whole truth gets tricky when you have to make a claim. If the insurance assessor comes around to check your bent/burnt/stolen-and-recovered "standard" Golf, and finds he's looking at a vehicle kitted out with mods, he's not going to turn a blind eye, and you're not going to get your claim paid.

One more thing - even if you think your car isn't worth a great deal, and you could stand not having the insurance pay out - be careful what you hit. If your insurance is declared void by your company, they won't pay out for the repairs to the other car you smacked. We'll say it again - without insurance cover, you'll have to pay. Probably for a long, long time. Think about it.

Big Brother in a Box

Speed cameras have to be one of the most unpopular things ever. We're talking worse than exams, dentists, alcohol-free beer, and the Budget. Does anyone actually like them? Well, the makers do - they should all be living it up on a beach in the Bahamas. The people making speed camera signs are obviously lovin' it. And the Chancellor? Nuff said.

Speed, of course, is fun. The sensation of speed is the main reason we enjoy driving, and it's one of the best ways to show off your motor. There's nothing like giving your ride a good caning, being pushed back in the seat, exhaust snarling, engine singing. Sounds like fun to me - so these things are really fun cameras, then?

Like it or not, we live in a world obsessed with limiting speed. Excess speed, we're told, causes accidents and costs lives. As most of us have realised by now, excess speed really means more money for the Government. What causes accidents is driving like a tw*t. But they don't have cameras for that.

Before we get ourselves in too much trouble, we have to admit the cameras might save lives in built-up areas with lots of peds, kids and old folk about. Driving like a hooligan in those situations probably should get you a slap on the wrist for 'endangering lives'. But at night, on a dead-straight road with no traffic? We think not.

Pay attention

The best you can say about cameras is that they're a necessary evil which we all have to live with. So what's the best way of avoiding the 'bad news' letter in the post?

There is one 100% foolproof method, which is totally legal, and it's dead simple - don't ever speed. That should do the trick. Yeah, right. Back in the real world, everyone speeds some time, even if it's only by a few mph. Add a few more miles-per because you weren't really watching your speed, and then do it somewhere there's a camera (or a sneaky mobile trap you'd never spotted before), and you're nicked. Is it any wonder that clean licences are getting as rare as rocking-horse leftovers?

Even on roads you know well, the do-gooders are forever lowering the limits, so if you don't watch it, you'll be sailing through more than 10 mph over today's new limit. And that's definitely worth a few points! You've gotta concentrate, to stay clean.

Know your enemy

First of all, you've got to know what you're up against. It's the only way (short of the fantasy world of never, ever speeding) that you stand a chance. And the first thing to know is - not all cameras are the same. Some can even be beaten.

Gatso (and PEEK)

The first, the best-known, the most common, and probably the most-hated. Invented by the winner of the 1953 Monte Carlo Rally, Gatsos are the familiar large, square box in stealth grey or high-viz yellow, with a square lens and flash unit (the later, less-common PEEK cameras have two round items, set one above the other). These are radar-operated (type 24) and can only 'get' you from behind, because they use a flash to take the photo, and this would blind you if it went off with you coming towards it. These cameras, therefore, cannot in theory catch you speeding towards them (don't quote us on that). As a result of this limitation, some authorities will turn the cameras round from time to time, to catch you out.

RLCs are also Gatso-based, but they work through sensors in the road, which are active when the lights are on red. If your car passes over them in this condition, it's gotcha. Some RLCs use radar too, so if you speed through on red, you'll also get a speeding fine. Gee, thanks.

Truvelo

Oooh, nasty. The forward-facing 'gatso' is particularly unpleasant, but luckily for us, it's also more expensive than the rear-facing Gatso, so not as common. Yet. The Truvelo camera can be recognised by two round lenses side by side in the centre of its box, and one of these is a pinky-red colour (hence the 'pinkeye' nickname). The unusual pink 'lens' is actually a flash unit, fitted with a red filter to avoid blinding the driver. Because the photo's taken from the front, it's hard for the driver to claim someone else was driving, or that they 'don't know'

who was driving (a common ploy to try and 'get off' Gatso offences). The less-visible flash gives less warning to following motorists, too. Not that we're suggesting they're out to get us. Oh no.

These babies are triggered by the car passing over piezo sensors set into the road, not radar. If you see three stripes across your path, slow the heck down.

Gatsos have 35 mm film inside, with about 400 shots possible before the film runs out. It's obviously vital that the film is recovered from the camera, or a prosecution can't be made - these cameras get vandalised for all sorts of reasons. Some cameras are rumoured not to contain any film, so they flash without recording any evidence (that bloke down the pub could be wrong, though).

If the radar detects excess speed, the flash is triggered twice as you pass over the measured line markings on the road. From the distance you travel between the set flashes, your speed can be proved. It's anyone's guess where the trigger speed for a camera will be set, but it's almost bound to be quite a few mph over the posted limit - if it wasn't, the camera would quickly catch dozens of speeders, and run out of film. Be more wary of inner-city Gatsos, as they're probably 'emptied' more often, allowing a lower speed tolerance.

tricks 'n' tips

In a thirty limit, you're less likely to speed if you hook a lower gear than normal. Most cars will comfortably cruise through a thirty in 4th gear, but it's too easy to add speed in 4th. Try using 3rd, and the natural engine braking (and extra engine/exhaust noise) will help you keep a lid on your speed. It's not foolproof, but give it a try anyway.

Red Light Cameras

Intended to catch people who go through traffic lights on red. Which, you have to say, is pretty dodgy. And have you ever risked it on a single amber? If you remember your Highway Code, this means stop, the same as a red light. 'Amber-gamblers' should also beware the traffic-light cams, 'cos they'll get you one day. Unlike (a few) points for speeding, points for traffic light offences will really hurt your insurance premiums, so watch it.

SPECS

Yikes - this really is Big Bro stuff. This system uses digital cameras (no film needed), mounted high on special gantries - these are a set distance apart, and create a speed monitoring zone. When you 'enter the zone', your number plate is recorded digitally, with a date and time stamp (regardless of whether you're speeding). When you leave the zone, another camera does the same thing. Because you've travelled a known distance between the two cameras, it's possible to calculate your average speed - if you're over the limit for the stretch of road, the computer spits out a fine in your direction.

What's really worrying about this technology is that it can be used to cross-check you and your car for other offences (whether your car's taxed and MoT'd, for instance). Anything dodgy, and the next time you pass by those cameras at that time of day, you could be in for a jam-sandwich surprise. Still, it could also catch the crims making off with your motor...

Mobile or temporary speed traps

These are either Gatso, Mini-Gatso, or laser type.

The potential Gatso sites are easy enough to spot - look for three shiny strips across the road, with a sturdy grey metal post alongside, on the pavement. Mr Plod comes along, sets up his camera (which uses sensors in the road strips not radar to detect your speed), catches his daily quota of speeders, and moves on. Don't give him a short day by being one of his victims.

Mini-Gatsos are just smaller, mobile versions of the UK's least-favourite roadside 'furniture', operated out of cop-cars and anonymous white vans - to get you, you have to be driving away from them.

More sinister (and much on the increase) are the laser cameras, which are aimed at your number plate (usually the front one) and record your speed on video. Often seen mounted on tripods, on bridges overlooking busy roads, or hidden inside those white 'safety camera partnership' vans. Lasers have quite a range (1000 metres, or over half a mile), so by the time you've spotted them, they've spotted you speeding. It's up to the operator to target likely speeding vehicles - so will they pick on your maxed motor? You bet!

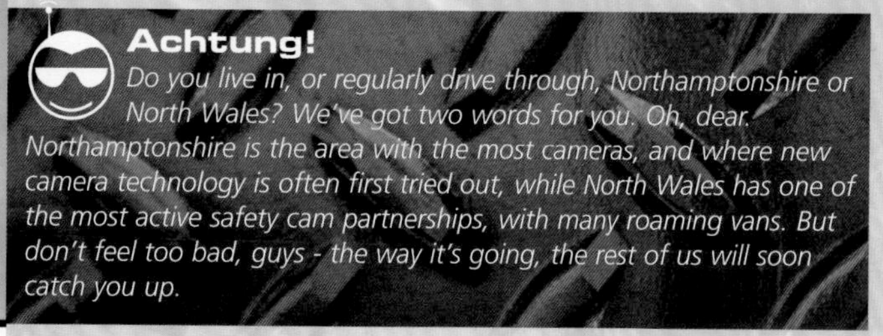

Achtung!

Do you live in, or regularly drive through, Northamptonshire or North Wales? We've got two words for you. Oh, dear. Northamptonshire is the area with the most cameras, and where new camera technology is often first tried out, while North Wales has one of the most active safety cam partnerships, with many roaming vans. But don't feel too bad, guys - the way it's going, the rest of us will soon catch you up.

Beating the system

No-one's condoning regular speeding, but these days, it's just too easy to get 'done' for a fairly minor speed infringement. Which hardly seems fair. There must be some way of fighting back, surely?

Cheap and legal

Don't. Ever. Speed. Simple, but not easy in the real world. Next!

Neither cheap nor legal

The James Bond option

One of 007's older cars had self-changing number plates - this may have been the inspiration for a highly-illegal speed camera dodge. Since all the detection systems rely heavily on your number plate, some skankers drive round with false plates - they might even have copied yours. Worth remembering if you ever get accused of speeding in the Outer Hebrides. Getting caught on false plates could be a £1000 fine, so is it worth the risk?

For ages now, companies have been advertising 'photo-reflective' plates (they're not illegal, but the dibble take a dim view). Most are a rip-off, but some do appear to work – on traps which flash. Speed cameras take very high-res pictures, however - even if your plates don't give you away, the coppers might i.d. your motor from its non-standard features. Money wasted, then.

Cloaking device?

The mobile laser speed trap is one of the most common, and most hated, in the UK. It sends out a laser beam which targets your front number plate. Wouldn't it be great if you could buy something to mess up its signal, so it couldn't 'lock on' ? You can - it's called a laser diffuser (sometimes marketed under the guise of a remote garage door-opener). And yes, they do work - but careful fitting is needed, and the lenses need regular cleaning. If you're caught using it for speed trap evasion, you can be done for obstruction, or perverting the course of justice - it pays to have a well-placed 'off' switch.

Gatso-beating radar 'scramblers' are said not to work, while radar jammers are an illegal transmitter - using one could see you inside for much longer than a speeding conviction.

A sound investment?

Radar detectors

These have been around for ages, and started life in the US. They're good for detecting radar-based speed cameras (most Gatsos), and any old police radar guns still in use, but that's all. Don't buy an old one (you'll get lots of false alerts if it's not meant for Euro/UK use), or a cheap one (it might not have enough range to give you a chance). ***Stop press: Looks like radar detectors are finally going to be made illegal later this year (2004) — only GPS systems will be legal after this.***

GPS systems

Using Global Positioning Satellite technology, these devices are really speed camera site locators, not detectors. Using an onboard database of camera locations, they constantly monitor your car's position, and warn when you're approaching a 'danger area'. Providing you keep your dash-mounted podule updated (by downloading the latest camera/blackspot info from the maker's website), these will warn you of virtually every potential camera in the country, including Truvelo and SPECS. The only limitations are a lack of laser detection, and it won't get all the mobile sites.

You must download new info regularly, and this costs (you buy a subscription to the website). Also, if your system hasn't been in use for a while, it can take quite a few minutes for the pod to pick up the satellites it needs - during this time, you're unprotected. Don't buy secondhand units with no subscription left, as the makers sometimes can't (won't?) re-activate them.

Laser detectors

The makers say this is essential kit to combat the roaming camera van threat, but be careful. We said earlier that laser cams have a range of up to 1000 metres, but most operators don't trigger theirs until you're much, much closer than that. Which means you have far less time to react. As long as you're not the first car along, your laser detector may pick up laser 'scatter' from cars in front, but there isn't much scatter with a laser. It's said that some laser detectors will only go off if your car's already been targeted - and of course, it's too late by then.

A final word

Don't rely too heavily on even the best anti-camera technology - try and drive within the spirit, if not the letter, of the Law, with a detector as backup.

Road **Angel**

The most effective way to 'detect' a camera is to know where it is. Yeah – obviously! But with cameras still being hidden behind road signs and bridges, and increasing numbers of camera-kitted white vans, knowing where the cams are ain't easy.

A GPS locator monitors your car's position relative to known camera sites, and warns you when you're getting close. The latest offerings also warn when you're approaching schools and other areas where extra care is needed. These devices are definitely not illegal. They increase road safety, by telling you where 'accident blackspots' are – not when to brake...

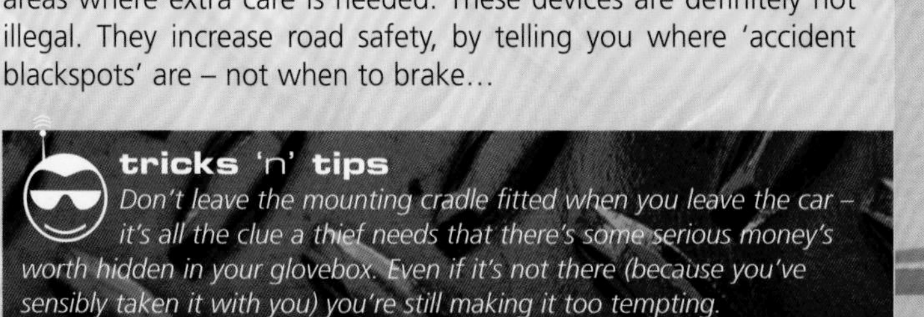

tricks 'n' tips
Don't leave the mounting cradle fitted when you leave the car – it's all the clue a thief needs that there's some serious money's worth hidden in your glovebox. Even if it's not there (because you've sensibly taken it with you) you're still making it too tempting.

01 This latest Road Angel offers two main mounting options – a sticky-backed magnetic mount directly on the dash, or this rather neat screen-mounted cradle (also with a mag mount). Either way, make sure the wipers don't obscure the unit's 'view', or the laser detection function won't stand a chance.

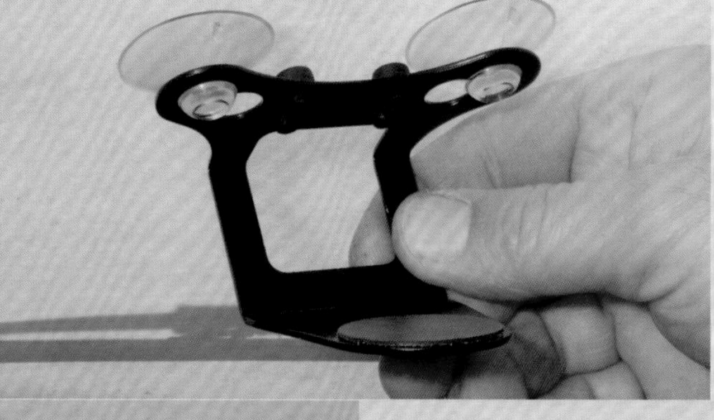

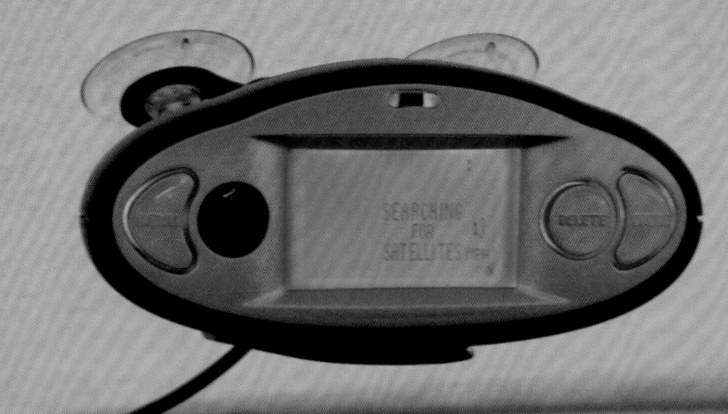

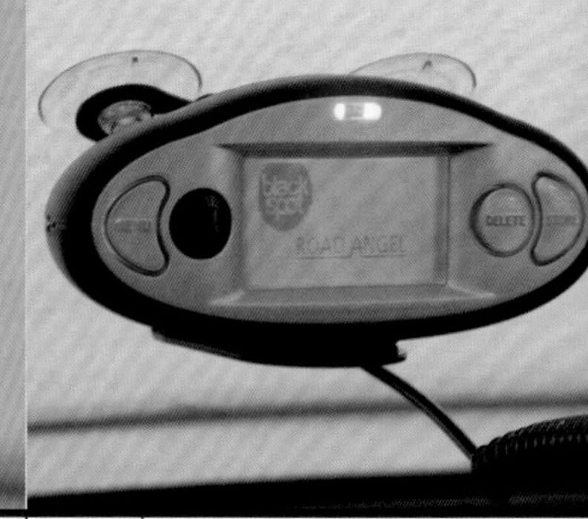

02 A GPS unit like this is only as good as the info it's working from – update it regularly by downloading the latest camera locations, or it's worse than useless. If you can use a PC well enough to download stuff from the Internet, you've got no worries.

03 Plug the unit into its lighter socket power supply (assuming it's not already taken by your phone charger or hands-free kit), then fit the unit to its bracket. First, you're greeted by a friendly message, then the unit starts searching for its satellites. While this is going on, remember that you're not protected.

04 Depending which system you've got, when you're getting near a camera site (sorry – accident blackspot), you'll get a warning beep or message, and the display will flash. If you miss all that lot, you probably need to downgrade your ICE install.

Look Mum, no hands!

As of December 2003 (okay, March 2004 really) it became illegal to hold your mobile while driving. Well, brilliant - something new to get done for. Like we were really getting short of that kind of thing. But you have to say, yipping and driving always was a pretty dodgy pastime, with driving coming off worse - if only all the UK's traffic legislation made this much sense.

Of course, the people who really benefit are the ones making hands-free car phone kits - you're looking at upwards of £50 (for a conventional kit) to get anything worth fitting. Which one do I go for? Will I have to make holes in my dash? Good questions. But we're jumping ahead - let's deal first with what the new law means in the real world.

Points of law

First, fitting a hands-free kit is merely a way of getting round part of the new legislation. They're not 'fully-legal', they're just 'not prohibited'. Even using a hands-free set-up is a distraction while you're piloting your machine, and if you start weaving about, carve up a cyclist, or run a red light, you're still likely to face a 'driving without due care' charge, or worse. The best solution for making a call is to stop where it's safe - have voicemail enabled if you get called while you're driving.

Answering a call, even with hands-free, might not be safe in all circumstances. Let it ring. As for what you're allowed to do with the phone itself - it's just pressing the buttons (and no, this doesn't mean it's ok 2 txt). Holding the phone in any way is not permitted. Even if you're stuck in traffic, completely stationary, the engine would have to be off before you can use your mobile normally - only then could you really say you weren't 'driving'.

At the moment, getting caught using a phone on the move only carries a fixed fine. But it looks like this hasn't worked, because it's soon going to be a bigger fine, and points on the licence. Use your moby sensibly (better still, don't use it, in the car at least), or it could mean re-sitting your driving test. Paying attention now, aren'tcha?

Achtung!

Don't just pull over and screech to a stop when the phone rings. If you do this somewhere stupid, you're just as likely to get fined as you would for using the phone on the move.

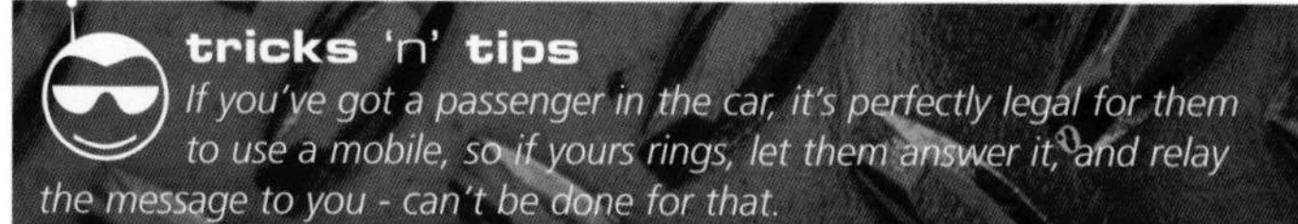

tricks 'n' tips

If you've got a passenger in the car, it's perfectly legal for them to use a mobile, so if yours rings, let them answer it, and relay the message to you - can't be done for that.

What's available?

Conventional kits

The new law has brought a whole range of new product to the market, so there's no need to settle for the old-style in-car kits, which leave holes all over your dash. Most of the latest kits have adhesive pads, and just plug into your fag lighter. The most essential item, to comply with the rules, is a phone holder or 'cradle' (holding phone bad - cradle good).

As no-one keeps the same phone for very long, it's worth looking for a kit which you can convert from one make of phone to another - by buying a different adapter lead, for instance.

Look for kits offering 'full duplex' operation - this means you can talk and listen at the same time. Just like real life. What it really means is conversations are easier and more natural - to understand fully why you need this feature, try one without it. Non-duplex kits cut out the speaker when they pick up any sound - this could be you talking (as intended), or it could just be noise inside the car. Very irritating, especially in an area where you've already got poor reception to deal with.

Some kits feature 'infra-red technology', which means you can answer/end calls by waving your hand in front of the phone. Proper hands-free operation, and great for impressing your passengers. Maybe not so good if you make lots of hand gestures while driving?

Car stereo kits

One of the newest ideas, and catching on fast. Uses a radio transmitter clipped over the phone speaker to transmit calls over a radio channel on your car stereo. When the phone rings, flick on the radio to the preset channel, speak into the phone's mike as normal, and hear your caller through your car speakers (since it's your stereo, you have easy control over call volume). They're cheap, and they appear to work, though there are potential problems with interference. Remember, this is a developing technology - it pays to buy the latest model you can find.

Bluetooth headsets

Bluetooth offers wireless operation, so get yourself a headset with mike, and you can chat away without having the phone up to your ear. Most modern handsets are Bluetooth-capable, and really new ones also have voice-activated dialling, which offers true hands-free operation in the car. Downsides? Some doubts over sound quality, and do you really want to wear a headset all the time you're driving?

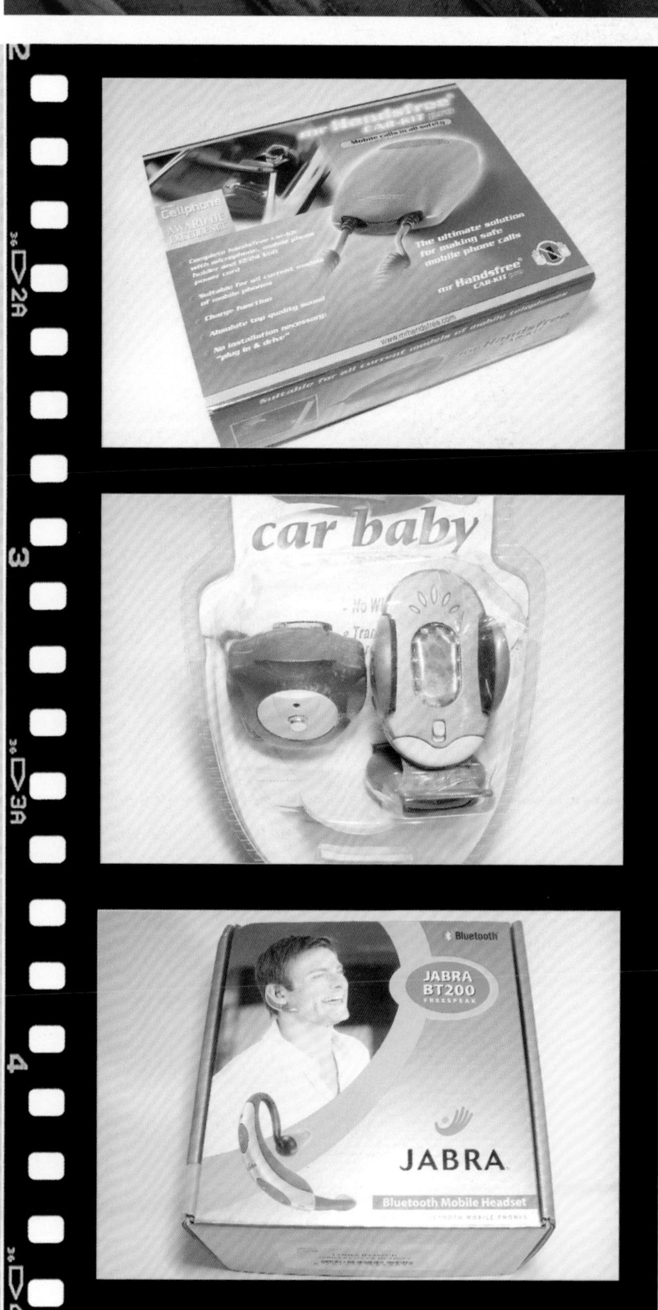

Kit fitting

Fitting details are obviously going to vary, depending on what you've bought – the main trick is to get one which doesn't require you to go drilling holes in your dash. Luckily, this is now so unpopular that most modern kits don't even offer hole-drilling as an option.

Mr Handsfree

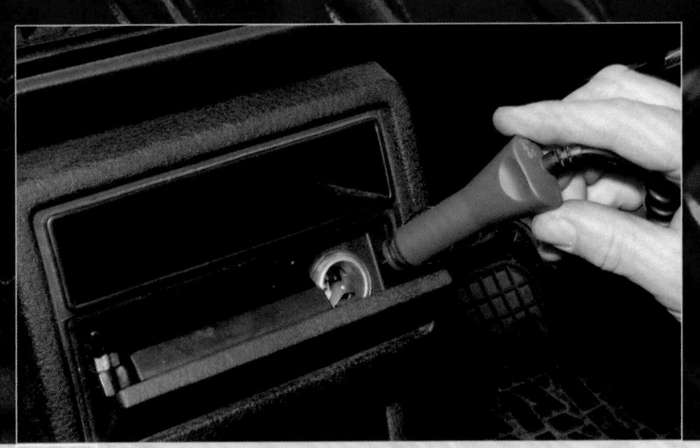

01 All these kits (apart from the Bluetooth headset) need power, usually conveniently taken from the fag lighter socket. Umm, yeah... right... Not easy getting the adapter in the socket, with the ashtray in place, is it? Proof that the Golf Mk 2 comes from a time before mobile phones.

02 If you're not going to drill holes, you'll be sticking stuff on. If you want things to stay stuck (and you usually only get one shot at this) a little cleaning is in order first.

03 Mostly, it's Velcro pads you get for sticking the various kit bits in place (so they can be easily ripped off and stashed when you leave the car). Leave the two 'halves' of Velcro stuck together while fitting. With the mounting area clean, it's peel . . .

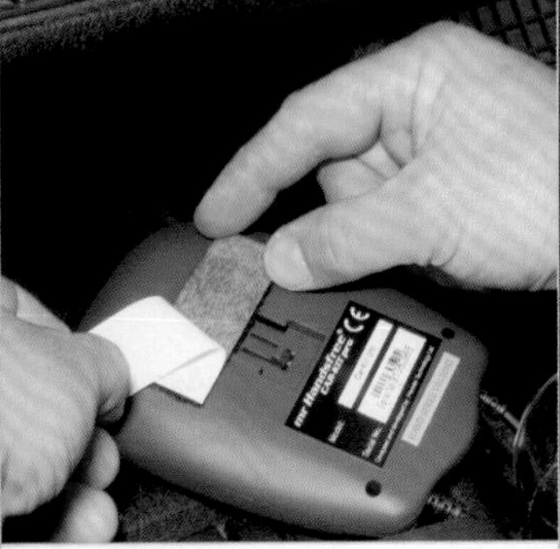

04 . . . and press firmly. This is the main unit, which contains the speaker. We thought the centre console was too good a spot to ignore. You only have to ensure the two curly-cords will reach the lighter socket and the phone.

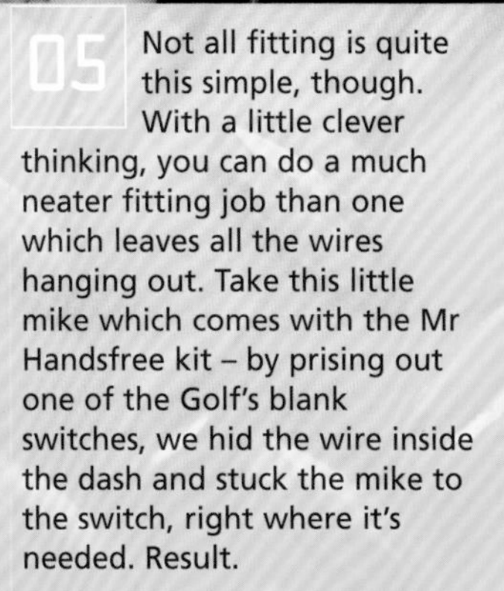

05 Not all fitting is quite this simple, though. With a little clever thinking, you can do a much neater fitting job than one which leaves all the wires hanging out. Take this little mike which comes with the Mr Handsfree kit – by prising out one of the Golf's blank switches, we hid the wire inside the dash and stuck the mike to the switch, right where it's needed. Result.

06 For mounting the phone itself, we have a magnetic bracket, again stuck with sticky pads. It's only an old Nokia, but we'd still better make sure it doesn't hit the deck, by making sure it's firmly attached.

07 And there it is – the phone's nice and handy, the mike's discreetly mounted, and the speaker unit's tucked in the console. And this is the first one of these we've fitted!

Pama Plug n Go

This is one neat unit – no dangling wires, a well-designed mounting bracket with a huge sucker for sticking to the windscreen, and a built-in speaker which faces the glass, so sound is 'reflected' back. The unit is self-contained, with a built-in battery (car charger supplied), so it can be used anywhere, not just in-car. Looks sweet, works a treat.

01

Jabra Bluetooth **headset**

Only any good to you if your phone's got Bluetooth, but like the Pama unit we fitted earlier, there's no mess. The headset needs charging before use, but after that, you just 'pair' your phone and headset together, and start jabbering. If your phone's trendy enough to have voice-activated dialling, this is about as hands-free as you'll get. You don't even need a cradle for your mobile with this one!

01

It's a sad fact, but making your car attractive to the opposite sex also tends to attract attention of a less-welcome kind from brainless thieves.

04

Security

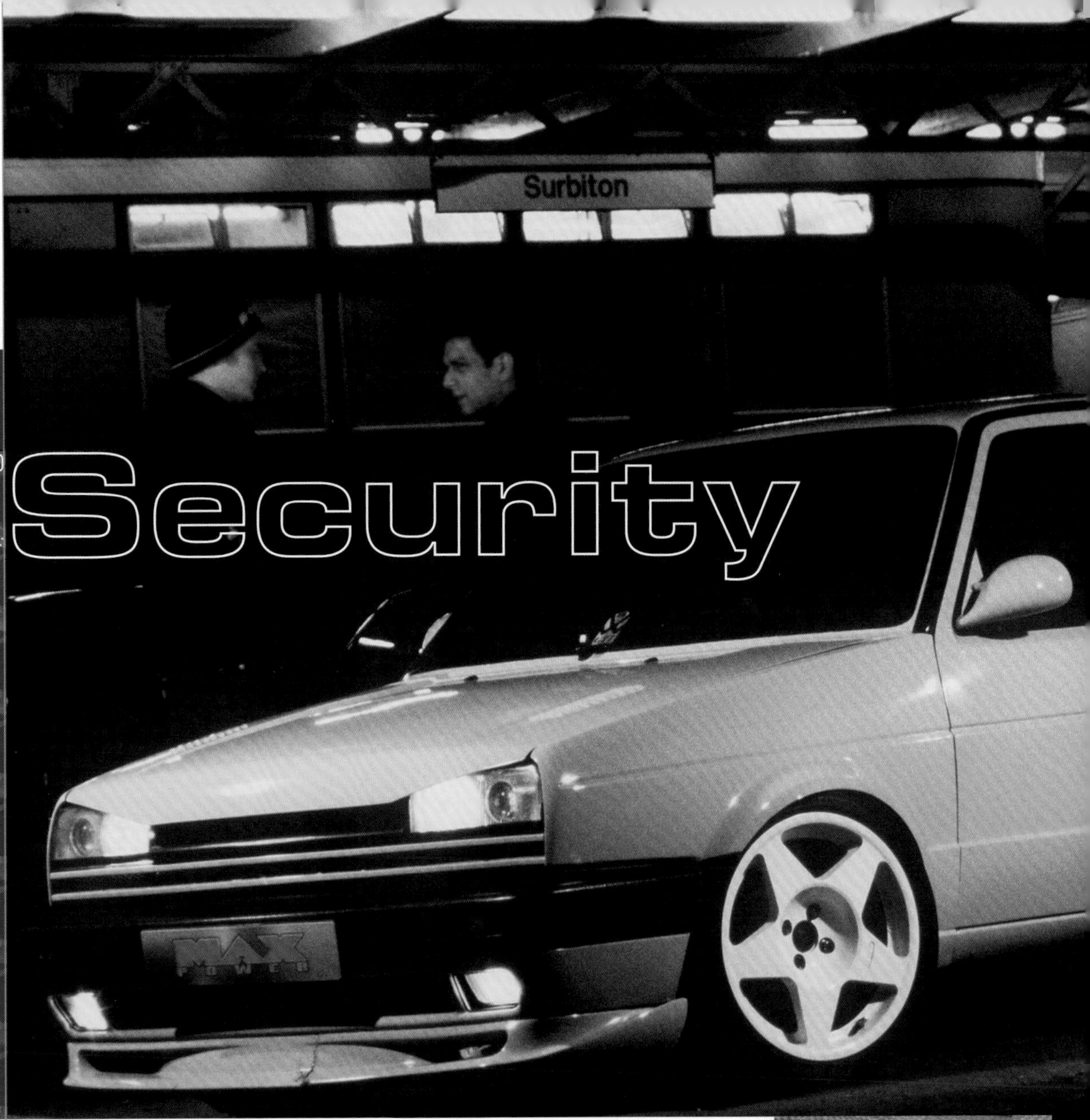

Security

Avoiding trouble

Now come on - you're modifying your car to look cool and to be seen in. Not a problem - but be careful where you choose to show your car off, and who to. Be especially discreet, the nearer you get to home - turn your system down before you get near home, for instance, or you'll draw unwelcome attention to where that car with the loud stereo's parked at night.

If you're going out, think about where you're parking – somewhere well-lit and reasonably well-populated is the best bet.

Hands up, who doesn't lock their car when they get petrol? Your insurance company has a term for this, and it's "contributory negligence". In English, this means you won't get a penny if your car goes missing when you haven't locked it.

If you're lucky enough to have a garage, use it and fit extra security to the garage door.

Always use all the security you have, whenever you leave the car, even if it's a bit of a chore fitting a steering lock, just do it.

A word about your stereo

From the moment you bolt on those nice alloys, it's taken as read that you've also got stereo gear that's worth nicking - and the thieves know it. All the discreet installation in the world isn't going to deter them from finding out what's inside that nice motor.

If you have a CD player, don't leave discs or empty CD cases lying around inside the car. 6x9s on the rear shelf are also very inviting to thieves, and very easy to steal. When you're fitting your system, give some thought to the clues you could accidentally leave in plain view. Oxygen-free speaker cable is great stuff, but it's also a bit bright against dark carpets, and is all the clue necessary that you're serious about your speakers.

Most modern sets are face-off or MASK, so if they've got security features like this, USE them - take your faceplate off when you leave the car, and take it with you rather than leaving it in the door pocket or glovebox (the first places a thief will look).

Things that go beep in the night

Don't skimp on an alarm, it may never even be put to the test, but if it is, you'll be glad you spent wisely ...

The simplest first step to car security is to fake it. It's obviously risky if the theif calls youre bluff, but if you really can't afford an alarm just an LED is cheap to buy and easy to fit, and can be rigged to a discreet switch inside the car (we show you how, later on).

Don't overlook the value of so-called "manual" immobilisers, such as steering wheel locks. These can be a worthwhile deterrent, in that a thief not specifically after your car (and yours alone) may move on to an easier target. Some of the items offered may be "Sold Secure" or Thatcham Cat 3, accolades well worth checking out, since it means they've withstood a full-on brute force attack for a useful length of time.

The only way to combat the more determined thief is to go for a well-specified and intelligently-installed alarm. Immobilisers alone have their place, but unfortunately, even a pro-fitted immobiliser on its own won't stop someone pinching your wheels, or breaking in and helping themselves to the stereo gear. Neither, incidentally, will every alarm , buit at least it gives you a fighting chance.

Finally, one other scam which you might fall victim to. If you find that your alarm is suddenly going off a lot at night, when previously it had been well-behaved, don't ignore the problem. It's an old trick for a thief to deliberately set off your alarm several times, each time hiding when you come out to investigate, then to wait until the fifth or sixth time when you don't reset, leaving him a clear run. If your alarm does keep false-alarming without outside assistance, find out the cause quickly, or your neighbours will quickly become "deaf" to it.

Thatcham categories and meanings:

1. Cat 1. For alarms and electronic immobilisers.
2. Cat 2. For electronic immobilisers only.
3. Cat 2-1. Electronic immobilisers which can be upgraded to Cat 1 alarms later.
4. Cat 3. Mechanical immobilisers, eg snap-off steering wheels, locking wheel bolts, window film, steering wheel locks/covers.
5. Q-class. Tracking devices.

Other alarm features to look out for are:

1 Two-stage anti-shock - means that the alarm shouldn't go off if your neighbour's cat jumps on your car roof. The alarm will only sound after a major shock, or after repeated shocks are detected.

2 Anti-tilt - detects any attempt to lift or jack up the car, preventing any attempt to pinch alloys. Alarm may sound if car is parked outside in windy conditions.

3 Anti-hijack - immobiliser with built-in delay. If your motor gets hi-jacked, the thieves responsible will only get so far down the road before the engine cuts out.

4 Rolling code - reduces the chance of your alarm remote control signal from being "grabbed" (copied) by special electronic equipment.

5 Total closure - module which connects to electric windows/ sunroof and central locking, which closes all items when alarm is set.

6 Pager control - alarm can be set to send a message to your a pager or mobile if your car gets tampered with.

7 Current-sensing disable - very useful feature on some cars which (like the Golf) have a cooling fan which can cut in after the ignition is switched off. Without this feature, your alarm will be triggered every time you leave it parked after a long run.

The knowledge

Attack 1 The first option to any thief is to smash glass - typically, the toughened-glass side windows, which will shatter, unlike the windscreen. Unfortunately for the thief, this makes a loud noise (not good), but is a quick and easy way in. The reason for taking this approach is that a basic car alarm will only go off if the doors are opened (voltage-drop alarm) - provided the doors aren't opened, the alarm won't go off.

Response 1 A more sophisticated alarm will feature shock sensing (which will be set off by the impact on the glass), and better still, ultrasonic sensing, which will be triggered by the brick coming in through the broken window.

Response 2 This kind of attack can also be stopped by applying security film to the inside of the glass, which holds it all together and prevents easy entry.

Attack 2 An alternative to smashing the glass is to pry open the door using a crowbar - this attack involves literally folding open the door's window frame by prising from the top corner. The glass will still shatter, but as long as the door stays shut, a voltage-drop alarm won't be triggered.

Response This method might not be defeated by a shock-sensing alarm, but an ultrasonic unit would pick it up. Incidentally, another bonus with ultrasonic alarms is that the sensors are visible from outside - and act as a deterrent.

Attack 3 Mk 2 Golfs are vulnerable to attacks involving prising behind the door handles, which works the lock and allows the door to be opened. Of course, this approach WILL trigger even a lowly voltage-drop system, but it's a common-enough problem.

Response Anti-prising armour door plates are available from several suppliers (ours came from C & R Enterprises of Radford). These not only prevent "pry-ins", but can also be used as a repair measure, covering up some of the damage caused! We show you how easy it is to fit these later on.

Attack 4 The next line of attack is to disable the alarm. The commonest way to kill the alarm is either to cut the wiring to the alarm itself, or to disconnect the battery after taking a crowbar to your bonnet catch.

Response 1 If your alarm has extra pin-switches, be sure to fit one to the bonnet, and fit it in the bonnet channel next the battery, so that it'll set off the alarm if the bonnet is prised up. Also make sure that the wire to the pin-switch cannot be cut easily though a partly-open bonnet.

Response 2 Make sure that the alarm module is well-hidden, and cannot be got at from underneath the car.

Response 3 Make the alarm power supply connection somewhere less obvious than directly at the battery terminal - any thief who knows his stuff will immediately cut any "spare" red wires at the battery. Try taking power from the fusebox, or if you must source it under the bonnet, trace the large red battery lead to the starter motor connections, and tap into the power there.

Response 4 Always disguise the new alarm wiring, by using black insulating tape to wrap it to the existing wiring loom. Tidying up in this way also helps to ensure the wires can't get trapped, cut, melted, or accidentally ripped out - any of which could leave you with an alarm siren which won't switch off, or an immobiliser you can't disable.

Response 5 An alarm which has a "battery back-up" facility is best. Even if he's successfully crow-barred your bonnet and snipped the battery connections, the alarm will still go off, powered by a separate battery of its own. A Cat 1 alarm has to have battery back-up.

To qualify for insurance discounts, your chosen alarm or immobiliser usually has to be to Thatcham-approved standards (Category 1 or 2). They have to be installed by qualified fitters to get you an insurance discount, so it's not a DIY task.

Fitting a basic **LED**

All you need for this is a permanent live feed, an earth, a switch if you want to be able to turn it on/off, and the flashing LED itself (very cheap, from any car accessory shop).

01 An LED draws very little current, so you'll be quite safe tapping into almost any live feed you fancy. If you've wired in your stereo, take a live feed from the permanent (radio memory supply) wire at the back of your head unit, or go into the fusebox with your test light (as featured in the alarm fitting procedure). An earth can easily be tapped, again from your head unit, or you can make one almost anywhere on the metal body of the car, by drilling a small hole, fitting a self-tapping screw, then wrapping the bared end of wire around and tightening it.

02 The best and easiest place to mount an LED is into one of the many blank switches the makers seem to love fitting. The blank switch is easily pried out, and a hole can then be drilled to take the LED (which usually comes in a separate little holder). Feed the LED wiring down behind the dashboard to where you've tapped your live and earth, taking care not to trap it anywhere, nor to accidentally wrap it around any moving parts.

03 Connect your live to the LED red wire, then rig your earth to one side of the switch, and connect the LED black wire to the other switch terminal. You should now have a switchable LED! Tidy up the wiring, and mount the switch somewhere discreet, but where you can still get at it. Switch on when you leave the car, and it looks as if you've got SOME sort of alarm - better than nothing!

Fitting an **Alarm**

We're fitting a MicroScan AN210 which offers decent protection, and useful features for a sensible price. In order to try and make this section as useful as possible, we won't show in detail how this particular alarm is fitted, but instead pick out some of the highlights and tips, in case your chosen alarm is different to ours.

01 Disconnect the battery negative lead, and move the lead away from the battery. Might screw up your stereo settings, but it's better than having sparks flying and your new alarm going the minute it's rigged up.

02 Decide where you're going to mount the alarm/siren. Like somewhere not easily reached from underneath, firstly. Will the wiring supplied with the alarm reach across to the fusebox on the driver's side? To give us more room, we unbolted the coolant expansion tank for the time being.

03 Loosely fit the alarm to the bracket, to help you decide how well it'll fit in your chosen spot, then take the alarm away. Mark the position of the first mounting hole.

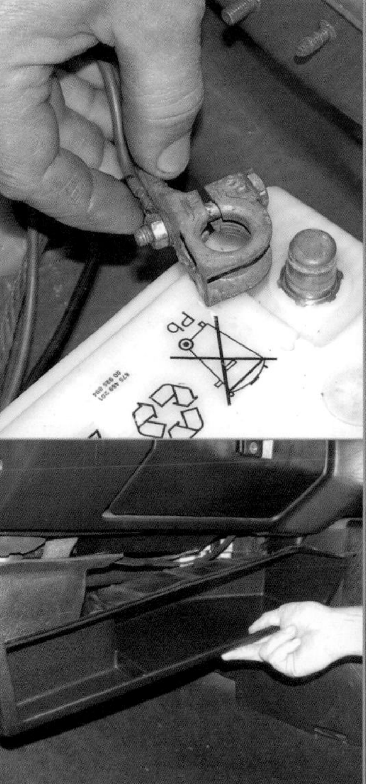

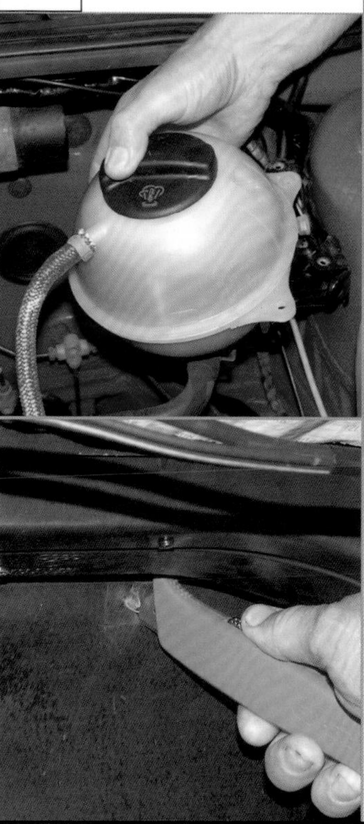

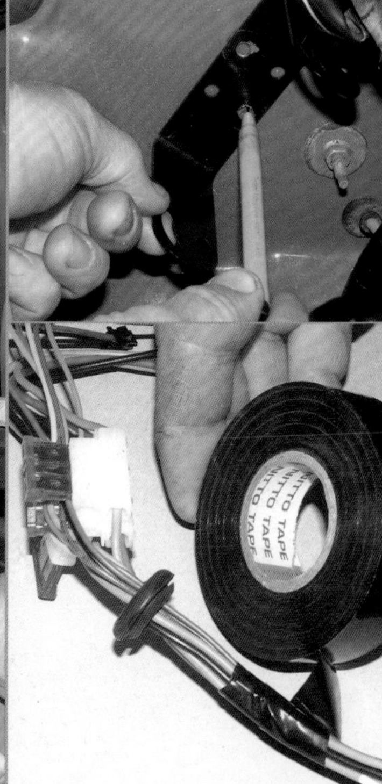

04 The next stage is to sort your wiring. The amount of wiring, and where you'll want to run it, will depend on your alarm. If, like us, you've got a bunch of wires which should be fed into the car, you'll need to feed them through somehow. We chose a ready-made grommet in the bulkhead, which we prised out, then poked a hole through the underfelt on the other side with a screwdriver.

05 Inside the car, remove the screws and take out the shelf below the glovebox . . .

06 . . . then pull down the carpet from the top of the footwell. If necessary, now you can cut a neat hole in the underfelt.

07 If you've got several wires to go through, as we did, tape them together into a makeshift "loom", which makes life much easier.

tricks 'n' tips

Drill one hole first, and fit the bolt loosely, then drill the second hole. If you drill all the holes at once, you might get one off-centre - this way, it'll definitely line up.

Feed the wires through, and pull them across towards the fusebox. Take care to feed them around the steering column and pedals, so that they won't get trapped or worn through, and so they won't interfere with

08 normal operation (could be VERY dodgy!).

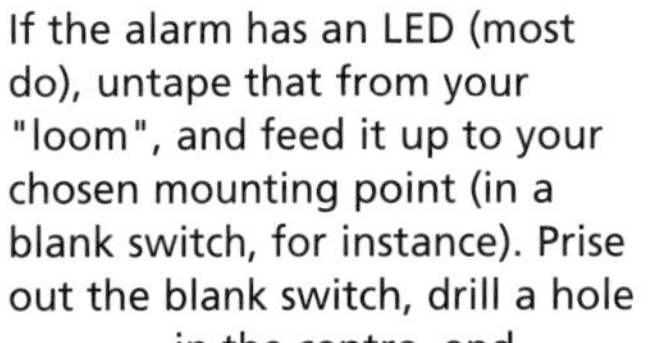

If the alarm has an LED (most do), untape that from your "loom", and feed it up to your chosen mounting point (in a blank switch, for instance). Prise out the blank switch, drill a hole

09 in the centre, and mount the LED and holder into it.

To get at the fusebox, take out

10 the screws and remove the driver's side lower dash panel first.

The fusebox is secured by two white clips - the left-hand one pivots towards you, while the right-hand one is a bit like a

11 clothes peg. Prise it free from the top, and pull it down.

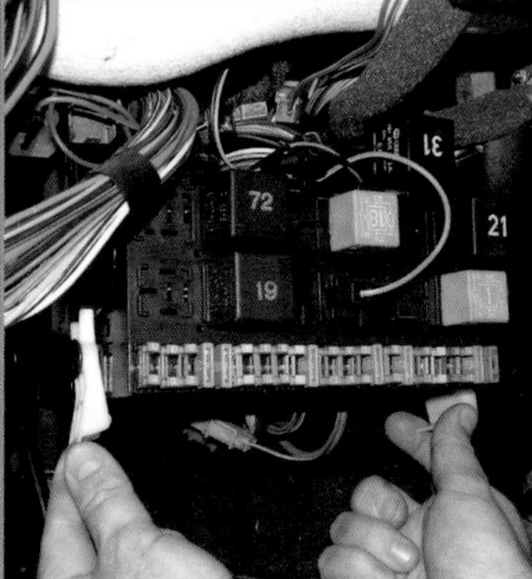

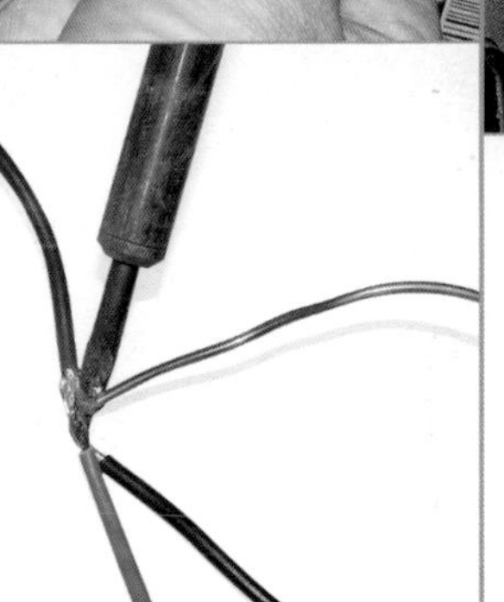

15 With your wires identified, how to tap into them? The three best options are:

a) Soldering - avoids cutting through your chosen wire - strip away a short section of insulation, wrap your new wire around the bared section, then apply solder to secure it. If you're a bit new to soldering, practice on a few offcuts of wire first.

b) Bullet connectors - cut and strip the end of your chosen wire, wrap your new one to it, push both into one half of the bullet. Connect the other end of your victim wire to the other bullet, and connect together. Always use the "female" half on any live feed - it'll be safer if you disconnect it than a male bullet, which could touch bare metal and send your motor up in smoke.

c) Block connectors - easy to use, just remember that the wires can come adrift if the screws aren't tight, and don't get too ambitious about how many wires you can stuff in one hole (block connectors, like bullets, are available in several sizes).

16 With any of these options, always insulate around your connection - especially when soldering, or you'll be leaving bare metal exposed. Remember that you'll probably be shoving all the wires up into the dark recesses of the under-dash area – if the wires get kinked/squashed together, that bit of protruding wire might just touch the metal bodywork, and cause a sparks. Steer clear of connectors like the above – they're convenient but can give rise to problems.

17 Any decent alarm should come with extra pin switches, and it's vital that you fit one to cover the bonnet at least. We found a ready-made hole near the battery, and enlarged it slightly.

12

As for tapping into the wiring, in the first place refer to the wiring diagrams in the Haynes manual, so you know which fuse to aim for in the fusebox, and which colour wire you're after. Most of it can be deduced without major brainwork. When you've found a likely suspect, use a 12V circuit tester (very cheap to buy) to confirm your suspicions. If you're after an ignition live, connect the tester probe to the wire (or push it carefully into the back of the wiring plug) and the croc clip to a good earth (like one of the door pin switch screws) - check that it's a switched live, not permanent, by temprarily reconnecting the battery and turning the ignition on and off. To check for an earth, use the same method, but connect the croc clip to a 12V supply.

13

Most alarms have a voltage-drop detection facility (ie it goes off when the interior light comes on, triggered by the door pin switches). Depending on which alarm you've chosen, you'll either be tapping into the positive side of the interior light circuit (ie the 12V live feed - check which fuse it's on, to start), or into the earth side. To get an easy tap into the earth side, unscrew and remove one of the door pin switches, and pull it out of the door frame - the wire attached is the earth circuit.

14

If you were thinking of taking a live direct from the battery, it's better to trace the red lead down to the starter motor, and tap in there. If a thief manages to get past your bonnet switch, his first thought will be to cut every additional live feed at the battery - of course, if he cuts all the battery leads, you're stuffed (without a battery back-up alarm), but at least you tried...

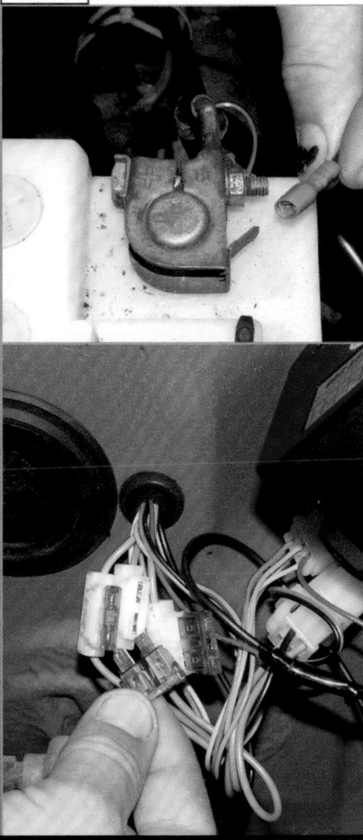

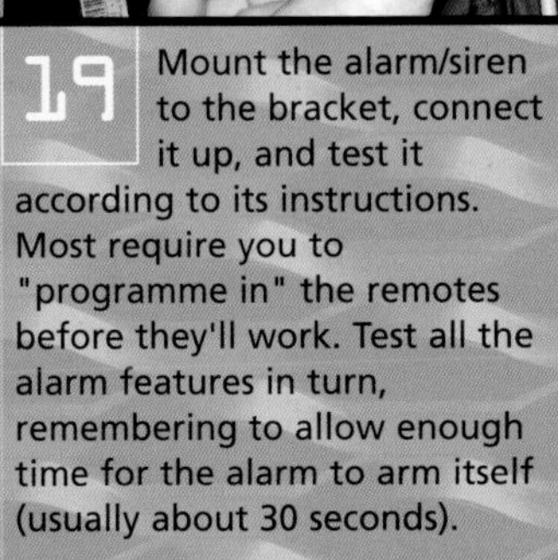

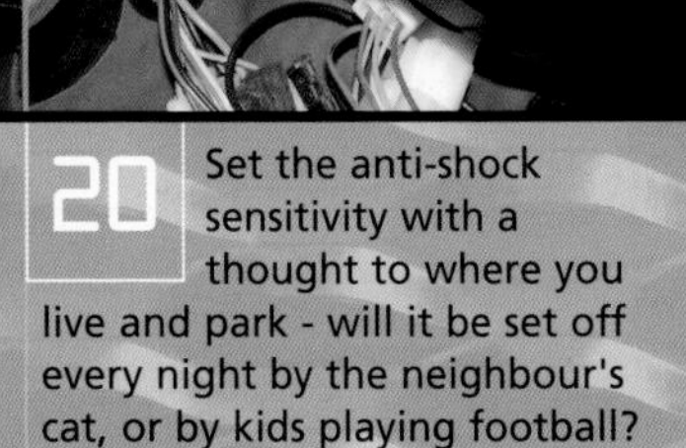

18

Run your wire round the engine, taping it up securely so it won't get chewed up or burned through, drop your switch into the hole, and connect up. The switch mounting screw is the earthing point, so must be into metal. It may be necessary to trim off the plastic top of the switch plunger, to allow the bonnet to close.

19

Mount the alarm/siren to the bracket, connect it up, and test it according to its instructions. Most require you to "programme in" the remotes before they'll work. Test all the alarm features in turn, remembering to allow enough time for the alarm to arm itself (usually about 30 seconds).

20

Set the anti-shock sensitivity with a thought to where you live and park - will it be set off every night by the neighbour's cat, or by kids playing football?

21

When you're happy all is well, go round and tidy up the wiring with tape and cable-ties. Hide the alarm fuses, but don't cover them in so much tape you can't get at them. Finally, and most important of all - next time you park up, remember to set it!

Fitting armour **door plates**

01 Prise off the outer trim strip from the door handle . . .

02 . . . to reveal the handle front mounting screw, which you remove.

03 Open the door, and remove the handle rear mounting screw visible through a hole in the rear edge of the door.

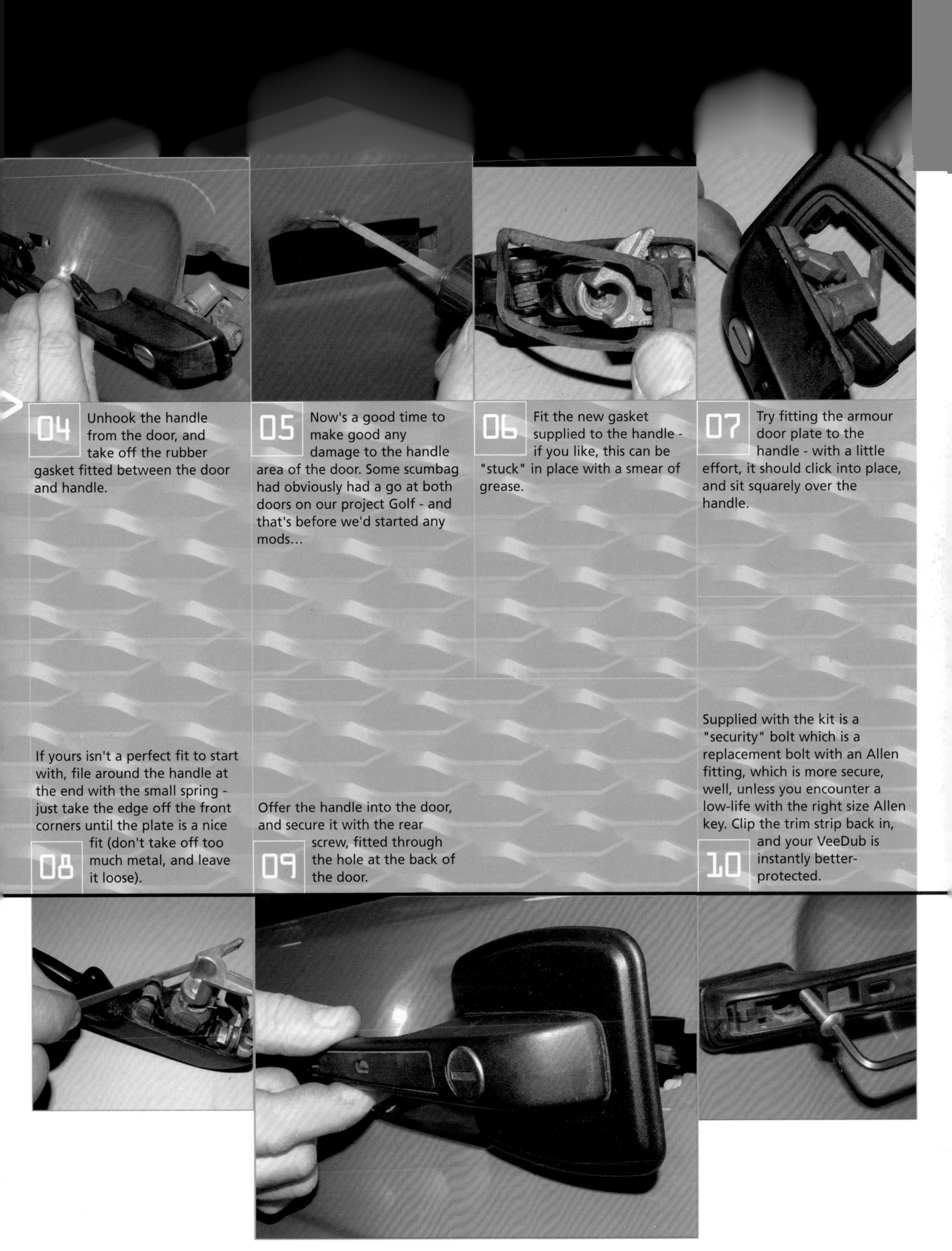

04 Unhook the handle from the door, and take off the rubber gasket fitted between the door and handle.

05 Now's a good time to make good any damage to the handle area of the door. Some scumbag had obviously had a go at both doors on our project Golf - and that's before we'd started any mods...

06 Fit the new gasket supplied to the handle - if you like, this can be "stuck" in place with a smear of grease.

07 Try fitting the armour door plate to the handle - with a little effort, it should click into place, and sit squarely over the handle.

08 If yours isn't a perfect fit to start with, file around the handle at the end with the small spring - just take the edge off the front corners until the plate is a nice fit (don't take off too much metal, and leave it loose).

09 Offer the handle into the door, and secure it with the rear screw, fitted through the hole at the back of the door.

10 Supplied with the kit is a "security" bolt which is a replacement bolt with an Allen fitting, which is more secure, well, unless you encounter a low-life with the right size Allen key. Clip the trim strip back in, and your VeeDub is instantly better-protected.

Body styling

There's loads of mods and established products that you can use on your Mk2, we've covered most of the stuff you can do at home. If you're feeling confident you could also have a go at mods like flushing the bootlid. If you can't spray, why not prep it for the bodyshop yourself and get them to spray it? Same goes for any other body mods you might do, save some money and spend it on other bits instead. Where there's a Golf, there's a way.

Single-light, **debadged grille**

At the front, an afternoon's work will see you change the grille. Whatever you fancy, from single headlight to grille spoilers, you get a big visual change, minimum effort.

01 Remove two screws (one either side) first.

02 Release plastic catches at the top of the grille, and the clips at the side

03 If you've got the extra set of grille lights, disconnect the wiring plugs from these, and the old grille is history.

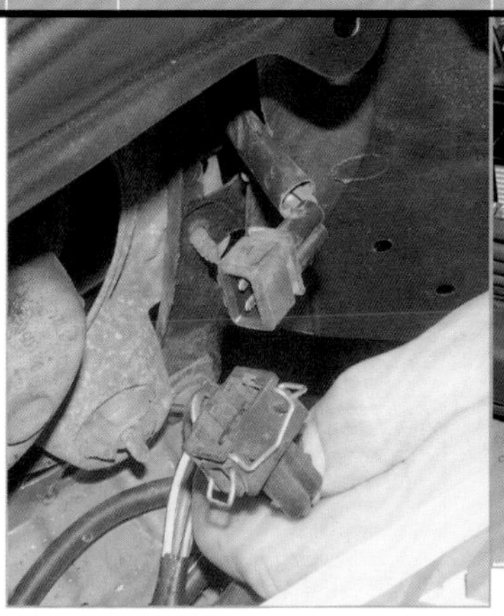

04 Some of you may be fitting a twin-headlight grille to a basic Golf. But remember - if you fit extra lights, they have to work, or you'll fail an MOT. Assuming you've got your grille from a scrapyard, did you also get the wiring for the lights? And you'll need a relay - see the section in "Lights & bulbs" on how to fit the front fogs, for guidance on wiring-up.

05 First, prise off the body-colour trim strip at the base of your old grille, and transfer it to the new one - it's held in place by a bunch of clips.

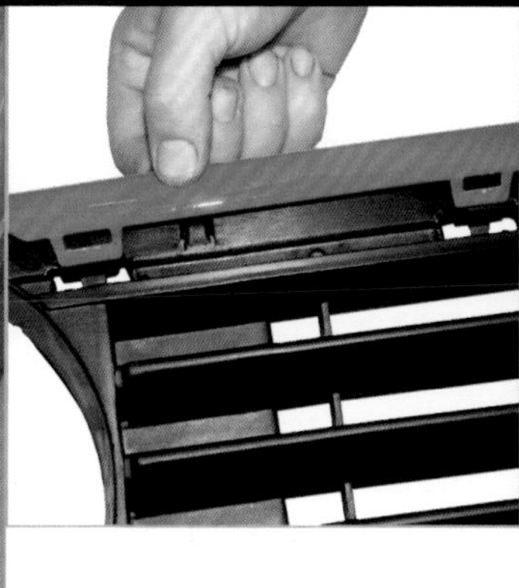

06 If you've got a decent new grille, it now fits into place like a dream, using the original clips and screws. Looking good.

'Badboy' headlight spoiler

The popular "badboy" look is a great way to toughen up the look of your Golf, without ruining its cool understated style.

Our spoiler was a little unusual in that it fits to the bonnet - it's more normal (and less work) to have them fitted to the grille - but hey - we like a challenge!

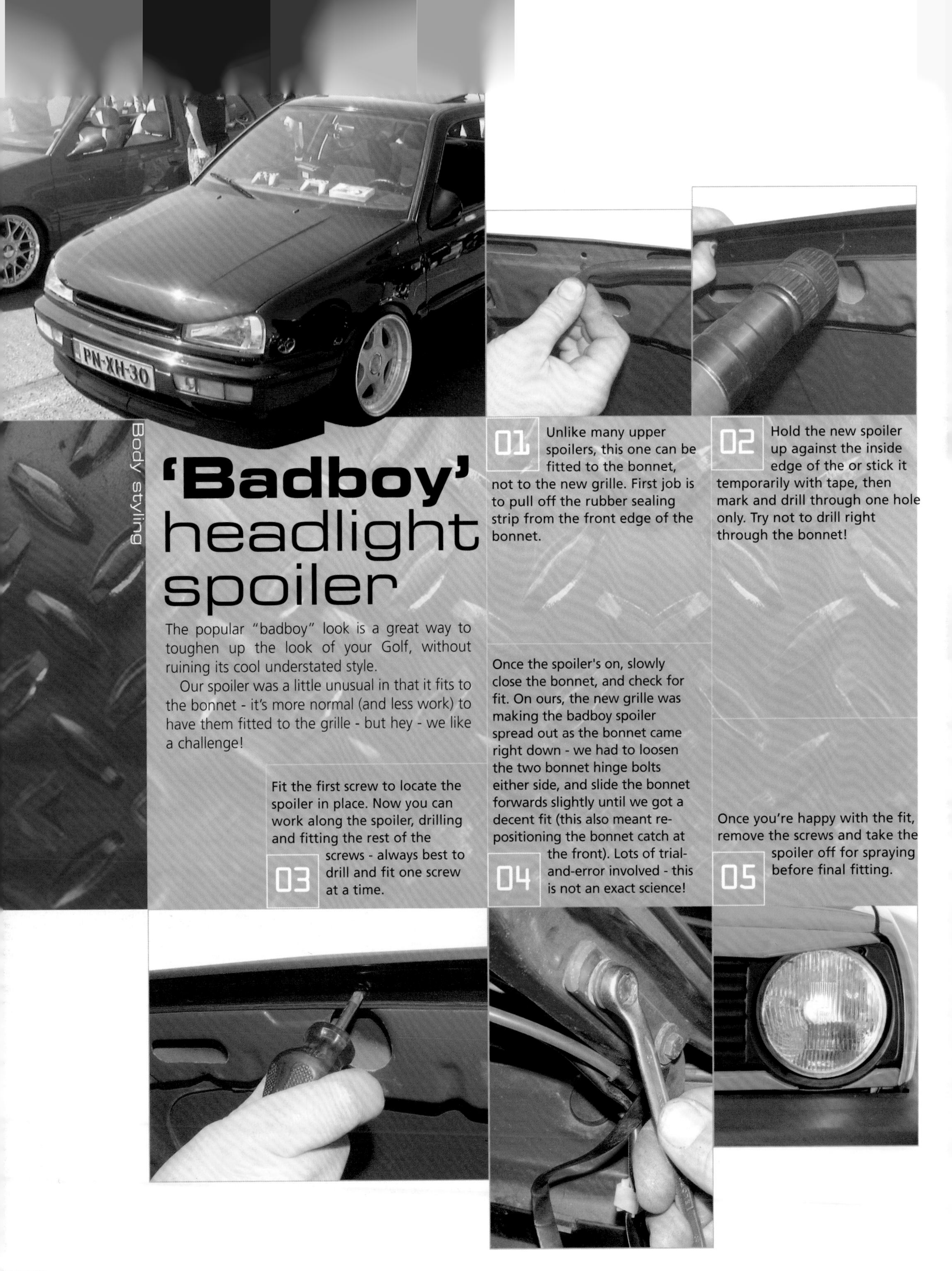

01 Unlike many upper spoilers, this one can be fitted to the bonnet, not to the new grille. First job is to pull off the rubber sealing strip from the front edge of the bonnet.

02 Hold the new spoiler up against the inside edge of the or stick it temporarily with tape, then mark and drill through one hole only. Try not to drill right through the bonnet!

03 Fit the first screw to locate the spoiler in place. Now you can work along the spoiler, drilling and fitting the rest of the screws - always best to drill and fit one screw at a time.

04 Once the spoiler's on, slowly close the bonnet, and check for fit. On ours, the new grille was making the badboy spoiler spread out as the bonnet came right down - we had to loosen the two bonnet hinge bolts either side, and slide the bonnet forwards slightly until we got a decent fit (this also meant re-positioning the bonnet catch at the front). Lots of trial-and-error involved - this is not an exact science!

05 Once you're happy with the fit, remove the screws and take the spoiler off for spraying before final fitting.

Meshing a front big bumper

01 First, take your sheet of mesh, and cut it to just bigger than your hole.

02 Drill some small holes next to your big hole . . .

03 . . . and attach your mesh along one edge with a few stumpy self-tappers and washers.

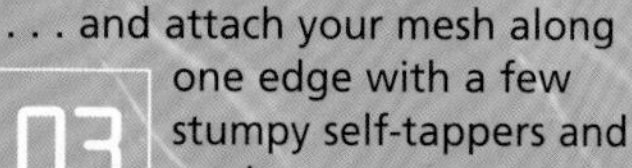

04 With one edge of your mesh pinned by the screws, fold the rest over your hole . . .

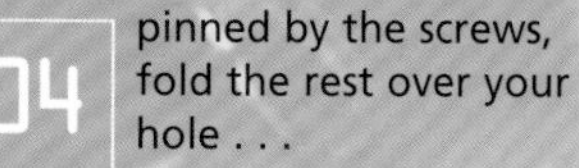

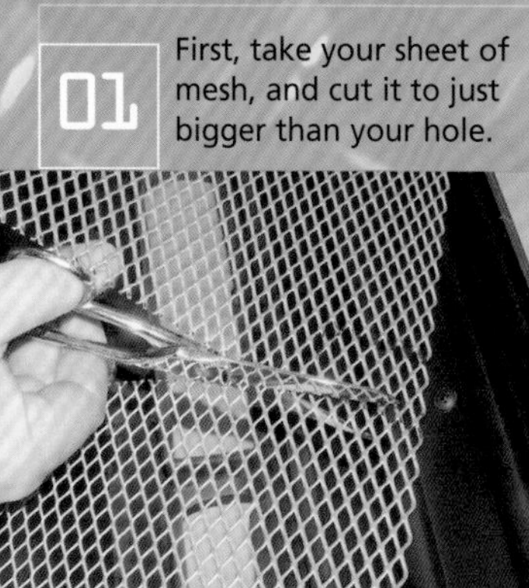

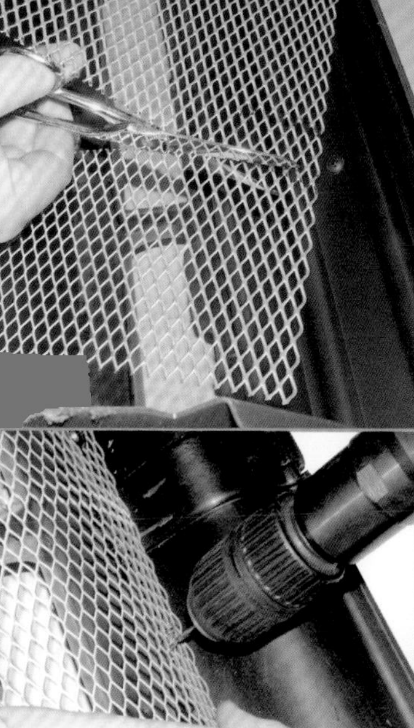

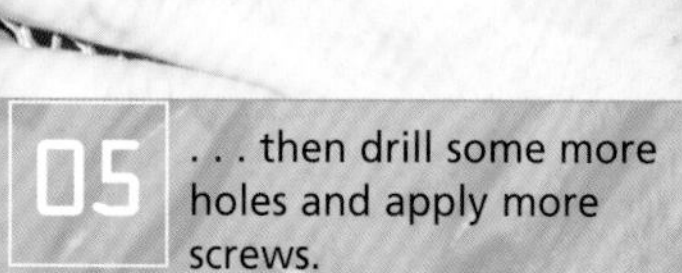

05 . . . then drill some more holes and apply more screws.

06 When you refit your bumper, you'll find that the front towing eye spoils the party, so cut it a hole with some snips and let it stick out through the mesh.

07 Of course, it's not always quite this simple. Some applications for mesh are not self-tapper-friendly, 'cos even the shortest of screw threads will poke through. In this case, you may have to pin your mesh with glass-fibre (if you're stuck, even "No-Nails" works).

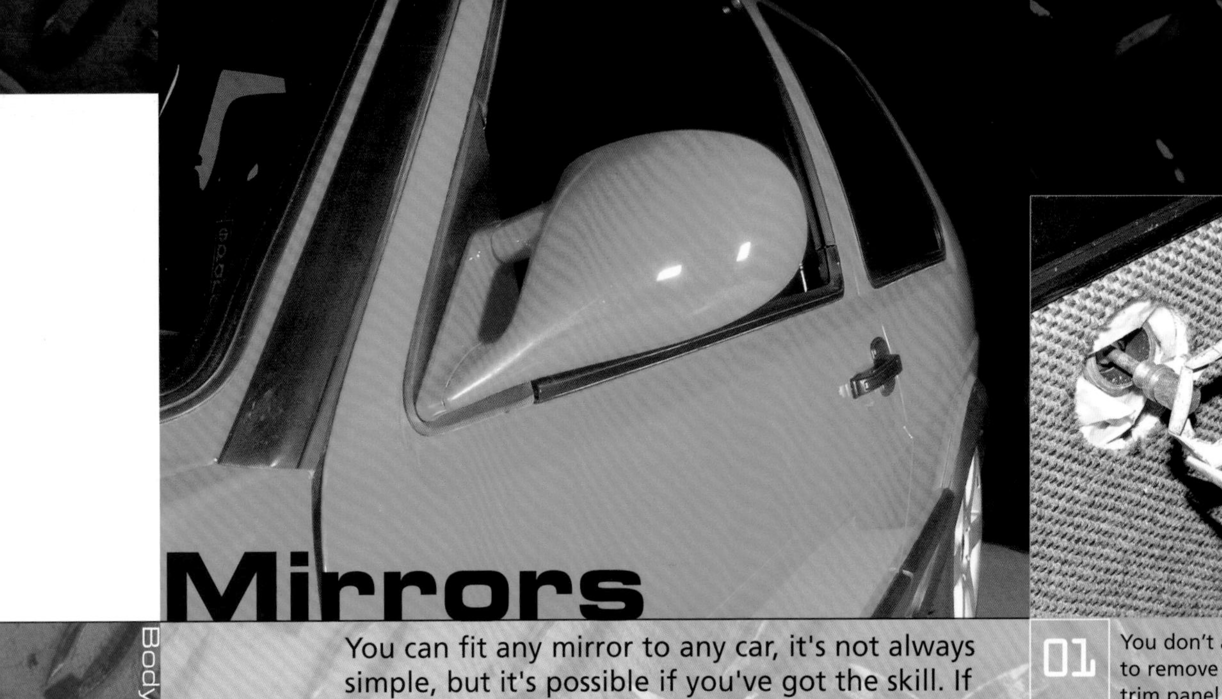

Mirrors

You can fit any mirror to any car, it's not always simple, but it's possible if you've got the skill. If you've got an early car with two-piece windows, then make sure before you buy what will fit. If you don't fancy following any trends, hunt around car parks, see something you like and order it up from the relevant manufacturer.

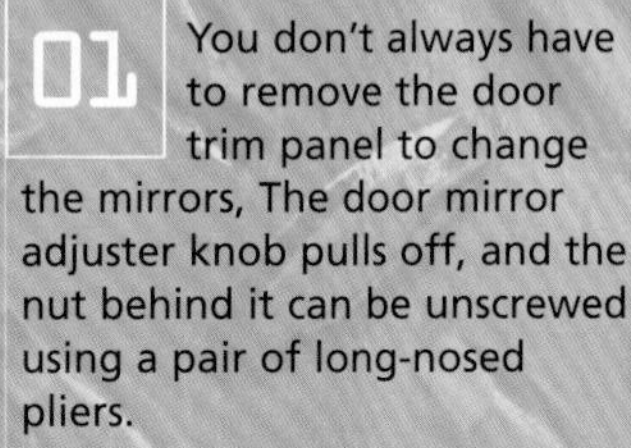

01 You don't always have to remove the door trim panel to change the mirrors, The door mirror adjuster knob pulls off, and the nut behind it can be unscrewed using a pair of long-nosed pliers.

06 Final shaping of the mounting plate will take time - work carefully, and keep offering the plate up to the car so you don't lose track. The Foamex can be sanded very easily, to achieve decent curves - also round off the edges of the plate as required. We found that the plate would only fit neatly after trimming up the window rubber and the door window top outer trim strip - take great care here, or you'll be ordering up a new window surround!

07 With the mirror held in the required position (check you can see behind from the driver's seat), mark around the base onto the new mounting plate.

08 Judging where to drill the three holes for attaching the mirror to the mounting plate is not easy, especially if, like our mirror, the base won't come off. Mark round the mirror base onto a piece of paper, then cut the paper out and fit it back onto the base of the mirror. Use a sharp object to "feel" for the three screw holes, and push them through the paper - only make a small hole, to ensure accuracy.

09 When all the screw holes have been found and marked this way, take the paper "template" off the mirror, turn it over, and fit it accurately inside the outline you marked on the mounting plate earlier. Now you can use the three punched holes to mark the hole positions for drilling the mounting plate. Drill the three holes...

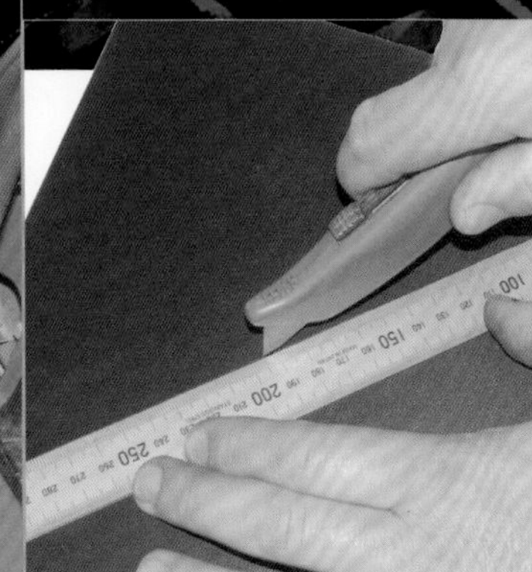

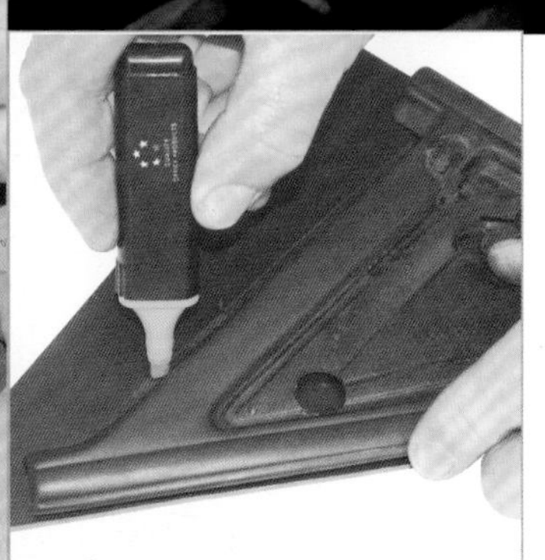

02 Prise off the triangular trim panel on the inside of the door, behind the mirror, then remove the three mounting screws.

03 Remove the mirror from the door (feed the operating cable through from inside). Peel off the old mirror mounting plate. What about the hole left in the trim panel by the now-missing mirror adjuster knob? One option is to cut the end section of the mirror operating cable off, attach it to the door using the nut, and refit the knob (or a new ally one) as a "fake". Some kits come with a rubber grommet to fill the hole. It's either that, or you re-trim your whole door panel to cover the hole.

04 Before you start properly, establish clearly how the new mirror is fitted. In the case of our featured universal mirror (supplied by Ripspeed), the mirror is screwed to a new mounting plate, and the mounting plate is screwed to the car - ie two separate operations. First job is to make up a new mirror mounting plate. Cut the square of Foamex in half diagonally to start.

05 Use the old mounting plate as a template to mark up the rough shape required. Trim the Foamex roughly to shape, then hold it and the new mirror up to the car, to judge how it'll look. Don't remove the protective film at this stage - leave that on until final, final fitting.

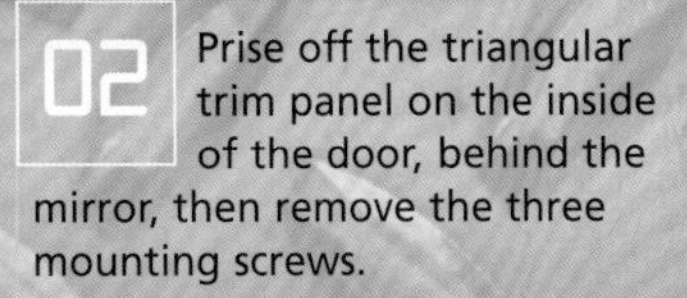

tricks 'n' tips

We found that the top corner of the mounting plate stuck out from the line of the door frame, which looked a bit cheap. Two choices here:

A *Pull down the window rubber and drill a tiny hole for a teeny self-tapping screw to fit, biting into the rear of the mounting plate.*

B *Before finally, finally offering the mirror into position (ie AFTER it's been painted), run a bead of black mastic sealant around the edge of the mounting plate, and on the door around the existing hole that the adjuster cable ran through. If clamped while the sealant sets, the top corner should be effectively stuck in position by the sealant. It's a good idea to use sealant of some kind anyway, as there's otherwise no waterproofing at all to stop water getting in around the original holes. Better-quality kits come with a rubber gasket (which you might like to stick on using a smear of mastic/sealant).*

10 ...and fit the mirror to the mounting plate using the shorter screws provided. Now mark the positions of the three holes you'll need to secure the mirror and mounting plate to the car. Have a mate hold the mirror and plate up to the car on the outside, while you hold the paper template you made earlier on the inside. It's important not to hit the three screws securing the mirror to the mounting plate. Aim slightly off the positions of the three screws marked on the paper template, and you should be fine.

11 Mark the three new holes for position (we were able to use at least one of the original mirror's mounting holes), then drill them through the door into the mounting plate (still held accurately in place by your mate).

12 Fit the longer screws and washers through from inside into the mounting plate, and tighten firmly. You can remove the mirror to cut the sharp ends of the screws off from outside, but we found this wasn't necessary. When you're happy, take the screws out again, and remove the mounting plate. Fit the mirror to the mounting plate again, then fit them to the car using the longer screws and washers.
Unless you particularly like black mirrors, you'll now have to remove the lot again, and prep it for spraying. For spraying details, see "Spraying stuff" further on.

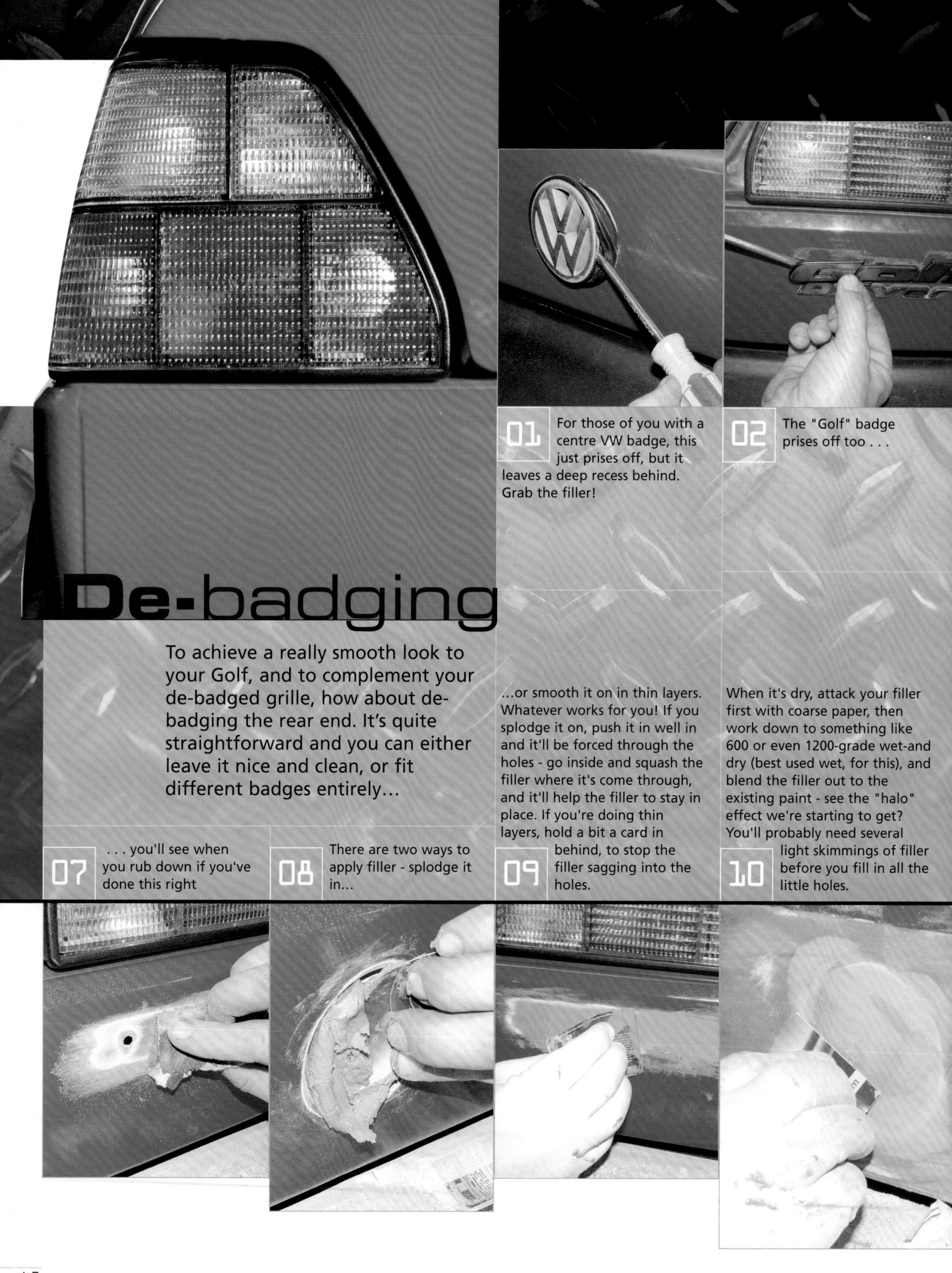

De-badging

To achieve a really smooth look to your Golf, and to complement your de-badged grille, how about de-badging the rear end. It's quite straightforward and you can either leave it nice and clean, or fit different badges entirely...

01 For those of you with a centre VW badge, this just prises off, but it leaves a deep recess behind. Grab the filler!

02 The "Golf" badge prises off too . . .

07 . . . you'll see when you rub down if you've done this right

08 There are two ways to apply filler - splodge it in...

09 ...or smooth it on in thin layers. Whatever works for you! If you splodge it on, push it in well in and it'll be forced through the holes - go inside and squash the filler where it's come through, and it'll help the filler to stay in place. If you're doing thin layers, hold a bit a card in behind, to stop the filler sagging into the holes.

10 When it's dry, attack your filler first with coarse paper, then work down to something like 600 or even 1200-grade wet-and dry (best used wet, for this), and blend the filler out to the existing paint - see the "halo" effect we're starting to get? You'll probably need several light skimmings of filler before you fill in all the little holes.

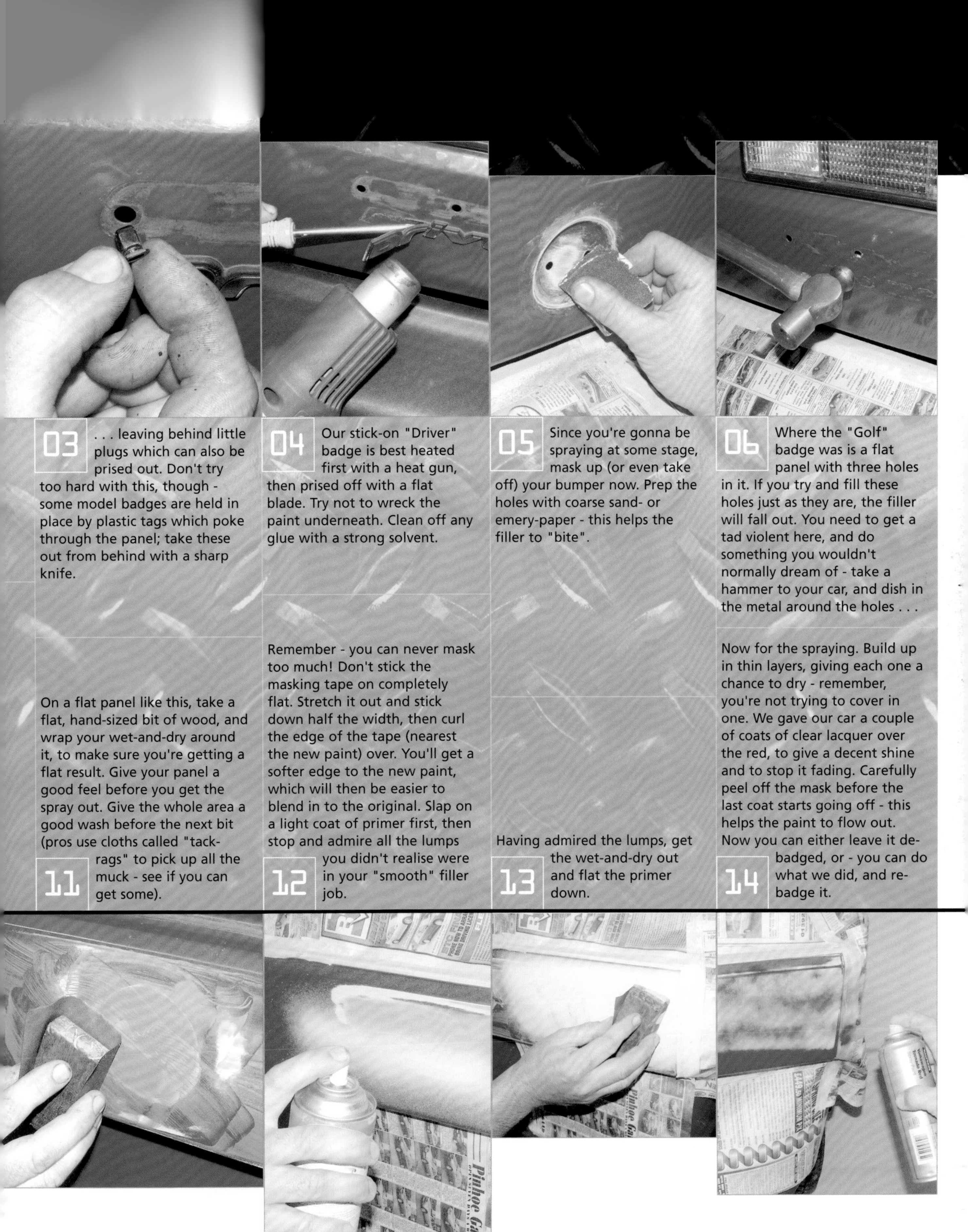

03 . . . leaving behind little plugs which can also be prised out. Don't try too hard with this, though - some model badges are held in place by plastic tags which poke through the panel; take these out from behind with a sharp knife.

04 Our stick-on "Driver" badge is best heated first with a heat gun, then prised off with a flat blade. Try not to wreck the paint underneath. Clean off any glue with a strong solvent.

05 Since you're gonna be spraying at some stage, mask up (or even take off) your bumper now. Prep the holes with coarse sand- or emery-paper - this helps the filler to "bite".

06 Where the "Golf" badge was is a flat panel with three holes in it. If you try and fill these holes just as they are, the filler will fall out. You need to get a tad violent here, and do something you wouldn't normally dream of - take a hammer to your car, and dish in the metal around the holes . . .

11 On a flat panel like this, take a flat, hand-sized bit of wood, and wrap your wet-and-dry around it, to make sure you're getting a flat result. Give your panel a good feel before you get the spray out. Give the whole area a good wash before the next bit (pros use cloths called "tack-rags" to pick up all the muck - see if you can get some).

12 Remember - you can never mask too much! Don't stick the masking tape on completely flat. Stretch it out and stick down half the width, then curl the edge of the tape (nearest the new paint) over. You'll get a softer edge to the new paint, which will then be easier to blend in to the original. Slap on a light coat of primer first, then stop and admire all the lumps you didn't realise were in your "smooth" filler job.

13 Having admired the lumps, get the wet-and-dry out and flat the primer down.

14 Now for the spraying. Build up in thin layers, giving each one a chance to dry - remember, you're not trying to cover in one. We gave our car a couple of coats of clear lacquer over the red, to give a decent shine and to stop it fading. Carefully peel off the mask before the last coat starts going off - this helps the paint to flow out. Now you can either leave it de-badged, or - you can do what we did, and re-badge it.

Body styling

Re-badging

If you've made your Driver look like a GTI like us, why not let the world think it is, and when modern badges look good, use them. You can also go for some genuine VW Motorsport items or Audi RS badges, there's loads out there to choose from and it's a simple job.

01 You could just stick your new badges on by eye, but be warned - the sticky is very sticky, so you won't be moving them even slightly once they're on. Offer the badges up, and mark the position required with masking tape. Our new Mk 4 badges came on a backing paper, which is a great aid to lining-up.

02 It's a good idea to give the badge area a good clean before you go any further - something quick-drying like meths is a good bet.

03 Peel off the protective backing, and offer the badge into place, using the mask as a guide . . .

04 . . . then, when you're feeling lucky, carefully press it all on firmly. In the case of a multi-letter badge like this, keep the whole thing square to the car as it goes on, or one of the letters might go on crooked. Peel off the top layer, and admire.

05 If you're putting another badge on the opposite side, get it lined up with the first one by careful measurement and use of the masking tape . . .

06 . . . before sticking it in place using the same method.

Cup-wings & splitters

You might want a full-on bodykit, but the theory for fitting any body add-on is the same. So we've fitted a few simple bits to keep the lines of our Mk2 uncluttered.

01 These are easier to fit with the bumper off (see section on fitting big bumpers, page 54). Lay the wings or splitter in position then clamp them gently with Mole grips.

02 Judging exactly where to drill through is a bit tricky, but you'll get the hang of it. See how many screws you've got, and space them evenly.

03 As you go along, fit the screw and U-nut to each hole you've just made – don't go mad and drill all the holes at once, because they may not all line up if you do...

04 When you're happy with the fit, take them off again and prep for spraying.

05 We found the best way is to hang them up - gives you access to both sides, but watch for runs!

06 Finally, fit your sprayed bits to the bumper - we didn't bother spraying all of it - remember, this is seen from underneath, or rabbit's-eye-view, as you might say...

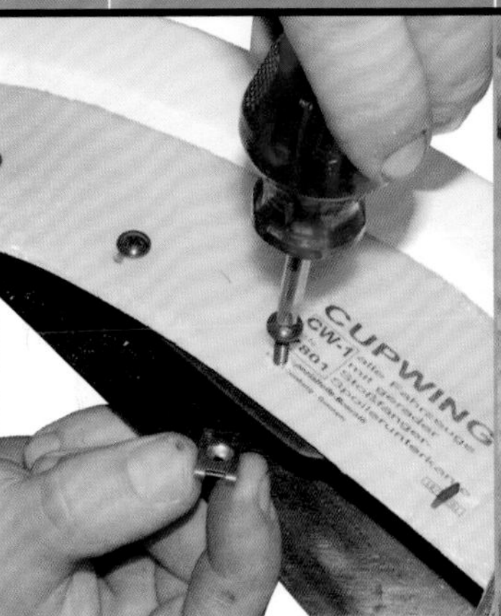

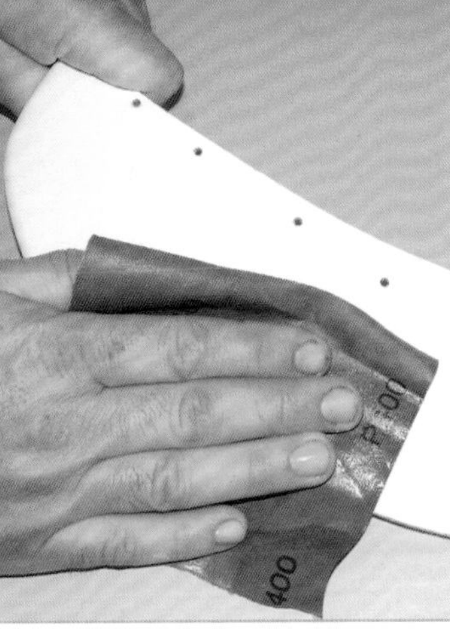

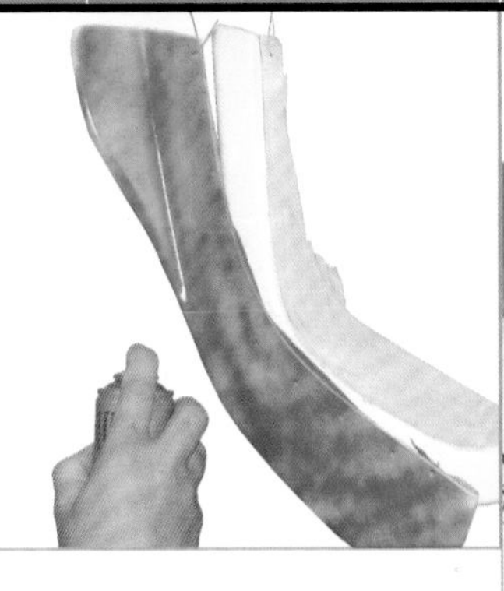

Is this the ultimate Golf rear spoiler? It's exclusive - one of only six made, ever!

Body styling

Rear spoiler

01 Our spoiler has three mounting brackets which clip under the top edge of the hatch window rubber, with a total of six screws holding it in place. The first job is to offer the spoiler up in place, and mark where the spoiler's screw holes will fall, using a few strips of masking tape.

06 Hold the spoiler up to the car and mark the position of the hole to be drilled in the tailgate. With the spoiler held like this, we're making a "mirror-image" of the hole in the spoiler.

07 Drill the hole in the tailgate, and don't forget to fit a grommet - if the wire chafes through, you'll blow fuses and have no brake lights at all.

08 Fit the metal screw clips over the spoiler screw holes.

09 Screw on the brake light mounting plate (three screws).

Using the masking tape as a guide, you can now fit the metal brackets. First, lift the window rubber with a screwdriver, and spray in some WD-40 (or similar) - this makes fitting the brackets easier.

02

Slide the brackets in under the rubber, and push firmly upwards until they "click" into place. The brackets have a curved lip at the top, which actually curls over the top edge of the glass for a really solid fit.

03

Put the spoiler on loosely, and check the alignment of the holes - the brackets can be moved sideways if necessary.

04

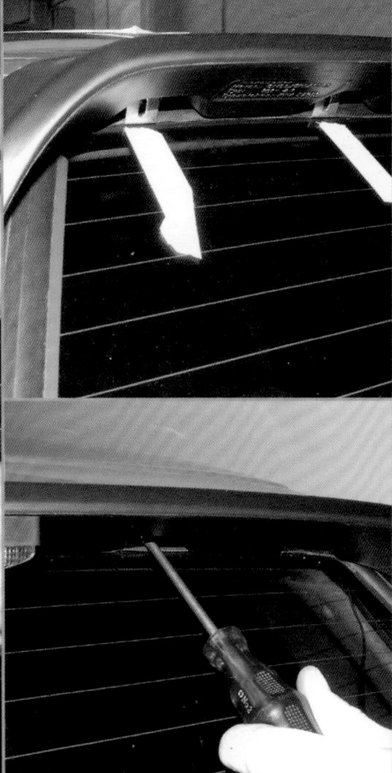

If you've got a brake light spoiler, you now have to drill holes in your spoiler and tailgate, for feeding the wires through. Our spoiler came with a template as a rough guide.

05

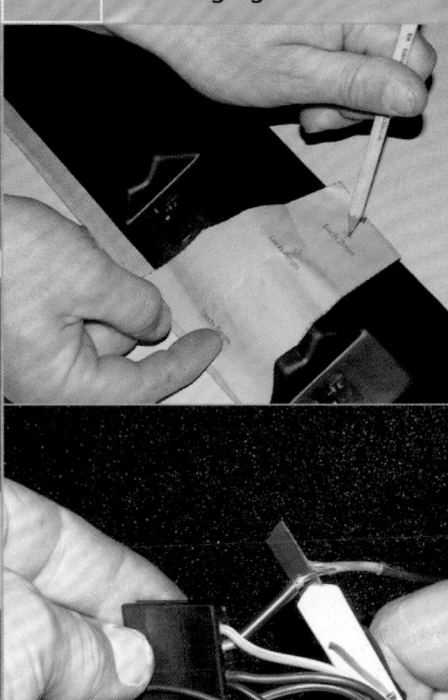

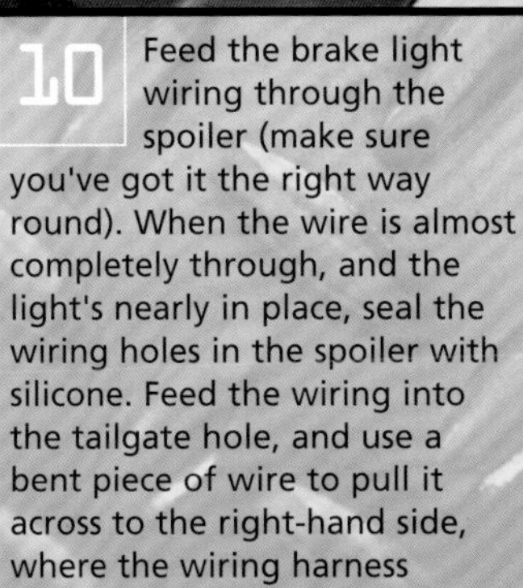

10

Feed the brake light wiring through the spoiler (make sure you've got it the right way round). When the wire is almost completely through, and the light's nearly in place, seal the wiring holes in the spoiler with silicone. Feed the wiring into the tailgate hole, and use a bent piece of wire to pull it across to the right-hand side, where the wiring harness rubber boot is located.

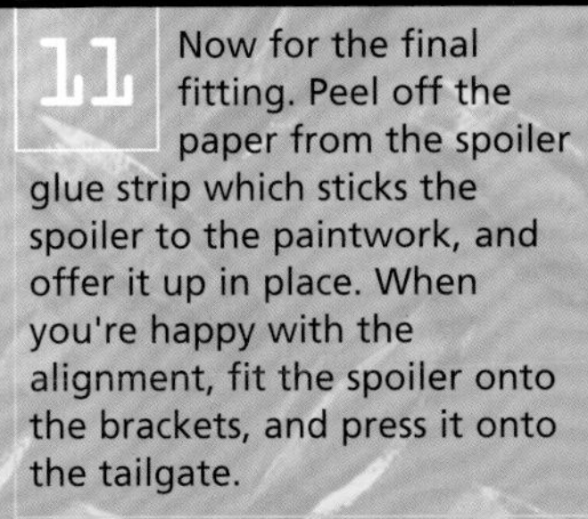

11

Now for the final fitting. Peel off the paper from the spoiler glue strip which sticks the spoiler to the paintwork, and offer it up in place. When you're happy with the alignment, fit the spoiler onto the brackets, and press it onto the tailgate.

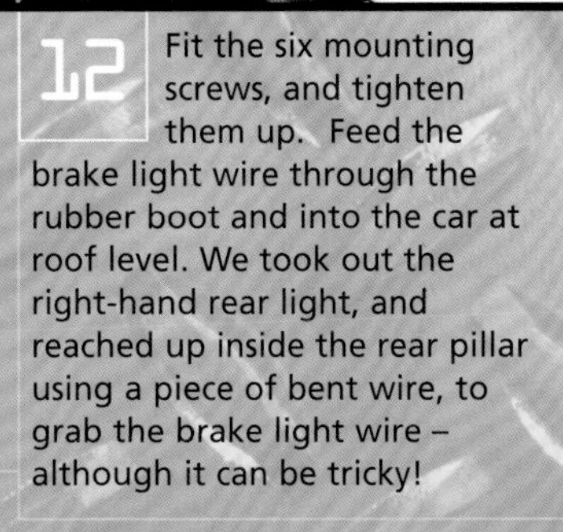

12

Fit the six mounting screws, and tighten them up. Feed the brake light wire through the rubber boot and into the car at roof level. We took out the right-hand rear light, and reached up inside the rear pillar using a piece of bent wire, to grab the brake light wire – although it can be tricky!

13

To make the light work, tap into the wiring at the rear light. Pull off the wiring plug from the bulbholder, and check the wire colours - on ours, the brake light live was red/black, and the earth wire was brown. Check the Haynes wiring diagram, or use a test light. It's best to strip a little insulation from the live and earth wires, and join in the new wiring using solder. Insulate the new connection with proper electrical tape, and the job's done!

Bee-sting aerial

Body styling

One style icon spawns another - the bee-sting aerial now features on many a modded motor. But the Mk 2 Golf had it first. So there.

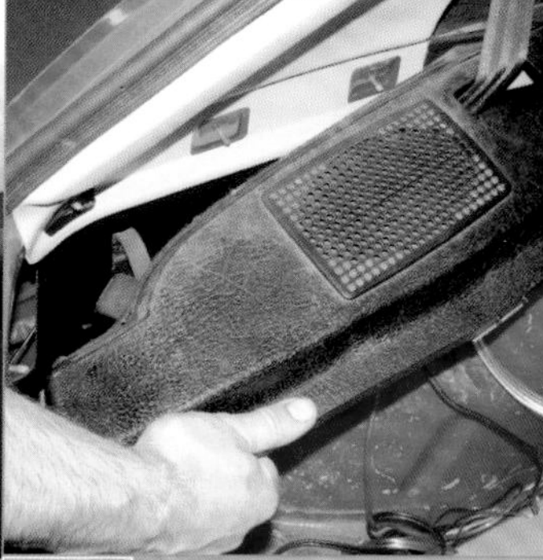

01 Before you remove anything, or drill any holes, think about where the aerial lead from the bee-sting's going to run. Ideally, it should be away from any speaker or amp leads. Ultimately, it'll be down one side of the car or the other - which side is up to you. We chose the left. Five nuts, and out comes the parcel shelf support.

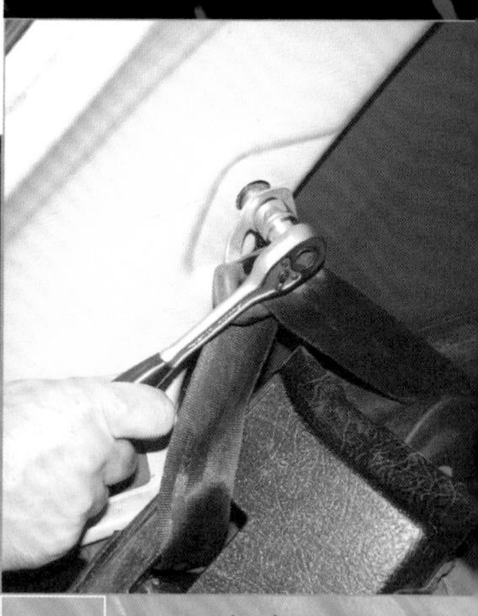

02 Now undo the rear seat belt upper mounting - as the bolt comes away, note how the washers and spacers fit on, 'cos they should go back on the same way, later.

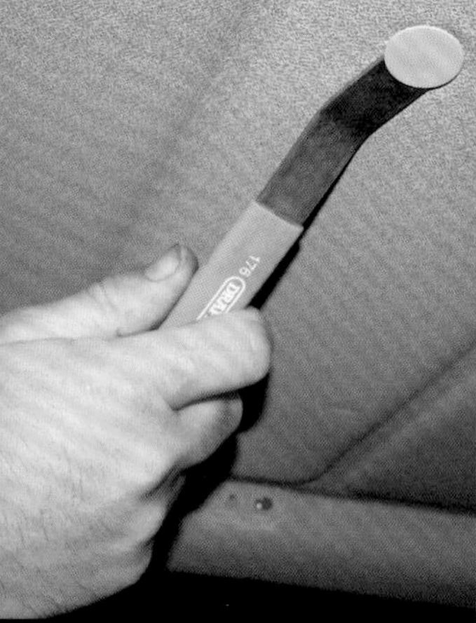

07 Prise out the two plug/clip things in the middle of the headlining, and now the headlining can be dropped. Pull it down at the back, and peel it from the top of the rear window rubbers so you can get your hand well in at the back edge.

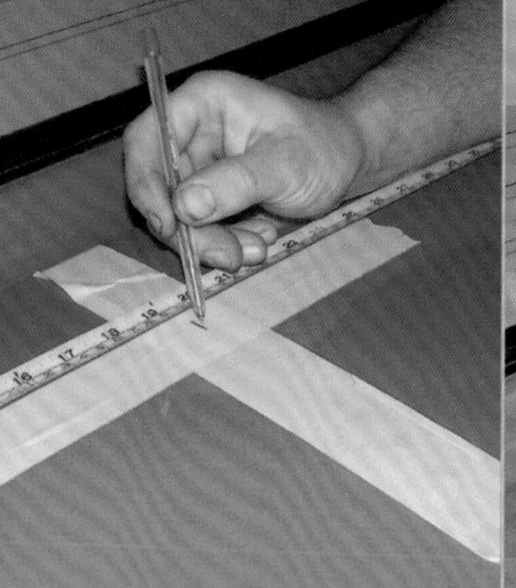

08 Now you're gonna need nerves of steel - you've gotta drill a hole in your roof! The first bit of this requires no nerve whatsoever – stick some tape on, and work out where halfway across the roof is. To work out how far back on the roof to go - stick your hand in at the back of the headlining, and feel for the crossmember at the very back of the roof - you don't want to drill through that. By feeling and eyeing the roof outside at the same time (tricky, but not impossible), you should be able to figure where's safe to drill.

09 To confirm it, hold the aerial roughly in place on the roof. Now's also a good time to check that the aerial won't get clobbered by the tailgate when it's open.

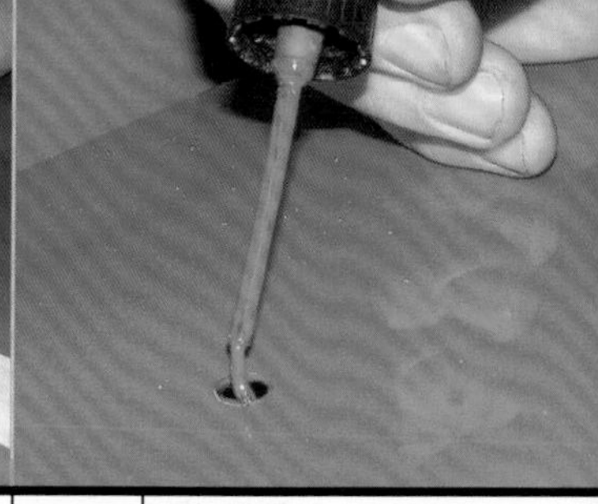

10 Drill the roof. You may actually need a bigger hole than the aerial "bolt" - on our bee-sting the plug on the rubber grommet was quite a bit bigger than the bolt. But start off small on the drill - you can always go bigger. Once you've made your hole, it's a good plan to paint around the bare edge, to stop the dreaded rust.

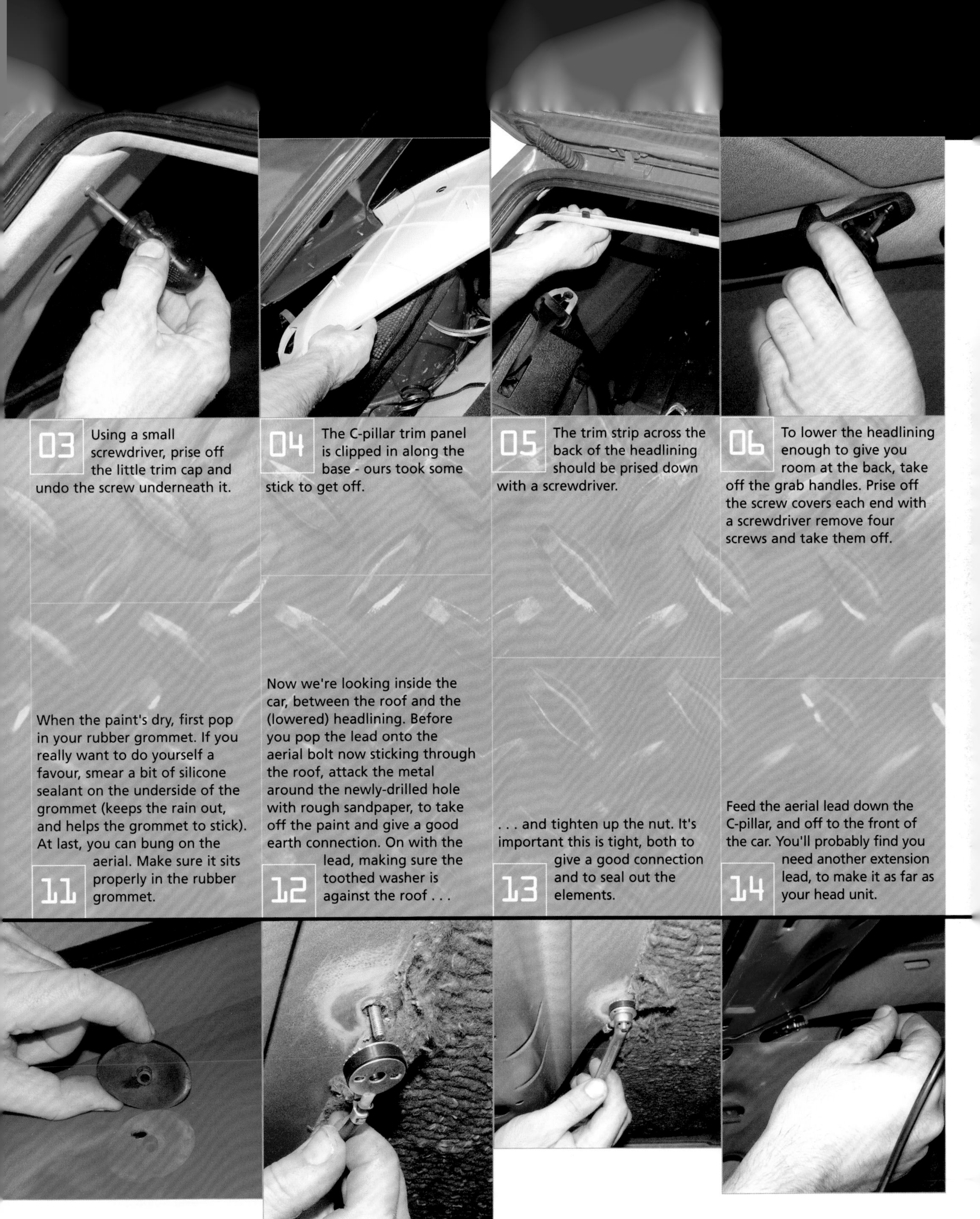

03 Using a small screwdriver, prise off the little trim cap and undo the screw underneath it.

04 The C-pillar trim panel is clipped in along the base - ours took some stick to get off.

05 The trim strip across the back of the headlining should be prised down with a screwdriver.

06 To lower the headlining enough to give you room at the back, take off the grab handles. Prise off the screw covers each end with a screwdriver remove four screws and take them off.

11 When the paint's dry, first pop in your rubber grommet. If you really want to do yourself a favour, smear a bit of silicone sealant on the underside of the grommet (keeps the rain out, and helps the grommet to stick). At last, you can bung on the aerial. Make sure it sits properly in the rubber grommet.

12 Now we're looking inside the car, between the roof and the (lowered) headlining. Before you pop the lead onto the aerial bolt now sticking through the roof, attack the metal around the newly-drilled hole with rough sandpaper, to take off the paint and give a good earth connection. On with the lead, making sure the toothed washer is against the roof . . .

13 . . . and tighten up the nut. It's important this is tight, both to give a good connection and to seal out the elements.

14 Feed the aerial lead down the C-pillar, and off to the front of the car. You'll probably find you need another extension lead, to make it as far as your head unit.

Removing the old **aerial**

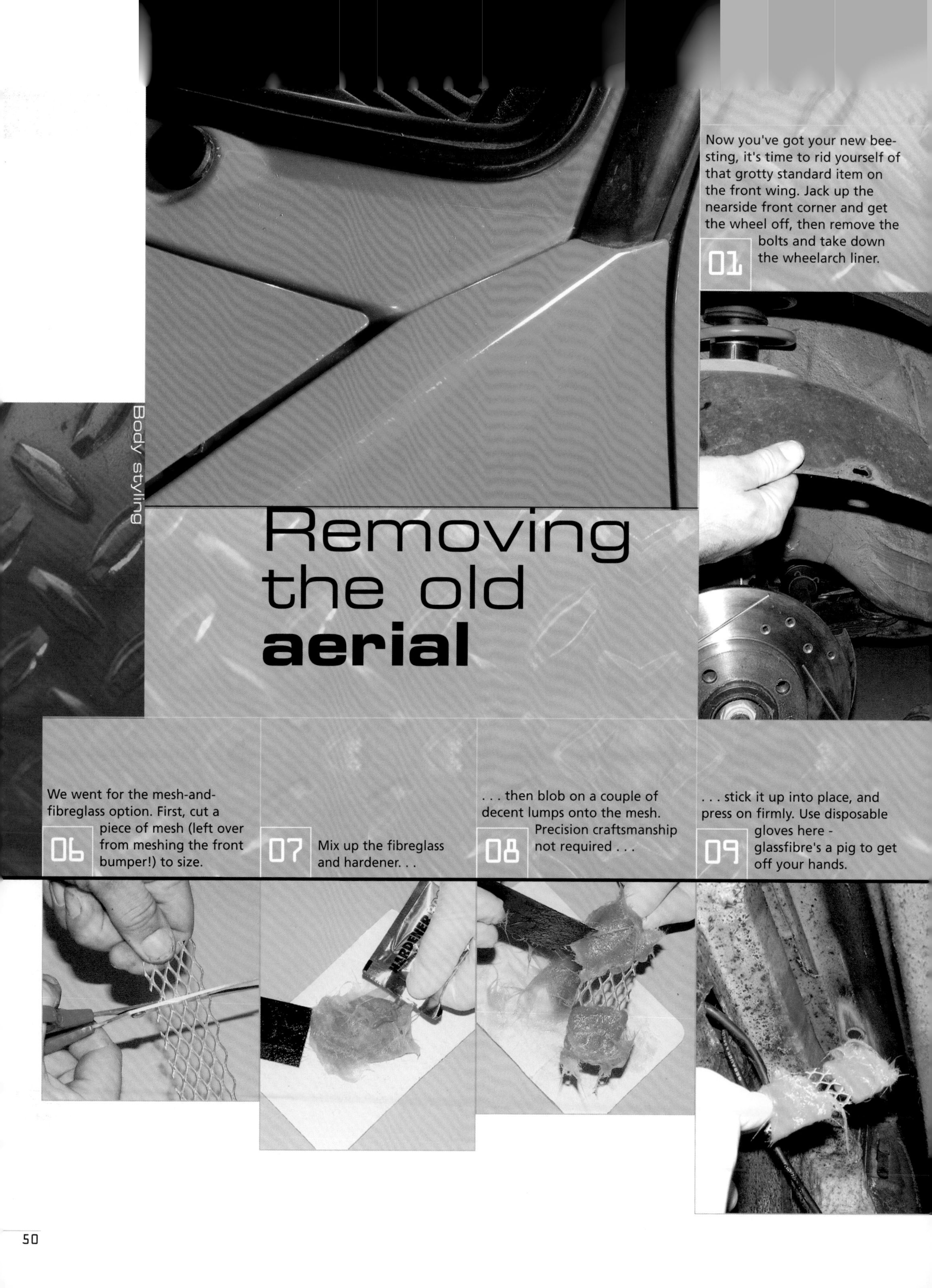

Now you've got your new bee-sting, it's time to rid yourself of that grotty standard item on the front wing. Jack up the nearside front corner and get the wheel off, then remove the bolts and take down the wheelarch liner.

01

We went for the mesh-and-fibreglass option. First, cut a piece of mesh (left over from meshing the front bumper!) to size.

06

Mix up the fibreglass and hardener. . .

07

. . . then blob on a couple of decent lumps onto the mesh. Precision craftsmanship not required . . .

08

. . . stick it up into place, and press on firmly. Use disposable gloves here - glassfibre's a pig to get off your hands.

09

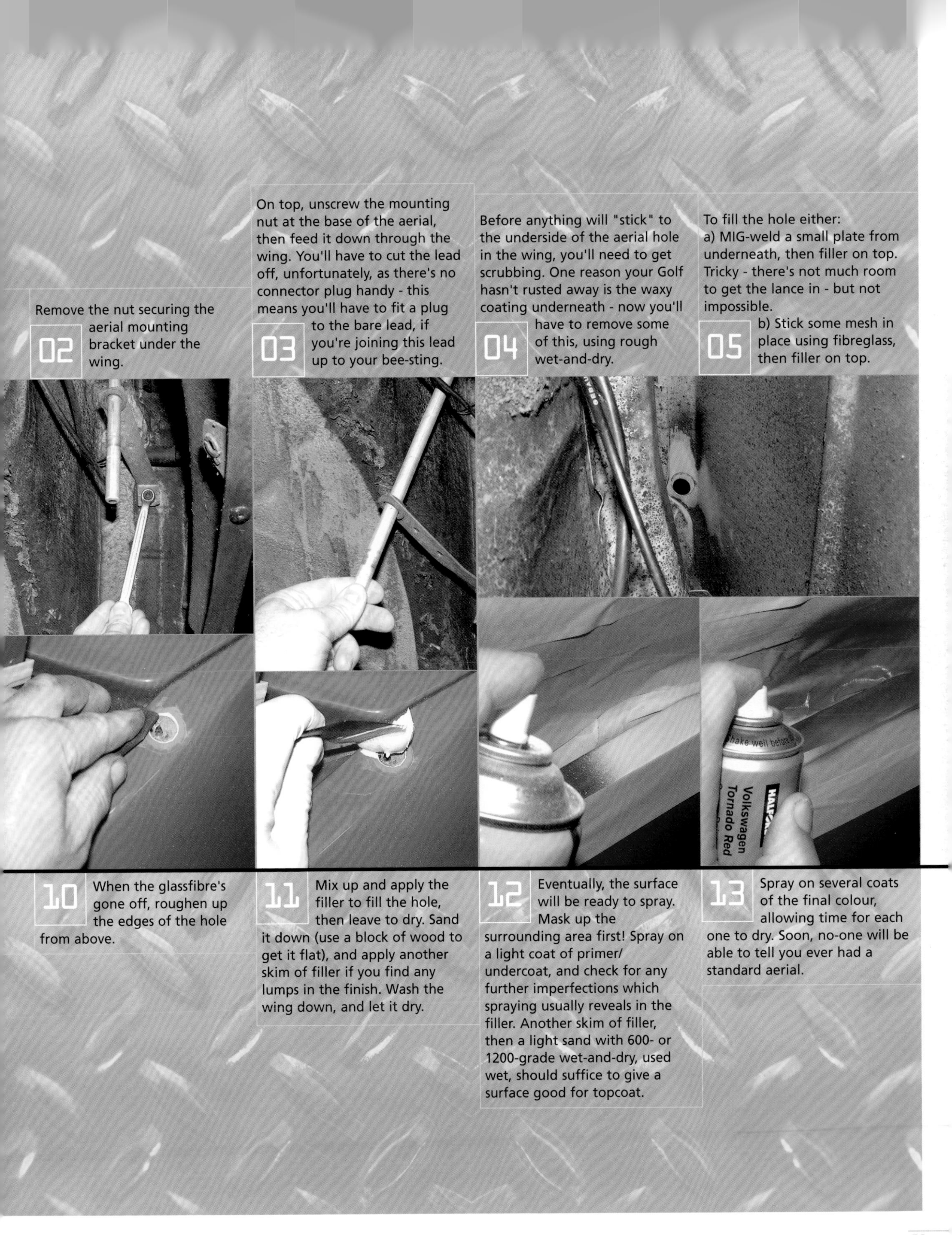

02 Remove the nut securing the aerial mounting bracket under the wing.

03 On top, unscrew the mounting nut at the base of the aerial, then feed it down through the wing. You'll have to cut the lead off, unfortunately, as there's no connector plug handy - this means you'll have to fit a plug to the bare lead, if you're joining this lead up to your bee-sting.

04 Before anything will "stick" to the underside of the aerial hole in the wing, you'll need to get scrubbing. One reason your Golf hasn't rusted away is the waxy coating underneath - now you'll have to remove some of this, using rough wet-and-dry.

05 To fill the hole either:
a) MIG-weld a small plate from underneath, then filler on top. Tricky - there's not much room to get the lance in - but not impossible.
b) Stick some mesh in place using fibreglass, then filler on top.

10 When the glassfibre's gone off, roughen up the edges of the hole from above.

11 Mix up and apply the filler to fill the hole, then leave to dry. Sand it down (use a block of wood to get it flat), and apply another skim of filler if you find any lumps in the finish. Wash the wing down, and let it dry.

12 Eventually, the surface will be ready to spray. Mask up the surrounding area first! Spray on a light coat of primer/ undercoat, and check for any further imperfections which spraying usually reveals in the filler. Another skim of filler, then a light sand with 600- or 1200-grade wet-and-dry, used wet, should suffice to give a surface good for topcoat.

13 Spray on several coats of the final colour, allowing time for each one to dry. Soon, no-one will be able to tell you ever had a standard aerial.

Window tinting

As with so much in modifying, window tinting is a matter of personal taste - it can look right with the right car and colour. There are also a wide variety of films available including coloured films, security films and films which reflect UV rays. The only downside is that it might not be legal use some tints on ther road which is why many are advertised as "for show cars only".

The law on window tinting currently is that there must be no tint on the front screen, no more than 25% reduction in light transmission through front side windows and whatever you like on the rear and rear windows. Also, consider that many cars come with tinted glass as standard which has to be taken into account before the tint film is fitted. If in doubt ask before you buy, and if you can, get a letter from the company to support the legality of the kit, to use in your defence. Some forces now have portable test equipment they can use at the roadside - if your car fails, it's an on-the-spot fine.

Kits fall into two main groups - one where you get a roll of film, which you then cut to shape, or a pre-cut kit where the film pieces are supplied to suit your car. In theory, the second (slightly more expensive) option is better, but it leaves little margin for error. The roll-of-film kit may leave enough over for a few false starts... Check when buying how many windows you'll be able to do - our kit was good for two Golf windows.

Photo courtesy of Volkswagen Driver *magazine*

Sunstrip

This is stuck to the outside, so only the outside of the screen needs cleaning. Do a good job of cleaning, though - any dirt stuck under the strip will ruin the effect.

01

02

Spray the screen with water, then lay the strip on top, with the protective film part touching the glass.

03

Check to see if the strip's level - use the top corners of the windscreen rubber as a guide for measuring from. How deep down the screen you go is up to you - how badly do you want to undo all your hard work, if the police object? Our strip was a bit skinny to start with.

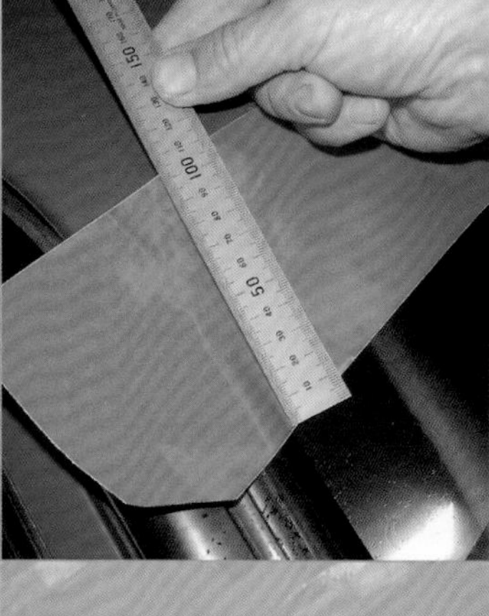

04

Trim the strip into place, tucking it into the windscreen rubber with your non-vital plastic. As you work around, try to make a tidy job of the corners by cutting in one movement, rather than lots of little nicks.

05

When trimming an opaque strip like this, it's not easy to judge where the rubber ends, and you'll end up trimming the rubber if you try to do too perfect a job at this stage.

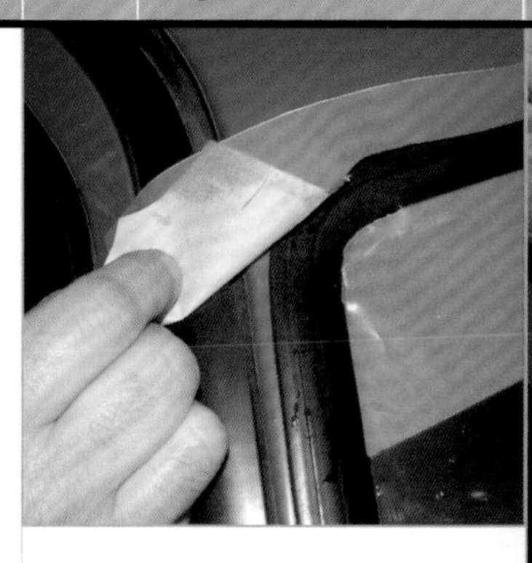

06

When you're happy with the fit, use the spray-and-peel method (as seen in "Top tint visor" over the page) to remove the protective film backing, and slide the strip into place.

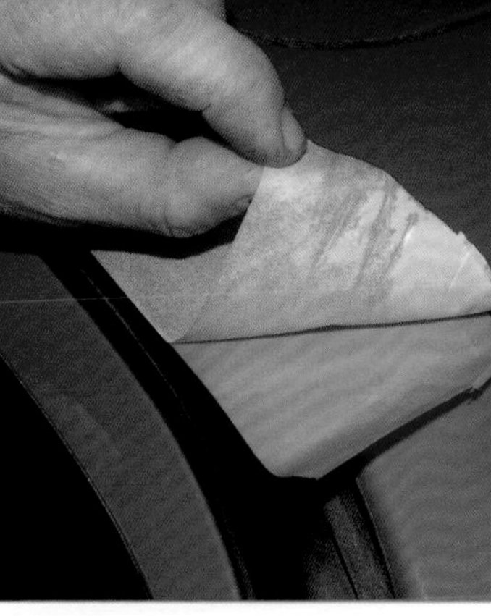

07

If you're still not happy with the fit, you can slide the strip a tiny bit further up (keeping it level) and try again (see Step 6 first, though). Spray and squeegee out all the air bubbles and creases.

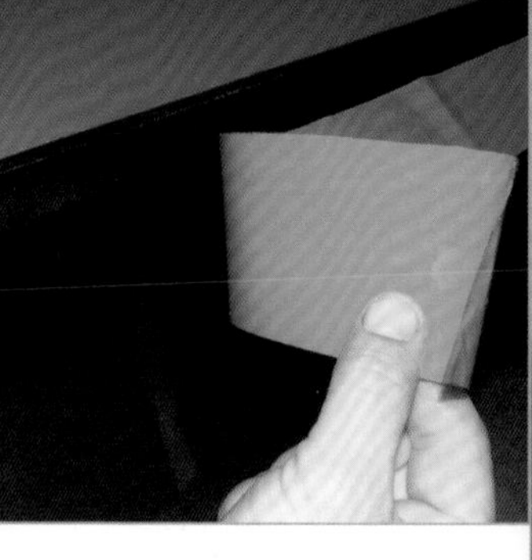

08

Don't be in too much of a hurry to trim the strip dead accurately to the windscreen rubber. It's better to use a small screwdriver to gently lift the edge of the windscreen rubber off the glass, then tuck the edge of the sunstrip underneath. If you haven't been too brutal with the knife (and made the rubber edge itself ragged), you should have a neat result with minimal effort.

Tinting

First, pick your day, and your working area carefully – don't attempt it on a windy day, and it's best on a warm day (or in a warm environment because the adhesive will begin to dry sooner). Don't try tinting when it's starting to get dark either! It's a good idea to have a mate to help out with this job too.

Step one is to get the window being tinted clean, really clean, inside and out. Don't use glass cleaners (or any other product) containing ammonia or vinegar, since both these will react with the film or its adhesive, and muck it up. It's also worth cleaning the working area around the window, because it's easy for stray dirt to attach itself to the film - and by the time you've noticed it, it could be too late. On door windows, wind them down slightly, to

01 clean all of the top edge, then close them tight to fit the film.

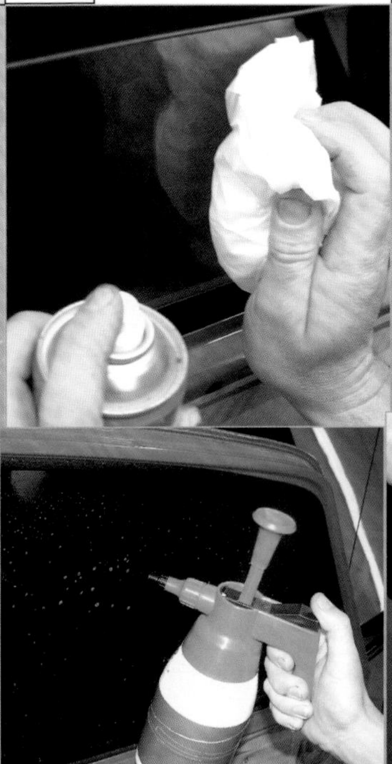

Before you even unroll the film, take note - handle it carefully and don't crease it. If you've got a pre-cut kit, you can probably ignore this bit - it's cut to size (go to step 12). Hold the roll of film up to the outside of the glass, and cut off a piece just slightly longer than the

02 window. Tape it in place at the top corners.

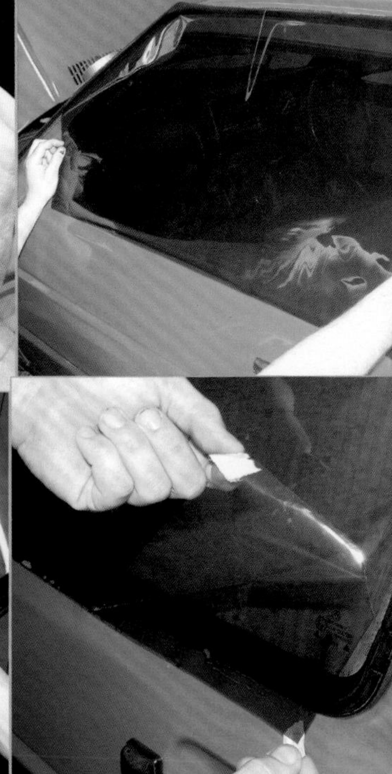

07 . . . then use a small squeegee to squeeze the water out from behind the film. Use the squeegee gently, in downward strokes - never use the squeegee on dry film, or you'll stretch it (maybe even tear it).

08 For trimming it accurately to the glass, we used a old store points card to press the film right into the corners - make sure it's nice and flexible. Though it's not easy, try and make a good job of the corners! It's absolutely vital that you don't trim right to the edge - leave a gap of about 2 mm - or the water won't be able to escape from under the film when you squeegee it. On wind-up windows, leave about an inch extra along the bottom edge, to tuck down into the window frame.

09 Before you remove the film from the window, spray the inside of the glass with the soapy water. It's a good idea to waterproof the trim panel in anticipation of the water by taping on some plastic sheet, or when doing a door window remove the door trim panel first (see "Interiors" for door trim removal).

10 Using the tape trick described earlier, separate the protective film from the tint film - as this is done, spray more water onto the outside of the film, to help it separate cleanly. Try not to lift the tint film too much off the glass when separating, as this increases the risk of creasing.

The next step is to establish which way up the film is - ie which is the tint, and which is the protective (clear) film. With our roll, the clear film was on the outside of the roll. The tinted film should be against the glass at this stage (clear side facing you). Take one corner of your cut piece, and apply a small bit of really sticky tape to the front and back side - use the tape to pull the films apart, just at one

03 corner. Once apart, the identity of the films will be obvious.

Using scissors (not a knife, or you'll damage your paint or the window rubber), trim round the outside of the window (for now, follow the outside of the window rubber). You should end up with a window-shaped

04 piece of film, just bigger than the glass.

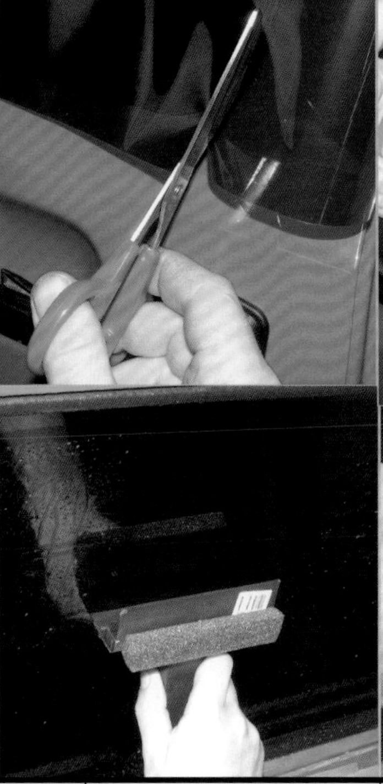

Now, and not for the last time, the window and film must be sprayed with soapy water. Use one of those plant sprayers you can buy cheap in any DIY store, and fill it with a weak solution of ordinary washing-up liquid (the soap keeps things clean and stops it from sticking).

05 Spray the outside of the glass, and "stick" the film to it.

06 Spray the outside of the film . . .

11 Have your mate on standby, to assist with transferring the film to the inside (be careful here). Peel the tint film off the glass, keeping it as flat as you can. Without letting it fold onto itself, move it inside the car and place it fairly accurately on the inside of the glass. The surface which was outside should now be on the inside of the glass (now that you've cut it, it will only fit one way!). Carefully slide the film into the corners, keeping it flat (don't crease it) and remembering that there must be a tiny gap all round (most important at the bottom).

12 Spray the film with the soapy water, then carefully start to squeegee it into place, working from top to bottom.

13 We found that, to get into the corners (and for tucking the bottom edge of the film into the door), it was easier to unscrew the blade from the squeegee, and use that on its own for some of it.

14 Have ready some soft towels (not paper towels) to soak up the excess water at the base of the window - if the excess is not removed as you go, it will seep back up under the film. Remember not to squeegee the film when it's dry.

15 Once you've got the film basically in place, it's time to chase out air bubbles and bits which won't stick down - sometimes this is best seen from outside. We found that, after a while, we gave up on the squeegee, and chased some of the bubbles out just using fingers. Don't lift the film off the glass unless absolutely necessary. Hopefully, you've now got a successfully-tinted window!
Don't be tempted to wind the window down for a day or two, and remember that the adhesive can take a week to cure fully. Once it's fully cured, it should be safe to give it a final clean. Be careful when cleaning only to use a totally-clean, soft cloth, and no vinegar or ammonia.

Top tint **visor**

In motorsports, where roll-cages mean you can't have sunvisors, they developed tints for the top of their screen. They look cool on road cars, and are cheap and easy to fit.

01 Remove the interior mirror – be careful, it may be stiff, but makes cleaning the inside of the screen much easier. It'd also be tricky to fiddle the tint in behind it! Using a small screwdriver, prise out the mirror base at the front, then tilt it down and pull it from the roof (ideally, without breaking it).

06 Our Foliatec sunvisor came with instructions that the bottom edge should be no more than 11 cm down from the top of the screen for legal reasons. It's up to you how far you go. Spray the top of the tint, then squeegee it onto the glass as flat as possible.

07 Using a sharp knife, trim the sunvisor to the inside of the windscreen rubber - use the plastic spreader provided, or other card, to tuck the film right into the rubber.

08 As you trim it up, make sure the tint doesn't move. You'll have to lean across the car to trim the centre bit, so watch where you put your hands.

09 Spray the inside of the screen with the soapy solution

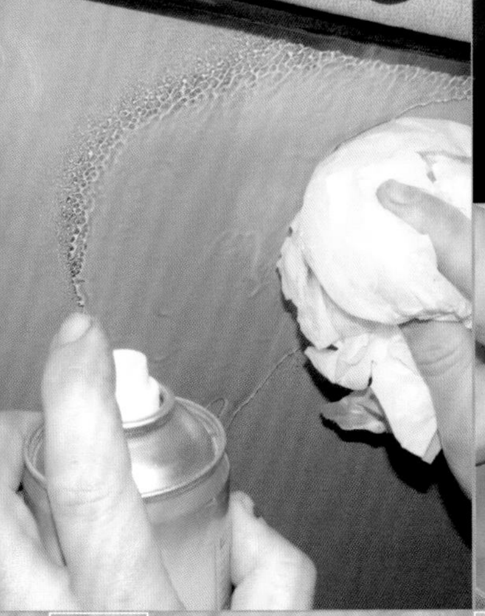

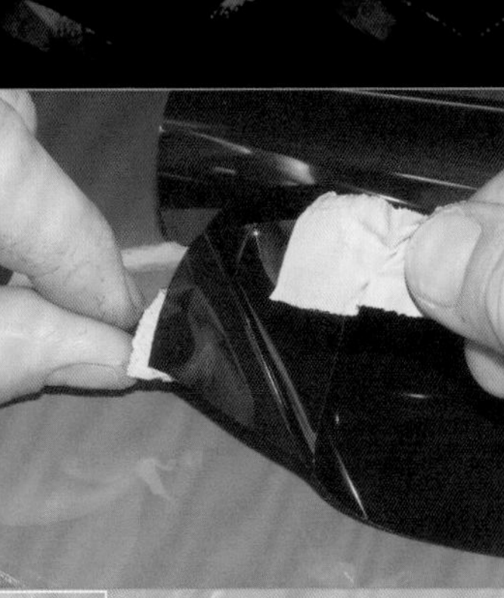

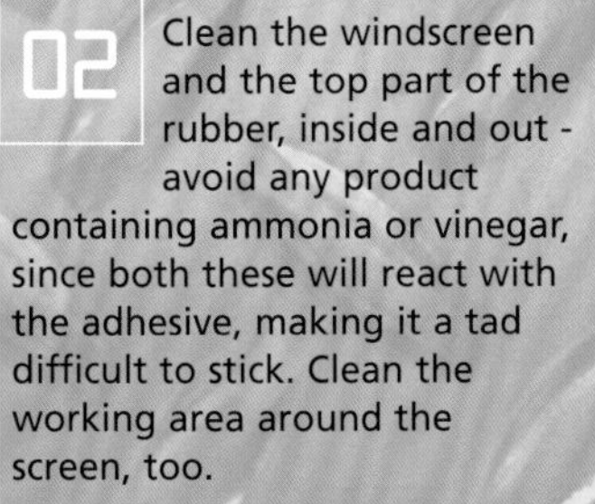

02 Clean the windscreen and the top part of the rubber, inside and out - avoid any product containing ammonia or vinegar, since both these will react with the adhesive, making it a tad difficult to stick. Clean the working area around the screen, too.

03 Next, roll out your tint, and establish which way up it needs to be. What you need to find out here is which bit's the tint, and which is the clear protective film (on top) - same trick as with the window tints. Take one corner, and apply a small bit of really sticky tape to the front and back side - use the tape to pull the films apart, just at one corner. Once apart, the identity of the films will be obvious.

04 Spray the outside top of the screen with a weak soapy water solution (washing-up liquid).

05 Lay the tint onto the outside, and slide it into position – get a mate to help you get it level. Tape it to the car roof, if it helps.

10 Using the tape trick again if necessary, peel off the top layer of protective film, spraying on a bit more as you go, and trying not to let the tint lift off the screen which is a bit awkward.

11 With a mate transfer the tint to the inside of the car, keeping the adhesive side facing forwards. Quickly slide it approximately into place (or even exactly into place, if you're feeling clever).

12 Using the squeegee or the plastic spreader and more spray, work the air bubbles and creases out from under the tint. As with tinting windows, remember that the tint will stick in the end - patience may well be needed, though.

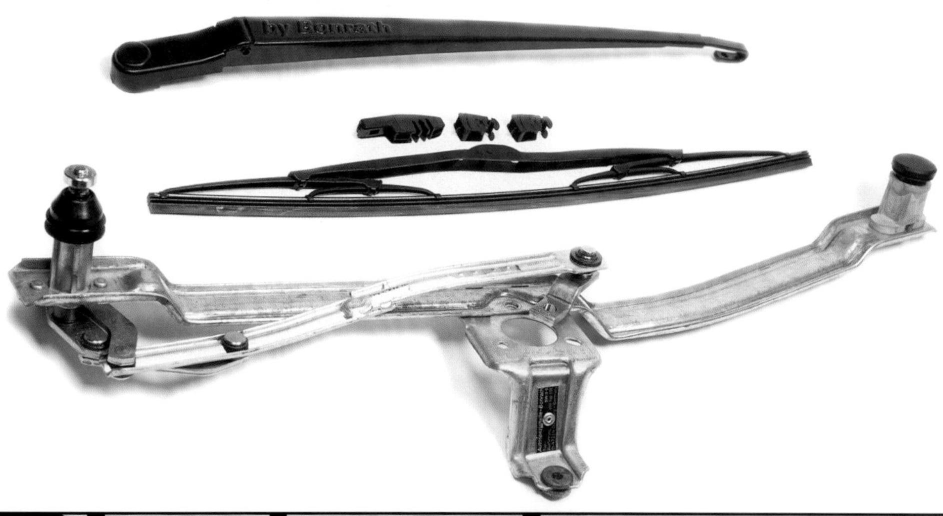

Single wiper conversion

Another race-inspired mod is the single wiper conversion. It replaces the two-arm factory wiper, with one central wiper to give a much cleaner look to the front of your Golf. Be wary of cheap kits however, as they won't stand up to much use.

01 For the most part, this job can be tackled with the bonnet open. Inside the engine bay, pull off the rubber seal at the back . . .

02 . . . and unclip the plastic scuttle panel which sits over the wiper linkage. If you've got a carb engine, you'll probably have to move the lurid green vacuum tank at the same time (just clips over the metal flange).

03 Prise up the cover on each wiper arm, and unscrew the nut below. Pull off the wiper arms.

04 Unscrew and remove the nut and washer below each wiper arm.

05 On the passenger side, prise up what looks like a blanking grommet, and carefully extract the two-part plug which is used to locate one end of the wiper frame. Try not to bust it, you'll need it again if your kit doesn't come with a replacement.

06 Back under the bonnet, unscrew the bolt which secures the wiper frame to the body.

07 Reach in and disconnect the wiring plug from the wiper motor.

08 The wiper assembly is now free to come out. First, wiggle it slightly to detach it from the body, then feed it out to the passenger side. Try not to scratch the paint as it comes out…

09 With the wiper assembly out, you now have to transfer the wiper motor to the new single-wiper linkage. Unscrew the nut which secures the linkage to the motor shaft, then prise the linkage off with a small screwdriver.

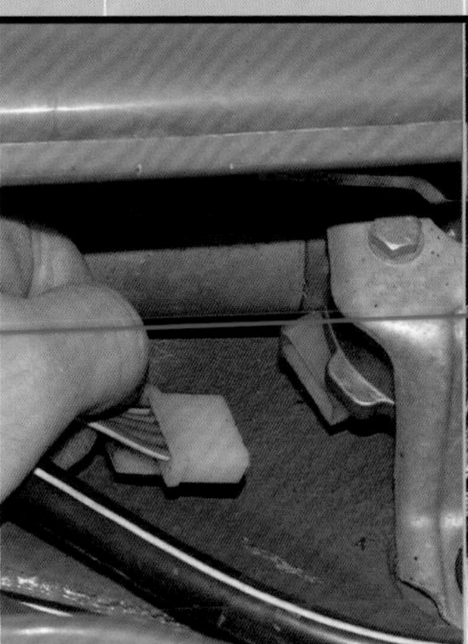

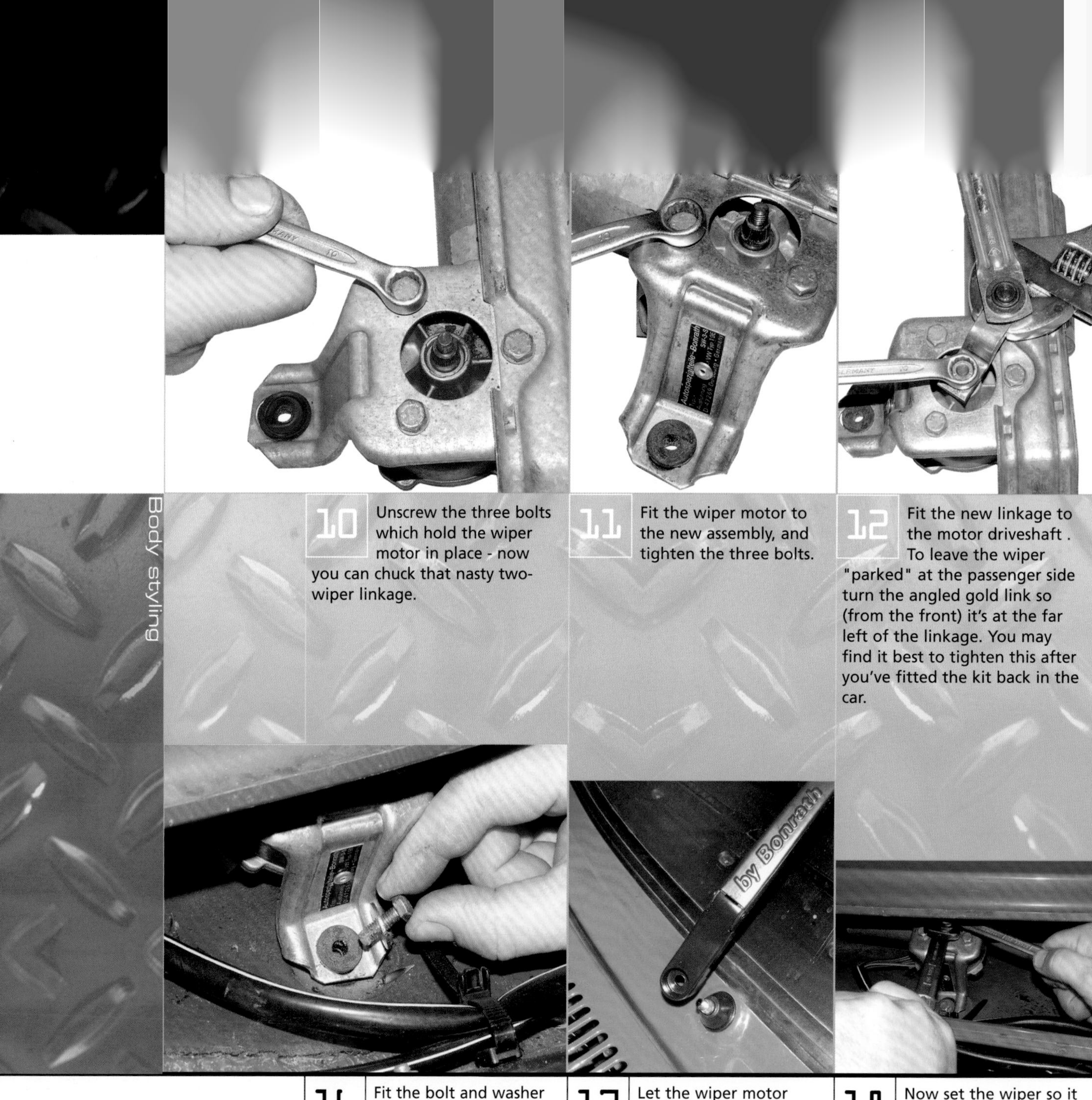

10 Unscrew the three bolts which hold the wiper motor in place - now you can chuck that nasty two-wiper linkage.

11 Fit the wiper motor to the new assembly, and tighten the three bolts.

12 Fit the new linkage to the motor driveshaft . To leave the wiper "parked" at the passenger side turn the angled gold link so (from the front) it's at the far left of the linkage. You may find it best to tighten this after you've fitted the kit back in the car.

16 Fit the bolt and washer to the wiper frame, and tighten it by hand - again, don't tighten it fully for now. Plug in the wiper motor, and you're ready to test the new linkage. Without fitting the wiper arm, flick on the wiper switch and let the motor run. To see whether the linkage clouts the bodywork - See "Bum notes".

17 Let the wiper motor park, by switching it on, then off. Loosely fit the wiper blade to the arm, to see where you want it, whether it's to one side or DTM-style centre parking (which is technically illegal). The wiper motor on some Golfs parks in two different places, depending on whether it's switched off from intermittent or continuous. Check to see if yours does, then account for it when setting the linkage.

18 Now set the wiper so it clears the screen properly and parks in the desired spot. Adjust the sweep by unscrewing the nut which holds the link arm to the motor shaft (see Step 12). The wiper arm can of course be re-positioned on the spindle by undoing the nut and lifting it off.

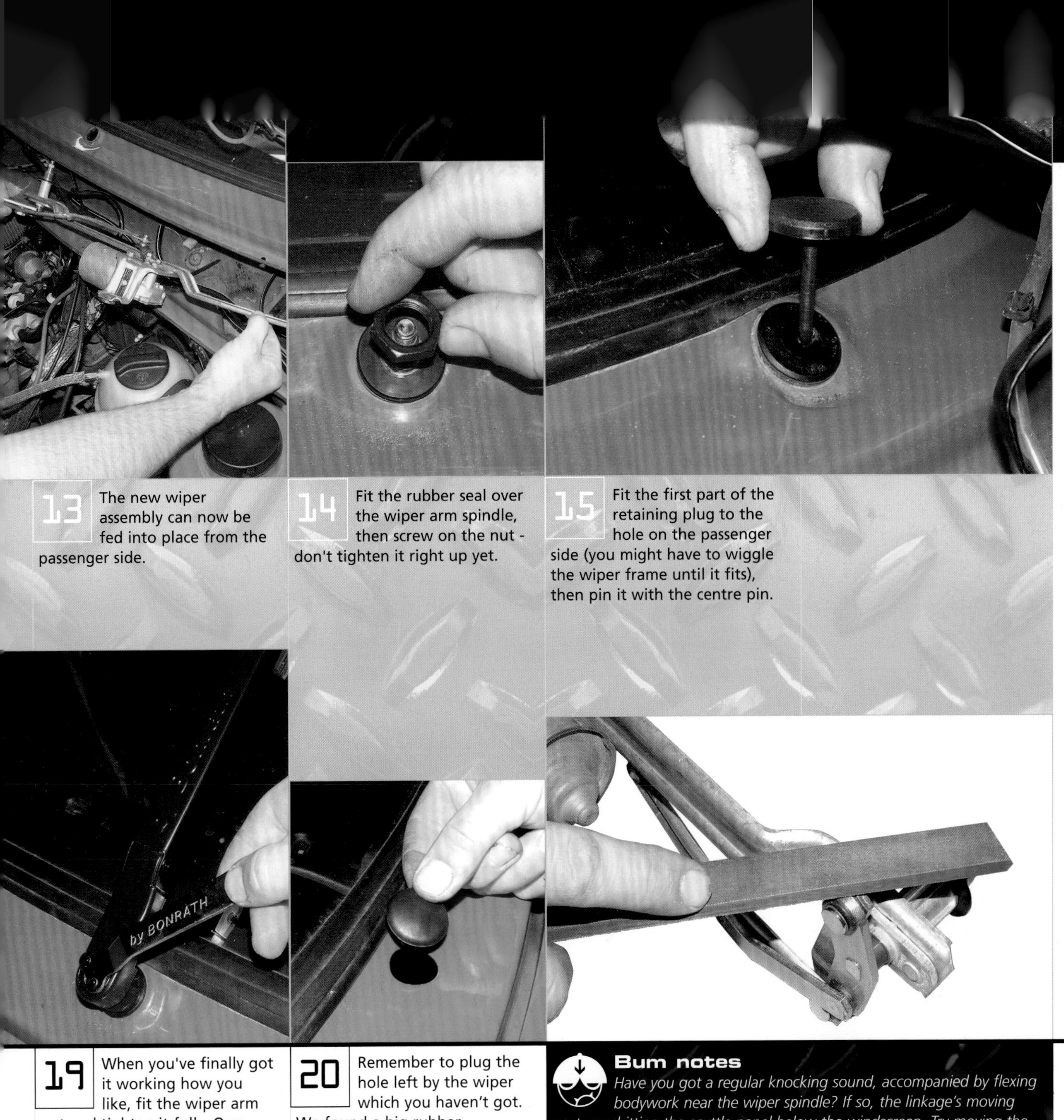

13 The new wiper assembly can now be fed into place from the passenger side.

14 Fit the rubber seal over the wiper arm spindle, then screw on the nut - don't tighten it right up yet.

15 Fit the first part of the retaining plug to the hole on the passenger side (you might have to wiggle the wiper frame until it fits), then pin it with the centre pin.

19 When you've finally got it working how you like, fit the wiper arm nut and tighten it fully. Our Bonrath single wiper was held by a "security" nut, which could only be tightened using the special peg spanner supplied - if yours is the same, don't lose the spanner! Fit the cap over the nut to finish the job.

20 Remember to plug the hole left by the wiper which you haven't got. We found a big rubber grommet did the job.

Bum notes

Have you got a regular knocking sound, accompanied by flexing bodywork near the wiper spindle? If so, the linkage's moving parts are hitting the scuttle panel below the windscreen. Try moving the assembly slightly, to see if this helps. The instructions with our wiper kit appeared to suggest bending the whole assembly in some way - not sure this is a good idea, or that it'll work. You could try filing the top edges off the wiper linkage, or if necessary beat out the panel from inside, like we did (not easy, and be careful not to crack the windscreen...)

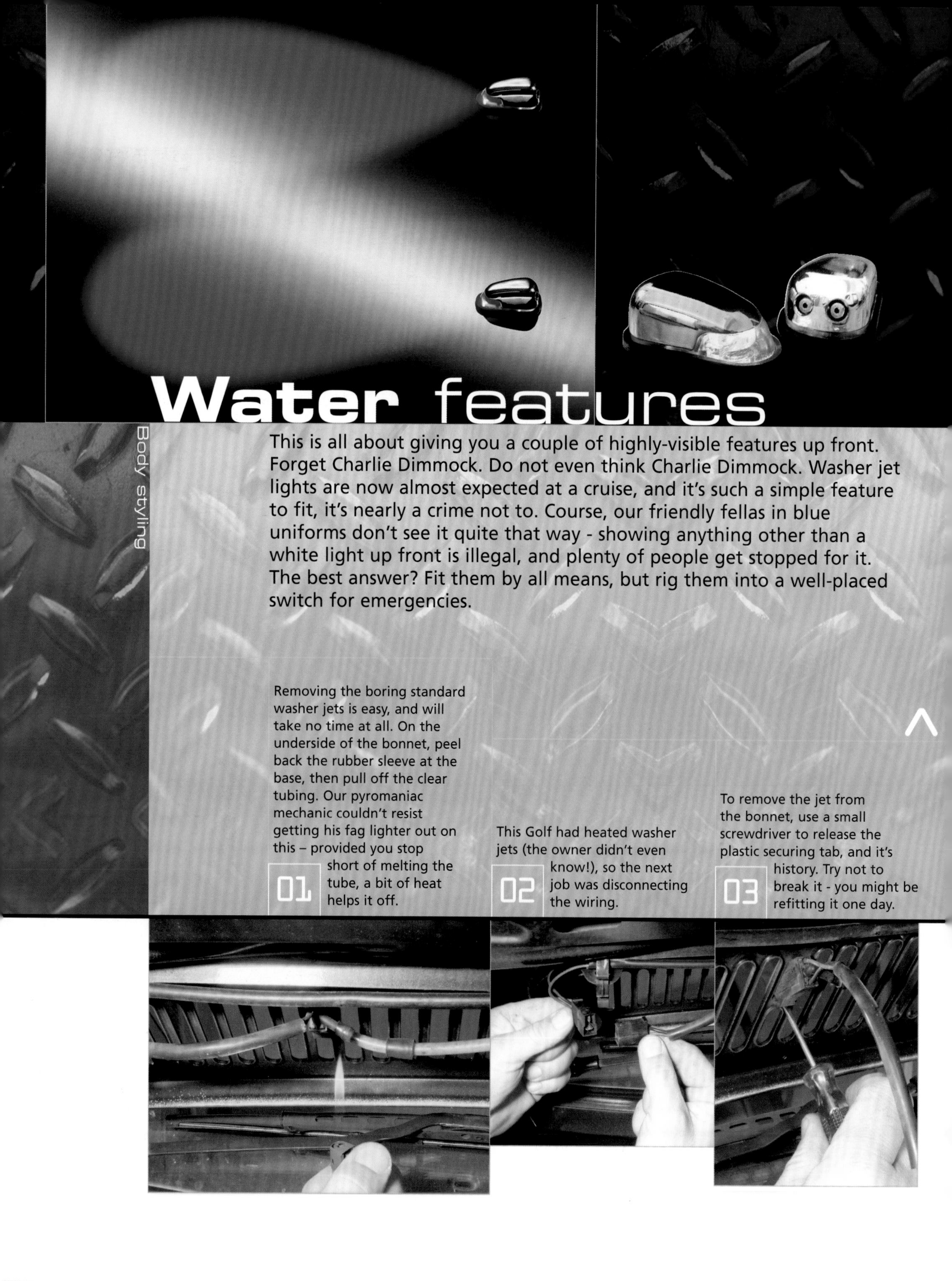

Water features

Body styling

This is all about giving you a couple of highly-visible features up front. Forget Charlie Dimmock. Do not even think Charlie Dimmock. Washer jet lights are now almost expected at a cruise, and it's such a simple feature to fit, it's nearly a crime not to. Course, our friendly fellas in blue uniforms don't see it quite that way - showing anything other than a white light up front is illegal, and plenty of people get stopped for it. The best answer? Fit them by all means, but rig them into a well-placed switch for emergencies.

01 Removing the boring standard washer jets is easy, and will take no time at all. On the underside of the bonnet, peel back the rubber sleeve at the base, then pull off the clear tubing. Our pyromaniac mechanic couldn't resist getting his fag lighter out on this – provided you stop short of melting the tube, a bit of heat helps it off.

02 This Golf had heated washer jets (the owner didn't even know!), so the next job was disconnecting the wiring.

03 To remove the jet from the bonnet, use a small screwdriver to release the plastic securing tab, and it's history. Try not to break it - you might be refitting it one day.

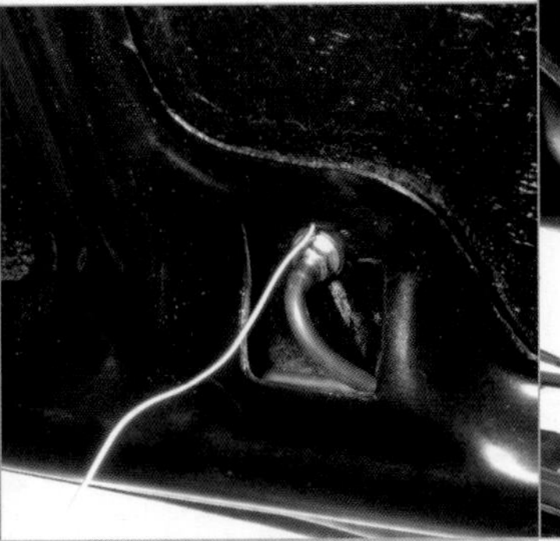

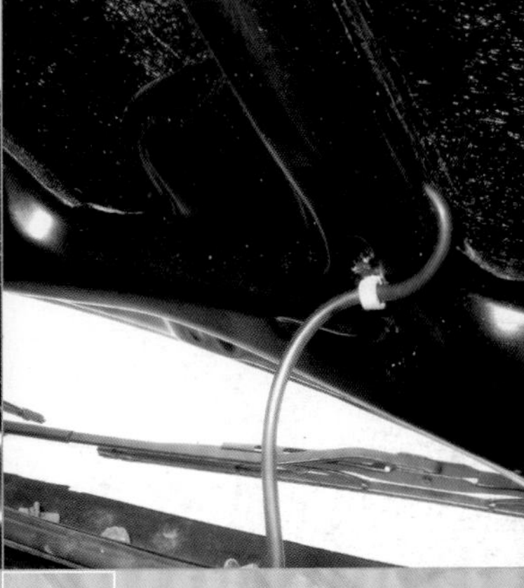

04 Slide the rubber base gasket up the wire and onto the bottom of the new washer jet. On a Golf bonnet, all this washer really does is save your paint from getting scratched.

05 Pop the new jet into the bonnet and slide the rubber washer up the wire. The rubber washer has a small recess cut out to stop the retaining nut crushing the wire.

06 Add the metal washer and retaining nut and tighten. With the old washer pipe refitted, the end result should look something like this.

07 This next bit is really fiddly, so take your time. The wires from the jets need to be routed into the engine bay, where they will be passed through the bulkhead to the switch on the dash. Use a length of welding wire and attach the end of each wire to it, then pull them through behind the bonnet braces. Using cable-ties attach the two wires to the existing washer pipe until you reach the battery.

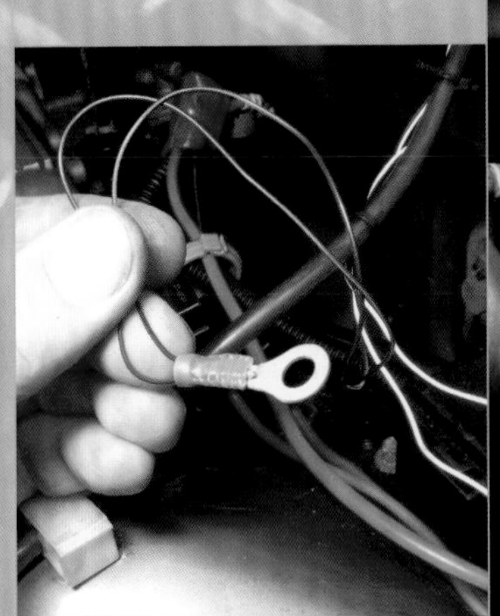

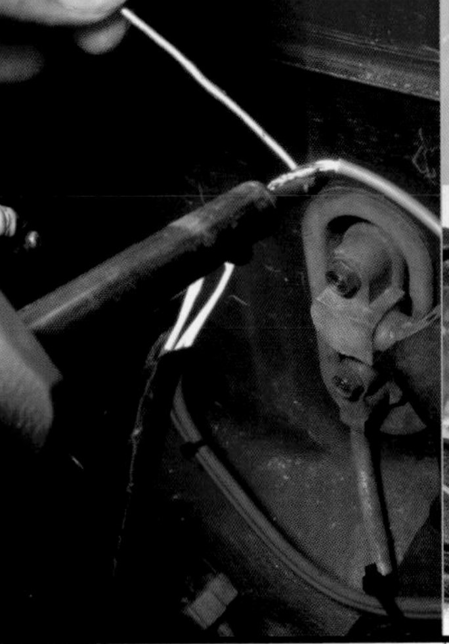

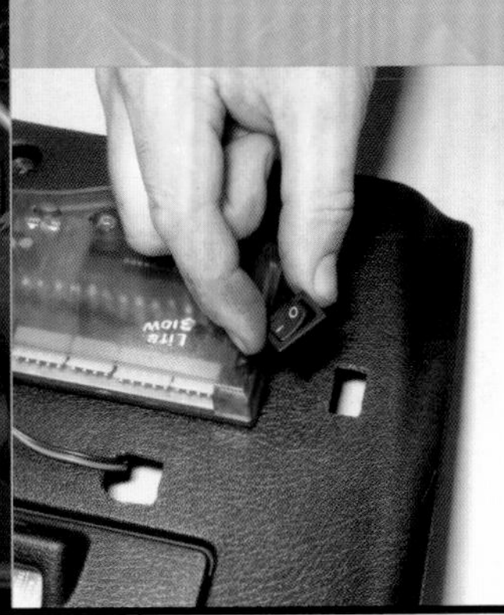

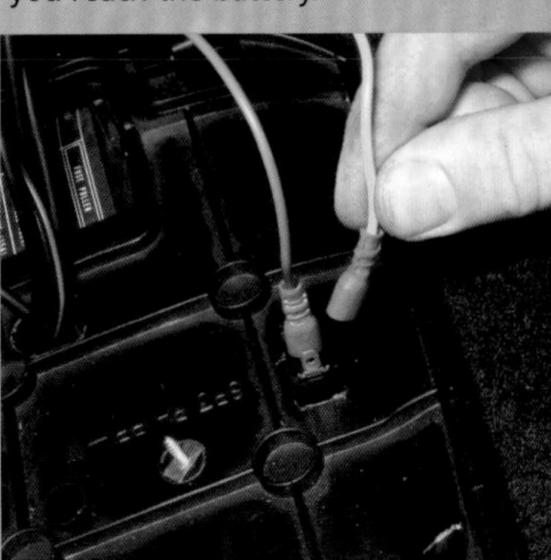

08 Each jet has a black and a white wire - according to the instructions, the blacks are earths. Using a ring terminal, connect the two black wires together, then fit them to a convenient earth point (should be lots available under the bonnet, or make your own by drilling a hole in the metalwork).

09 Now to the two white wires (the live feeds). At this point, we have to add a length of our own wire, as the wire supplied is not long enough to get it to its final resting place inside the car. Solder the two white wires to the new wire, remembering to insulate the joint afterwards. Or you could use crimps.

10 We've decided to add a switch to the jets (good idea, seeing as they're for show use only, thus illegal). So the next job is to mount the switch to a suitable area inside the car. After removing your chosen panel, mark and cut out a hole for the switch to sit in.

11 Feed the new wire through the bulkhead, under the dash and into the driver's footwell, where a female connector will join the wire to the back of the switch. The final stage of the wiring is to find yourself a live feed. We've taken one from our fusebox, but a fused feed from the battery will be fine. Another female crimp joins our yellow live wire to the switch and completes the circuit.

Late style big bumpers

Body styling

With the last of the Mk 2 Golfs, VW finally acknowledged that the front and rear bumpers were letting the looks down a little, and fitted the now famous 'big bumpers'. Unless you bought a late-model GTI (or GL), your Mk 2 Golf will be looking seriously under-endowed in the bumper department. One of the most convincing mods for any 'lesser' Golf, the big bumper kit is also not expensive, and is easy to fit. Don't be in too big a hurry to paint your new bumpers when you get them – check that the bumpers will fit first, then take them off and spray them (use the info in "Spraying stuff" if you like).

01 The bumpers are mounted on brackets which slide into the chassis legs, and secured by two bolts up from below either side. Unclipping the round plastic covers in the front panel below the bumper this gives you access to the front bolt . . .

02 . . . though you can reach both bolts from further back without removing the covers.

07 Use a punch (a small screwdriver will do) to push out the centre plugs on the bumper side mounts - the plugs go through and fall out inside. The mounts fall off outside.

08 When you get your big bumper kit, note that the bumper side mounts for the front and back are different - look closely, and in our pic you'll see that the front mount (which is at the bottom) has a stepped profile, to match the curve of the front wing.

09 Clip the front side mounts into the two wing holes . . .

10 . . . then tap in the centre plugs (so that the ends are flush) to secure them.

03 Have a mate help you off with the bumper. Pull the bumper forwards slowly, and it will slide off the side mounts; let it rest on the floor while you disconnect the wiring.

04 Trace the indicator wires back through the front panel, and separate the wiring plugs. The bumper can now be completely removed.

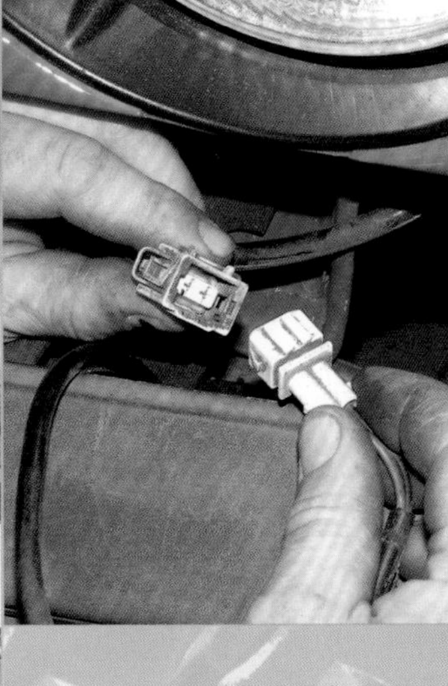

05 Prise out the lower front grille, which is just clipped in, and take it away for scrapping!

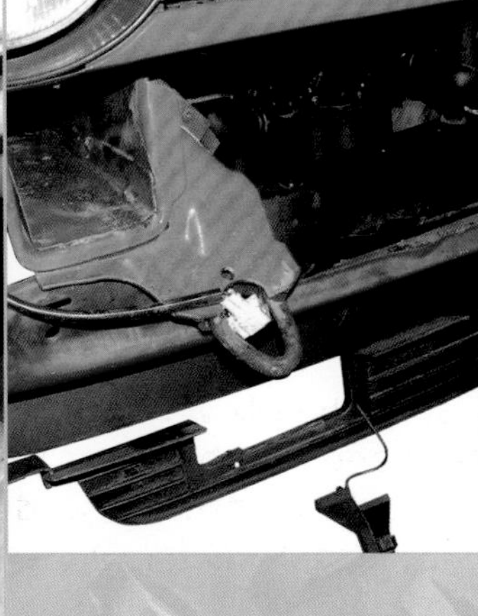

06 On Drivers and GTIs (and other special editions), the chin spoiler is held on by a row of small bolts.

11 With your mate, lift the bumper and slide it over the top and bottom lips on the side mounts, while feeding the two brackets into the chassis legs. Push the bumper fully home, and make sure it's sitting straight before you try the bolts in.

12 The hardest bit about fitting these bumpers is getting the bolts to feed up through into the bumper brackets from underneath. The first three are easy, but the fourth one can be awkward - on our front bumper, we found we had to put both left-hand bolts in first, then the rear right, then the front right. Find a sequence which works for you, and check our tips out, too.

13 When you're happy with the fit of the new bumpers - take them off! Now they can be sprayed. If you're having the bumpers sprayed by a bodyshop, make sure they know which sections of the big bumpers are to be done body colour, and which bits get left black. You can stick your newly-sprayed bumpers straight on now, but if you're fitting front fogs, or a splitter, the bumper will have to come off again. Remember to refit your indicators and number plates...

Tricks 'n' tips

To align the bumper bolt holes, work a screwdriver up into one of the holes from below - it should also go through the bumper bracket. Now slide the bumper in and out, and use the angle of the screwdriver shaft to tell you when you've found the mid-point (the shaft should be vertical). Now take out the screwdriver, and try the bolt. When you've got one in, each side, the other two should be easy. You can also see the bolts (or the screwdriver) by shining a torch down the chassis legs. Good luck!

Spraying stuff

This is not the section where we tell you how to respray your entire Golf in a weekend, using only spray cans. This bit's all about how to spray up your various plastic bits before final fitting – door mirrors, spoilers, splitters, even bumpers if you like. As we've no doubt said before, fit your unpainted bits first. Make sure everything fits properly (shape and tidy up as necessary), that all holes have been drilled, and all screws, etc. are doing their job. Then and only when you're totally, completely happy with the fit – take them off, and get busy with the spray cans.

01 The first job is to mask off any areas you don't want painted. Do this right at the start, or you could be sorry; on our door mirrors, we decided to mask off just at the lip before the glass, to leave a black unpainted edge - if we hadn't masked it as the very first job, we would've roughed up all the shiny black plastic next, and wrecked the edge finish.

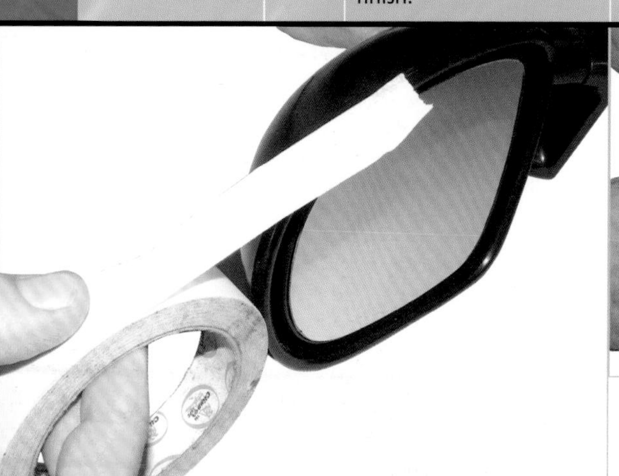

02 Remove any unwanted "seams" in the plastic, using fine sandpaper or wet-and-dry. Some of these seams look okay, others don't - you decide. Also worth tidying up any other areas you're not happy with, fit-wise, while you're at it.

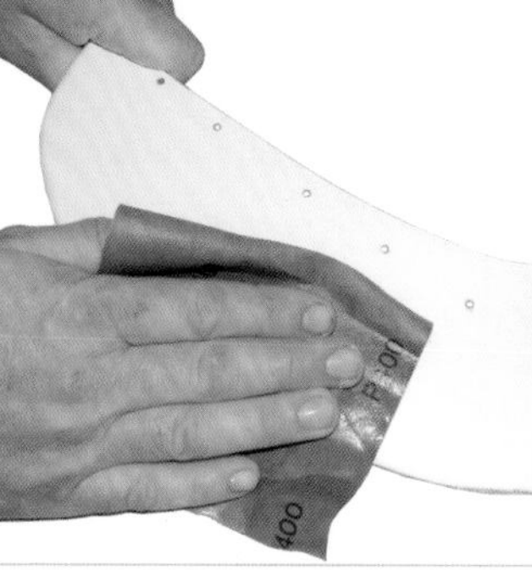

03 Especially with "shiny" plastic, you must rough-up the surface before spray will "bite" to it, or - it'll flake off. Just take off the shine, no more. You can use fine wet-and-dry for this (used dry), but we prefer Scotch-Brite. This stuff, which looks much like a scouring pad, is available from motor factors and bodyshops, in several grades - we used ultra-fine, which is grey. One advantage of Scotch-Brite is that it's a bit easier to work into awkward corners than paper.

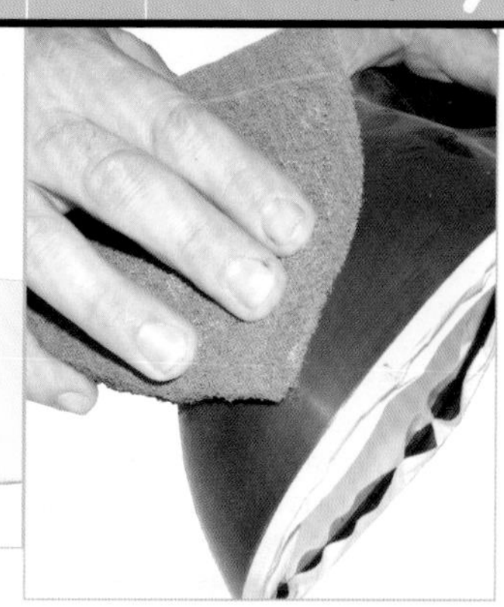

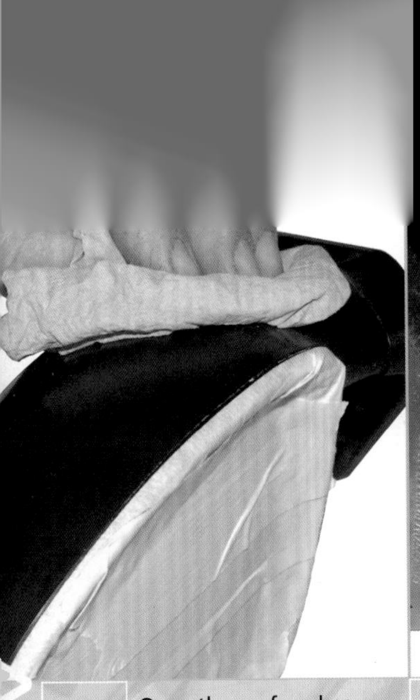

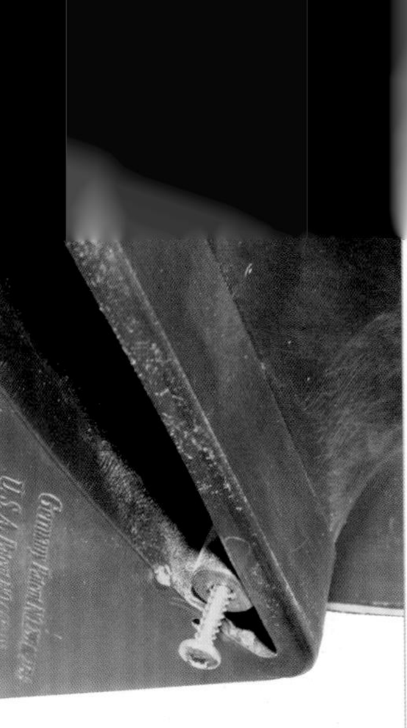

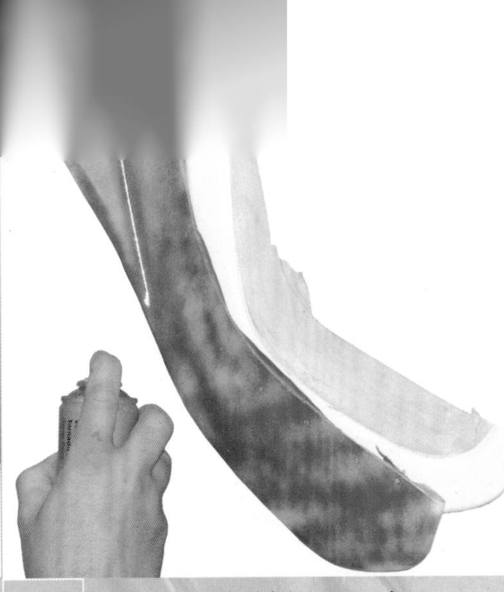

04 Once the surface has been nicely "roughened", clean up the surface using a suitable degreaser. Generally, it's ok to use methylated spirit or cellulose thinners but test it on a not-so-visible bit first, so you don't have a disaster.

05 Before you start spraying (if it's something smaller than a bumper) it's a good idea to try a work a screw into one of the mounting holes, to use as a "handle", so you can turn the item to spray all sides.

06 Another good trick is to use the screw to hang the item up on a piece of string or wire - then you can spin the item round to get the spray into awkward areas. If it's at all windy, you'll end up with a really awful finish and overspray on everything. Even indoors, if it's damp weather, you'll have real problems trying to get a shine - some kind of heater is essential if it's cold and wet (but not one with a fan - stirring up the dust is the last thing you want).

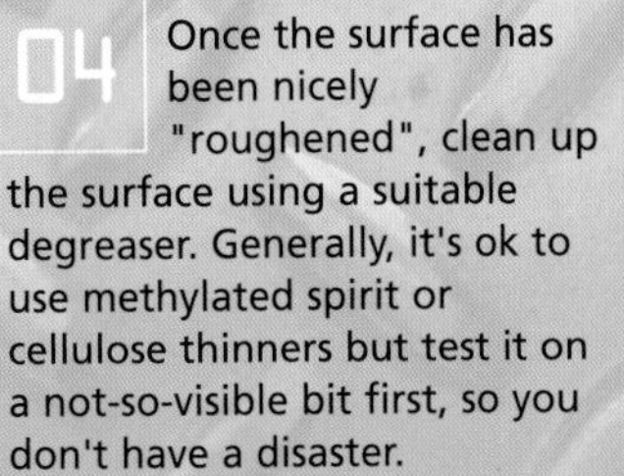

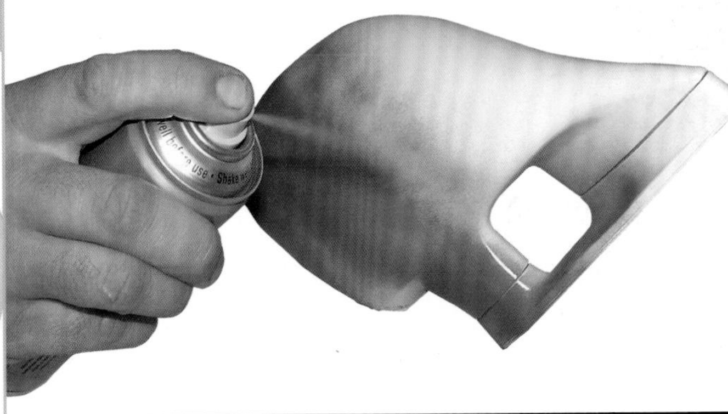

07 Thoroughly mix the paint by shaking the can. If you're new at spraying, practise your technique first. Working left-right, then right-left, press the nozzle so you start spraying just before you pass the item, and follow through just past it the other side. Keep the nozzle a constant distance from the item - not in a curved arc. Don't blast the paint on too thick, or it'll run - hold the can about 6 inches away - you're not trying to paint the whole thing in one sweep. Once you've got a patchy "mist coat" on - stop, and let it dry (primer dries pretty quickly).

08 Continue building up thin coats until you've got full coverage, then let it dry for half an hour or more. Using 1000- or 1200-grade wet-and-dry paper (used wet), very lightly sand the whole primered surface, to take out any minor imperfections (blobs, where the nozzle was spitting) in the primer. Try not to go through the primer to the plastic, but this doesn't matter too much in small areas. Rinse off thoroughly, then dry the surfaces - let it stand for a while to make sure it's completely dry, before starting on the top coat.

09 Make sure once again that the surfaces are clean, with no bits left behind from the drying operations. As with the primer, work up from an initial thin mist coat, allowing time for each pass to dry. As you spray, you'll soon learn how to build a nice shine without runs - any "dry" (dull) patches are usually due to overspray landing on still-wet shiny paint. Don't worry if you can't eliminate all of these - a light cutting polish will sort it out once the paint's hardened (after several hours). Especially with a colour like red (which is notorious for fading easily), it's a good idea to blow on a coat or two of clear lacquer over the top - this will also give you your shine, if you're stuck with a very "dry" finish. It's best to apply lacquer before the final top coat is fully hardened. The spraying technique is identical, although pro sprayers say that lacquer should be applied pretty thick - just watch those runs! Lacquer also takes a good long while to dry – so don't pick up your item too soon.

Tailgate smoothing

Achieving the "smooth-tailgate" look isn't too involved a procedure, providing you know someone who can weld, and are handy with filler and spray. It's a logical extension of de-badging - the first thing to go is the rear wiper. Remove the rear wiper arm, motor and washer jet, and the lock/trim, and fill over the holes - easy? Well, yes, except that most of the holes are too big to just fill over, and will probably need glassfibre matting or welding. The final act of smoothing is to weld a plate over the rear number plate recess, and finish with filler and spray.

If you're going to de-lock the tailgate as well, you'll need to devise a means of opening it afterwards. Options range from attaching a cable to the lock itself, feeding it through for manual operation, to fitting a solenoid kit and wiring it up to a convenient switch.

01 Prise up the hinged cover over the rear wiper nut, then undo the nut and pull the wiper arm off its splines (persuade it by levering with a screwdriver if you have to).

06 Unscrew the single nut securing the wiper link arm to the motor, and prise the arm off the motor with a screwdriver.

07 With some fiddling, the wiper motor should now come out of the tailgate.

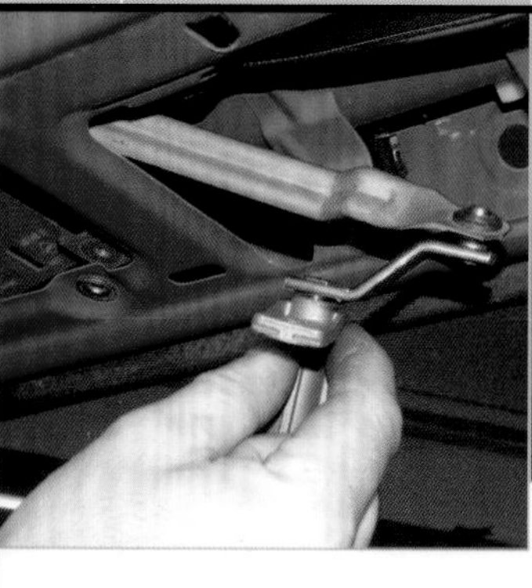

08 Once you've got the motor so far, stop and disconnect the wiring from it. Release the wiring harness from the clip using a screwdriver.

09 Unclip the lock operating rod from behind the lock button.

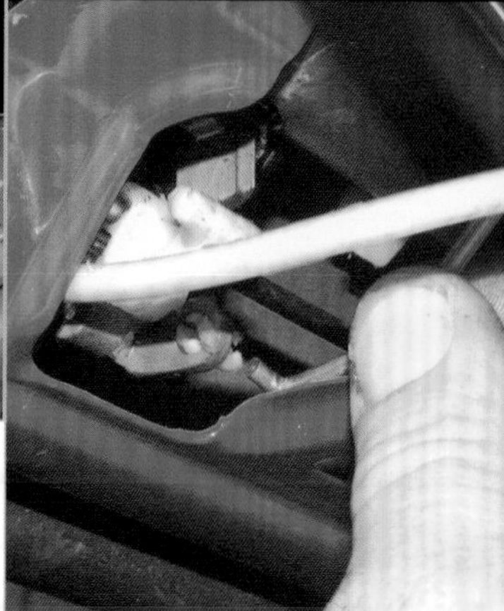

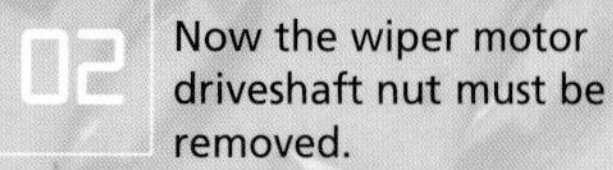

02 Now the wiper motor driveshaft nut must be removed.

03 With the tailgate open, prise out the trim clips and drop down the inner trim panel.

04 Remove the two bolts which hold the wiper arm end of the wiper linkage in place.

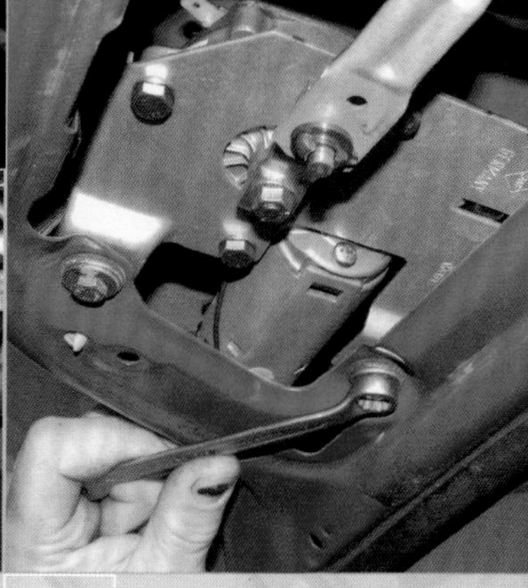

05 Now remove the three wiper motor mounting bolts, and loosen the whole motor and linkage (probably "stuck" to the inside of the tailgate).

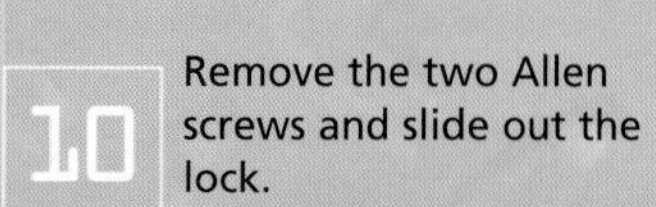

10 Remove the two Allen screws and slide out the lock.

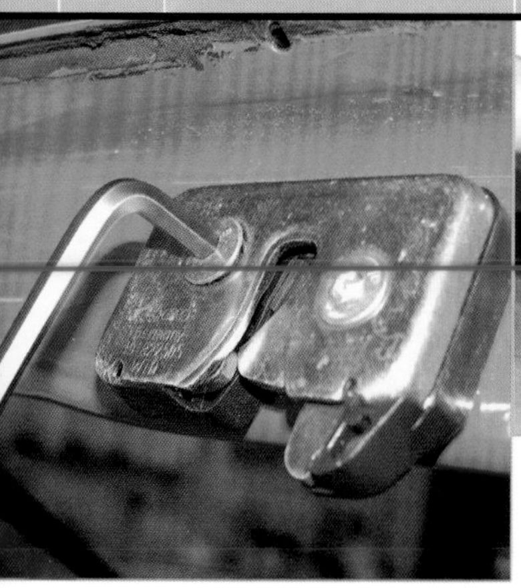

11 The lock trim panel on the outside of the tailgate is held on by four screws, accessed from inside. Remove the screws and take off the trim panel.

12 If your Golf has central locking, undo the screws securing the vacuum motor (ours was blue). Unclip the operating rod from the motor, and pull off the vacuum hose as you remove it.

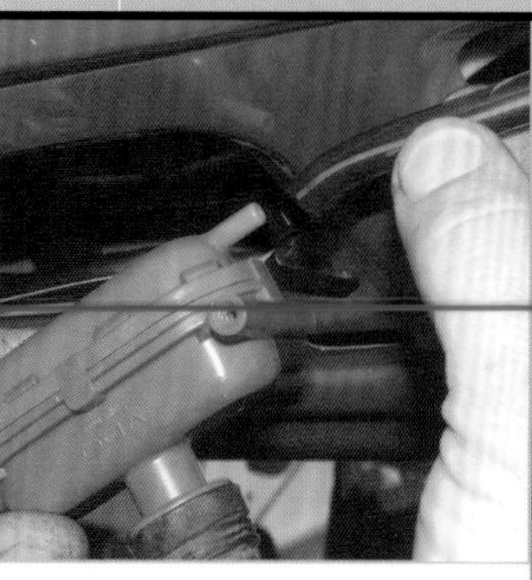

13 Unclip the lock operating rod from the right-hand-side of the tailgate.

>>

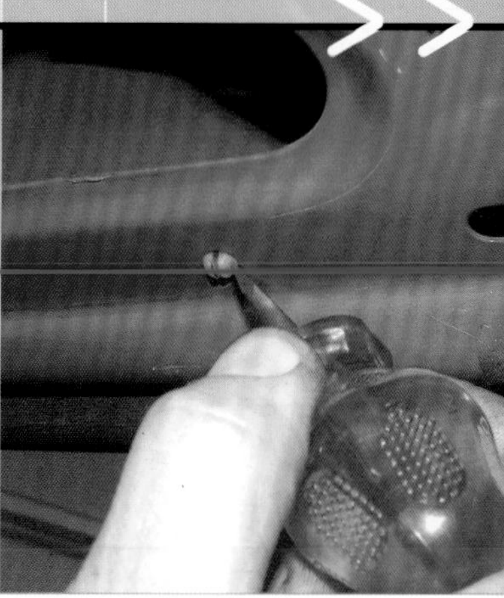

14 Press the clips either side of the lock pushbutton, and slide it out of the tailgate.

15 Squeeze together the tags which hold the washer jet in place, then slide it out of the tailgate. Pull the jet out of the washer hose. Once the tailgate's been removed, plug the end of the pipe to stop water leaking into the tailgate - the pipe could be tied in a knot, or alternatively, seal the pipe end using a close-fitting screw and some waterproof silicone sealant.

16 Remove the screws securing the number plate light lenses, then pull out the lights and disconnect the wiring. Your tailgate is now nearly stripped for smoothing - all that remains is removing the tailgate itself!

17 Work around the inside of the tailgate, releasing the wiring harness from the plastic clips. Unplug the spade connectors for the heated rear window (one plug either side). The HRW connectors are just too big to feed back through their holes, so the plugs must be cut off. If you're planning to re-connect the HRW, you'll need to fit new spades when you refit the tailgate.

22 Around the lock hole, dish in the metal slightly (this makes it easier to fill over later), then cut a circle of metal to sit in your newly-made recess. Run a neat line of weld around the metal circle, to pin it to the tailgate.

23 Now for a proper job on the number plate recess. Chop out a piece of metal which just sits down inside the recess.

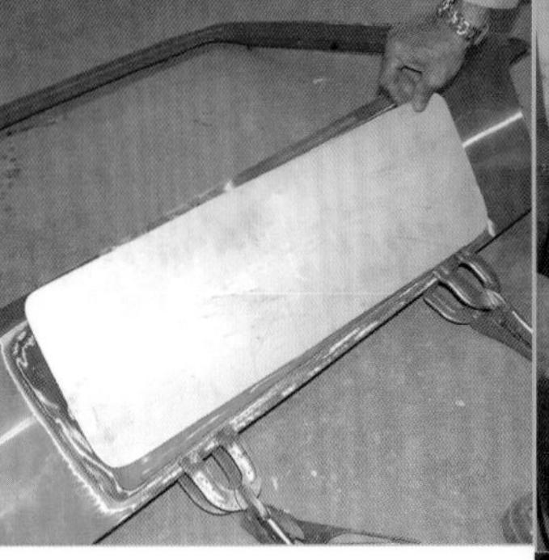

24 Tack the panel in place with a few blobs of weld (gloves would be sensible, but our man's feeling lucky) then run around the whole piece, with a nice run of weld.

Achtung!

Regardless of what you see going on here, always wear proper gloves and eye protection when welding. Same applies when filling, spraying and sanding. Well, just don't say we didn't warn you . . .

25 Now you can get the filler out. Just a light skim should be all that's needed. If the welding didn't go as well as ours, you might need the grinder...

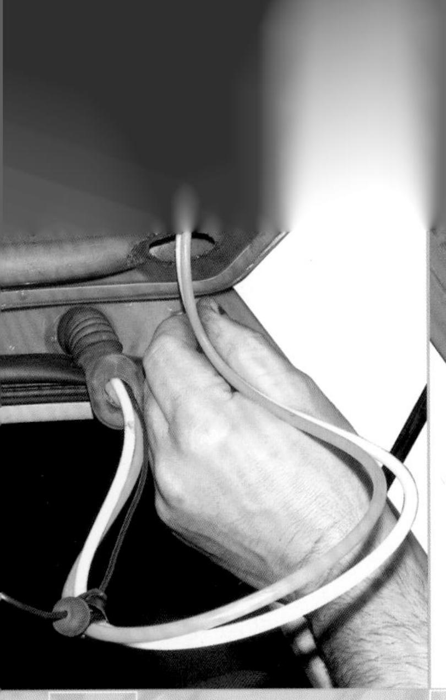

18 Feed all the wiring and the washer tube through the holes in the tailgate.

19 Get a mate to hold the tailgate up. At one end of each tailgate lift strut, prise off the retaining clip, then prise the strut off the ball-end fitting.

20 With the tailgate being held by your willing volunteer, unscrew the four hinge bolts at the top of the tailgate. Carefully lift the tailgate clear of the car.

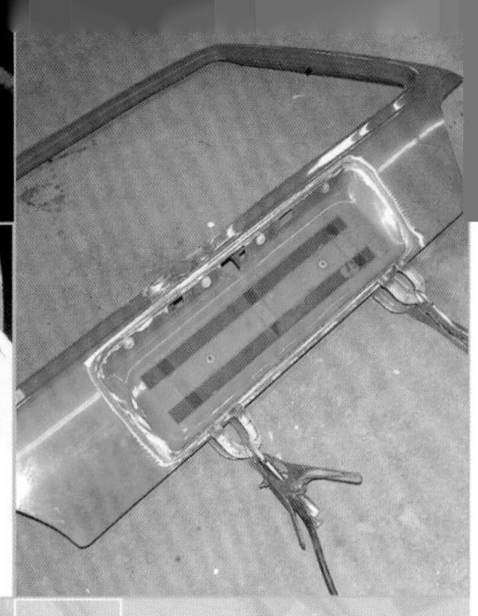

21 We booked our tailgate in for its facelift with our local bodyshop - but if you're a bit handy with a welder, you could have a go at some of it yourself. Don't try filling in the entire number plate recess with filler, it won't work. First rub down the lock hole and edge of the number plate recess to bare metal, for welding.

26 We didn't spray the entire tailgate with cans. And here's the proof - some things are better left to the pros.

27 To refit the tailgate you need patience, and not a little stamina, as you get the tailgate hinge bolts to bite back in. Get a mate to help.

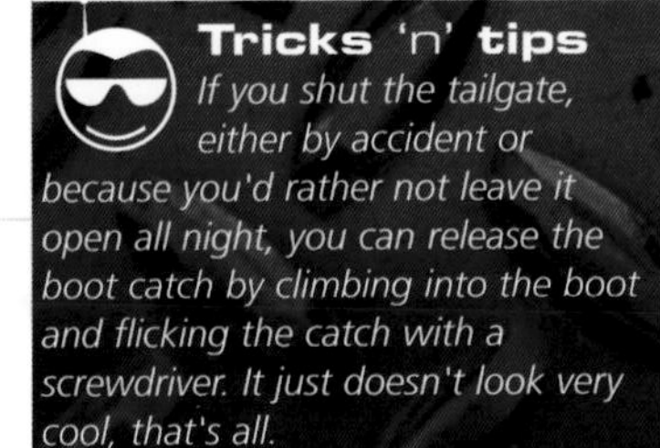

Tricks 'n' tips

If you shut the tailgate, either by accident or because you'd rather not leave it open all night, you can release the boot catch by climbing into the boot and flicking the catch with a screwdriver. It just doesn't look very cool, that's all.

28 Feed the heated rear window wires back through the rubber boot, and then into the sides of the tailgate. It's not an easy task but soldering wire worked for us.

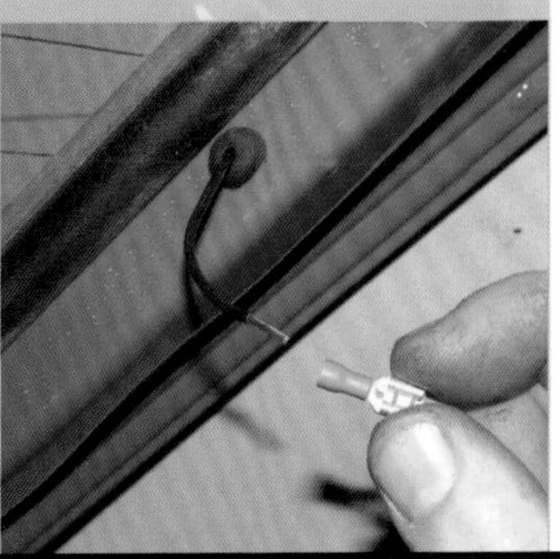

29 Make sure you pop a wiring grommet into each of the tailgate wiring holes. Don't assume you can do without these, because the HRW takes a lot of current, and if that little wire rubs through and shorts onto the metal, you will have a fire or a fusebox meltdown! Fit a new spade to the wire, then connect it up. Refer to the "De-locking" section before you refit the tailgate inner trim panel. Remember - you'd better have some way to open the tailgate before you shut it to admire your handiwork.

Numberplate **recess**

Now you've carefully rid your tailgate of its number plate recess, the bad news is that the plate's got to go somewhere. Fortunately, you can buy a ready-made recess from Venom Motorsport, for cutting into a big rear bumper.

Cut the hole for the recess, making sure you get it central. Besides the plastic, the metal bumper behind will also need a chop. Stick the recess in place from behind, using glassfibre. Self-tappers are only an option if you're desperate.

Depending on how good a fit your recess is, you might need to tidy the edges with a little filler. Completely smoothing-in the recess might be a time-consuming exercise, even for a bodyshop - very thin skims of filler on a plastic bumper will tend to flake off. And now it's time to spray.

Having "moved" your plate, you're now going to need a means of lighting it up after dark - otherwise your mods will fail the MOT.

01 The biggest difficulty we found was sourcing a pair of suitable lights - the problem is, they must not show any white light to the rear - meaning there's no re-using the old lights. A couple of trips round the scrapyard later, we found these on a Citroën XM, of all things! Remember to get the wiring plugs as well (chop off the loom).

02 Before you get the bumper off, measure up the lights to work out what size hole you'll need. This isn't necessarily the overall size of the light - ours are held by two clips on the back, so we measured the length and width of the mounting clips instead.

03 With the bumper off, decide first on the spacing of the two lights, and mark their centres with one strip of masking tape each. Then transfer your measured sizes for the holes, remembering that each light is a bit bigger than the holes you'll be making.

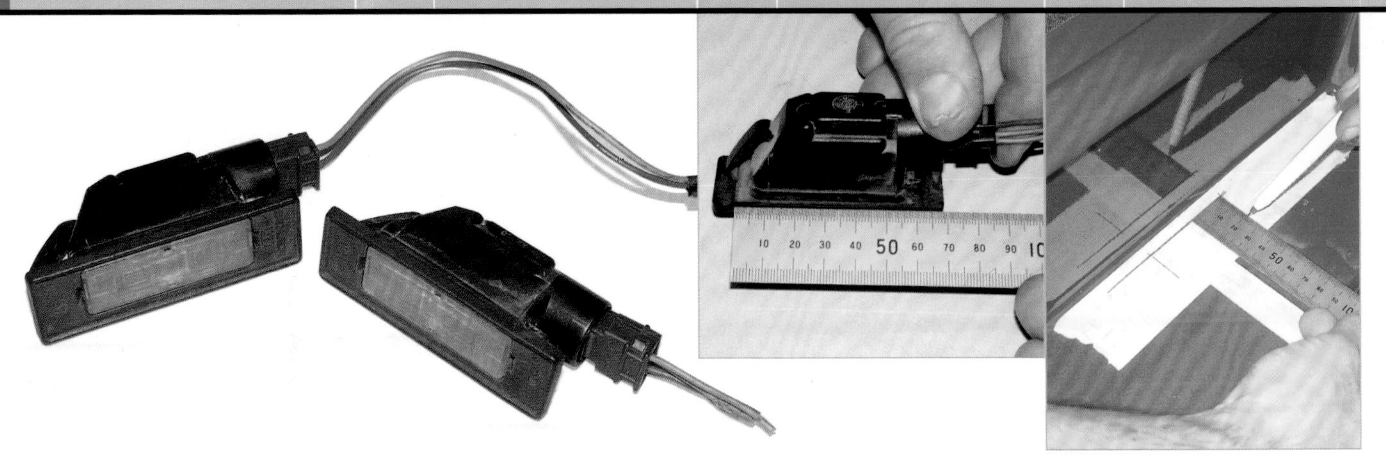

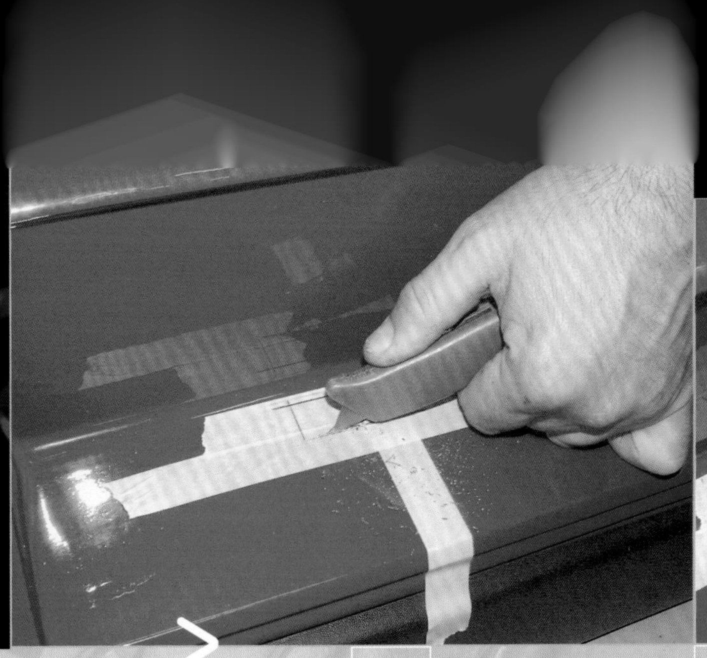

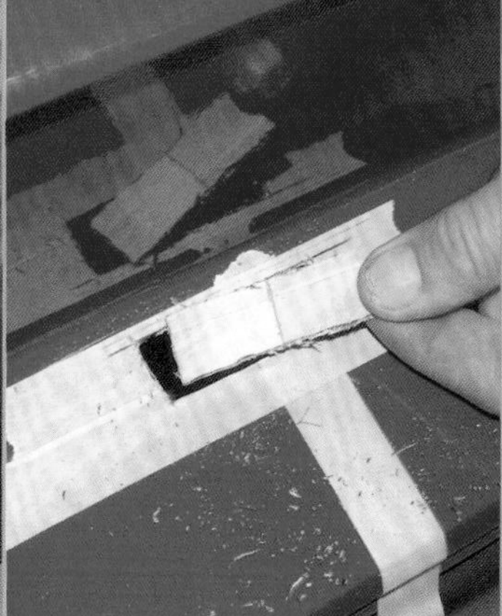

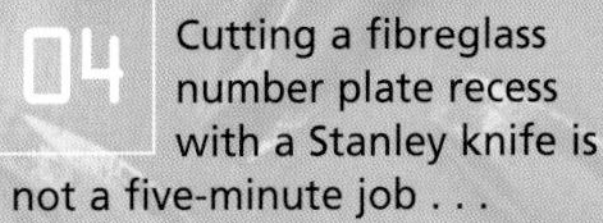

04 Cutting a fibreglass number plate recess with a Stanley knife is not a five-minute job . . .

05 . . . but we got us a hole in the end. One more tip, if you're making two holes like us - by all means mark both holes, but only cut one to start with. That way, you can test the fit of the lights and adjust the size of the second hole if you need to.

06 Test fit the lights into the hole as you go so you don't take off more than you need.

07 The lights are wired up in parallel, which means you can join the wires from each light together, and add on your own lengths to get connected to the wiring harness inside the boot.

08 Feed your new wires in through this grommet in the back panel (in the centre, behind the bumper), which takes you directly into the boot. It's a good idea to seal up the hole you make in the grommet, using a little silicone sealant. The original number plate light wiring comes into the boot area on the right-hand side, goes right across the rear of the boot, and up to the tailgate on the left-hand side. Our live was a grey/green wire - check your Haynes wiring diagram if you're not sure. Any brown wire should do for the earth.

09 All that's left is to fit the number plate, and try the lights. Stylish and 100% legal.

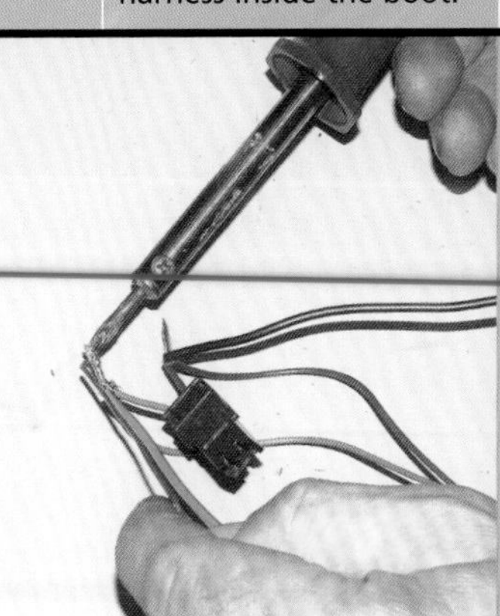

De-locking

One very popular way to tidy up the Golf lines is to do away with the door locks, and even the door handles. Removing the rear door handles (on 5-door models) is okay, legally/MOT-speaking, but removing the front door handles will land you in trouble, come MOT time.

The easiest route to de-locked standard handles is to fit a pair of rear door handles from a 5-door to the front doors - these look identical to the front handles, but have no locks. Other aftermarket handles are available - Audi handles, for instance, are available ready-fitted to a metal panel; fitting involves cutting out your old ones, welding in and blending the new.

So you can lock and unlock your de-locked doors, you'll need to get a remote central locking kit, which are available from several Golf parts suppliers. If your Golf already has central locking it works on vacuum, and is not readily compatible with remote operation. We chose to do ours this way, to show how to fit central locking to a Golf without it as standard.

01 First, remove the door trim panel (see "Removing stuff" in "Interiors"). Push out the centre pins from the two white plastic clips at the front and rear of the doors, and remove the clips (the pins fall down inside the doors, but don't panic!).

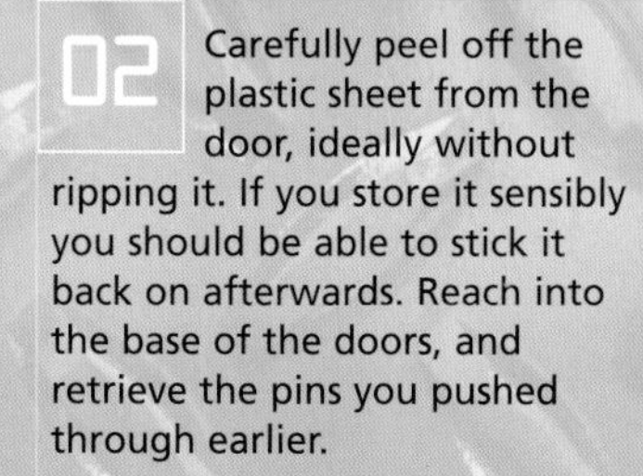

02 Carefully peel off the plastic sheet from the door, ideally without ripping it. If you store it sensibly you should be able to stick it back on afterwards. Reach into the base of the doors, and retrieve the pins you pushed through earlier.

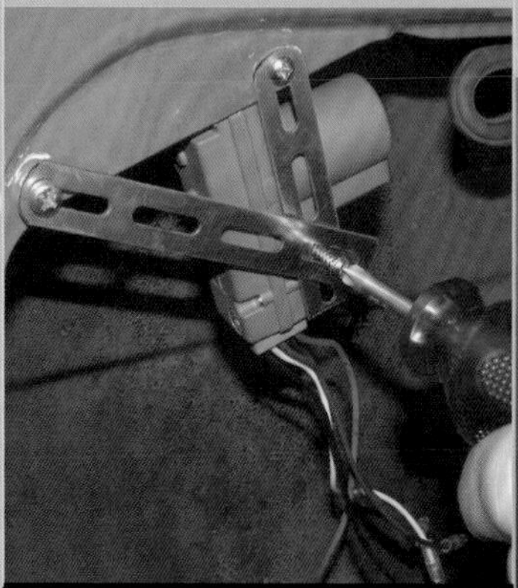

07 The new lock solenoids must be mounted so they work in the same plane as the door lock buttons. It's no good having the lock solenoid plungers moving horizontally, to work a button and rod which operates vertically. Make up the mounting brackets from the metal bits provided in the kit, and screw them in place loosely. Wind the window down, then up, to check that the window mech and glass won't hit it.

08 The kit contains several items which look like bike spokes - these are lock operating rods, which have to be cut to length, then joined onto the old rods with the small metal clamps. It's best to join the old and new rods at a straight piece of the old rod, so feed the new rod in, and mark it for cutting.

03 If you've got central locking, pull off the vacuum pipe from the vacuum unit.

Remove the two screws and take out the vacuum unit - unclip the operating rod at the top. Before you start fitting your new lock solenoids, test them. Connect them all together as described in your kit's instructions - if they talk about a trigger wire, don't worry about this just now. With power connected to all the solenoids, pull up on the

04 operating plunger of one, and all the rest should pop up too.

Decide where you're going to mount the lock control unit - we fitted ours by taking out the right-hand end vent from the dash, and it slipped in below

05 that, with some double-sided tape to hold it.

Identify the various looms, and feed them out to the doors - there's a handy rubber boot at the door front edge you can prise out and feed wires through into the door. We had a 4-door locking kit for our 3-door Golf, and used the two rear door solenoids (the ones

06 with less wires) for the filler flap and tailgate - so can you.

09 Cut the new rod to the marked length.

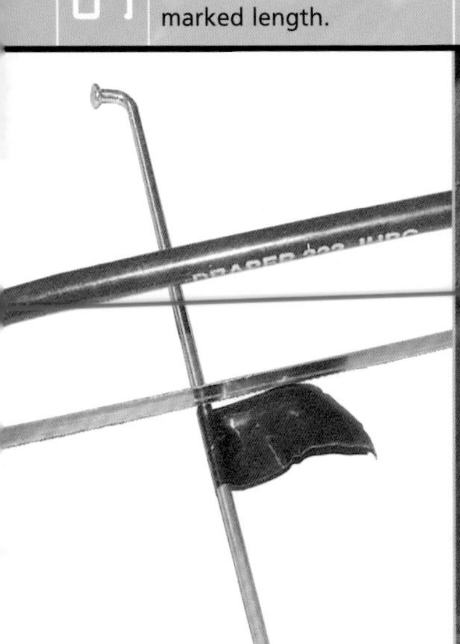

Fit the cut rod to the solenoid, then slip the joiner onto it. Fit the solenoid onto its bracket,

10 and offer the rod into place, to connect to the old rod.

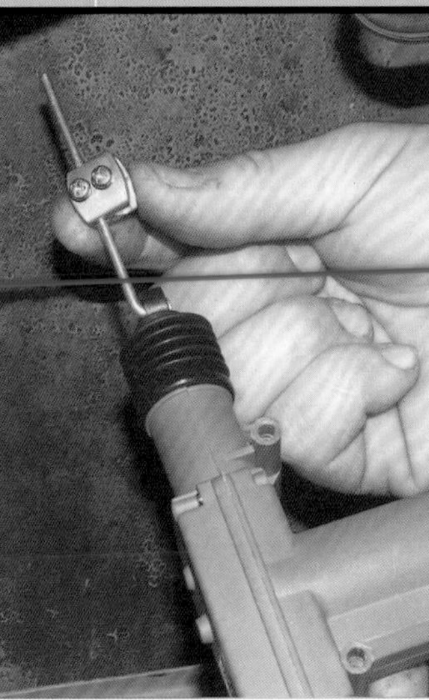

Working inside the door (where there's not a lot of room!), join the new rod and old rod together, and fasten the clamp screws tight. If the clamp screws come loose, you're going to be locked out. The only way we could tighten the screws was by using a small "cranked" screwdriver (a bit like an Allen key) - our pic shows all the bits

11 removed from the door, so you can see what's involved.

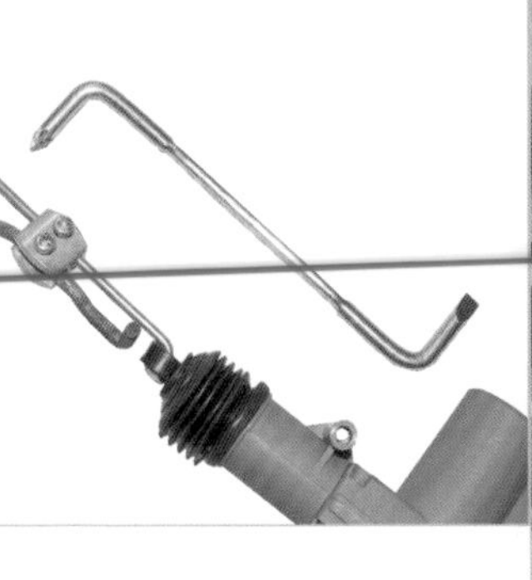

Once you've managed that, you can connect up the wires - the easy bit is joining up inside the door. Hopefully, your kit's instructions should be sufficient, but if not, you'll have to resort to the Haynes manual to identify the standard wiring (basically, everything off the

12 driver's door motor will be needed for the lock control unit).

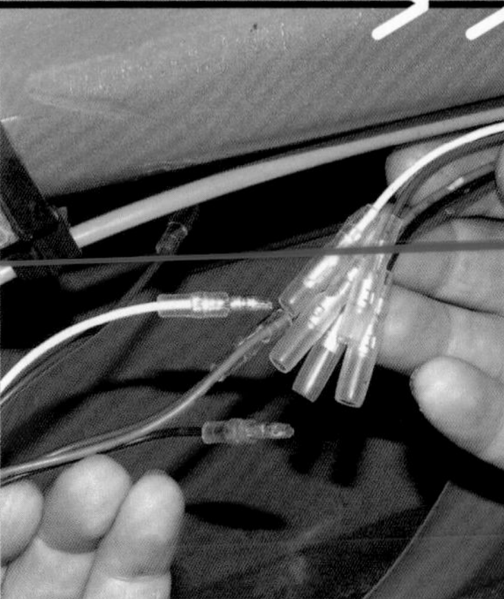

13 Fitting the tailgate lock is much the same as doing a door lock. The tailgate lock comes off after removing two screws and unhooking the operating rod.

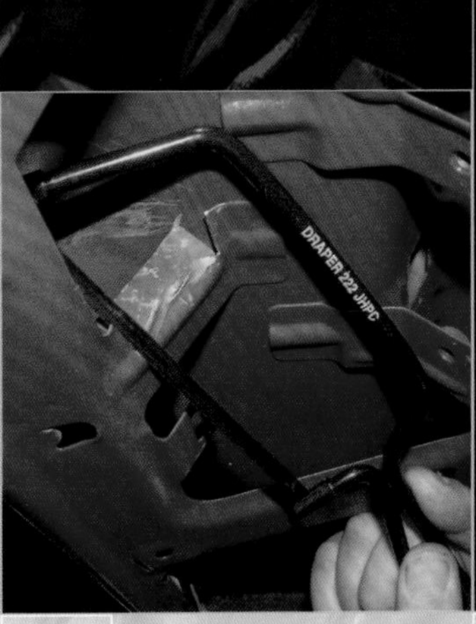

14 The tricky bit with the tailgate lock is that the solenoid has to be set vertically - we found some vandalism of the tailgate inner panels was required.

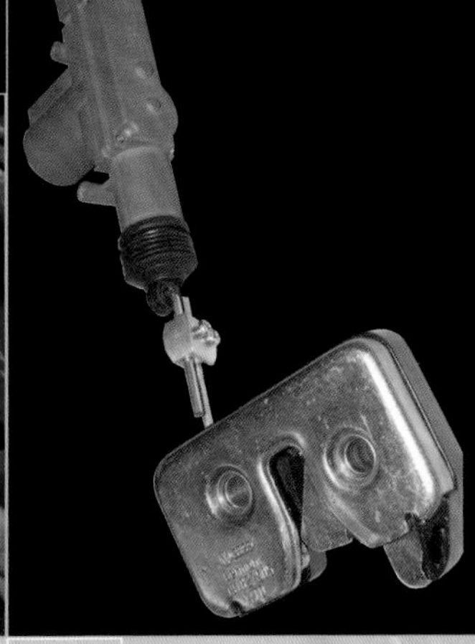

15 Cut and connect up your new and old operating rods as for the door locks - again, here's a shot of the assembled lot to start with.

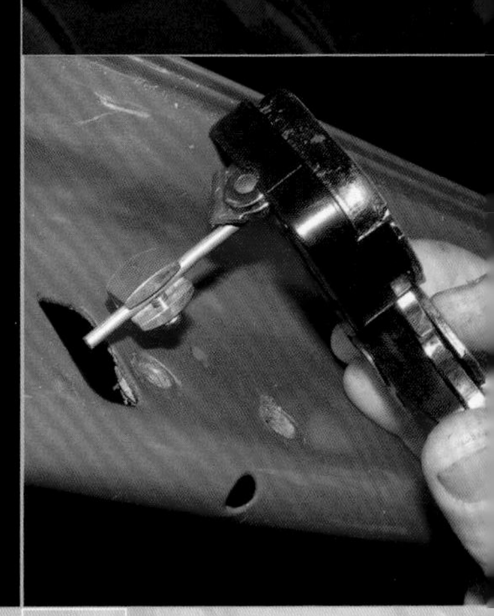

16 Offer in the lock with joiner attached . . .

20 All that's needed to open a de-locked tailgate is a separate live and earth connected to the newly-fitted lock solenoid, operated by a switch on the dash. We found some unused live feeds on the back of the fusebox . . .

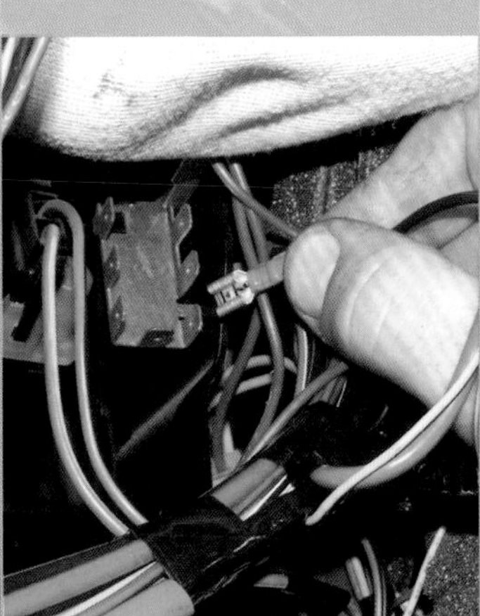

21 . . . and there's a handy connector block of earths tucked up above the fusebox.

22 Our switch arrangement consists of a switch we got from our local Lucas branch, it has a flick action (it only takes a quick flick for the solenoid to pop the tailgate). A good switch mounting point can be found by working in behind the dash, taking out the screw holding the blanking plate for the manual choke control . . .

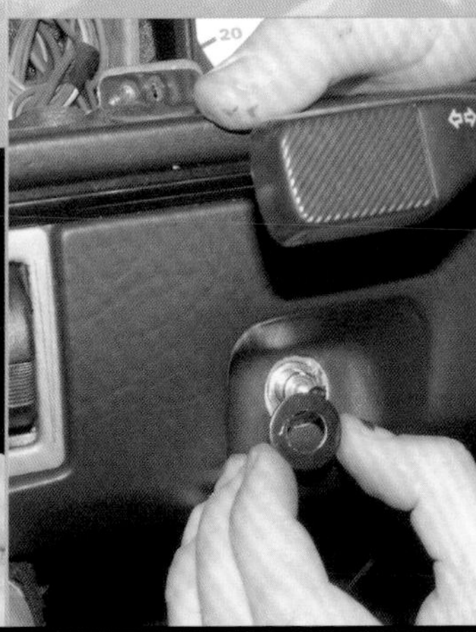

23 . . . and mounting your switch into the ready-provided hole.

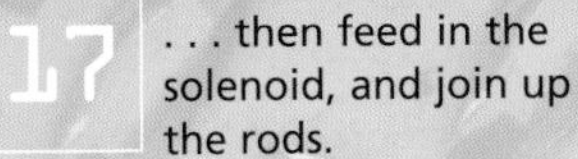

17 . . . then feed in the solenoid, and join up the rods.

18 Now you've got to feed the solenoid wires down through the tailgate, and out at the rubber boot at the top. Use a piece of wire to help poke the wires through (gravity won't do the whole job, unfortunately) - see "Tricks 'n' Tips".

Tricks 'n' tips

A handy discovery we made is that solder works really well for feeding wires through. A length of solder is flexible (for going round corners), but just strong enough that you can push it round obstacles. You can even tie knots in it, but taping wires to it is better, to go through small holes. Well, it worked for us, anyway...

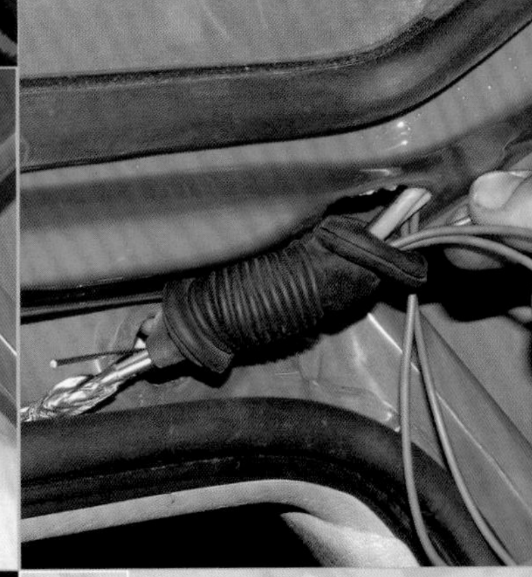

19 Once you've got the wires through the tailgate, feed them into and through the rubber boot, and into the car. From there, you can take the wires through to the front, for connection to the lock control unit. If you're de-locking the tailgate, however, you need to do something just a bit different.

24 Don't forget the filler flap if your Golf had vacuum central locking as standard, or you'll look stupid when you next want to fill up. Disabling the standard locking will also mean that the filler flap stays locked, with no way of opening it manually. So first remove the trim clips and take out the black side panel on the right-hand side of the boot.

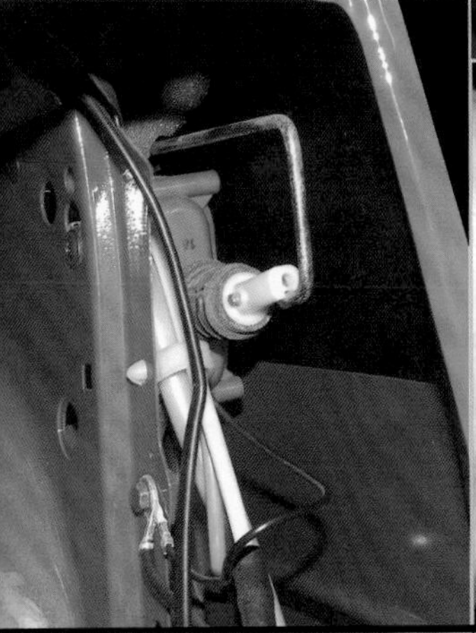

25 Unscrew the three nuts holding in the right-hand rear light cluster, and take out the light. Just so you've some idea what a fun job this part is, here's a view of the vacuum unit.

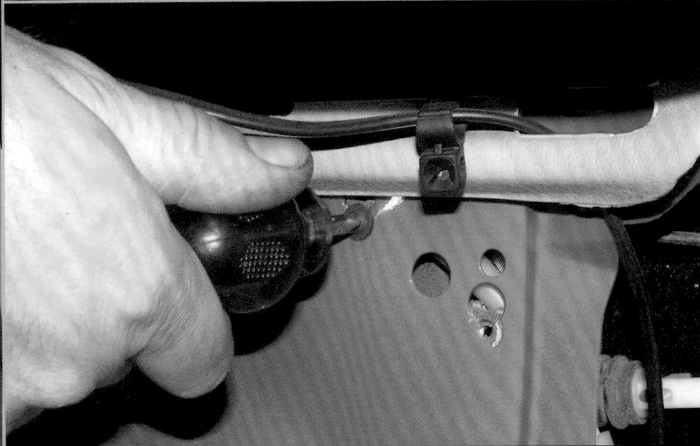

26 Remove the two screws holding the unit inside the boot . . .

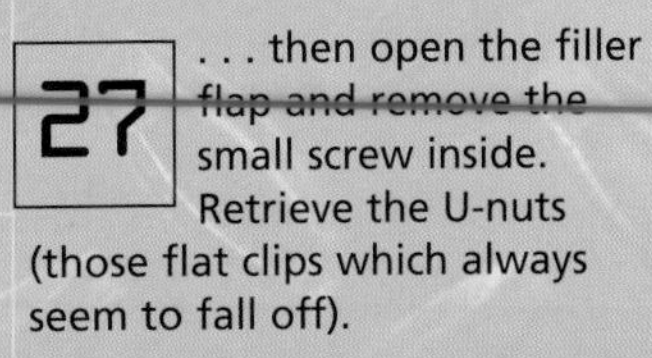

27 . . . then open the filler flap and remove the small screw inside. Retrieve the U-nuts (those flat clips which always seem to fall off).

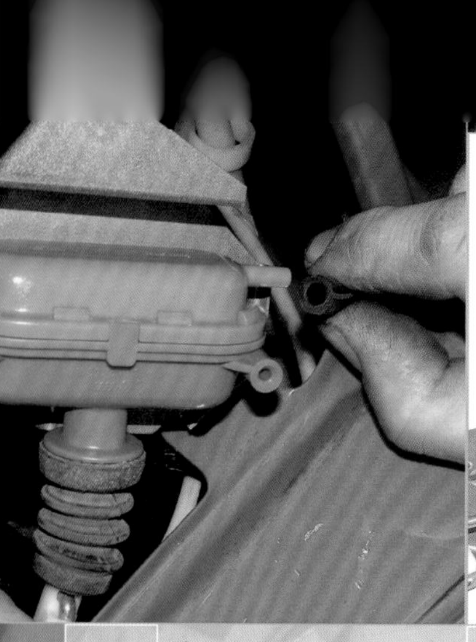

28 The vacuum unit is mounted on a plate. Pull the plate down inside the boot, and disconnect the vacuum pipe from it. The whole plate can now be wangled out of the car.

29 Remove the two screws holding the vacuum unit to the plate . . .

30 . . . and unhook the operating rod from the unit (don't remove the rod at the other end).

31 Mounting the new solenoid to the plate requires some thought. It has to work the operating rod the same way as before, and it can't take up too much room. Use our photos as a guide. Drill holes as necessary, and screw the solenoid loosely onto the plate.

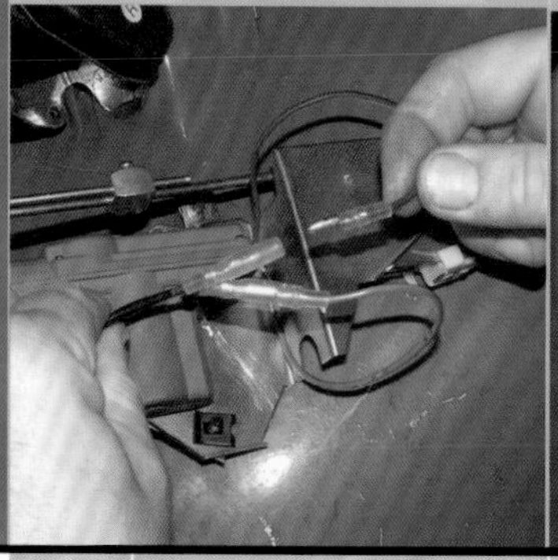

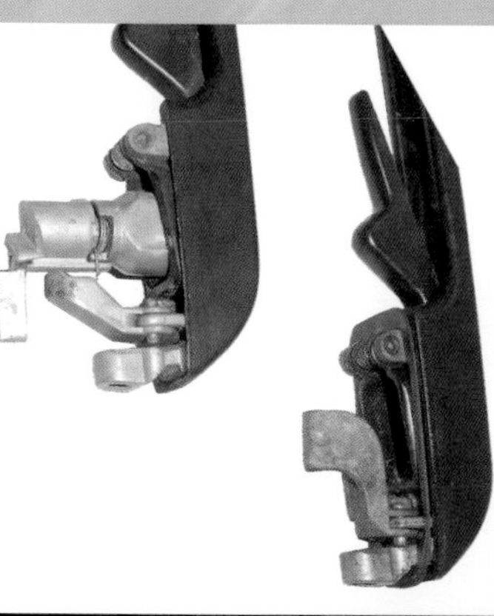

36 Feed the wires down the side of the car, and connect them up.

37 Manoeuvre the whole lot in through the back, and pray there's enough room for it all. The two screws inside the boot can be fitted loosely to the plate before feeding it in (the mounting holes are slotted, so the bolt heads can fit through and then down into place for tightening). Tighten the screws inside, and the one inside the filler flap, then check to make sure it works. You may find you have to adjust the rods if there's not enough clearance between the rods and the rear light cluster.

38 Removing the old handles is simple - see the section on fitting armour door plates in "Security". You can of course fit Audi handles (or any others you fancy) to your Golf, but you're gonna have some serious work to do.

39 You'll have read about the neat trick of fitting 5-door Golf rear handles (which don't have locks) to the front doors, although it's not a straight swap. Study the photo, and spot the difference - the front door handle is the one on the left.

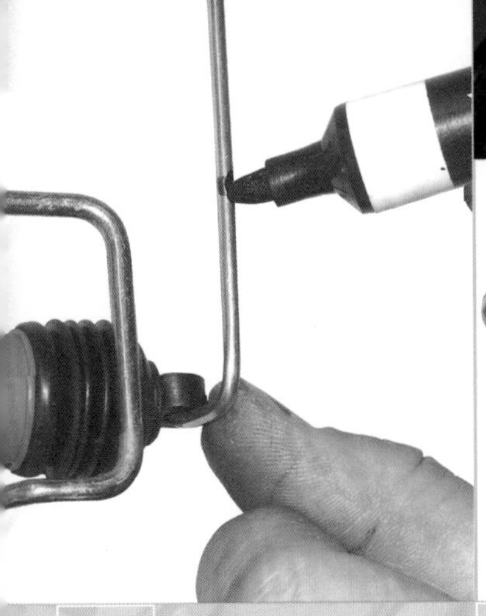

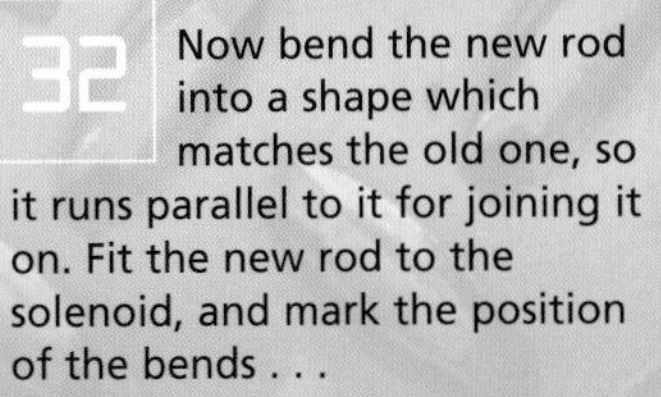

32 Now bend the new rod into a shape which matches the old one, so it runs parallel to it for joining it on. Fit the new rod to the solenoid, and mark the position of the bends . . .

33 . . . then bend it round at ninety degrees. Twice.

34 Trim off the excess new rod, then fit it on and clamp it to the old rod.

35 It's a good idea to fit another bit of metal bracket, to strengthen the whole thing up.

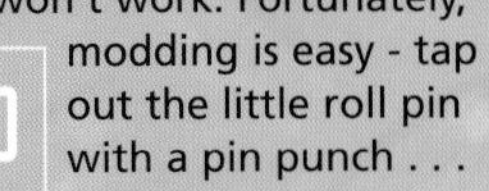

40 The difference is the lock operating levers. If you try a rear handle in a front door, the lock won't work. Fortunately, modding is easy - tap out the little roll pin with a pin punch . . .

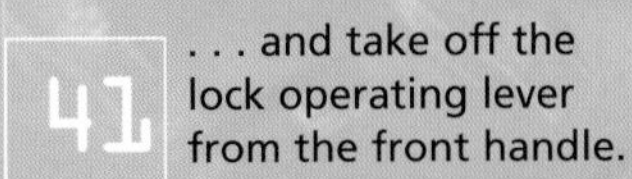

41 . . . and take off the lock operating lever from the front handle.

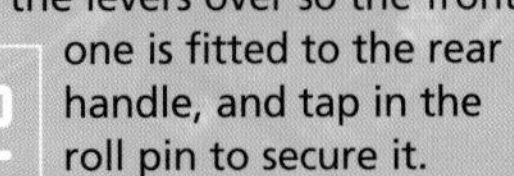

42 Remove the lock lever from the rear handle in the same way. Swap the levers over so the front one is fitted to the rear handle, and tap in the roll pin to secure it.

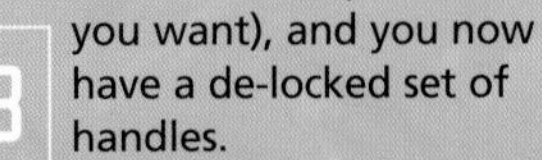

43 Fit the handle to the front door (with the armour door plate, if you want), and you now have a de-locked set of handles.

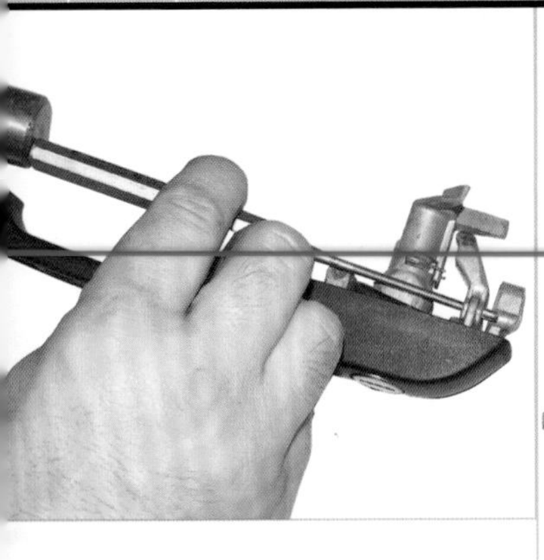

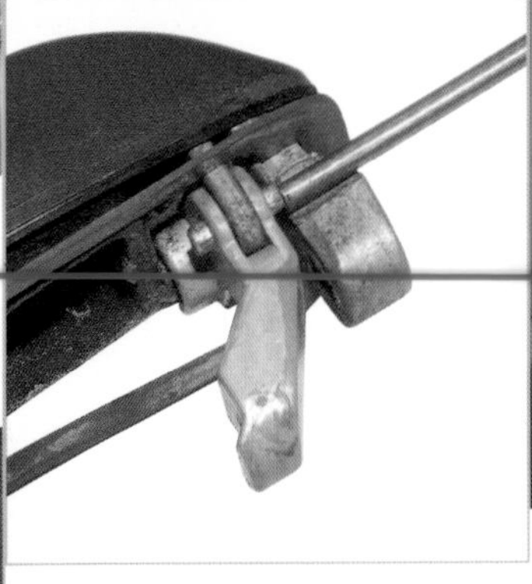

Glow **for it**

Ever since 'The Fast and the Furious' first glued us to our screens, every cruise-goer wants a cool neon glow under their car. Wanting's one thing - make it a reality, and you'll have to explain it to the Law. Under-car neons are totally illegal on the road, and rather an obvious 'come-and-nick-me' to Plod (who will then have a field day with any other semi-legal features on your Golf). So - you have been warned. But we know you still want them, anyway...

01 First, the car's got to get airborne - look in 'Wheels & tyres' for info on jacking the car up, and supporting it safely. Offer the first tube in place, and see where it fits best. It mustn't interfere with the jacking points on the sills (but you're probably using these already). Those tubes are fragile (no - really?), so don't drop 'em...

02 The Folia Tec neons we used came with these plastic mounting clips, which you just slip onto the tubes (use three on the longer tubes). With the tubes fitted inside the sill flange, we marked through the clips for the mounting holes.

03 Yes, we're drilling holes in the floor. Are we bothered about making our Golf rust? Well, maybe we should be - before subjecting your hole-y Golf to the British weather, get some silicone or underseal on round those clips (without plastering it on your tubes, of course).

04 Inside the car, take the door sill plastic trims off (only a few clips), and lift the edges of carpet, to find where your holes ended up. Poke a bolt down through, then go underneath and fit the tube and its clip to the bolt. Tightening the nut and bolt is one time when an assistant comes in pretty handy.

05 The neon across the front of the car's about the easiest to fit. First, make up a small bracket (we used some cut-down brackets from our local DIY store) to fit to the plastic clamp, with one small nut and bolt, then offer the tube and clamps under the front crossmember, and you should find something you can attach the bracket to, by screwing on an extra nut.

06 At the back, the exhaust and rear bumper cause problems fitting our last tube. We trimmed away part of the plastic bumper, and fitted two more of our DIY-store brackets, then attached the tube using its plastic clamps, and some more small bolts.

07 Tubes nicely mounted, but plenty of heavy cables dragging on the floor? Time to wire it all up, then. Decide where the control box is going (ours went next to the battery), and start feeding the two nearest tube cables in towards the battery (okay, so this isn't a Golf. but you get the idea).

08 Drilling holes may well be necessary as part of the wire-routing process - for this one, we were lucky to get our cordless back out! The most important bit is fitting a grommet to the new hole. If you study the neon's control box, you'll see it mentions something about 6000 volts. If one of those cables rubs through on a sharp-edged hole - we'll leave the rest to your imagination.

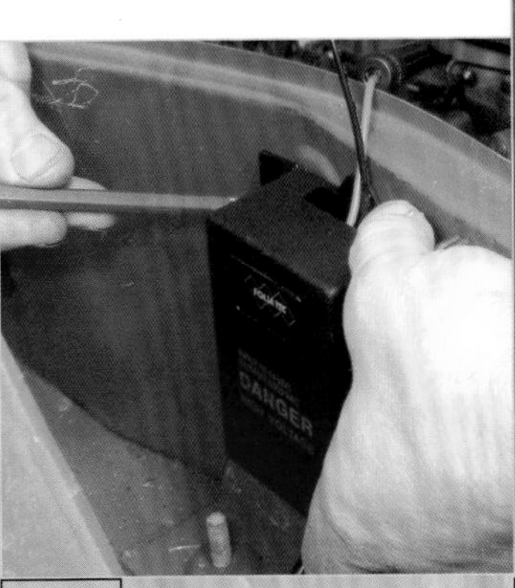

09 Mounting the control box somewhere near the battery seems a good move - lots of lives and earths close to hand. However, if you remove the battery (like we did) to give yourself more room, check before finally fitting the box that the battery will go back in. That's what we call a Homer moment.

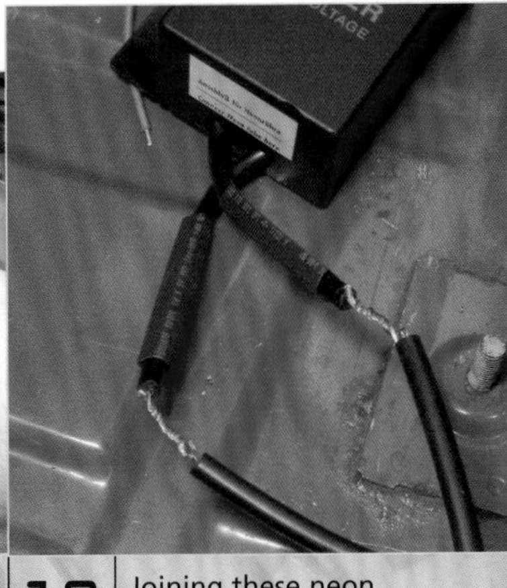

10 Joining these neon cables together requires a special technique - strip about an inch off the thick insulation of each wire, and twist the bared ends together. Do not use solder. Do not use bullets, terminal blocks, or any other joiners. Do not pass Go. Apparently, any method other than the wires-twisted-together one might cause the tubes to malfunction. So there.

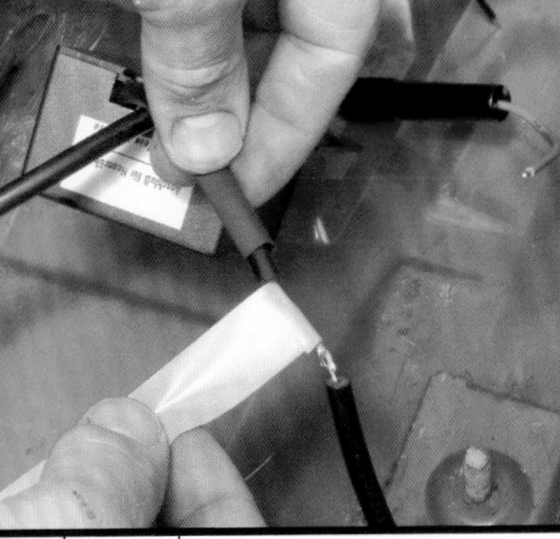

11 You are allowed to tape up the joint - which is just as well, with all those volts going through it. Don't be shy with the tape. And tidy all that wiring up, with some cable-ties – we don't want a high-voltage wire flapping around in the engine bay...

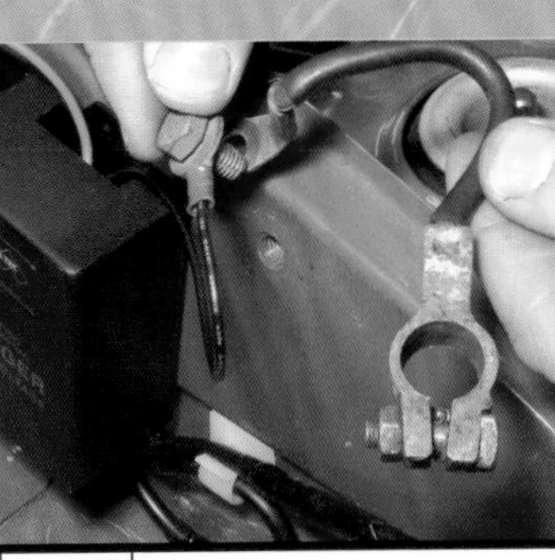

12 Two more wires to go now, at the control box - a red live, and a black earth. We've got the battery earth lead right in front of us - shame not to use it. Unbolt it from the car, and fit the black wire to the earth lead mounting bolt, using a ring terminal.

13 You must be able to control under-car neons - a switch is essential. Run the red wire from the control box into the car, and feed it to one side of your new switch (this red wire became a blue wire by the time it reached the switch). Here, we're joining on another red wire, which is going to be our live feed. We fitted our switch in the centre console, on a new alloy plate.

14 To get a live feed, you have two options. You can poke about behind the fusebox with a test light and your Haynes wiring diagrams for an existing wire to join onto (tricky, but check out the section on de-locking), or you can run one into the car from the battery (easy).

Wheelarches

The law states that your tyres shouldn't stick out wider than the arches. This presents something of a problem, especially to a car with really wide wheels, or spacers. There are some relatively simple options to stop your rubber from rubbing, assuming you don't own a Rallye, which had mega-blistered arches in the first place!

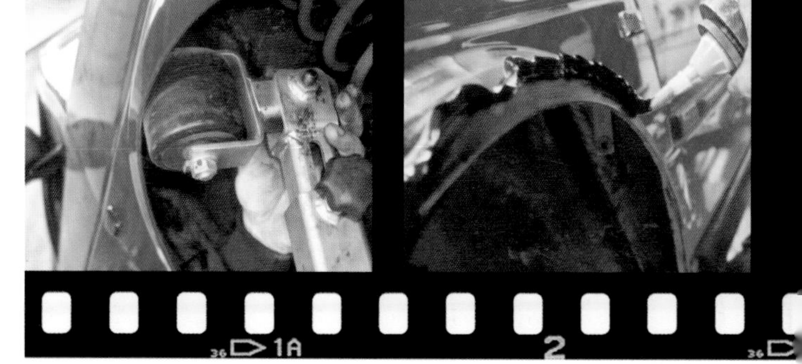

The first option, which should accommodate most wide alloys, is to fit a set of G60 wheelarch extensions. These really suit the Golf - hardly surprising, since they're based on items originally fitted to a real Golf, albeit a rare one. If you're not going for 17s, and don't need to roll the arches, the G60 arch extensions can be DIY-fitted fairly easily. If you've got (or intend to fit) the big bumpers, you can also buy the matching "1990-spec" wheelarch and sill extensions from various suppliers.

Sometimes, all you need to stop your tyres rubbing is to remove the plastic wheelarch liners. These are usually held on by a few simple clips and screws. Tyres can sometimes be rubbing on the liner clips alone - once they're trimmed off, problem gone.

If you need to accommodate bigger-than-16-inch wheels on a lowered car, your arches must be "rolled", and this is a job for a pro bodyshop. The arch return lips are first heated, to soften the metal and ensure that the paint doesn't crack. The lips are then rolled out using a special tool, and can then either be cut off or flared out to provide a mounting for arch extensions (such as the G60s). The new extensions are then attached using mastic and pop-rivets. The alternative option is even less DIY-friendly - fitting replacement Rallye arches, or another alternative full bodykit.

Venting

We're not talking about bonnet vents here. If you've spent out on an induction kit for your GTI, you may be wondering what to do with the length of air hose which probably came with it. The idea with an induction kit is that the incoming air should be as cool as possible, since this will give more power when the engine's hot.

Normally, the intake air gets heated by having passed through the radiator at the front, so the end of the air hose must be mounted out of the airflow from the radiator. Most standard Golfs take a cool air supply from an intake in the inner wing, and this can be re-used with an induction kit quite effectively.

A more obvious way to ensure cooler air is to cut the offside outer front wing, and mount the air hose close to it - that way, you're drawing in cool air from the outside. It's possible to buy a ready-made vented panel, which is cut in and welded to the wing; although cutting your own wing vents needn't be that scary. A steady hand, a file to smooth off the rough edges, and a can of spray to cover the bare metal, should be all you need. Some cars actually mount the induction kit filter cone so that it pokes through the wing - this looks good, but is not so great in wet weather...

Another possibility when providing an intake for your induction kit (if you have the big bumpers) is to buy an air scoop which fits into the foglight hole, or just next to them if you have foglights already...

'Crosshair' headlights - a very cool and subtle Golf mod indeed. Just make sure the ones you buy are UK-legal (lots aren't).

Lights & bulbs

Lights - one of the easiest ways to trick up your Golf. So many options here, we'll start at the front, and work back. Almost nothing influences the look of your Golf more than the front end, so the headlights play a crucial role.

On the Mk 2s, you can buy the rectangular Rallye lights, or Jetta lights. Many owners whose cars started out with four headlights (GTI, Driver, etc) dump the inner pair of lights, which with a de-badged grille, nicely reduces the clutter at the front. But fashions change, and the badges and inner lights could easily make a comeback...

For the headlights, you can get ones with black reflectors and crosshairs on the glass, or the "clear-glass" option - similar to the Mk 4 headlights, where the glass has no pattern on it. Quite a cool, subtle mod. When you're buying lights, make sure they're UK-legal - they must be E-marked, and right-hand-drive fitment.

Blue Headlight bulbs

Currently very popular, the new high-power and "blue" headlight bulbs are an excellent way to boost headlight performance, and to give more of a unique "look". However, fitting these bulbs is not without its pitfalls.

Some of the bulbs on sale are illegal for road use - they give off masses of heat and can even melt your headlights, so watch out. Reputable brands are recommended to keep you on the right side of the law (and your lights intact).

01 At the back of the headlight, pull off the plug, then whip off the rubber.

02 You'll now find a wire clip with two prongs on it, which you squeeze together - there's this sort, which comes right off . . .

Tricks 'n' tips

Put the old bulbs in the glovebox - carrying spare bulbs is a good way to get a let-off from Plod, if they stop you for having a bulb gone. "Yes, officer, I'll replace it right now!".

03 . . . and this sort, which just hinges to one side. Yes, our Golf had two completely different headlights.

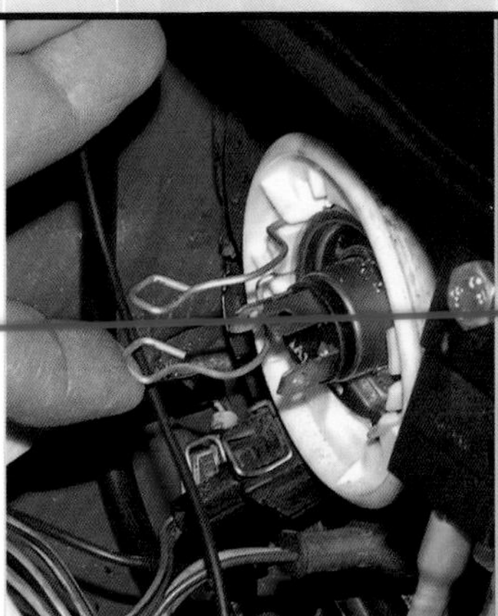

04 And now the bulb comes out. If you've any plans to re-use it, hold it only by the metal bits, not the glass.

05 The correct way to open this box is from below. If you touch the bulb glass, wipe it clean with a little meths (methylated spirit). Otherwise, your new bulb will burn out even faster than stated on the packet.

06 Fit the new bulb. Looks the same as the old bulb, only shinier. Secure with the wire clip, fit the rubber boot over the bulb connectors, and plug in.

Front **fog & spotlights**

The only popular fitments here are the discreet foglights which fit directly into the later Mk 2 big bumpers - these lights are also available in different colours.

01 If you're fitting fogs, they must be wired in to work on dipped-beam only. The opposite is true for spotlights. Pop out the main light switch (or pull down the fusebox, as described in the alarm fitting section in "Security"), and check for a wire which is live only when the dipped beams are on (or main beam for spotlights). The Haynes wiring diagrams will help here.

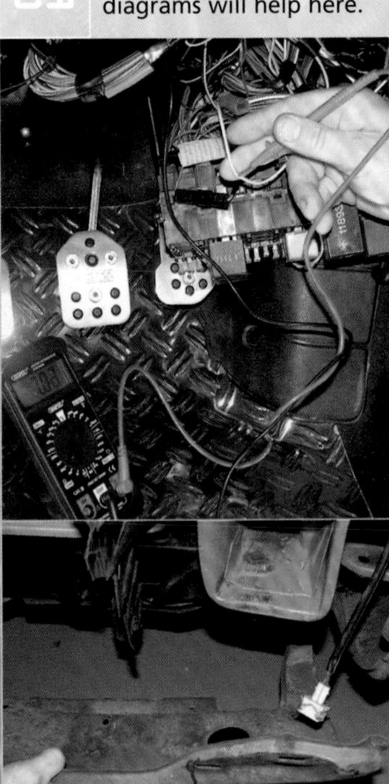

02 Once you've traced your wire, this is the live (+ve) feed for your foglight relay. Did we mention you'll need a relay? You'll need a relay. A four-pin one will do nicely. Splice a new wire onto the feed you've found . . .

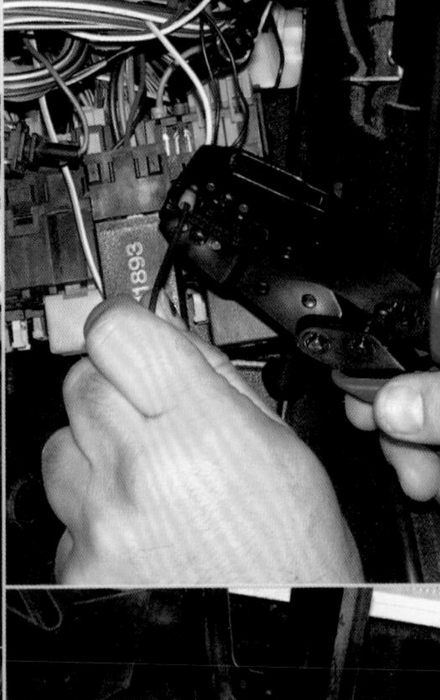

03 . . . and feed it through to the engine (lift the carpet, and go through one of the bulkhead grommets). Decide where you'll mount the relay (next to the battery seems obvious) and plug the wire into terminal 86.

04 For your other relay connections, you'll need an earth to terminal 85 (we found a good spot next to the battery) . . .

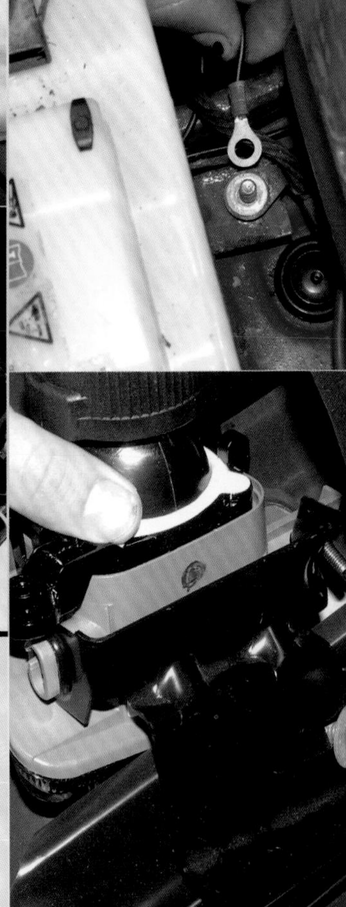

09 . . . and one right in the middle. Take off the full-width metal panel (more scrap!) . . .

10 . . . then refit the middle bolt, as this supports the front "slam" panel.

11 Hook the foglight mounting bracket onto the rear of the light, and tighten the bolts.

12 The bolts for fitting the mounting brackets to the bumper must be "coach" bolts, with a square section under the bolt head - the square bit locks into the bumper, and means you only have to tighten the nut (the bolt stays still). Fit the bolts, then slide the bracket in place and tighten the nuts.

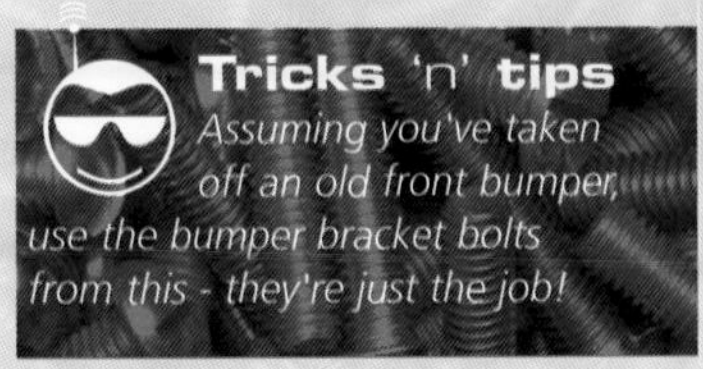

Tricks 'n' tips

Assuming you've taken off an old front bumper, use the bumper bracket bolts from this - they're just the job!

. . . and a live supply, which must be fused (15 or 20 amps should be enough) - VW kindly supply this little spade terminal on the battery lead, so we took

05 full advantage. This goes to terminal 30 on your relay.

Now, terminal 87 on your relay is the live output to the fogs - split this into two wires, and feed it out to where the lights will go. Each foglight will also need an earth - either pick a point on the body next to each light, or run a pair of wires back

06 to the earth point you used earlier for your relay.

With the wiring sorted, now you'd best fit the lights. First problem - the pukka VeeDub-style fogs won't sit deep enough into the front bumper holes. Why? Because there's a metal panel behind, in the way.

07 This is held by five bolts - one at each side . . .

08 . . . one each side underneath . . .

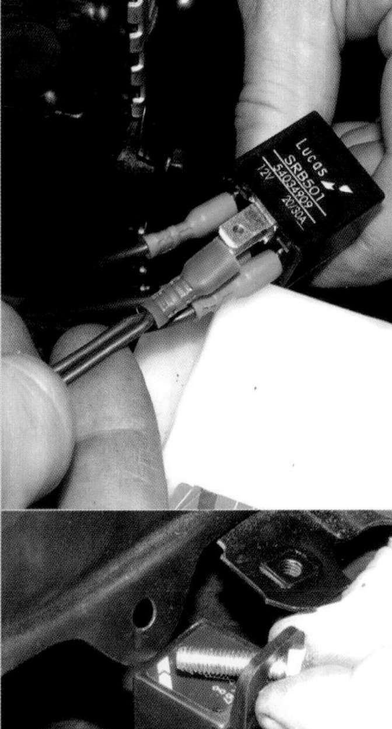

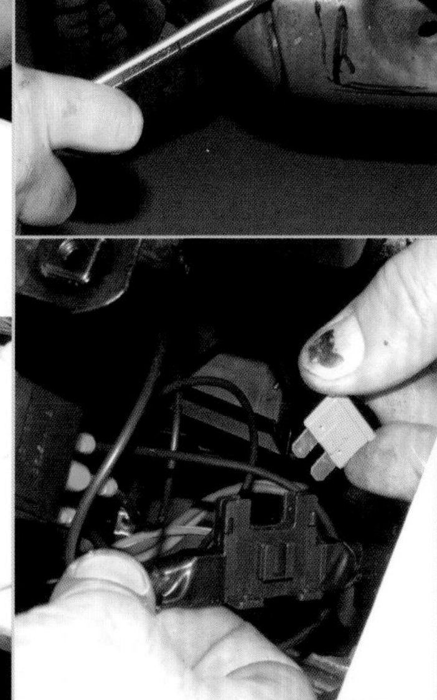

13 To connect the wiring, you'll probably need to pinch a proper wiring plug (or two, even!) from somewhere. We chopped the plugs from our inner pair of headlights (now scrap, after fitting our de-badged single-light grille) and spliced on the wires rigged up earlier. Connect the wiring to the lights . . .

14 . . . fit the remaining connector to the relay (terminal 87), mount the relay . . .

15 . . . and fit the fuse to your live supply from the battery.

16 Finally test to see if they work and it's job done!

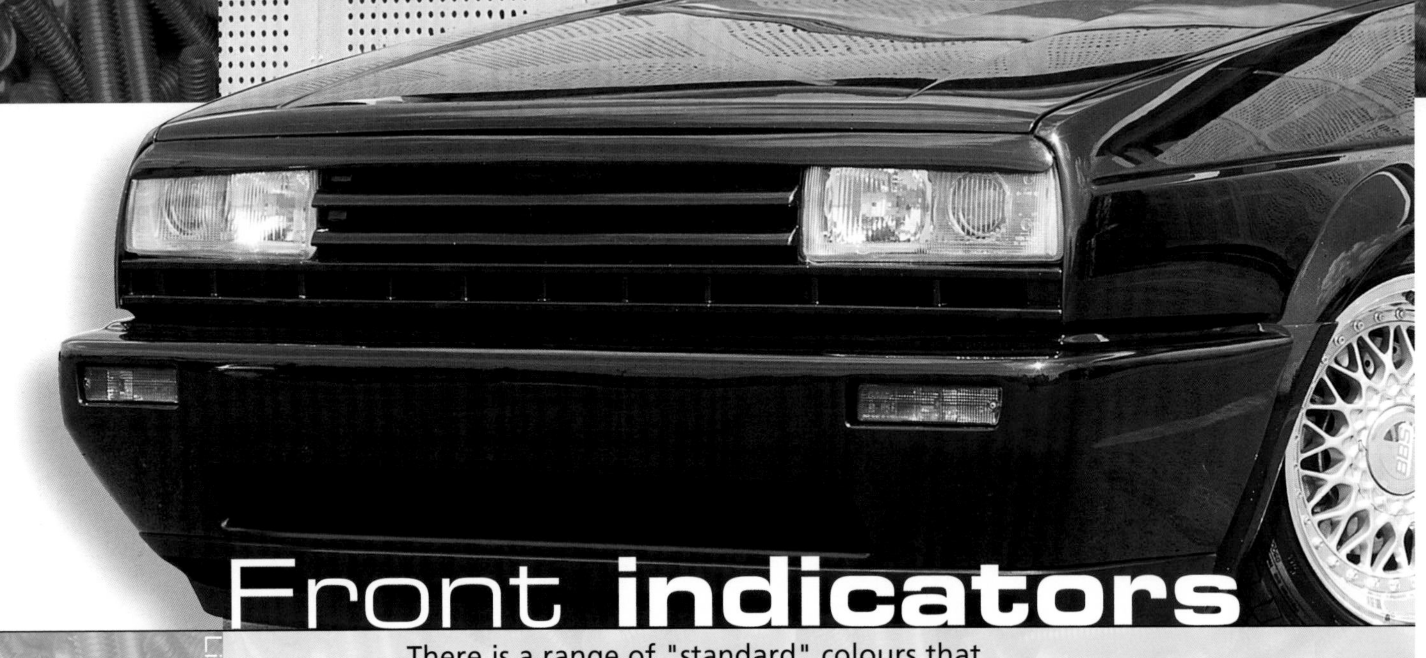

Front indicators

There is a range of "standard" colours that indicators come in (clear, red, smoked, green and blue). One potential problem here is that the indicators must still show an orange light when the indicators are on, and they must be sufficiently bright. Providing you buy good-quality lenses, and use the recommended bulbs with them, there should be no problem.

Especially if you've decided on the clear lenses, note that you'll have to change the bulbs too, to orange ones or preferably special bulbs which provide the orange light without being as obviously orange from outside.

01 If you're fitting indicators to new front bumpers, collect these little plugs from the old ones, and fit them to the new.

02 Plug the bulbholders into the existing wiring, then fit the holder to the light.

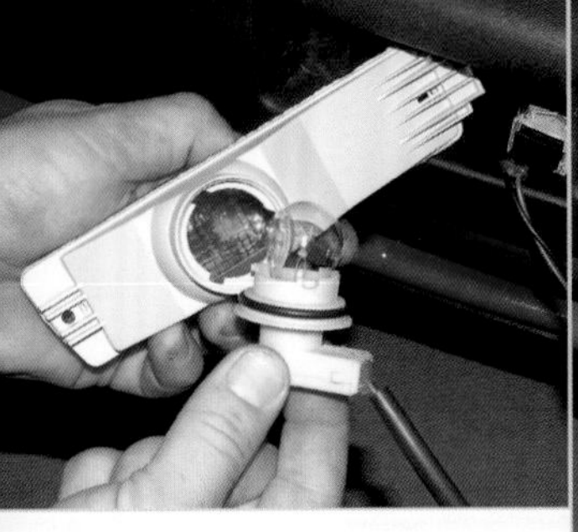

03 Pop the light into the bumper, and screw it in. Make sure you don't do it too tight as this will crack the plastic.

Side **repeaters**

Besides the various colour effects, side repeater lights are available in different shapes. Any shape goes, really it's up to you.

01 Fitting side repeaters, in theory, is dead easy - as long as you've bought the right units! Check the photo here before you buy - the one on the right will fit easily, the other will need work to fit.

02 Remove the old repeater by prising it rearwards and out at the front edge.

03 Peel back the rubber boot over the wiring connectors, then disconnect them.

04 Connect up the wiring (doesn't matter which wire goes to which terminal), fold back the boot and fit the light into the back edge of the hole. Secure by pressing rearwards and in at the front edge.

05 The "wrong" units can still be made to fit if required. Visit your local scrapyard, and grab two of the two-pin wiring plugs which are fitted to the various coolant temperature sensors/switches around the Golf engine. Take your "wrong" side repeaters along, to check that you get the right plugs. Using spade connectors, connect the wires on the switch plugs to the existing repeater light wiring. This type of repeater is then fed into the wing, and stuck in place using the sticky pad provided - make sure it's properly lined up first!

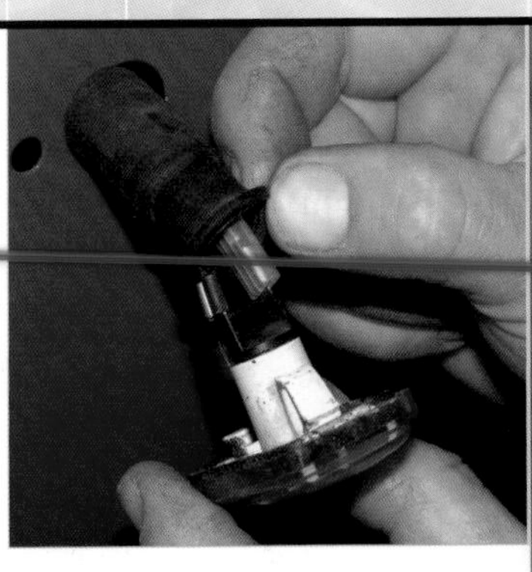

Rear **light clusters**

Rear lights are available in as many (if not more) colours than the front and side indicators. The most popular colours are clear/white, red, green, yellow, blue, and red/white BMW M3-style units.

When buying rear lights, avoid LHD clusters as your foglight will be on the wrong side, and they won't have red reflectors which are a legal requirement. Our "illegal" rear light clusters came with separate stick-on reflectors (proper mounts were also supplied, for more permanent fixing) - but would you fit these? We don't think so. The only way to avoid all this unnecessary grief is to stump up the cash for some pukka UK-legal lights in the first place. Hella make UK-legal lights (they also made the Golf originals), and they've also been in touch with all UK police forces, to advise them that their lights are legal.

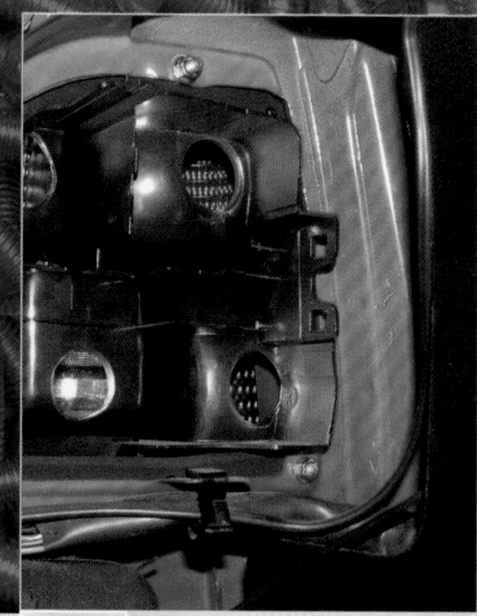

01 Open the tailgate and release the big bulbholder from the back of the light by squeezing the tabs. Remove the three nuts - hold onto the light while the last one's being undone.

02 Take out the light unit. If it didn't come off with the light, peel off the foam/rubber gasket from the car.

03 Fit the new gasket to the new light unit, and offer it up to the car. Refit the mounting nuts, and tighten them firmly. Clip the bulbholder into the rear of the light unit, then test all the lights.

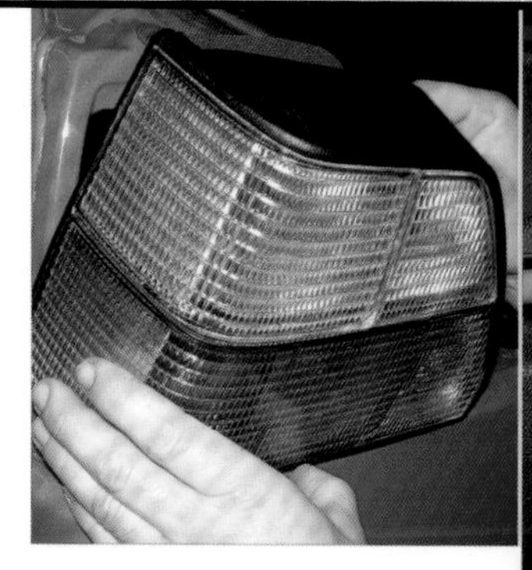

04 If you've fitted left-hand-drive lights, strictly speaking, you must fit these rear reflectors - here, we chose the least-offensive option (sticking them directly to the bumpers). You could try mounting them either side of the number plate. Trouble is, they look so cheap you'd probably only want them on for the MOT.

05 You'll also need a rear foglight of some sort. Try this approach if you like - drill a hole in the blanking plate for the bulb (taking care not to go too deep, and totally knack the light lens) get Stanley out and enlarge the hole . . .

06 . . . then refit the bulbholder with a 21-watt red bulb. If it looks pink however, it may not satisfy the MOT crew.

Rear **foglight**

01 One option is to try and fit a separate rear fog that doesn't look a complete mess. Rear big bumpers come with a handy recess for the rear towing eye - if you can get a foglight to fit inside this, it looks neat and you can fit a cover over it!

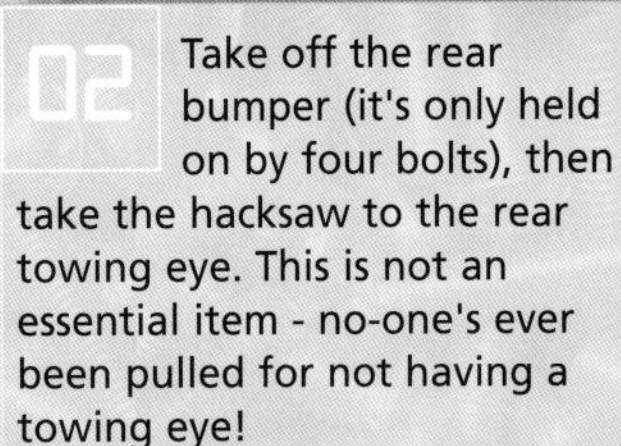

02 Take off the rear bumper (it's only held on by four bolts), then take the hacksaw to the rear towing eye. This is not an essential item - no-one's ever been pulled for not having a towing eye!

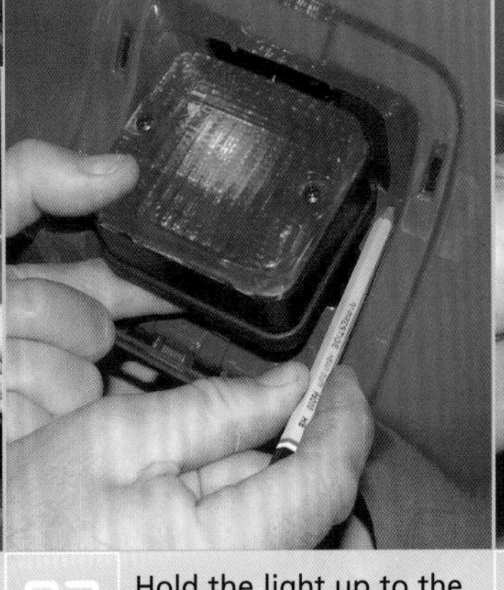

03 Hold the light up to the recess, and mark the recess for cutting. You'll need to cut the "back" of the recess out, so the bumper will slip over the foglight - give yourself some room to play with, too (an exact fit is not what you want).

04 Now hold the light in place, and mark where the hole for the mounting bracket needs to be. Take your time - this bit must be accurate. Drill the hole, and fit the light. We packed a few washers behind our bracket, to allow the light to tilt down slightly (this lets it fit better into the bumper recess).

Connect up two lengths of wire to the terminals on the light, using spade connectors. If your light isn't marked for live and earth, don't worry - it's not important which wire does which.
05

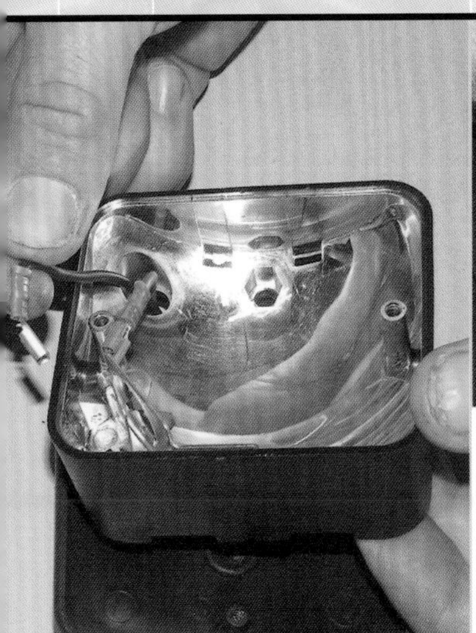

The new wires must be routed through the rear body panel (avoid using the bumper mounting bracket holes, as you might crush the wire and get a short-circuit when you refit the bumper). To get the wires up to the rear light bulbholder, you'll have to lift the boot carpet and drill a hole in the boot floor. Remember to fit a grommet to the hole, to protect the wires.
06

Unplug the wiring connector from the rear light cluster, and connect the new wires to the foglight live and earth. On our car, live was a grey/white wire, and the earth was brown. Check with the Haynes wiring diagrams, or switch on the old foglight (ignition and dipped beams on) and check using a test light or meter.
07

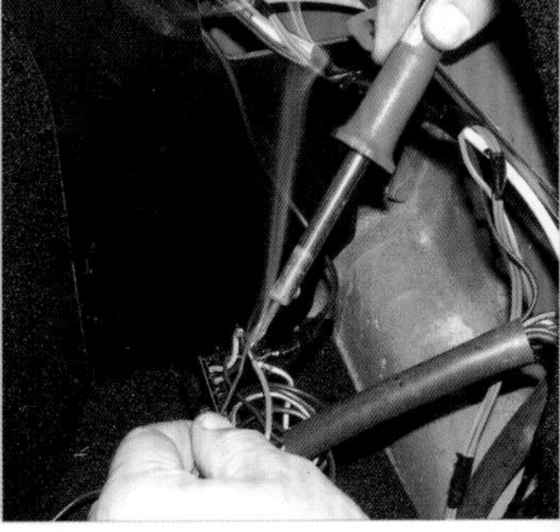

Now you've got a foglight that'll make Mr MOT happy, and (although this isn't strictly legal) you can pop the cover over it for the other 364 days of the year!
08

07 Wheels & tyres

Surely the classic Golf alloy, the timeless BBS RS split-rim just shouts "Look at my wad!"

Alloy wheels are the most important styling decision you'll make. No matter how good the rest of your car is, choose some naff rims and your car will never look right. Choose a good set and you're already well on the way to creating a sorted motor. Take your time and pick wisely - wheel fashions change like the weather, and you don't want to spend shedloads on a set of uncool alloys.

Don't forget to tell your insurance company what you're fitting, you may find you're not charged a penny more, especially if you've fitted some locking wheel nuts/bolts. Not all companies are the same, though - some charge an admin fee, and yes, some will start loading your premium. If you want the rims covered, it's best to talk to a company specialising in modified cars.

Keep them clean

It's a small point maybe, but you'll obviously want your wheels to look as smart as possible, as often as possible - so how easy are they going to be to clean? The multi-spokers and BBS style are hell to clean - a fiddly toothbrush job - do you really want that much aggro every week? The simpler the design, the easier time you'll have. For those who like nothing better than counting their spokes, though, there are several really good products out there to make your life less of a cleaning nightmare.

It's worth applying a bit of car polish to the wheels - provided it's good stuff, and you can be sure of getting the residue out of the corners and edges, a polished wheel will always be easier to clean off than an unpolished one.

Check your bolts

Most steel-wheel bolts are NOT suitable for use with alloy wheels (and vice-versa). Make sure you ask about this when buying new wheels, and if necessary, bargain a set of bolts into the price.

Another point to watch for is that the new wheel bolts are the correct length for your fitment, taking into account whether you've fitted spacers or not. Bolts that are too short are obviously dangerous, and ones that are too long can foul on drum brakes, and generally get in the way of any turning activities. If in doubt ask the retailer for advice. Always check that the wheels turn freely once they've been put on, and investigate any strange noises before you go off for a ride.

If you're keeping a steel wheel as your spare (or even if you're keeping an original GTI alloy), keep a set of your original wheel bolts in a bag inside the spare wheel. Locking bolts especially might be too long when fitted to a thin steel wheel, and might jam up your brakes!

Other options

If you're on a really tight budget, and perhaps own a real "basic" model Golf, don't overlook the possibility of fitting a discarded set of standard alloys, possibly from another VW entirely - check that the stud pattern's the same, obviously.

If the VW range of wheels is too limiting, don't be too quick buying (for instance) BMW or Vauxhall alloys - they might appear to bolt on okay, but the offset is often different. In the case of BMW alloys on VWs, the pitch circle diameter on the Beemer's rims is often fractionally less - if you bolt these on, the strain on the bolts is too great, and they can fracture or work themselves loose...

Size matters

The trend in wheel size is an interesting one. It seems that, for us Brits, biggest is best - there are many Golfs with 18s and in extreme cases 19s. But in general it's safe to say that you can't be seen with anything less than 17-inchers.

In Europe they often go for the small-wheel look, still with seriously dropped suspension of course, but on 14- and 15-inch rims. On many cars (the Golf included), 16-inch rims are the biggest you can sensibly fit before you have to start looking at sorting the arches, but it's not too major a task to roll the arches to accept 17s.

Width is the key

Successfully fitting big wheels in combination with lowered suspension is one of the major challenges to the modifier. At least the Golf has reasonably roomy arches, so there are less problems than you'll find with a Nova or Saxo. As much as anything, tyre width is what ultimately leads to problems, not so much the increased wheel diameter.

If the tyres are too wide, they will first of all rub on the suspension strut (ie on the inside edge of the tyre). Also, the inside edges may rub on the arches on full steering lock. Rubbing on the inside edges can be cured by fitting offsets or spacers between the wheel and hub, which effectively pull the wheel outwards, "spacing" it away from its normal position. Fitting spacers must be done using longer wheel bolts, as the standard ones may only engage into the hubs by a few threads, which is highly dangerous (also check that your locking bolts are long enough).

Rubbing on the outside edges is a simple case of wheelarch lip fouling, which is cured by rolling out the wheelarch return edge. If you've gone for really wide tyres, or have already had to fit spacers, the outer edge of the tyre will probably be visible outside the wheelarch, and this is a no-no (it's illegal, I'm afraid, and you must cover it up!). With Golfs, most people opt for G60 wheelarch extensions.

The other trick with fitting big alloys is of course to avoid the "Golf 4x4 off-road" look, which you will achieve remarkably easily just by bolting on a set of 17s with standard suspension. Overcoming this problem by lowering is essential (see "Suspension").

Fitting locking wheel bolts shows a very responsible attitude to the theft threat, which your insurance company will appreciate. Which is nice.

Jargon explained

PCD – Is your Pitch Circle Diameter, which relates to the spacing of your wheel bolt holes, or "stud pattern". It is expressed by the diameter of a notional circle which passes through the centre of your wheel bolts, and the number of bolts. On a Mk 2 Golf, the PCD is 100 mm with four bolts, which is given as 100/4.

ROLLING RADIUS – is the distance from the wheel centre to the outer edge of the tyre, or effectively, half the overall diameter.

OFFSET - this is determined by the distance from the wheel mounting face in relation to its centre-line. The offset figure is denoted by ET (no, I mustn't), which stands for einpress tiefe in German, or pressed-in depth (now I know you're asleep). The lower the offset, the more the wheels will stick out. Fitting wheels with the wrong offset might bring the wheel into too-close contact with the brake and suspension bits, or with the arches. Very specialised area - seek advice from the wheel manufacturers if you're going for a very radical size (or even if you're not). The correct offset for Golfs of all sizes is ET 35.

Hold onto your wheels

The minute you bolt on your alloys, your car becomes a target. If you don't make life difficult for thieves you risk losing them.The market and demand for stolen alloys is huge, but since most people don't bother having them security-marked in any way, once a set of wheels disappears, they're almost impossible to trace.

Locking wheel bolts combined with a good car alarm which detects if the car is being moved are your best bets. If you fit a cheap set of locking bolts, thieves may use a hammer and thin chisel to crack off the locking bolt, or hammer a socket onto the bolt head, and undo the locking bolt as normal. So - choose the best bolts you can.

There is some debate as to whether it's okay to fit more than one set of locking bolts to a car - the feeling against doing this is that the replacement locking bolts may not be made to the same standard as factory originals, and while it's okay to fit one set on security grounds, fitting more than could lead to the bolts failing. Obviously, you must carry the special key or tool which came with your bolts with you at all times, in case of a puncture, or if you're having any other work done, such as new brakes or tyres. But don't just sling it in the glovebox or the boot where a thief could easily find it. Either keep it with you, or find a very good hiding place in the car.

Don't try this at home. Find somewhere more original than the glovebox for your tool!

How to change a set of wheels

It's all fairly straightforward stuff, but we'll run through the basics, where the jacking points are, and what happens if you want to take more than one wheel off at a time.

What to use

If you don't already have one, invest in a decent hydraulic (trolley) jack. This is way more use than the standard car jack, which is really only for emergencies, and which isn't stable enough to rely on. Trolley jacks have a valve, usually at the rear, which must be fully tightened (using the end of the jack handle) before raising the jack, and which is carefully loosened to lower the car.

Axle stands are placed under the car, once it's been lifted using the jack. Stands are an important accessory to a trolley jack, because once they're in place, there's no way the car can come down on you - even a brand new trolley jack could creep down (if you haven't tightened the valve), or could even fail completely under load (if it's a cheap one, or knackered, or both).

Under no circumstances use bricks, wooden blocks or anything else which you have to pile up, to support the car - this is just plain stupid. A Golf weighs around a ton - if you want to find out just how solidly it's built, try crawling under it when it's resting on a few bricks.

Where to use it

Only ever jack the car up on a solid, level surface (ideally, a concrete or Tarmac driveway, or quiet car park). If there's a slope, the car could move as the wheels are lifted off the ground. Jacking up on a rough or gravelled surface is not recommended, as the jack could slip at an awkward moment - such as when you've just got underneath...

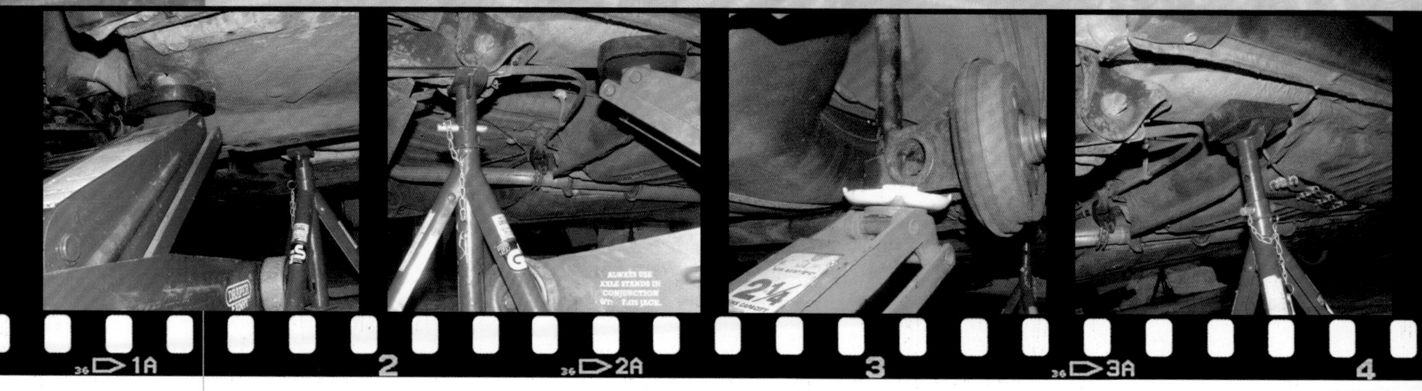

Trolley jack under one of the front support points, and an axle stand under the front subframe.

Rear jacking point in use, and axle stand under the trailing arm pivot - ok, but not the best.

Another jacking point that's not in the manual, but ok in the real world - under the rear shock.

Very safe, very secure - axle stand under rear jacking point, with a block of wood.

wheel centre.

Tricks 'n' tips

Whenever you have your wheels off, clean off any corrosion with wet-and-dry paper, then coat the hub mating surfaces with copper (brake) grease - this "sticks" better than ordinary grease, and is temperature-resistant. There's no way you'll suffer stuck-on wheels again. "Proper" alloys come with a plastic collar which fits inside the wheel - this is an essential item which should not be discarded, as it centres the wheel properly and prevents wheel-to-hub corrosion.

Jacking up the front

Before jacking up the front of the car, pull the handbrake on firmly (you can also chock the rear wheels, if you don't trust your handbrake).

If you're taking the wheels off, loosen the wheel bolts slightly before you start jacking up the car.

Assuming you've got a trolley jack, the next question is - where do you stick it? VW provide two support points at the front, behind the front wheels and inside the sill flanges, and they look like cups welded to the floor. Put a flat offcut of wood on your jack head, and get it under there! You can jack on the sill jacking points (which are marked by little notches above the sill edges), but it's worth making up a block of wood with a slot cut in it, to relieve the stress on the sill edge.

Once you've got the car up, pop an axle stand or two under the front subframe (the bit the triangular-looking front wishbones are attached to, don't put stands under the wishbones though). With the stands in place, you can lower the jack so the car's weight rests on the stands.

Don't jack up the car, or stick stands under the car, anywhere other than the correct jacking and support points. This means - not the floorpan or the sump, and not under the brake/fuel pipes for obvious reasons.

Jacking up the rear

When jacking up the rear of the car, place wooden chocks in front of the front wheels to stop it rolling forwards, and engage first gear.

If you're taking the wheels off, it's better to loosen the rear wheel bolts on the ground, as with the fronts.

Jacking and supporting the rear end is a little trickier. There's a jacking point provided just inside the sill jacking point at the back, but once you've got your trolley jack head on it there's nowhere to put the axle stand. Try either under the pivot point for the rear trailing arm, but this isn't the greatest place, or jack up under the back end of the trailing arm, where the rear shock mounts on. If you jack under there, you can then pop an axle stand right under the approved jacking point inside of the sill edge (with a block of wood, if you like).

Remember not to put your axle stands under any pipes, the spare wheel well, or the fuel tank.

Even with the plastic, wheels can still corrode on. Smear on some copper brake grease.

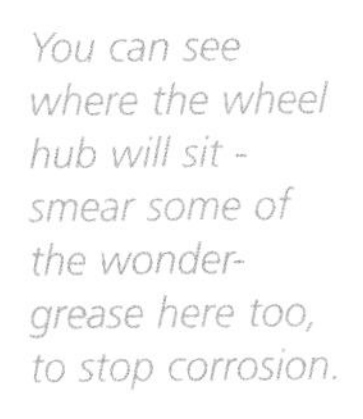

You can see where the wheel hub will sit - smear some of the wonder-grease here too, to stop corrosion.

Do yourself a favour and pop some grease on the wheel bolt threads as well.

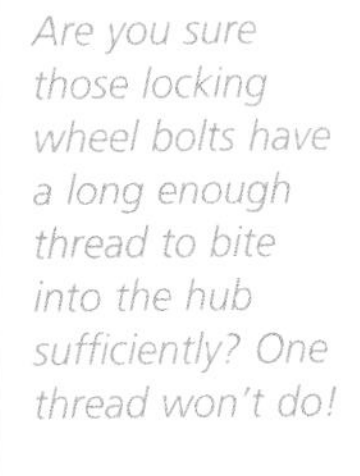

Are you sure those locking wheel bolts have a long enough thread to bite into the hub sufficiently? One thread won't do!

The centre cap looks good, and might stop thieves getting at the wheel bolts. Fit it!

Always nice to see a decent brand of tyre on a decent alloy. How cool do cheap tyres look, on a car like the Golf?

Tyres

Without wanting to sound like an old advert, choosing a known brand of tyre will prove to be one of your better decisions. Tyres are the only thing keeping you on the road, as in steering, braking and helping you round corners - what's the point of trying to improve the handling by sorting the suspension if you're going to throw the gains away by fitting cheap tyres?

The combination of stiff suspension and cheap tyres is inherently dangerous - because the front end dives less with reduced suspension travel, the front tyres are far more likely to lock and skid under heavy braking. So steer clear of cheapies and especially remoulds.

A problem with really wide tyres is aquaplaning - fitting good tyres won't prevent it, but it might increase your chances of staying in control. The sexiest modern low profile tyres have a V-tread pattern, designed specifically to aid water dispersal, which is exactly what you need to prevent aquaplaning. Also make sure, before you splash your cash on decent tyres, that you've cured all your rubbing and scrubbing issues, as nothing will rip your new tyres out faster.

When buying tyres, look out for ones which feature a rubbing strip on the sidewall (such as our Toyo Proxes) - these extend over the edge of the wheel rims, and the idea is that they protect the rim edges from damage by 'kerbing'.

The size markings are obviously the most important, but take note of the directional marks too, if swapping wheels round. Most of the other markings are for anoraks only.

Marks on your sidewalls

Tyre sizes are expressed in a strange mixture of metric and imperial specs - we'll take a typical tyre size as an example:

205/40 R 17 V
for a 7-inch wide 17-inch rim

205 width of tyre in millimetres

40 this is the "aspect ratio" (or "profile") of the tyre, or the sidewall height in relation to tyre width, expressed as a percentage, in this case 40%. So - 40% of 205 mm = 82 mm, or the height of the tyre sidewall from the edge of the locating bead to the top of the tread. Not very relevant to the amount of sidewall actually visible, then.

R Radial.

17 Wheel diameter in inches.

V Speed rating (in this case, suitable for use up to 150 mph).

Tyre pressure

Don't forget, when you're having your new tyres fitted, to ask what the recommended pressures should be, front and rear – the VW specs won't be relevant any more. Running the tyres at the wrong pressures is not a good idea (you'll stand to wear them out much faster) and can be very dangerous (too soft - tyre rolls off the rim, too hard - tyre slides, no grip).

Speed ratings

Besides the tyre size, tyres are marked with a maximum speed rating, expressed as a letter code:

T up to 190 km/h (118 mph)

U up to 200 km/h (124 mph)

H up to 210 km/h (130 mph)

V inside tyre size markings (225/50 VR 16) over 210 km/h (130 mph)

V outside tyre size markings (185/55 R 15 V) up to 240 km/h (150 mph)

Z inside tyre size markings (255/40 ZR 17) over 240 km/h (150 mph)

Aquaplaning is a very scary feature associated with wide tyres. Total loss of grip in the wet is best avoided by fitting decent tyres in the first place.

Photo courtesy of Volkswagen Driver magazine

08

Suspension

Lower your Golf

If your Golf's still sitting on standard suspension, but you've decided you couldn't wait to fit your big alloys, the chances are it is now doing a passable impression of a tractor. Lowered suspension is an essential fitment, then - so how low do you go, and what side-effects will a lowering kit have?

As for what to buy, there are basically three main options when it comes to lowering, arranged in order of ascending cost below:

1 Set of lowering springs.

2 Matched set of lowering springs and shock absorbers.

3 Set of "coilovers".

Lowering springs

The cheapest option by far, but with the most pitfalls and some unpleasant side-effects. Lowering springs are, effectively, shorter versions of the standard items fitted to your Golf at the factory. However, not only are they shorter (lower), they are also of necessity uprated (stiffer) - if lowering springs were simply shorter than standard and the same stiffness (the same "rate"), you'd be hitting the bump-stops over every set of catseyes.

With just a set of lowering springs, you fit new springs and keep the original shock absorbers ("dampers") - even if the originals aren't completely knackered, you're creating a problem caused by mis-matched components. The original dampers were carefully chosen to work in harmony with the original-rate springs - by increasing the spring rate without changing the dampers, you end up with a situation where the dampers will not be in full and effective control of the spring motion. What this usually does before long is wreck the dampers, so you really don't save any money in the end.

Assuming you want to slam your suspension so that your arches just clear the tops of your new rims, assess the required drop by measuring the tyre-to-wheelarch gap, to start with. Springs are generally only available in a very few sizes, expressed by the amount of (fixed) drop they'll produce - 60mm, 40mm and, if you're less brave, 30 and 35mm springs are all available. If you want to try and avoid any arch work, take as many measurements as possible, and ask around your mates - suppliers and manufacturers may be your best source of help in special cases.

Suspension kit

A far better choice - a matched set of springs and dampers - is a genuine "upgrade". There are several kits available, so go for the best you can afford. With a properly-sorted conversion, your Golf will handle even better, and you'll still be able to negotiate a set of roadworks without the risk of dental work afterwards.

Some of the kits are billed as "adjustable", but this only applies to the damper rates, which can often be set to your own taste by a few minutes' work with a spanner (don't mistake them for coilovers). This feature can be quite good fun to play around with - but be careful you don't get carried away and set it too stiff, or you'll end up with an evil-handling car!

Although you'll undoubtedly end up with a fine-handling car eventually, there are problems with suspension kits. They are guilty of causing changes to steering geometry so you'll have to have it reset if you don't want your tyres to wear out at an alarming rate. The kit we bought is available in several "drops" - 40 mm, 60 mm, and 60 mm front/40 mm rear. We chose the 60 mm drop all round.

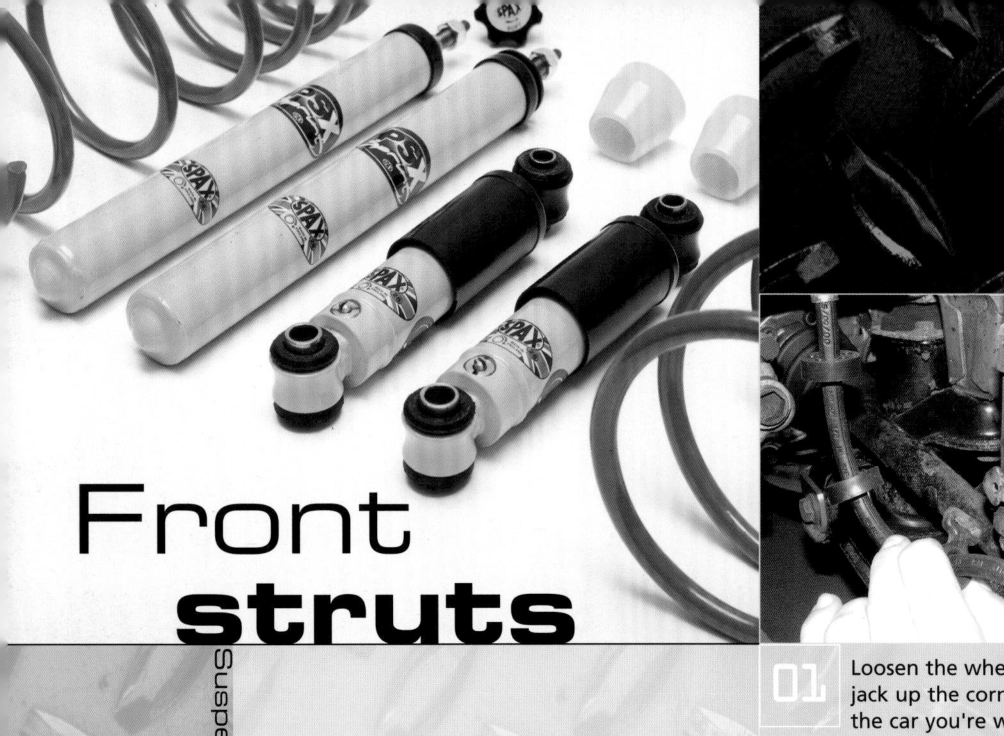

Front struts

01 Loosen the wheel bolts, jack up the corner of the car you're working on, and take off the wheel. Make sure you've got an axle stand under a solid part of the car (like the front subframe) in case the jack gives out. Have a look in "Wheels & tyres" for more info on jacking up. The first bit's easy - unclip the brake hose from the strut.

02 In theory, you're supposed to mark these two strut-to-hub bolts before loosening them, because they're used to set the front camber. We found that the new strut holes were so "baggy", the camber setting gets lost anyway. Note which way round the bolts fit, then loosen them off. Don't remove them yet - leave them loose.

Tricks 'n' tips
Don't start this job without coil spring compressors or the special tool for loosening the front strut internal nut, or you'll be sorry!

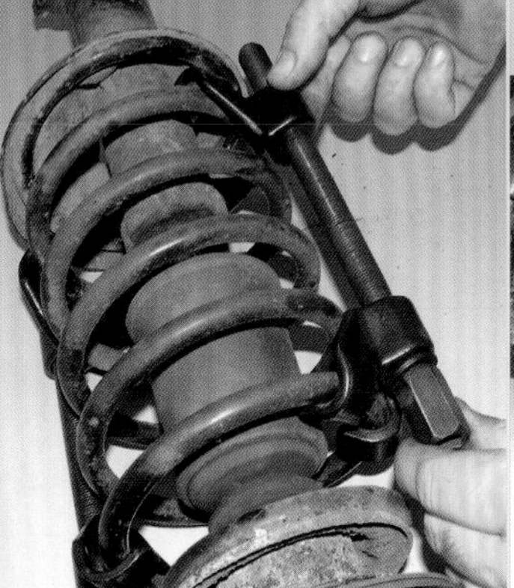

Achtung!
For the next bit, you MUST use coil spring compressors ("spring clamps"). It's the only way to get the springs off, but means they're under a lot of tension so be very careful if you don't want to get damaged by a flying spring.

07 There are two clamps, each with two hooks, which sit over one of the spring coils. You won't get the hooks over the top and bottom coils, but try the next nearest. Get the two clamps opposite each other, then tighten the big bolt up the middle of each to compress one side of the spring - this must be done evenly, one side after the other, or the un-clamped side might fly off.

08 Compress the spring carefully until the tension is off the top spring seat. Now you need this tool to undo the internal piston nut, which has two slots in the top. Some of the more expensive kits come with the tool. But if not a motor factor should be able to sort you out.

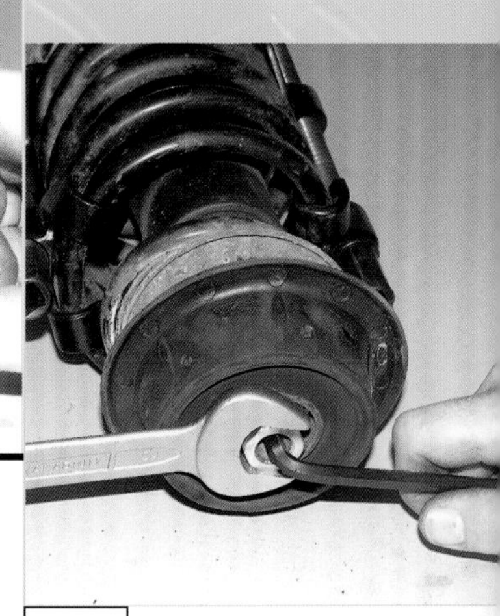

09 Use the tool to unscrew the internal nut, again holding the strut piston with the hefty Allen key.

03 Under the bonnet, pop off the plastic cap on the strut top mount, and loosen the centre nut. You'll need a hefty Allen key to hold the strut piston against turning.

04 Remove the nut completely, and take off the upper mounting plate. Now all that's holding the strut in are the two bolts down below.

05 Back under the car, put something under the lower wishbone to support it, and slide out the two strut-to-hub bolts.

06 Slip the strut off the hub, and slide it on out from the wheelarch.

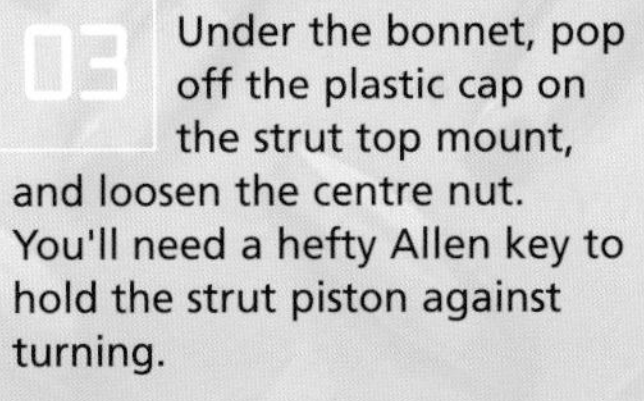

10 Remove the nut, and take off the strut bearing. Pay attention, because you'll be refitting most of this stuff in a minute! Check the strut bearing for slop and roughness. Apparently, some slop is normal. If your Golf's done mega-miles, it might be best to assume the strut bearings either are shot, or soon will be. You can get uprated replacements, if standards won't do.

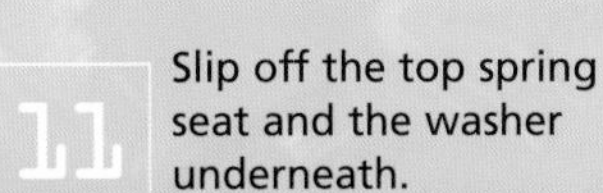

11 Slip off the top spring seat and the washer underneath.

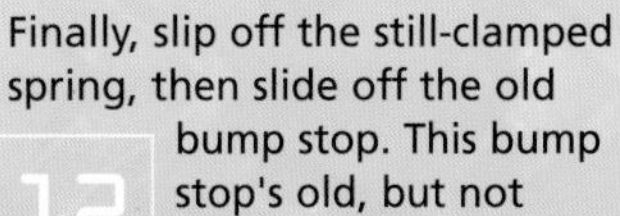

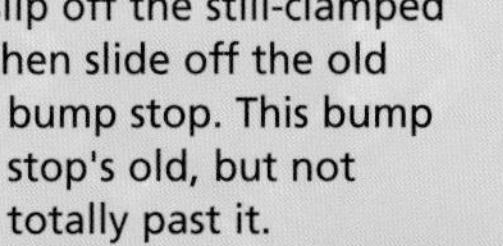

12 Finally, slip off the still-clamped spring, then slide off the old bump stop. This bump stop's old, but not totally past it.

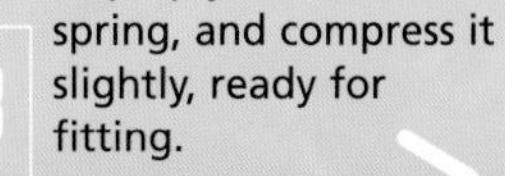

13 Slowly, carefully, loosen the bolts on the spring clamps, until the old springs are uncompressed - then scrap them. Clamp up your new spring, and compress it slightly, ready for fitting.

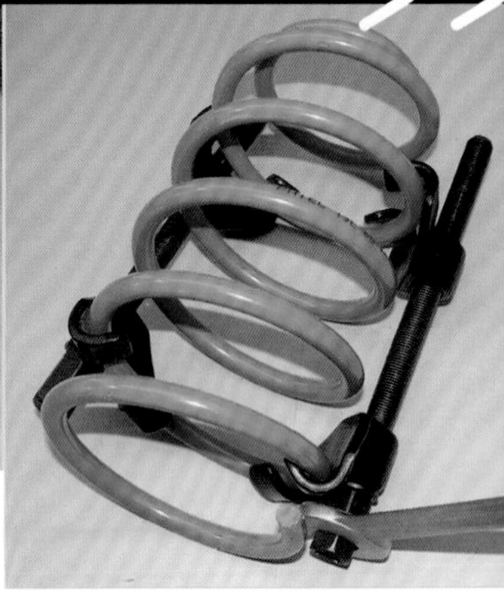

14 If you're going to fit uprated bump stops like these, fit them onto the new strut now . . .

15 . . . followed (if you like) by the old bump stop, and its washer. You don't have to fit both bump stops so seek advice on this point from your parts supplier.

16 Now you're ready to slip the clamped new spring onto the new strut. The spring end should sit into the notch in the lower spring seat - turn the spring round until it does. Generally, the slightly narrower end of the spring is the bottom end.

17 When you offer on the top spring seat, you'll see it too has a little notch for the spring end to fit into. Make sure it does. This is the same spring seat we took off - we just shot-blasted and painted it.

21 Feed the strut up into the wheelarch, and . . .

22 . . . (it's best to have an assistant for this) refit the upper mounting plate and the nut - it only needs tightening by hand at this stage. Just so the strut doesn't fall out.

23 Lift the hub and lower wishbone so that the holes line up again . . .

18 Slip on the strut bearing . . .

19 . . . then try fitting the internal nut, slots upwards. This is where you find out if you compressed the spring enough.

20 There is a torque for this nut (40 Nm), but using the special tool AND an Allen key makes using a torque wrench a bit tricky for the DIY-er. Just do it up tight.

When the nut's tight, you can unwind the spring clamps, and take 'em off - just make sure the spring ends stay in place, top and bottom.

24 . . . then slide in the bolts from the front - if new ones are provided, use them.

25 You should really fit new nuts to these bolts too, and torque them up to 80 Nm. Try and centralise everything now, or else wait until the car's back on its wheels before tightening up fully. Even so, the camber angles will need setting later or you'll be chewing tyres...

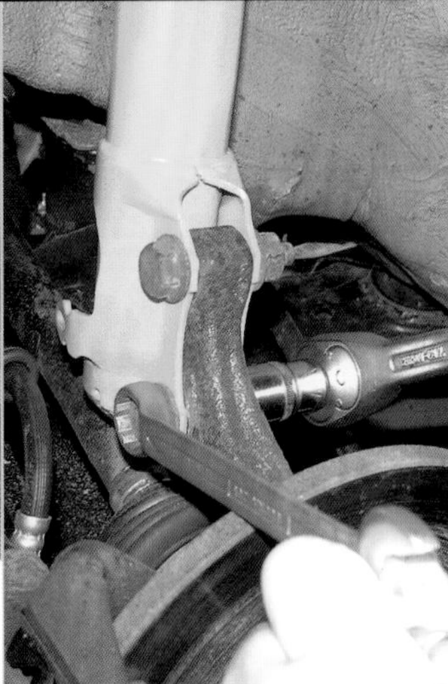

26 Clip on the brake hose before. . .

27 . . . tightening the top nut. For info, this should be 60 Nm, but the need for an Allen key again makes this a bit irrelevant. Just do it good and tight.

Rear **struts**

Loosen the rear wheel bolts, jack up the corner of the car you're working on, and take off the wheel. It's best to jack directly under the rear suspension arm for this, but make sure you can still get to the shock's lower bolt. Don't try this unless you've got a proper trolley jack, AND an axle stand to go under the rear jacking point. Have a look in "Wheels & tyres" for more info on jacking up.

01

Open the tailgate, and take out the parcel shelf. The shelf side supports have to be taken out next, and they're each held in by five nuts.

02

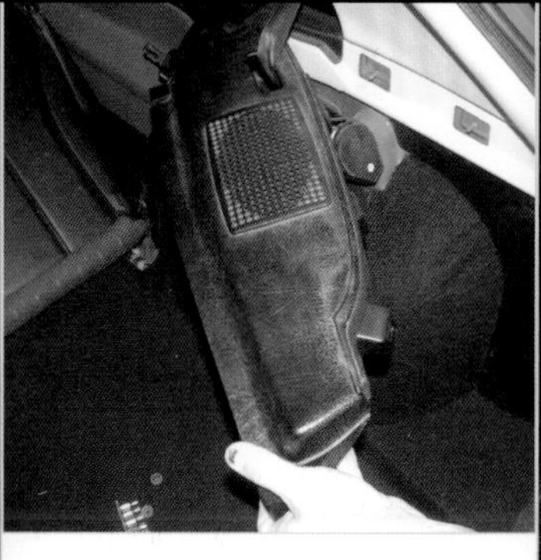

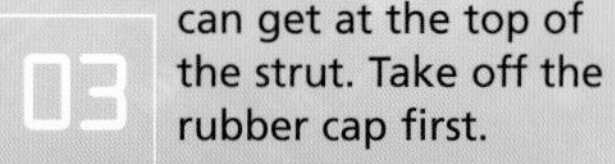

With the supports gone, you can get at the top of the strut. Take off the rubber cap first.

03

04 Loosen the top nut - you'll need two spanners for this (one very tiddly, approx 8 mm, to hold the flats on the strut piston).

05 Take off the nut, and the top mounting plate.

06 Now it's out with the same spanners again, to loosen the lower nut.

07 Take off the upper bearing (which has a dished washer inside) . . .

08 . . . followed by this dished washer (note how all these bits are fitted, for when you refit them).

09 Now loosen off the shock absorber lower mounting nut and bolt. This is a bit awkward, as you've got to stick a spanner up inside the rear arm, and fish about until you find the nut.

10 Slip out the bolt (retrieve the nut from inside) and the strut's ready to come off.

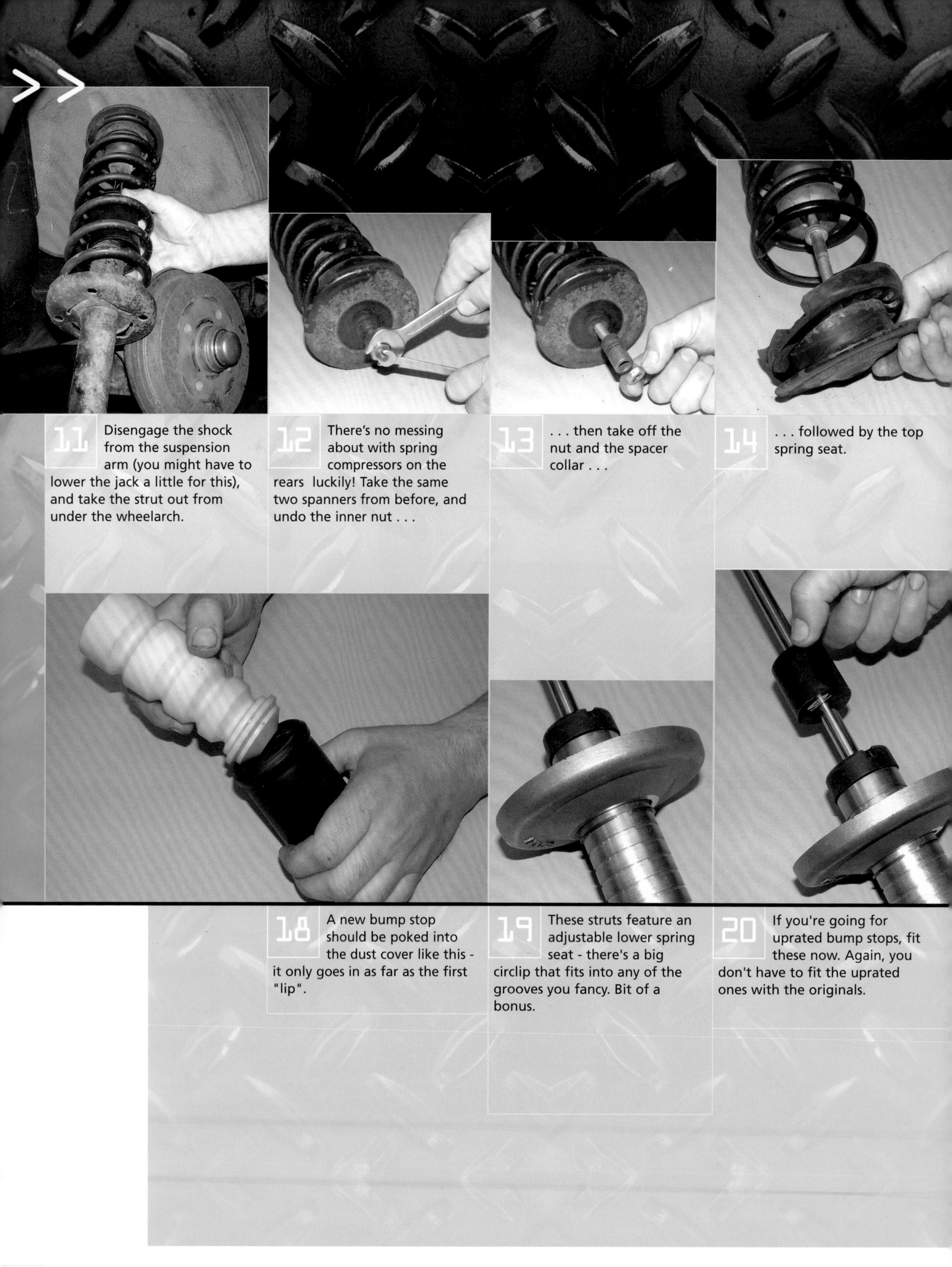

11 Disengage the shock from the suspension arm (you might have to lower the jack a little for this), and take the strut out from under the wheelarch.

12 There's no messing about with spring compressors on the rears luckily! Take the same two spanners from before, and undo the inner nut . . .

13 . . . then take off the nut and the spacer collar . . .

14 . . . followed by the top spring seat.

18 A new bump stop should be poked into the dust cover like this - it only goes in as far as the first "lip".

19 These struts feature an adjustable lower spring seat - there's a big circlip that fits into any of the grooves you fancy. Bit of a bonus.

20 If you're going for uprated bump stops, fit these now. Again, you don't have to fit the uprated ones with the originals.

15 Now there's a washer to come out . . .

16 . . . before the bump stop . . .

17 . . . or rather, what's left of it! This is what a severely-knacked example looks like. Don't refit anything which looks like this - get new ones.

21 Slip on the new spring (narrower end down) . . .

22 . . . then slide on the bump stop. If you have trouble doing this, take the spring off again, and fit the bump stop first - it's all the same in the end!

23 Now slip on the little washer . . .

24 . . . followed by the top spring seat . . .

>>

25 . . . making sure that the end of the spring fits in as shown, next to the just-visible arrow in the rubber.

26 Now it's time for the spacer collar . . .

27 . . . followed by the nut. On the new struts, you now need an Allen key to stop the piston from turning.

32 . . . and its own washer.

33 Tighten the nut which goes on next, holding the piston with the Allen key.

34 Now there's this washer to go on . . .

28 Your new strut can now be offered up into the wheelarch . . .

29 . . . then drop the shocker into the suspension arm, and slot in the bolt. Fit the nut up inside the suspension arm, and tighten it by hand only for now. Wait 'til the car's back on its wheels to fully tighten it.

30 Especially now it's been dropped, you might need to raise the jack under the suspension arm, to get the top of the strut up into its hole. First bit to go on is the dished washer . . .

31 . . . followed by the upper bearing . . .

35 . . . and (finally!) the top nut - use a new one if you got it.

36 Do it up nice and tight, then plonk on the rubber cap.

37 Put the wheel on, and let the car down off the jack and axle stands. Crawl underneath, and tighten up the shock lower mounting nut and bolt - should be 70 Nm, if you've a torque wrench.

Coilovers

This is the most expensive option, and it offers one vital feature that the other two can't - true adjustability of ride height. This gives you more scope to fit those big rims and spacers. Coilovers are a variation on the suspension kit theme, in that they are a set of matched variable-rate springs (some have separate "helper" springs too) and shocks, but they might not guarantee as good a ride/handling mix as a normal kit.

A coilover set replaces each spring and shock with a combined unit where the coil spring fits over the shocker (hence "coil" "over") - nothing too unusual in this, because so far, it's similar to a normal front strut. The difference lies in the adjustable spring lower seat, which can lower the spring to any desired height (within limits).

Coilovers are something of a compromise. Making a car go super-low is not going to be good for the ride or the handling. Coilover systems necessarily have very short, stiff springs, and this can lead to problems similar to those found with cheap lowering springs alone. If you go too far with coilovers, you can end up with a choppy ride, heavy steering and generally unpleasant handling.

Coilover sets are developing all the time, and advances in progressive-rate springs mean that good-quality sets from known makers are well worth the extra over cheaper solutions.

Coilover conversion

Another cheaper option is the "coilover conversion". Offering as much potential for lowering as genuine coilovers (and at far less cost), these items could be described as a cross between coilovers and lowering springs, because the standard dampers are retained. What you get is a new spring assembly, with adjustable top and bottom mounts - the whole thing slips over your standard damper. Two problems with this solution:

1 Your standard dampers will not be able to cope with the uprated springs, so the car will almost certainly ride (and possibly handle) like a pig if you go for a really serious drop.

2 The standard dampers are effectively being compressed, the lower you go. There is a limit to how far they will compress before being completely solid (and this could be the limit for your lowering activities). Even a partly-compressed damper won't be able to do much actual damping - the results of this could be dodgy.

Side-**effects**

Camber angle and tracking

With any lowering, it's likely that your suspension and steering geometry will be affected - this will be more of a problem the lower you go. This will manifest itself in steering which either becomes lighter or (more usually) heavier, and in tyres which scrub out their inner or outer edges in very short order. Sometimes, even the rear tyres can be affected in this way, but that's usually only after some serious lowering. Whenever you've fitted a set of springs (and this applies to all types), have the geometry checked ASAP afterwards.

If you've dropped the car by 60 mm or more, chances are your camber angle will need adjusting. There's not usually much scope for camber adjustment on standard suspension, which is why (for some cars) you can buy camber-adjustable top plates which fit to the strut tops. Setting the camber accurately is a job for a garage with experience of modified cars.

Rear brake pressure regulator

Some cars have a rear brake pressure limiting valve fitted, which is linked to the rear suspension. The idea is that, when the car's lightly loaded over the rear wheels, the braking effort to the rear is limited, to prevent the wheels locking up. With the boot full of luggage, the back end sinks down, and the valve lets full braking pressure through to the rear. When you slam the suspension, the valve is fooled into thinking the car's loaded up, and you might find the rear brakes locking up unexpectedly - could be a nasty surprise on a wet roundabout! The valves are quite simple devices - the best idea would be to get underneath and see how it looks when unloaded (on standard suspension), and try to re-create the same condition once the car's been dropped.

On the Golf, the brake pressure regulator is under the car, in front of the left-hand rear wheel. The upper part of the regulator linkage can be re-positioned on its mounting bracket.

The first thing to do is put the brace in its place. Lay it onto the strut tops, and see how much other stuff it interferes with. Almost certainly, you'll have to unbolt the coolant expansion tank - if so, don't disconnect any hoses. Adjust the length of the brace using the centre "screw" until it sits nicely over both struts, then mark the position of the bolt holes. Try and avoid the spot welds if you can.

01

fit a strut brace

The strut brace (in theory) does exactly what it says on the tin, by providing support between the strut tops, taking the load off the bodyshell. In truth the strut brace has a marginal effect, so one of the reasons to fit one is for show - and why not? Strut braces can be chromed, painted or anodised, and can be fitted with matching chromed/coloured strut top plates - a very tasty way to complement a detailed engine bay. People also fit strut braces to the rear suspension mounts, usually on cars where the rear seats have been junked.

tricks 'n' tips

If you're one of those really organised types, the best time to fit a strut brace is during fitting your new front struts. It's much easier bolting in a strut brace if the struts aren't stuck under their towers. Just make sure the front end's well supported.

05

Seriously tighten the four nuts and bolts on each strut top plate.

Now you've got to drill four dirty great holes in the top of the strut towers. As you've probably guessed, the strut towers ain't exactly the flimsiest metal parts to go attacking with your drill, and it's 8 mm holes you'll be drilling. Patience and some decent drill bits are a must. You may find that the drill wants to wander away from your chosen hole location - this is one time above all when you must fit the bolts (at least loose) in each hole as you go! You might need a decent round

02 file to adjust your holes slightly, to get them to line up.

03 When all the holes have been drilled on one side take off the brace, and slap some rust-proofing stuff (like Waxoyl) on your new holes. If you've got no rust-proofer, paint will do.

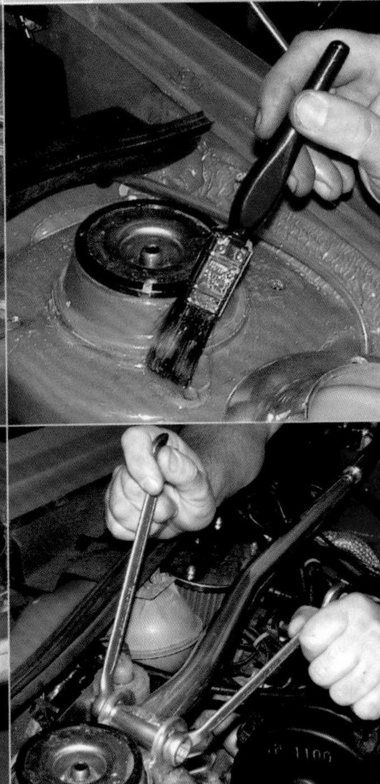

04 Refit the brace and drill through the other strut top, then you're ready for the final fitting. Bolt the brace to the strut top.

a Bolts in from below - fairly easy to fit the bolts, dead easy to screw on the nuts from above. But - to make it look neat under the bonnet you'll have to chop off the excess bolt thread, which, on four 8 mm bolts per side, isn't too funny.

b Bolts in from above - dead easy to fit the bolts, but fiddly to work the nuts on from below (not much room between the strut and the strut tower). No need to chop off the excess bolt thread.

06 If you fit an adjustable brace like this one, turn the "screw" adjuster using a stout screwdriver in the hole provided, so that the brace forces outwards. Don't go too mad (the brace is only made of ally). When you're happy, hold the adjuster and tighten the large nuts either side of it.

07 Before you tighten up the bolts at either end of the brace, where it mounts onto the strut plates, check whether you can shut the bonnet without it touching. Ours had to be mounted almost at the bottom of the slot each side.

08 We made up our own little extension piece to the standard mounting bracket for the expansion tank which could be bolted in the same place as before . . .

09 . . . but let the tank sit slightly lower, to clear the brace. Don't set it too low, or it won't do its job properly, and you'll have various cooling system problems.

Lower front **strut brace**

On a Golf, the one strut brace which will produce a noticeable benefit is the lower strut brace, fitted to the front subframe, in front of the lower wishbones.

Achtung!

Jack up the whole front end of the car, as high and as securely as you can - you'll be undoing (and doing up) two very tight bolts while the car's over your head! Have a look in "Wheels & tyres" for more info on jacking and supporting. Don't try this if all you've got is the standard jack! A trolley jack and at least one axle stand are essential for safety.

01 Those bolts you're undoing are the wishbone-to-subframe pivot bolts, and they're done up to 130 Nm. Which is tight. And which also means these bolts are seriously safety-related. You really ought to get hold of a torque wrench, to do these back up, but you don't need one to undo them.

02 The suspension could possibly move apart when the pivot bolt is pulled out, with the wheels hanging loose, so be careful. You might need to wiggle the wheels slightly, to get the bolts out.

03 When you've remove the pivot bolt either side, offer the strut brace into position, and adjust its length until the big holes line up.

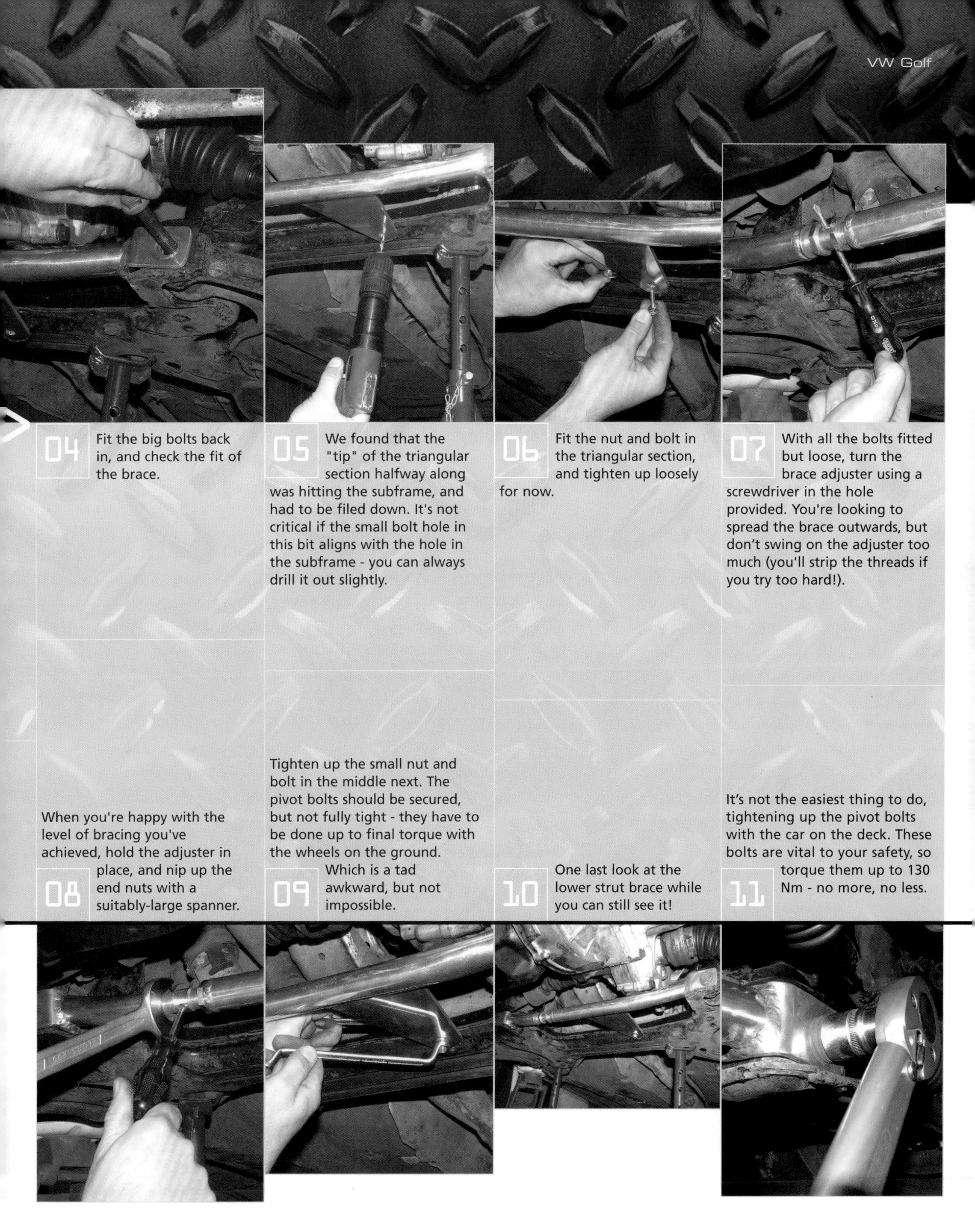

04 Fit the big bolts back in, and check the fit of the brace.

05 We found that the "tip" of the triangular section halfway along was hitting the subframe, and had to be filed down. It's not critical if the small bolt hole in this bit aligns with the hole in the subframe - you can always drill it out slightly.

06 Fit the nut and bolt in the triangular section, and tighten up loosely for now.

07 With all the bolts fitted but loose, turn the brace adjuster using a screwdriver in the hole provided. You're looking to spread the brace outwards, but don't swing on the adjuster too much (you'll strip the threads if you try too hard!).

08 When you're happy with the level of bracing you've achieved, hold the adjuster in place, and nip up the end nuts with a suitably-large spanner.

09 Tighten up the small nut and bolt in the middle next. The pivot bolts should be secured, but not fully tight - they have to be done up to final torque with the wheels on the ground. Which is a tad awkward, but not impossible.

10 One last look at the lower strut brace while you can still see it!

11 It's not the easiest thing to do, tightening up the pivot bolts with the car on the deck. These bolts are vital to your safety, so torque them up to 130 Nm - no more, no less.

The middle pedal

The original Mk 1 Golf won friends for its many talents, but good braking wasn't one of them. This was, of course, largely remedied on the Mk 2, but those of you without the all-disc GTI setup might still yearn for beefier brakes.

Uprating the brakes is actually a very easy bolt-on upgrade, but it'll be a complete waste of time if you're a cheapskate on tyres. Cheap, no-name tyres or remoulds won't be able to translate extra braking power into actual vehicle-stopping power - they'll give up their grip on the Tarmac and skid everywhere.

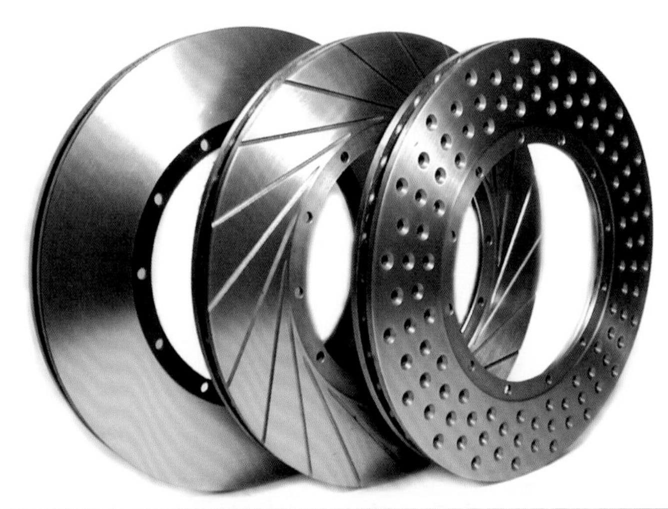

Grooved or drilled?

Besides the various brands of performance brake pads that go with them, the main brake upgrade is to fit performance front discs. Discs are available in three main types – grooved, cross-drilled and combinations of both.

Grooved discs (which can be had with varying numbers of grooves) serve a dual purpose - the grooves provide a "channel" to help the heat escape, and they also help to de-glaze the pad surface, cleaning up the pads every time they're used. Some of the discs are made from higher-friction metal than normal discs, too, and a good set can greatly improve braking performance.

Cross-drilled discs offer another route to heat dissipation, but one which can present some problems. In extreme cases cross-drilled discs can crack around the drilled holes, after serious use. The trouble is that the heat "migrates" to the drilled holes (as was intended), but the heat build-up can be extreme, and the constant heating/cooling cycle can stress the metal to the point where it will crack. Discs which have been damaged in this way are extremely dangerous. Only fit discs of this type from established manufacturers and check them regularly.

Performance discs also have a reputation for warping (nasty vibrations felt through the pedal). Now this may be so, but of course, the harder you use your brakes, the greater the heat you'll generate. Cheap discs, or ones which have had a hard time over umpteen thousands of miles, probably will warp. So buy quality, and don't get too heroic on the brakes for too long a period of time.

Performance pads can be fitted to any brake discs, including the standard ones, but are designed to work best with heat-dissipating discs. Don't be tempted to go much further than "fast road" pads - anything more competition-orientated may take too long to come up to temperature on the road, and might leave you with less braking than before!

Lastly, fitting all the performance brake bits in the world is no use if your calipers have seized up. If, when you strip out your old pads, you find that one pad's worn more than the other, or that both pads have worn more on the left wheel than the right, your caliper pistons are sticking. Sometimes you can free them off by pushing them back into the caliper, but this could be a garage job to fix. If you drive around with sticking calipers, you'll eat pads and discs. Your choice.

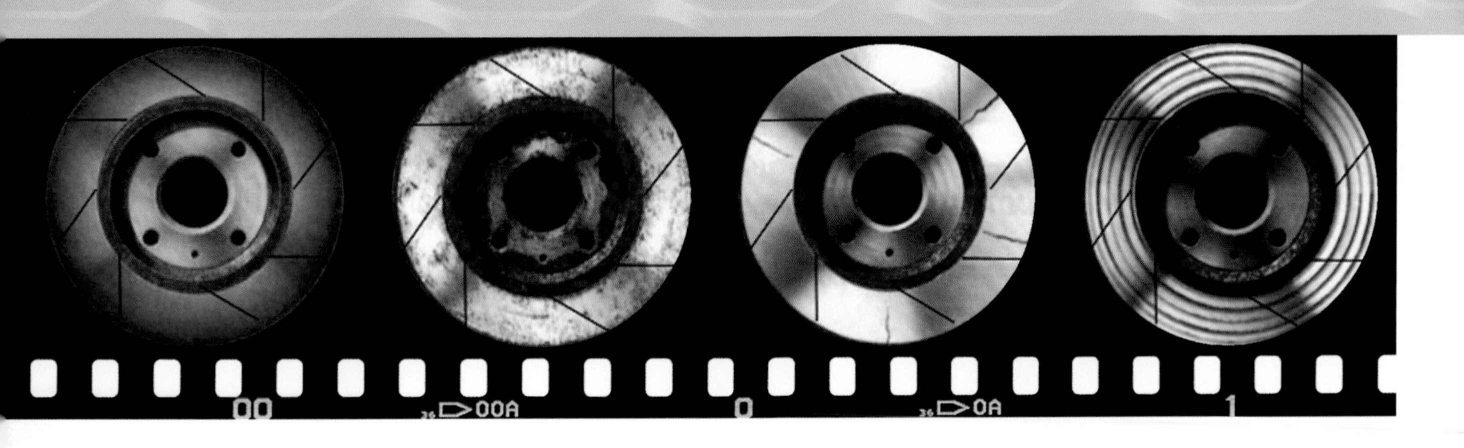

Brake discs
& pads

01 Loosen the wheel bolts, jack up the corner of the car you're working on, and take off the wheel. Make sure you've got an axle stand under a solid part of the car (like the front subframe) in case the jack gives out. Have a look in "Wheels & tyres" for more info on jacking up. You now need a 6 mm Allen key, to undo the two caliper mounting bolts. They're two different lengths, so watch which goes where.

06 Tighten the disc retaining screw as tight as poss (do get a new screw, if yours had to be drilled).

07 And here are our new pads. The smaller one fits to the inside of the disc.

08 So - fit the inner pad, together with the anti-rattle springs. These springs are fitted so their tabs face each other, and are roughly in line with the edge of the disc.

02 Lift away the caliper, and now you can see the pads. Don't leave the caliper swinging by its hose - that's a good way to end up needing a new hose. Tuck it away on the wishbone, or stick it on a spare axle stand.

03 Now you can take out the pads. Take note of how the pad anti-rattle springs fit, top and bottom, and that the inner pad is smaller (in surface area) than the outer one - all this info will come in handy later. You can buy brake pad spring sets off the shelf, if yours have disintegrated.

04 Taking off the disc itself should now be a easy - it's only held on by one screw. A good clout with a hammer (and a soak with WD-40) might free off a rusted-in screw, but an impact driver or even a drill may be needed. Lift off the old disc.

05 When you first take out your two new discs, you might think they're identical. Chances are, they're not, and each should only be fitted to one side of the car. Check your paperwork - these discs must be fitted as shown - this is the left front.

Achtung!

Brake dust from old pads may contain asbestos. Wear a mask to avoid inhaling it. Dispose of old braking system components safely at your local waste recycling centre - don't just put them in the bin.

09 On with the outer pad . . .

10 . . . and fit the caliper back over the lot. You'll probably have to push the caliper pistons back into their bores to make room for new pads. A pair of "water pump" (sliding jaw) pliers helps here - if you're stuck, sometimes a long spanner placed across the face of the piston can be used to press the piston in.

11 The long caliper bolt goes at the top. Do these bolts up good and tight (25 Nm, if you're torque-wrench-equipped). Job done! But those calipers look sad, against the posh brakes. How about a lick of paint, then?

Tricks 'n' tips

New discs or pads of any sort need careful bedding-in (over 100 miles of normal use) before they'll work properly - when first fitted, the pad surface won't have worn exactly to the contours of the disc, so it won't be touching it over its full area. Always follow the manufacturer's bedding-in guidelines, othewise your brakes will be nowhere near as effective as they should be.

Painting calipers

Painting the calipers requires that they are clean - really clean. Accessory stores sell aerosol brake cleaner although some caliper painting kits come complete with cleaner spray. Many of the kits advertise themselves on the strength of no dismantling being required, but for the best results it's wise to dismantle.

01 We removed the caliper and pads, then took off the disc, and re-mounted the caliper on its own. Doing it this way means no risk of paint going on the pads or disc.

02 Get the wire brush out, and attack the rust on the caliper. Watch you don't accidentally attack any rubber bits around the caliper. Remember - you won't get it looking shiny this way - just get rid of all the loose muck. While you're at it, try attacking the lumps and bumps with rough sandpaper - a smooth surface will look much better when painted.

03 Squirt on your brake cleaner (our kit came with its own can), giving the caliper a good dose - being high-octane stuff, it evaporates quickly, so get wiping as soon as possible. This is really vital to getting a clean surface - spraying alone will only loosen the muck.

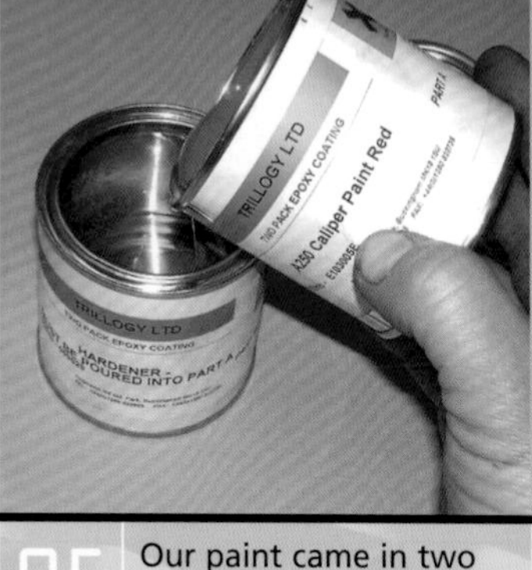

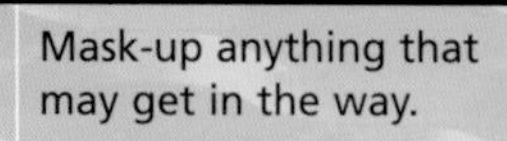

04 Mask-up anything that may get in the way.

05 Our paint came in two tins - one paint, one hardener. Pour one into the other, stir, and you then have about four hours max before the paint sets hard in the tin. If you're painting calipers and drums, make sure you do all the prep work, and are totally ready to start painting at all four corners of the car, before you mix the paint.

06 Stick some card or paper under where you're working, and get painting! Remember that you only have to paint the bits you'll see when the wheels are on (the disc will cover quite a lot too).

07 It's best to do more than one coat. Follow the instructions with your kit on how long to leave between coats, but remember the time limit before the paint in the tin's useless. Wait until the paint's totally dry (like overnight, or longer) before reassembling.

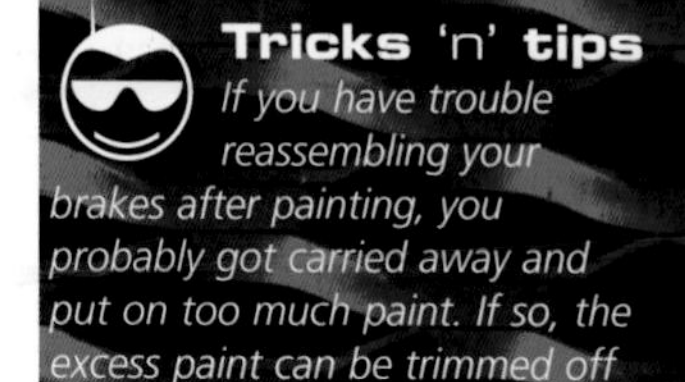

Tricks 'n' tips

If you have trouble reassembling your brakes after painting, you probably got carried away and put on too much paint. If so, the excess paint can be trimmed off with a knife.

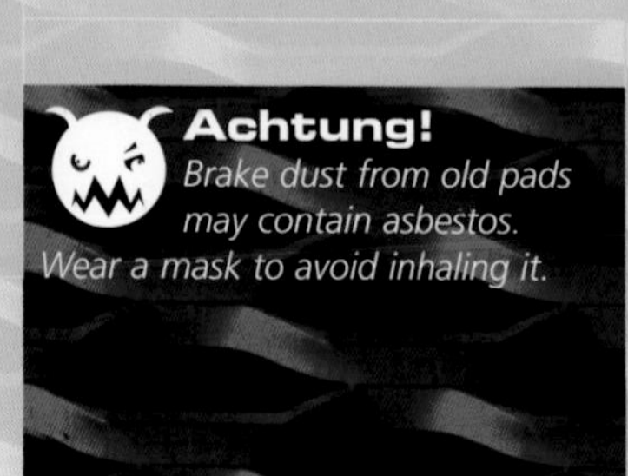

Achtung!

Brake dust from old pads may contain asbestos. Wear a mask to avoid inhaling it.

Painting **drums**

At least there's no dismantling with drums - get the rear end jacked up, wheels off (see "Wheels & tyres" if you need jacking info) and just

01 get stuck in with the wire brush . . .

02 . . . and with the sandpaper, if it's looking rough.

03 Then it's spray on the brake cleaner . . .

04 . . . and wipe thoroughly.

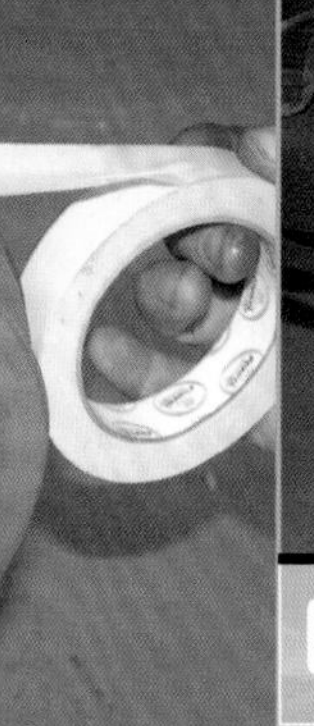

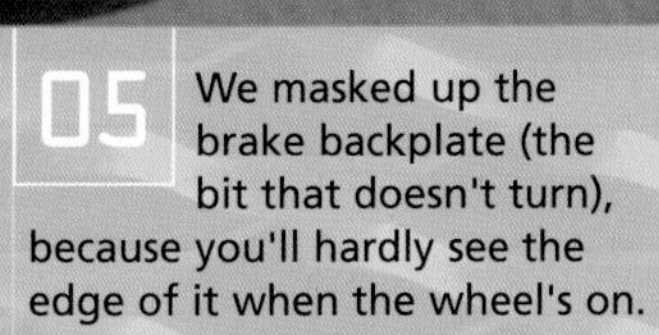

05 We masked up the brake backplate (the bit that doesn't turn), because you'll hardly see the edge of it when the wheel's on.

06 To keep the paint from getting into the wheel bolt threads, we made up this circle of cardboard to slip over the drum. Once the wheel's on, the centre part of the brake drum can't be seen - if you need to, hold the wheel up in place to check the size of card circle you'll need, but you can probably see from the drum itself where the wheel sits.

07 And on with the paint - again, two coats is a good idea. Another good idea is to let off the handbrake and turn the drum half a turn every so often until the paint's dry, to prevent runs.

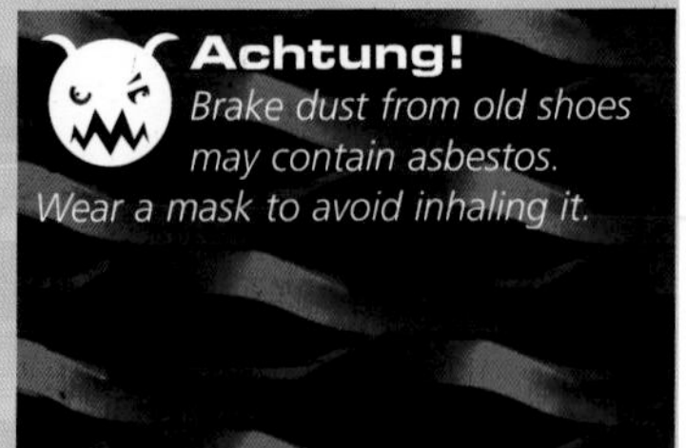

Achtung!
Brake dust from old shoes may contain asbestos. Wear a mask to avoid inhaling it.

10 Interiors

The standard Mk 2 interior may not be the most exciting dashboard to look at but you need suffer no longer, because the interior really is one area where most of the goodies are pretty easy to fit.

As with the exterior styling, though, remember that fashions can change very quickly - so don't be afraid to experiment with a look that you really like, because chances are, it'll be the next big thing anyway.

Removing stuff

Many of the procedures we're going to show involve removing interior trim panels (either for colouring or to fit other stuff), and this can be tricky. It's far too easy to break plastic trim, especially once it's had a chance to go a bit brittle with age. Another "problem" with the Golf is that the interior trim is especially well-attached, meaning that it can be a pig to get off, with more "hidden" screws, clips and fasteners (to stop it rattling) than you'd imagine. We'll try and avoid the immortal words "simply unclip the panel", and instead show you how properly, but inevitably at some stage, a piece of trim won't "simply" anything. So - take it steady, prise carefully, and think logically about how and where a plastic panel would have to be attached. You'll encounter all sorts of trim clips (some more fragile than others) in your travels - when these break, as they usually do, know that many of them can be bought in ready packs from accessory shops, and that the rarer ones will be available from a VW dealer.

Door trim panels

You'll find plenty of excuses for removing your door trim panels - fitting speakers, re-trimming, even window tinting...

01 Wind down the window, then if you've got wind-up windows:

02 Prise off the trim from the winder handle, remove the screw behind. Pull the handle from the splines (note roughly what angle the handle sits at, so you can fit it back in the same position).

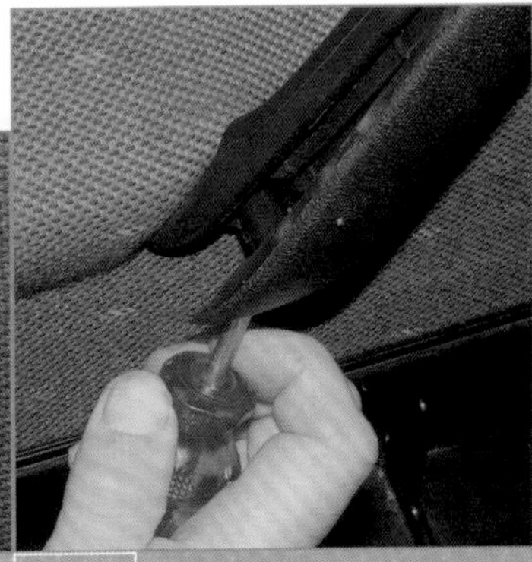

03 Prise off the centre trim from the door pull handle.

04 Remove the two screws – one above, one below – and take off the door pull handle.

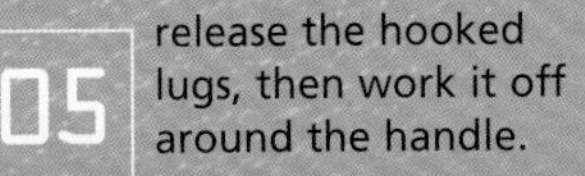

05 Prise the trim panel around the lock handle backwards, to release the hooked lugs, then work it off around the handle.

06 There are four screws around the edges of the door panel - two in front, two behind - take them out. Carefully pull out the base of the trim panel, to release the clips. Once the base of the panel's free, you can reach in behind and disconnect the speaker wiring.

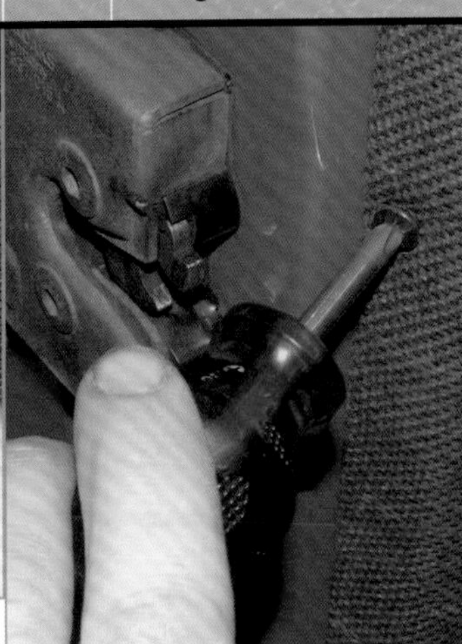

07 Using a screwdriver, prise up the top edge of the trim panel, to release it.

08 Unscrew the door lock button and remove it. Lift the trim panel upwards to clear the lock button's threaded rod, and remove it completely.

Instrument panel

Interiors

This describes how to strip the dash down as far as getting the clocks out, to fit the coloured-dial kit of your choice. This process includes removing the steering wheel and the switch panels, so use it for as much or as little as you want to do. If you've just bought a new wheel, but are going to fit new dials later, it would make more sense to fit the two things together, or you'll be taking a steering wheel off twice - up to you.

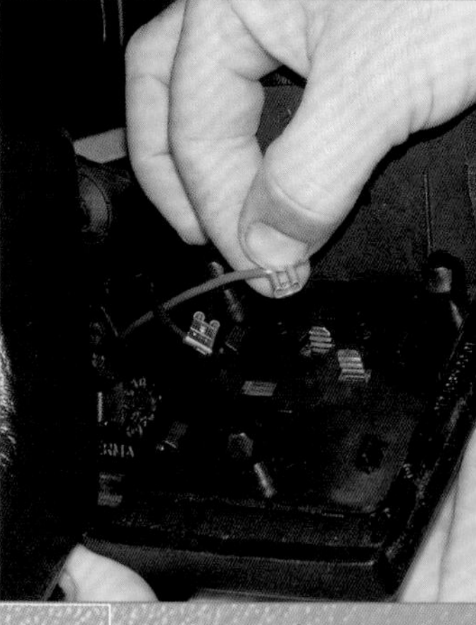

01 Disconnect the battery. Prise and pull off the horn push from the centre of the steering wheel, then disconnect the horn wiring behind.

02 Make sure the front wheels are pointing exactly straight-ahead (this makes it easier to refit the wheel straight). Take out the ignition key, and use the steering lock to hold the wheel while you unscrew the nut, then take off the nut, and the washer behind it . . .

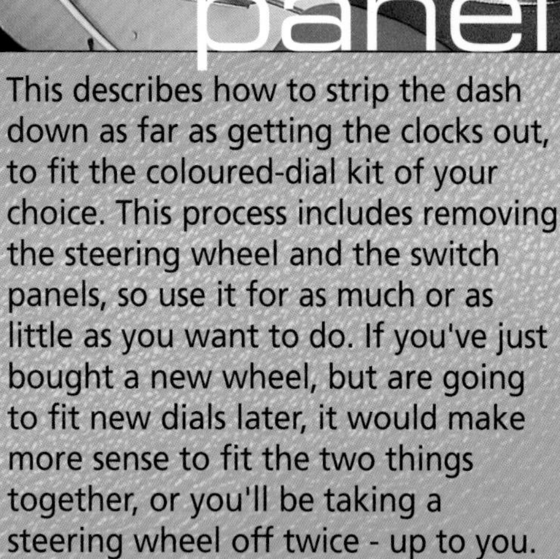

07 Now the instrument panel surround/switch panel can come out - this is secured by a total of eight small cross-head screws. Two screws above the instruments...

08 ...one below the light switch...

09 ...three below the heater control panel...

10 ...one behind the lower switch nearest the steering wheel...

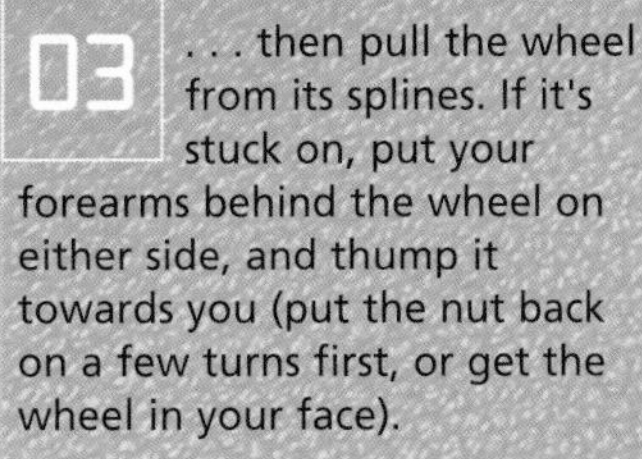

03 . . . then pull the wheel from its splines. If it's stuck on, put your forearms behind the wheel on either side, and thump it towards you (put the nut back on a few turns first, or get the wheel in your face).

04 Make a note of which switch fits where, before you start pulling them out. Prise out the switches in turn, and disconnect the wiring plugs behind them.

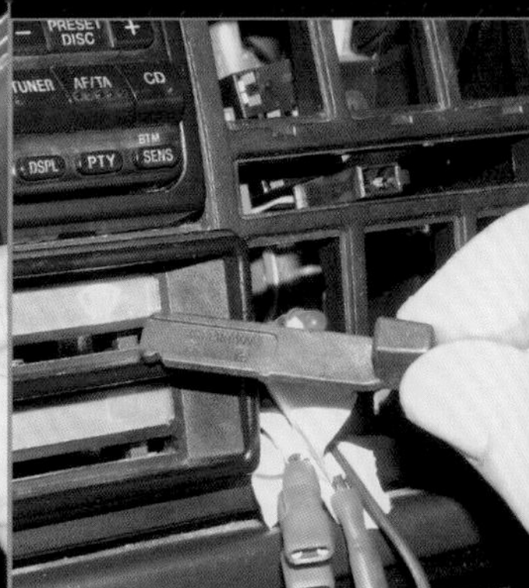

05 The heater control knobs/levers all pull off, but you might need to persuade the slide levers with a small screwdriver.

06 Prise out the heater control panel, then disconnect the fan switch wiring plug.

11 ...and one above the radio cage (bend up the tabs and slide out the cage for access).

12 Lift away the surround, feeding the wiring through as you pull it back.

13 The instrument cluster is held in by two screws - one each side at the top. Remove the screws, and tilt the panel towards you at the top.

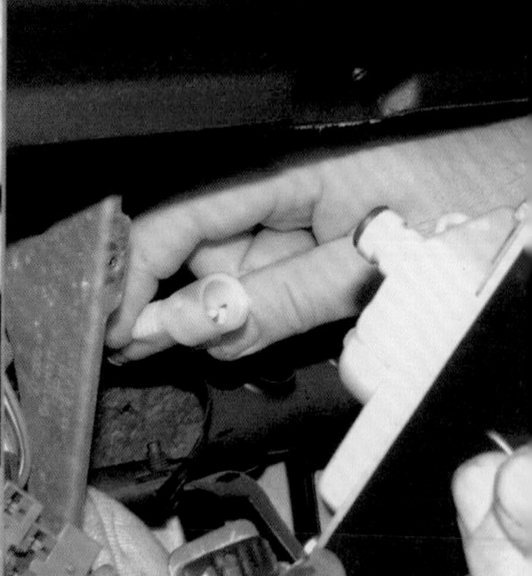

14 Disconnect the speedo cable by squeezing the plastic collar and pulling the cable backwards out of the panel. Disconnect the wiring plugs (and if fitted, the vacuum hose from the gearchange indicator) from the base of the panel, then remove it.

Glovebox lid

01 Open the glovebox. Using a very small precision-type screwdriver, prise the hinge pins from the two lid hinges sideways. This is a bit fiddly, but there is a flattened (outer) end to prise behind - watch the pins don't fly out and get lost!

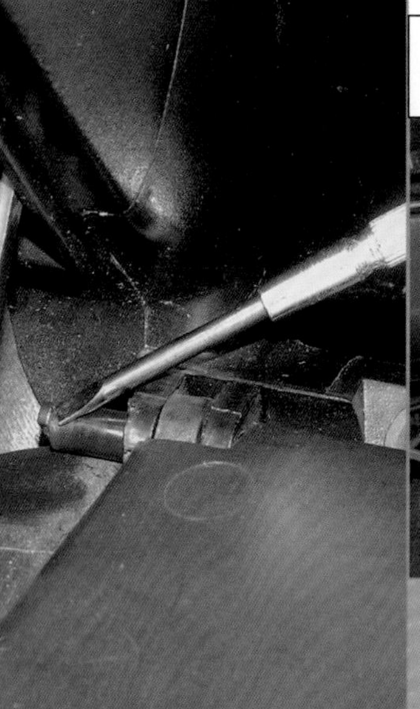

02 Release the two "stays" either side by pressing the centre sections of the stays towards each other - this will let the lid drop down so it can be removed.

03 If you want, you can remove the glovebox lock from the lid. Prise up the horseshoe-type lock retaining clip with the precision screwdriver and the lock falls out.

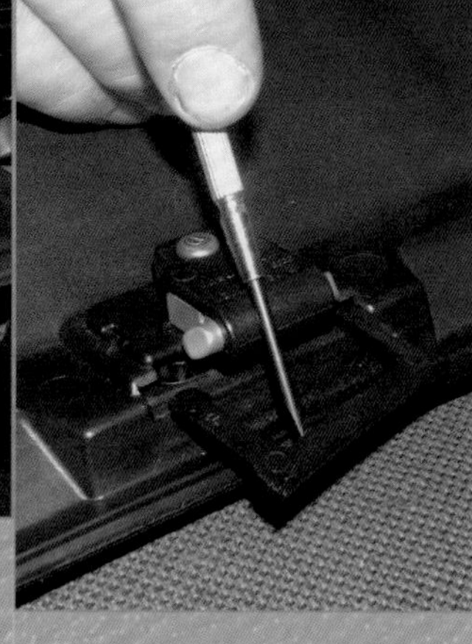

Interiors

Dash vents

01 Carefully prise out the vent grille from the side, using a small screwdriver.

02 Remove the screw at the top, inside (two screws, on the central twin vent).

03 Prise up the two tabs at the base of the vent hole with a small screwdriver . . .

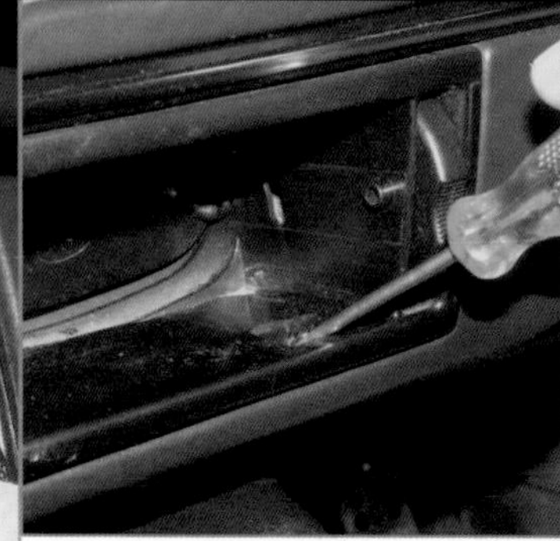

04 . . . and slide the vents out. This might take a bit of brute force, because you're actually separating the front part of the vent from the plastic nozzles which feed up under the dash (the centre twin vent's a real pig to move).

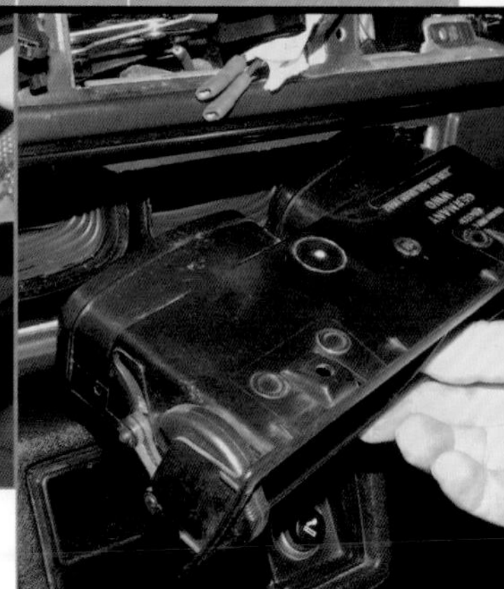

Centre console

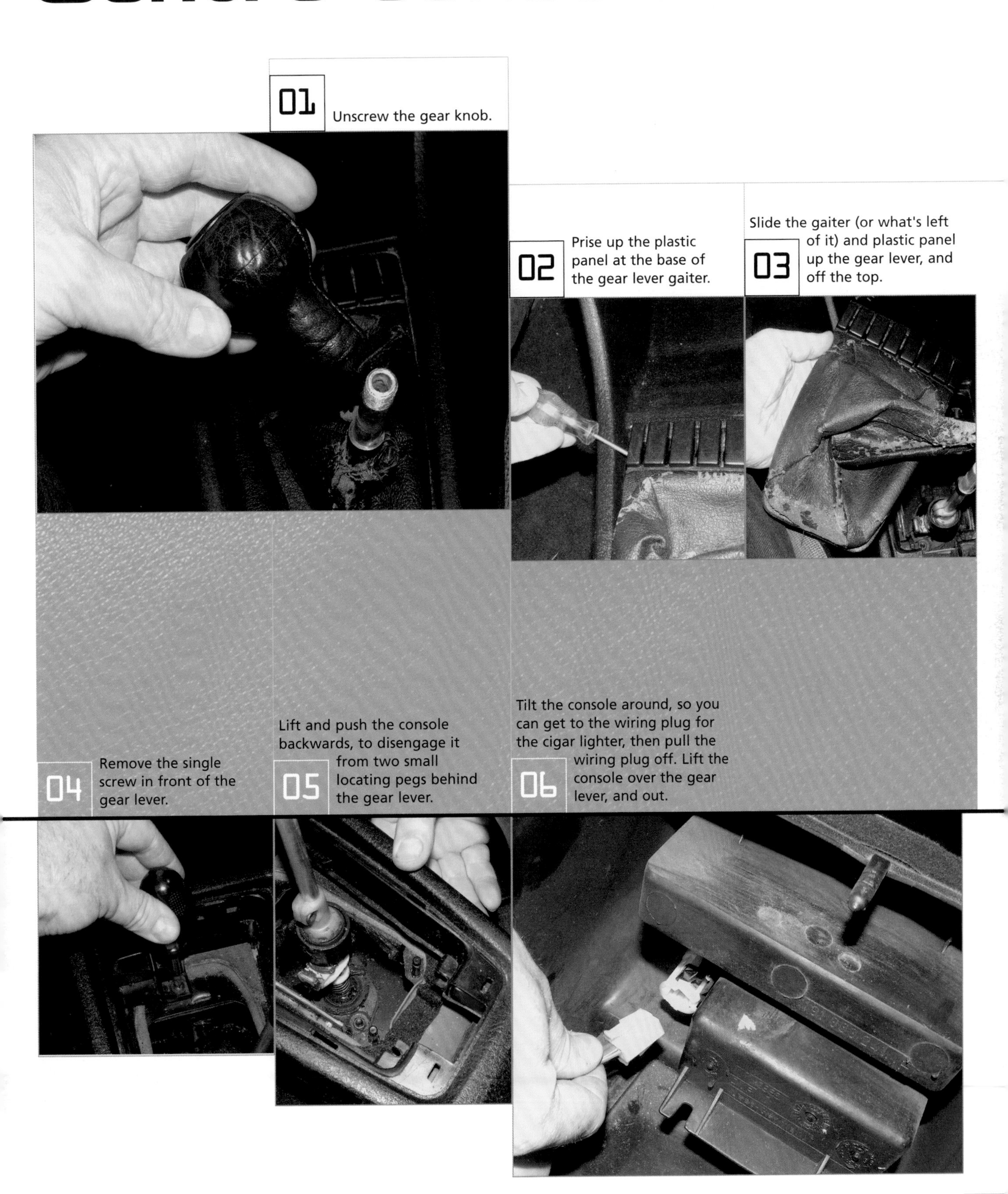

01 Unscrew the gear knob.

02 Prise up the plastic panel at the base of the gear lever gaiter.

03 Slide the gaiter (or what's left of it) and plastic panel up the gear lever, and off the top.

04 Remove the single screw in front of the gear lever.

05 Lift and push the console backwards, to disengage it from two small locating pegs behind the gear lever.

06 Tilt the console around, so you can get to the wiring plug for the cigar lighter, then pull the wiring plug off. Lift the console over the gear lever, and out.

Door dress-up

Okay, so you're definitely not happy with how the inside of your Golf looks, but you're not sold on any of the off-the-shelf options for modifying it, either. You know how you want it to look, though, so get creative!

There are any number of upholstery companies in Yellow Pages, who will be able to create any look you want. If your idea of Golf heaven is an interior swathed in black and purple leather, these guys can help. If you're even slightly handy with things like glue and scissors, you might be able to use this one example we've got here as inspiration to get brave and DIY. Any upholsterers will still be a useful source for your materials.

Very, very saucy - blue alcantara and leather. Mmm. Don't forget the rear side trim panels when creating your dream interior.

Other **options**

01 Instead of fitting ally parts we decided to remove a selection of bits from the door trim panel, and paint them. For more details on how to do this, see "Anything but black" later on. Here's the masked-up bits getting the spray treatment . . .

02 . . . and here's what the final fitted result looked like - discreet but tasty! Of course, there are other colours you could try...

Door lock **buttons**

One of the easiest bits to fit .

01 The first bit is easy - unscrew the old buttons.

Most kits simply screw on, but

02 others may not be an exact fit, and could require glueing.

If youy've chosen a chunky button it might not fit down the plastic collar, so prise out

03 the collar from the door trim with a small screwdriver . . .

04 . . . then you can screw the pins on.

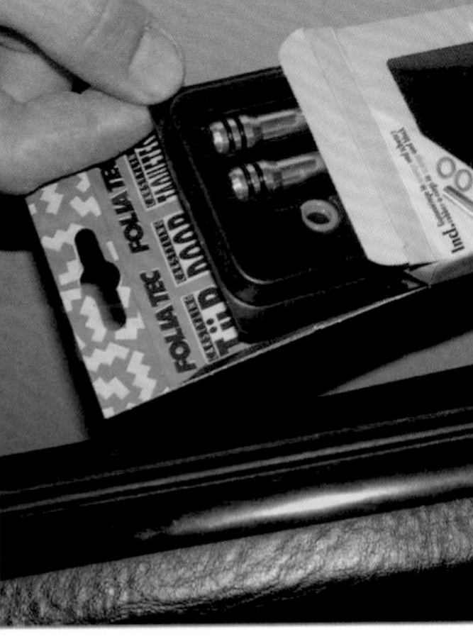

Mirror control knob

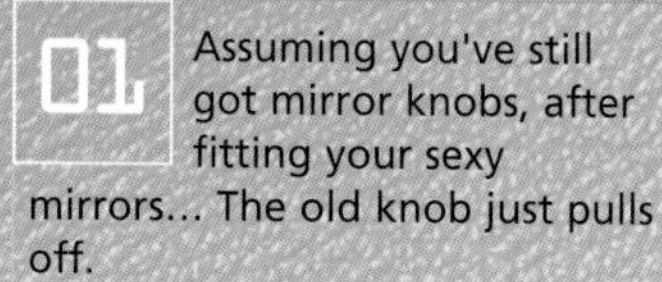

01 Assuming you've still got mirror knobs, after fitting your sexy mirrors... The old knob just pulls off.

02 Slip the new knob in place . . .

03 . . . and tighten the grub screw. Easy.

Window winder

01 If you've not got the luxury of electric windows and you want to sort your winder, removal's easy - prise off the cover . . .

02 . . . remove the cross-head screw underneath and slip it off the splines.

03 Fitting an ally replacement is also a doddle - slip the new winder over the splines, setting it in the desired position . . .

04 . . . and tighten the screw.

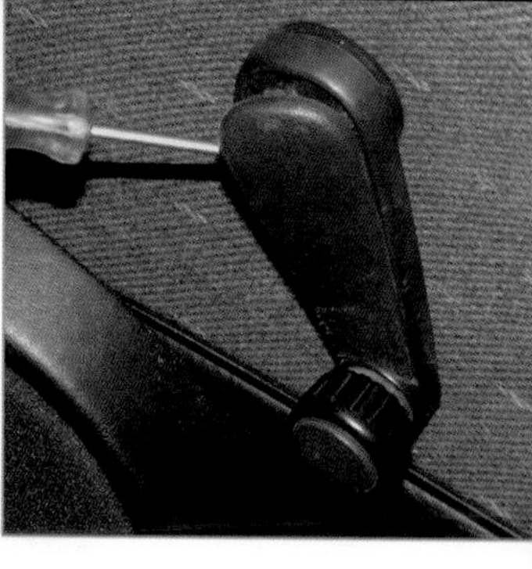

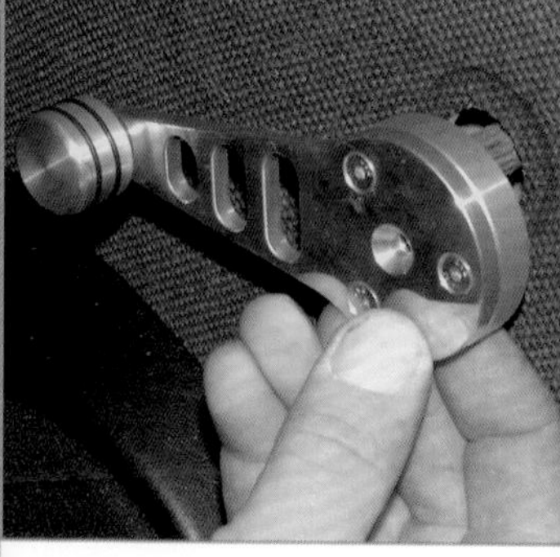

Door sill trims

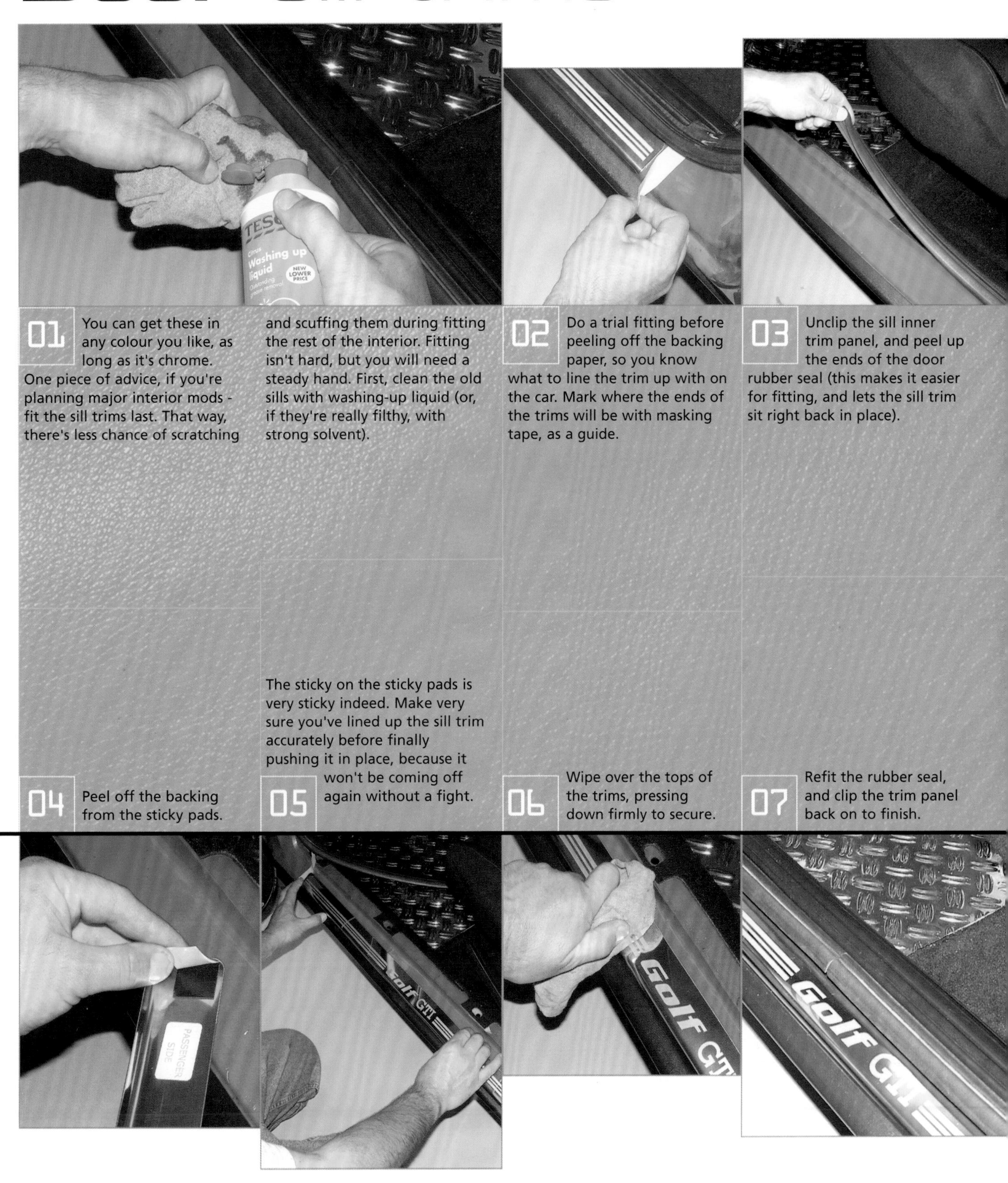

01 You can get these in any colour you like, as long as it's chrome. One piece of advice, if you're planning major interior mods - fit the sill trims last. That way, there's less chance of scratching and scuffing them during fitting the rest of the interior. Fitting isn't hard, but you will need a steady hand. First, clean the old sills with washing-up liquid (or, if they're really filthy, with strong solvent).

02 Do a trial fitting before peeling off the backing paper, so you know what to line the trim up with on the car. Mark where the ends of the trims will be with masking tape, as a guide.

03 Unclip the sill inner trim panel, and peel up the ends of the door rubber seal (this makes it easier for fitting, and lets the sill trim sit right back in place).

04 Peel off the backing from the sticky pads.

05 The sticky on the sticky pads is very sticky indeed. Make very sure you've lined up the sill trim accurately before finally pushing it in place, because it won't be coming off again without a fight.

06 Wipe over the tops of the trims, pressing down firmly to secure.

07 Refit the rubber seal, and clip the trim panel back on to finish.

Anything but black

The interior trim on the Golf is solid, and doesn't rattle much. But it is dull – fortunately, there's plenty you can do to personalise it, and there are three main routes to take:

Painting trim

For the Mk 2 Golf interior, we found that the interior spray approach was the most successful. We tried film for some things, and weren't as happy with the results as after painting.

One thing to realise with the painting process is that it's a multi-stage application. Just buying the top coat looks like a cheap option compared to film. But even the proper interior spray top coat won't stay on for long without the matching primer, and the finish won't be wear-resistant without the finishing sealer spray. So - buy the complete system! There's also a foaming cleaner you can buy, but you could use a degreaser, such as meths. Watch for the cloth turning too black when you're using your chosen solvent - if it does, you're damaging the finish.

Providing you're a dab hand with the masking tape, paint gives you the flexibility to be more creative. With our interior, we chose silver as our main theme, and as well as the obvious things like the instrument surround and glovebox lid, we wanted to "highlight" a few other items, like the vent and dash speaker surrounds, and the front lip of the centre console.

1 Spray paint available in any colour you like. Certain stuff actually dyes softer plastics and leather, and comes in a multi-stage treatment, to suit all plastic types. Remember that ordinary spray paint for bodywork won't "stick" too well to plastics. Make sure you also buy LOTS of masking tape.

2 Adhesive or shrink-fit film available in various colours, carbon, and, er... walnut (don't!). Probably best used on flatter surfaces, or at least those without complex curves, or you'll have to cut and join - spray is arguably better here.

3 Replacement panels are the easiest option, as the panels are supplied pre-cut, ready to fit. Of course, you're limited then to styling just the panels supplied.

If you fancy something unique, consider Alcantara or leather, although it won't be cheap.

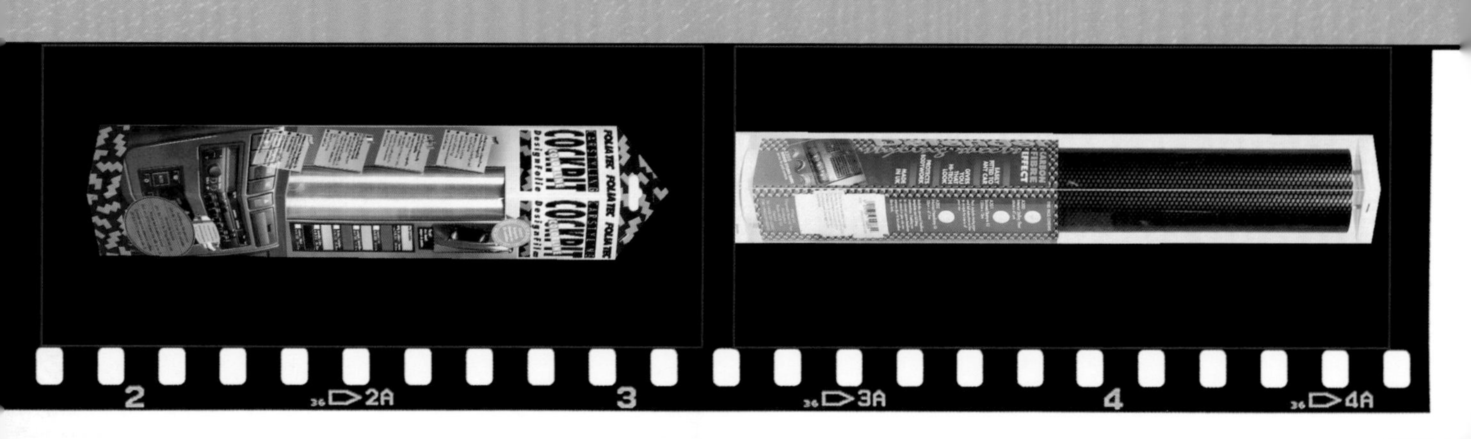

Get the **cans out**

01 Clean up the surface to be sprayed, using a suitable degreaser. You must use something fairly strong, to get off any silicone-based products you or the previous owner may have used, as these are death to paint adhesion.

02 Mask up the bits you don't want sprayed. Make sure you protect all surfaces from overspray, as Foliatec recommend putting the topcoat on very "dusty", which results in a lot of spray in the air. You can never do too much masking. Time taken masking will be repaid in time not spent re-doing the job.

03 Apply a mist coat of primer - this is essential to help the paint "stick" to the plastic. Allow plenty of time for the primer to dry.

04 Now for the topcoat - this should be applied very "dusty", which means you spray from slightly further away than normal, and let the paint fall onto the job, rather than blast it on using the full force of the aerosol spray. We found the silver needed several coats before it looked right - allow time for each one to dry (a few minutes) before applying some more.

05 Once you're happy that there's even coverage, let the last top coat dry, then put on the sealer coat. This improves wear-resistance. You should only need a light coat of sealer to finish the job.

06 Let the paint go tacky (rather than fully dry) before peeling off the masking, and take care when you do - if the paint's too dry, you'll peel some of the paint off with the mask! If you're in any doubt, take your steadiest hand and a sharp knife to the edges of the masking tape before peeling.

Filming your Golf

If you fancy creating a look that's a bit more special than plain paint colours, film is the answer - but be warned - it's not the easiest stuff in the world to use, and so isn't everyone's favourite. If you must have the brushed-aluminium look, or fancy giving your Golf the carbon-fibre treatment, there really is no alternative (apart from new panels, of course).

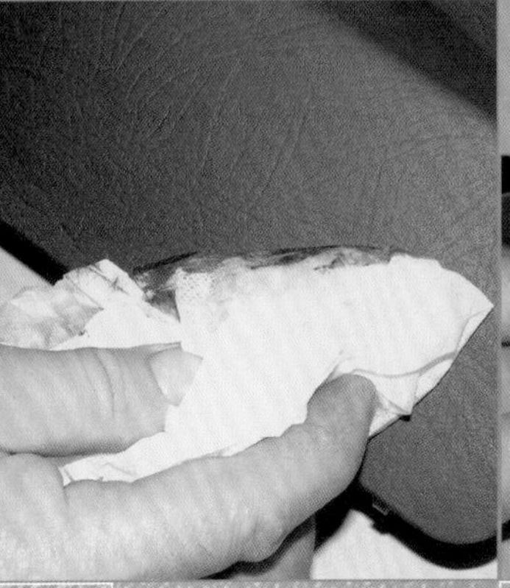

01 Step 1 is cleaning and degreasing - see the advice in Step 1 for painting. On a heavily-grained finish (such as the glovebox lid), remember that the grain will show through the film, and a deep grain means the film won't stick over all the surface. Not a good idea to rub stuff down with wet-and-dry, to get rid of the grain - you'll destroy the surface totally. Cut the film roughly to size, remembering to leave plenty of excess for trimming - it's also a good idea to have plenty to fold around the edges.

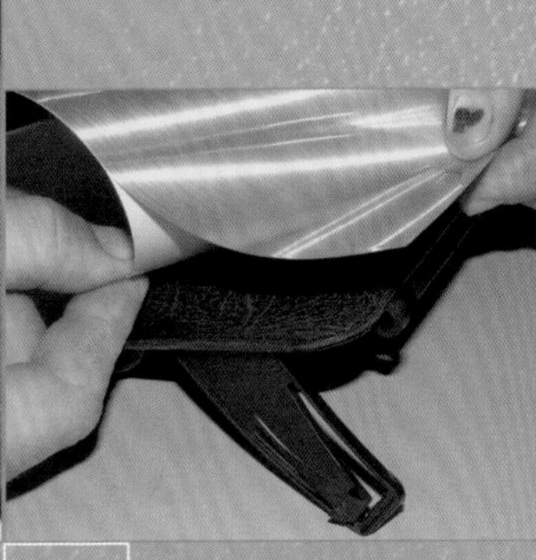

02 Peel off the backing, and stick the film on - start at one edge or corner, and work across, to keep the air bubbles and creases to a minimum. If you get a really bad crease, it's best to unpeel a bit and try again - the adhesive's very tacky, and won't slide.

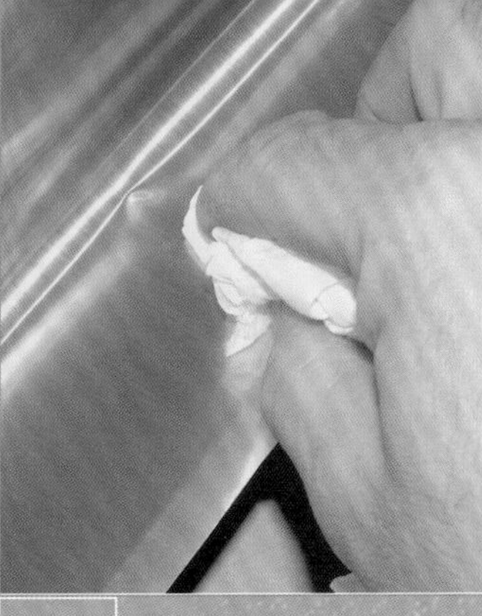

03 Work out the worst of the air bubbles with a soft cloth - get the stuff to stick as best you can before trimming, or it may go wrong.

04 Once the film's basically laid on, it's time for trimming - which is the tricky bit. It's much easier to trim up the tricky bits once the film had been warmed up using a hairdryer or heat gun, but don't overdo it - check first whether your film is shrink-fit, and don't warm it up unless you actually want it to shrink. Make sure you've also got a very sharp knife - a blunt one will ripple the film, and may tear it.

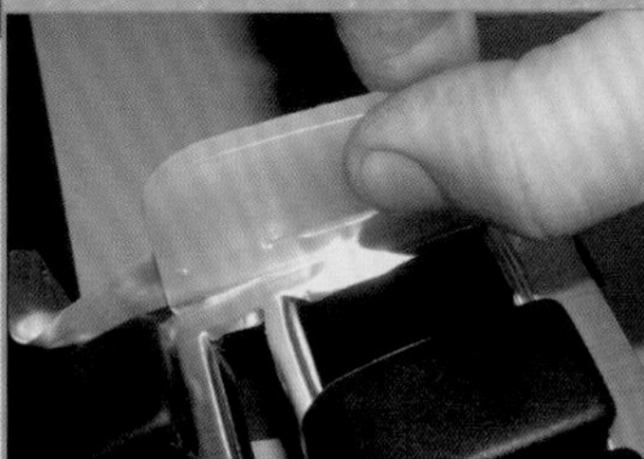

05 Use a flat spreader or card to press the film into the edges when cutting. If you're cutting out holes (as we did for the instrument panel surround) it's best to cut diagonally from corner to corner, then fold the film flaps into the hole. That way, you shouldn't get the ragged edges or the problem of the film peeling off - always have plenty to fold over any edge, or it will peel. It may even be worth applying a line of glue along any edge you're not sure of.

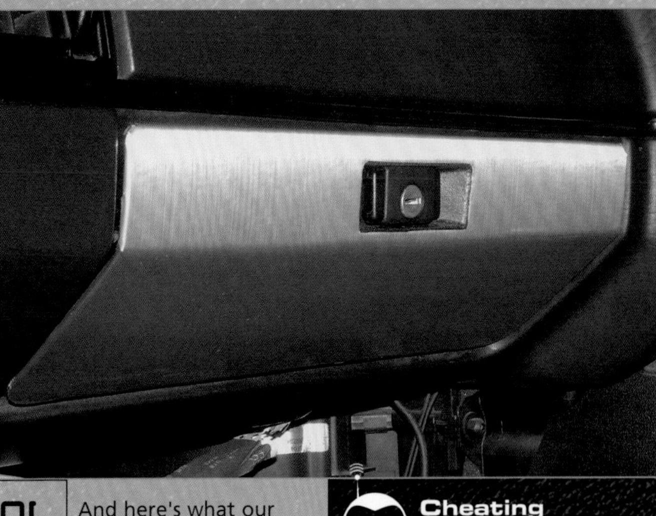

06 And here's what our glovebox lid came out like!

Cheating

A far easier route to the brushed-ally or carbon look is pre-finished panels which are available from various suppliers. Bit of a limited range from some places - you'll probably still have to do some work to achieve your idea of a full-on interior. Remember it's advisable not to mix styles.

Gear knobs & gaiters

There's a huge choice of gear knobs and gaiters - you can spend almost as much or as little as you want. Whatever you choose, start by unscrewing the old knob.

01 Check the centre console removal details and remove the gear lever, then take off your old gaiter and bin it. The new gaiter stretches over the lip provided on the base panel (if your gaiter has "laces" at the top, these should face forward so you don't see them when it's fitted).

02 If you're gonna fit a surround over your gaiter (like ours), slip it down over the gaiter and bottom lip . . .

03 . . . and use a screwdriver to tuck in any excess leather.

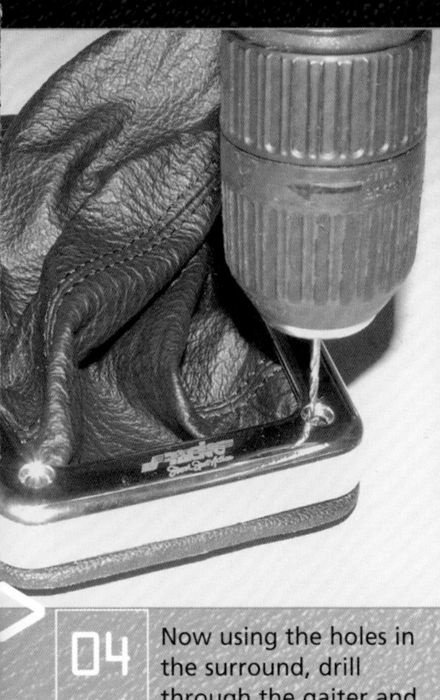

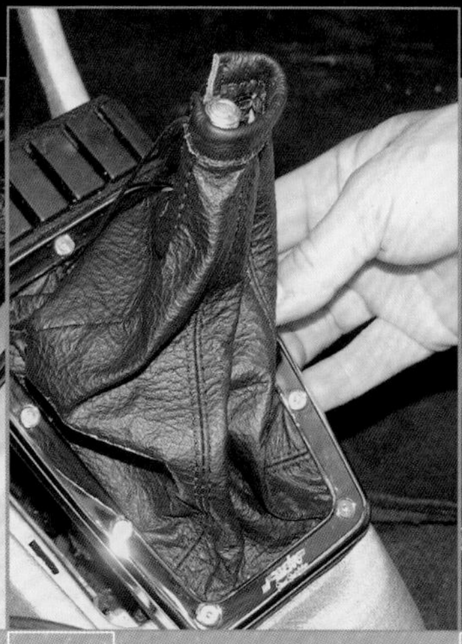

04 Now using the holes in the surround, drill through the gaiter and the lip on the base panel, to provide mounting holes for the surround screws. Try and keep the drill vertical while doing this, or your screws will go in wonky.

05 Fit the screws as straight as possible, and tighten up with an Allen key.

06 Fit the new gaiter over the gear lever. Some gaiters have a threaded top section built in, which attaches directly to the bottom of the gear knob.

07 On this knob you fit the collar over the gear stick, then choose the tightest-fitting rubber collar to go over the threaded end.

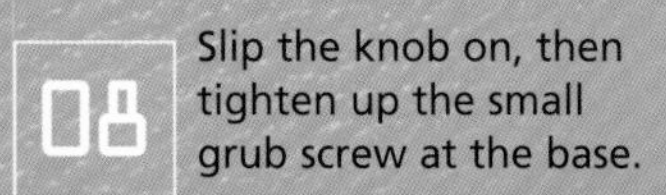

08 Slip the knob on, then tighten up the small grub screw at the base.

09 Screw on the collar, then tighten up your gaiter laces to finish the job.

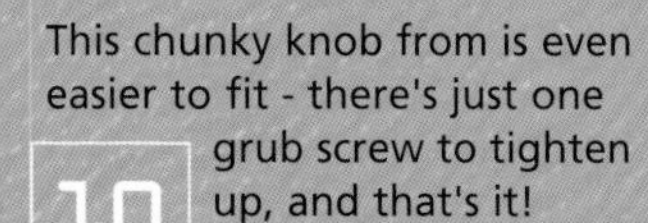

10 This chunky knob from is even easier to fit - there's just one grub screw to tighten up, and that's it!

11 Our final chosen knob was this very slinky item with a cool chrome collar.

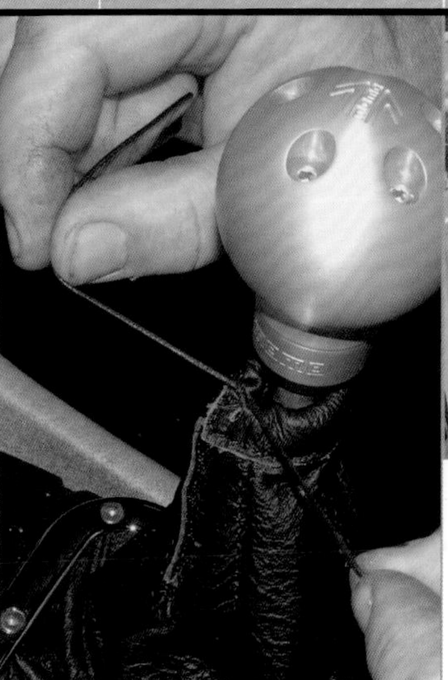

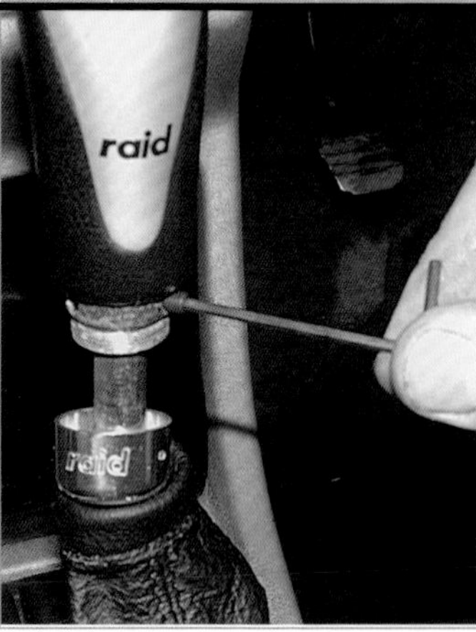

Handbrake knobs & gaiters

01 After having fitted a new gear knob and gaiter, you're going to want to spice up the handbrake too. So first, unclip and take off the plastic rear cover.

02 The knob itself is released by sticking a tiny screwdriver in to pop the catch at the base . . .

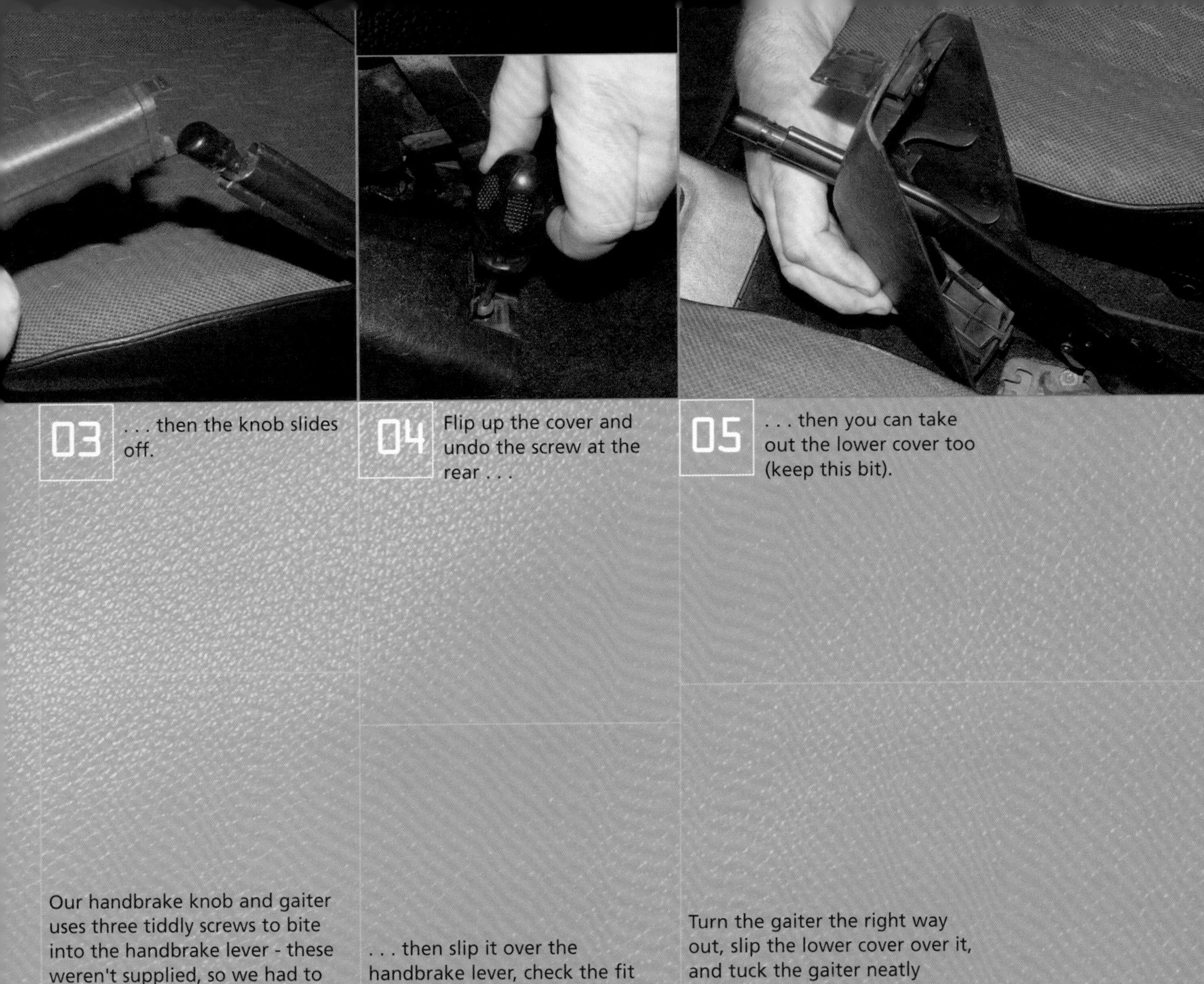

03 . . . then the knob slides off.

04 Flip up the cover and undo the screw at the rear . . .

05 . . . then you can take out the lower cover too (keep this bit).

06 Our handbrake knob and gaiter uses three tiddly screws to bite into the handbrake lever - these weren't supplied, so we had to chop down some already-small self-tappers. Turn the gaiter inside-out to fit the screws . . .

07 . . . then slip it over the handbrake lever, check the fit (make sure you can work the handbrake release button), and tighten them up.

08 Turn the gaiter the right way out, slip the lower cover over it, and tuck the gaiter neatly inside. You can now refit the lower cover (with the screw), and admire the finished result.

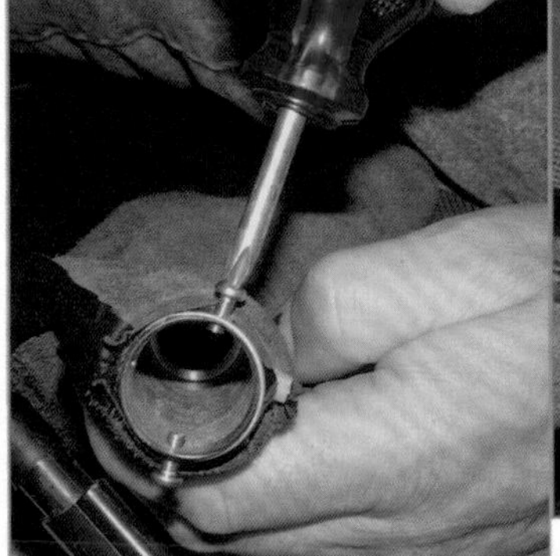

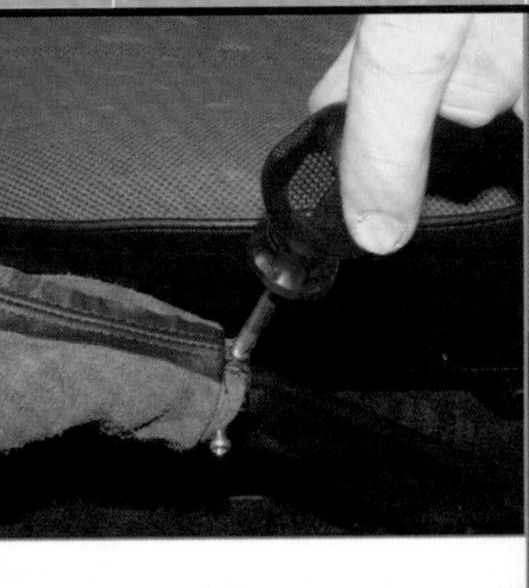

Coloured **dials**

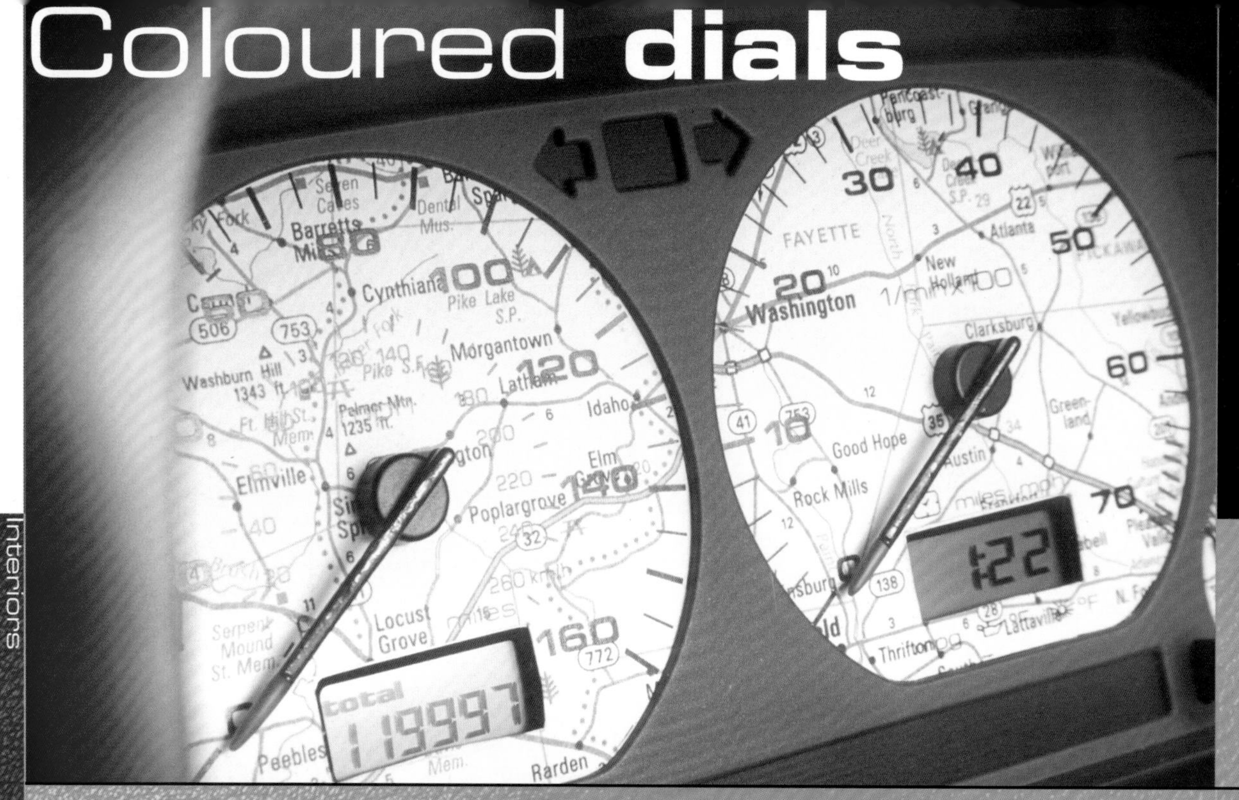

Interiors

Coloured dial kits are a good way to liven up your dark Golf dash. Just make sure you get the right kit for your car, and don't start stripping anything until you're sure it's the right one. Be very careful with the needles too, unless you want your dials to never read the same again.

01 Removing the clocks themselves is covered in "Removing stuff", so we'll start in by removing the eight tiny screws on the back of the clocks - get yourself a tub to put all the bits in.

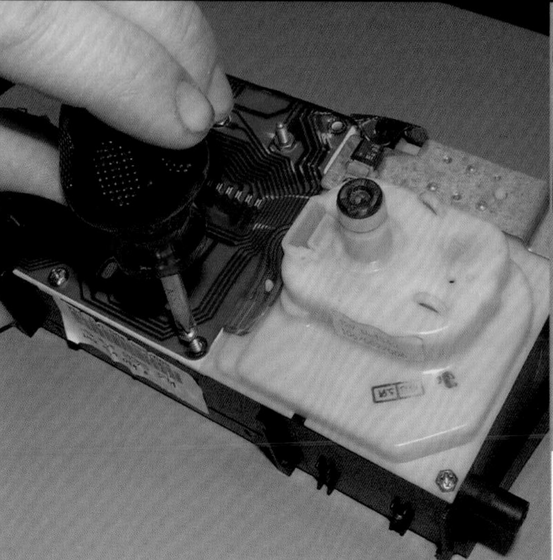

02 Prise up two clips and release the rev counter wiring plug, which in turn releases the printed circuit.

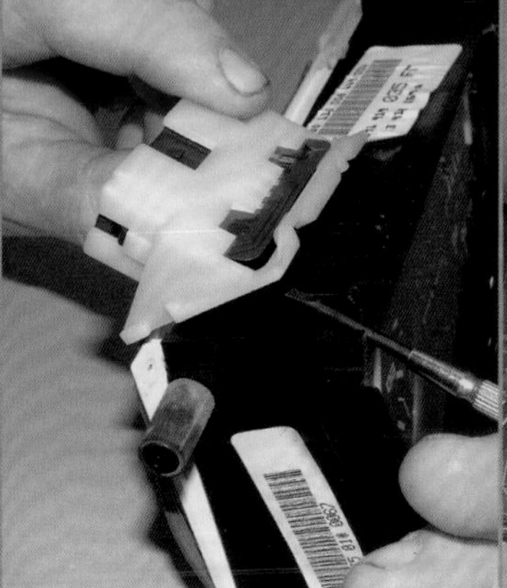

03 Twist and remove the bulbholders (they all seemed to be the same type on ours, but you might like to check!).

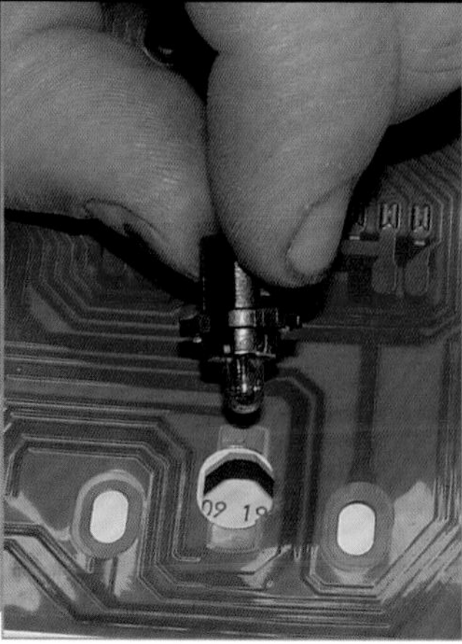

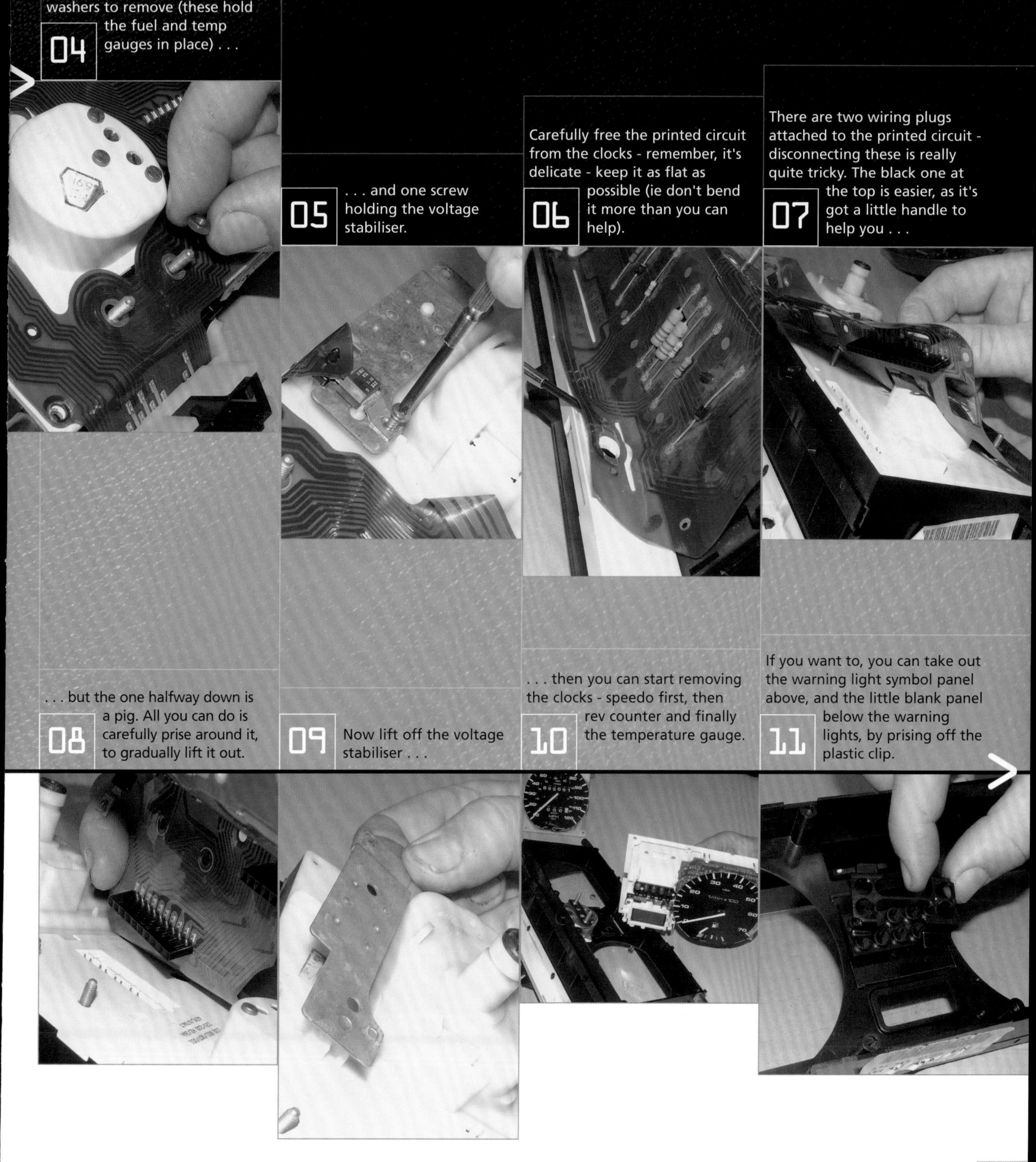

washers to remove (these hold
04 the fuel and temp gauges in place) . . .

05 . . . and one screw holding the voltage stabiliser.

06 Carefully free the printed circuit from the clocks - remember, it's delicate - keep it as flat as possible (ie don't bend it more than you can help).

07 There are two wiring plugs attached to the printed circuit - disconnecting these is really quite tricky. The black one at the top is easier, as it's got a little handle to help you . . .

08 . . . but the one halfway down is a pig. All you can do is carefully prise around it, to gradually lift it out.

09 Now lift off the voltage stabiliser . . .

10 . . . then you can start removing the clocks - speedo first, then rev counter and finally the temperature gauge.

11 If you want to, you can take out the warning light symbol panel above, and the little blank panel below the warning lights, by prising off the plastic clip.

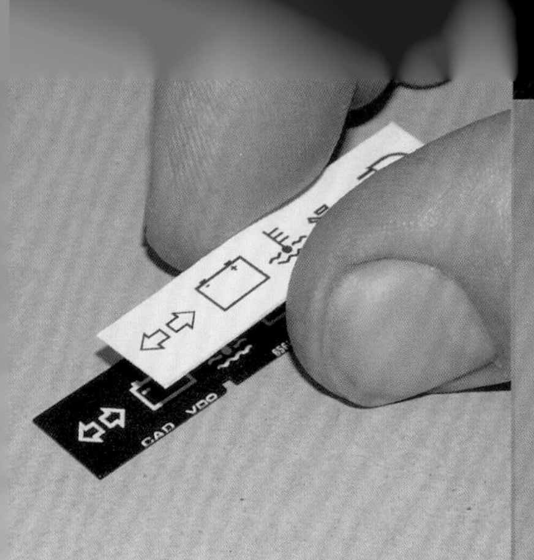

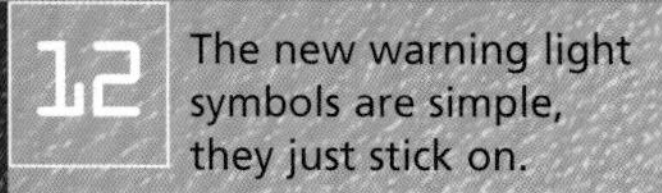

12 The new warning light symbols are simple, they just stick on.

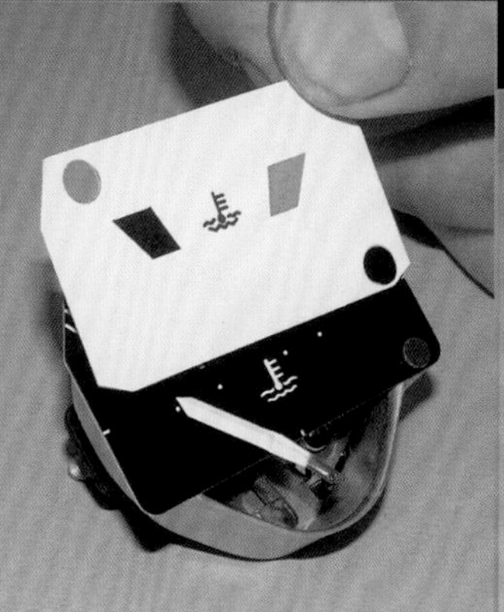

13 The temp gauge white dial is also one of the easier ones to do - peel off the backing, and feed it under the needle, trying to stop it sticking until it's in the right spot!

14 On some dial kits, you don't have to remove the needles, but we had to, be very careful if you do too. First, you lift the needle over the end stop (so it goes back past the "10"), then lever it off. It will come off this way – but it may fly off so watch where it lands!

15 Now remove these two little screws, to get the dial off.

On the fuel and temp gauges, it's not a good idea to remove the needles. So - when you come to paint them, slide the backing paper from the white dial (or any other bit of paper) behind the needle, to protect the new dials from paint. **20**

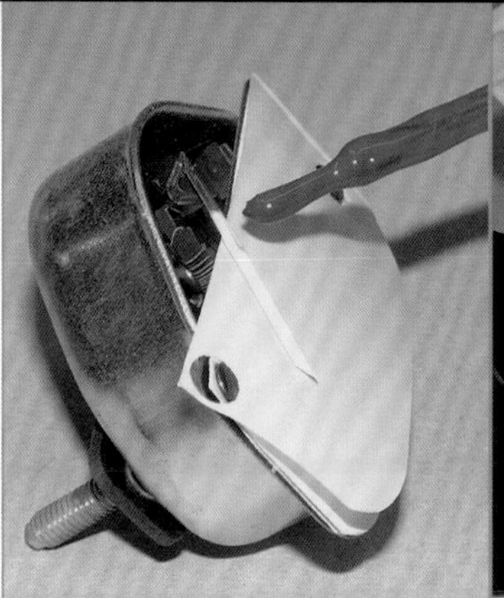

When reassembling your clocks, the order of refitting bits is the key. The panels above and below the warning lights go in first, then the speedo . . . **21**

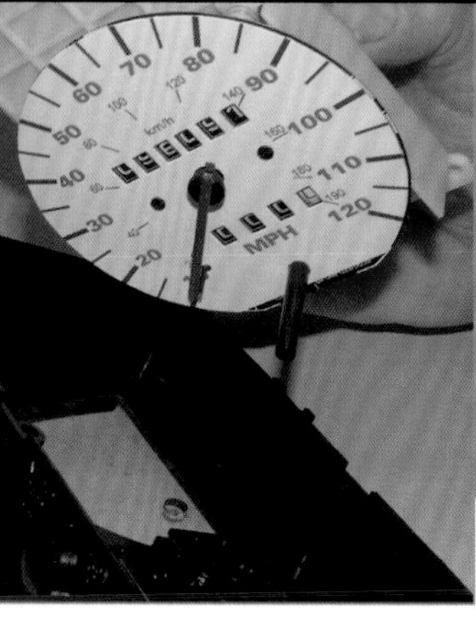

. . . followed by the temp gauge and the reassembled fuel gauge and rev counter. When it comes to refitting the printed circuit, the trickiest bit is again fitting the two wiring plugs attached to it - align the plug pins before pushing them in. **22**

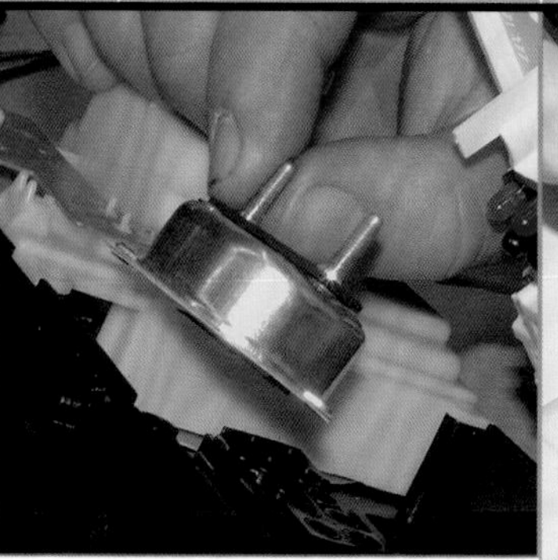

Our white dial kit also included white "dials" for the heater control panel. What you've got to do is separate the glued-on grey back piece from the panel - the trick is to crack the spots of glue, not the plastic. **23**

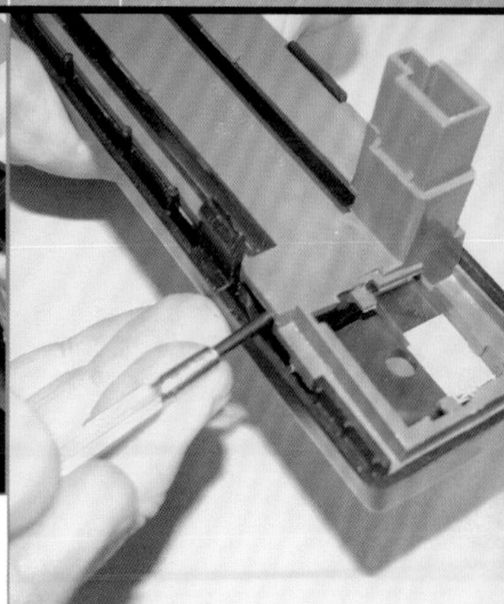

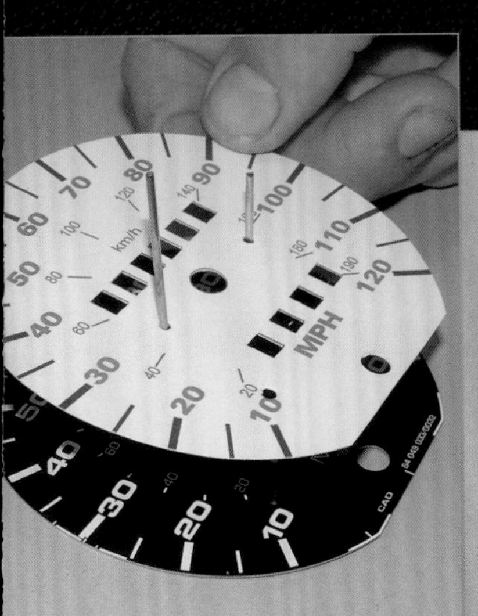

16 Getting the dial on straight is a challenge unless you poke two thin bits of wire through the screw holes in the dial, and feed the white dial on then refit the screws.

17 The needle you removed earlier must now be painted - red seems appropriate.

18 Fit the needle carefully back on (when the paint's dry) and remember to lift the needle back over the stop.

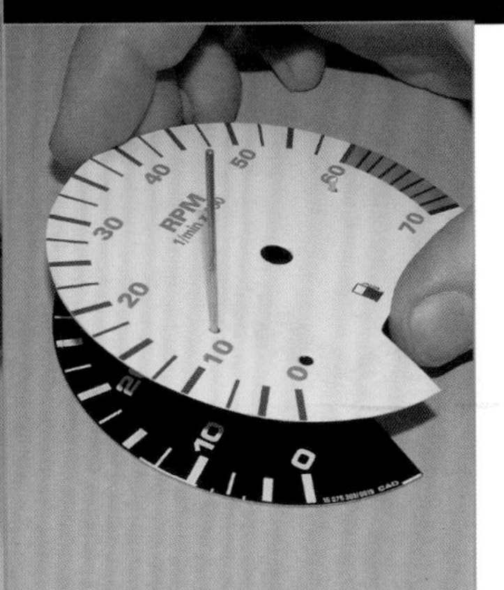

19 The rev counter can be tackled in much the same way as the speedo - the fuel gauge lifts out once the rev counter needle and dial are taken off. Here we are, fitting the white dial to the rev counter. When you're ready to refit the needle, it must be accurately fitted pointing to the "0", as there's no stop fitted - flick the needle around and back to check it sits on the zero.

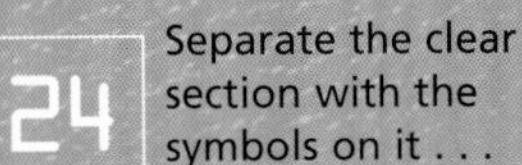

24 Separate the clear section with the symbols on it . . .

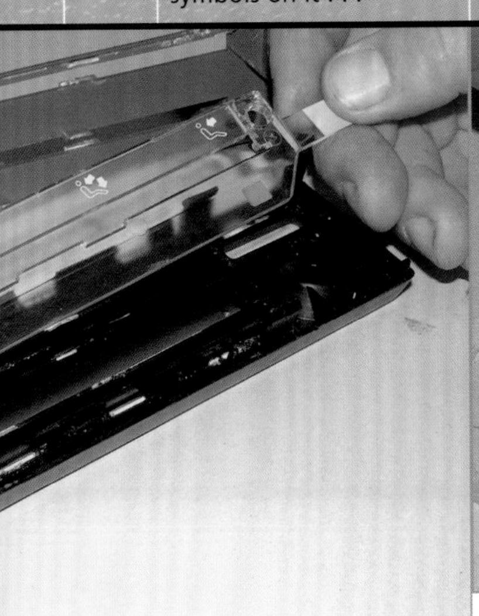

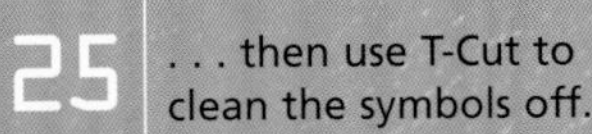

25 . . . then use T-Cut to clean the symbols off.

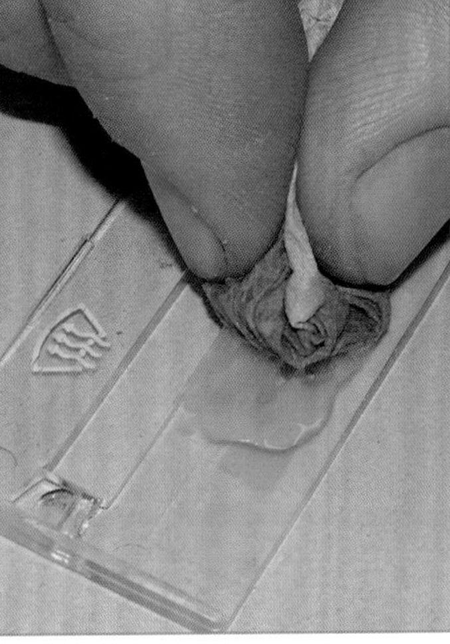

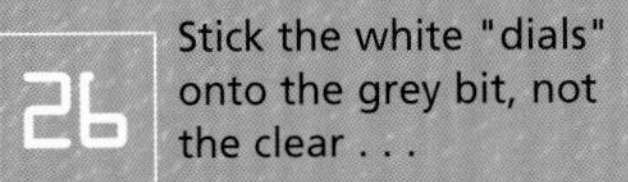

26 Stick the white "dials" onto the grey bit, not the clear . . .

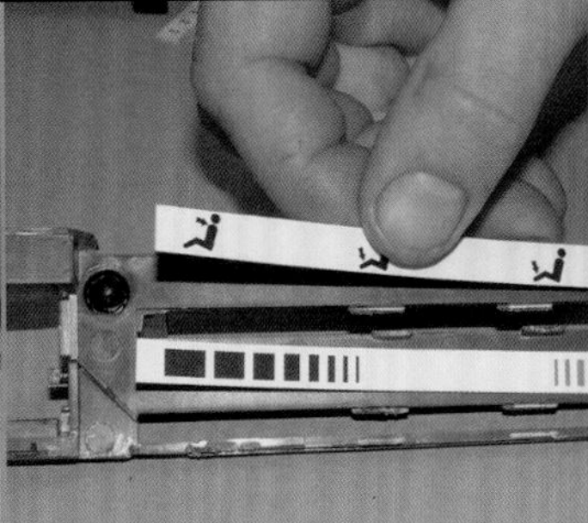

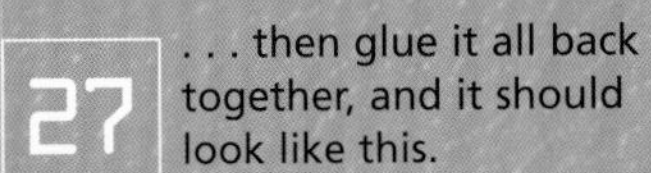

27 . . . then glue it all back together, and it should look like this.

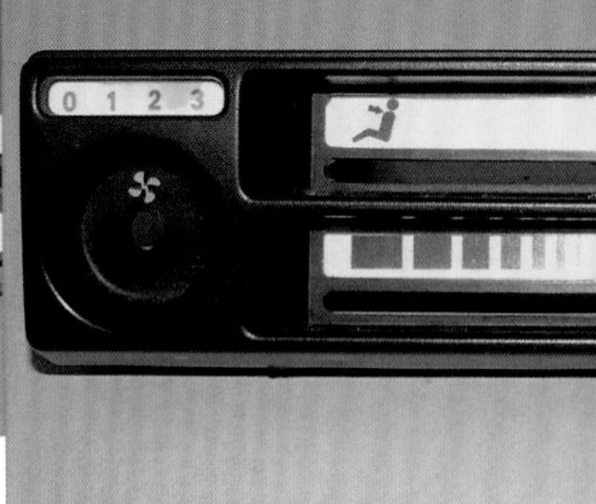

Chequerplate mats

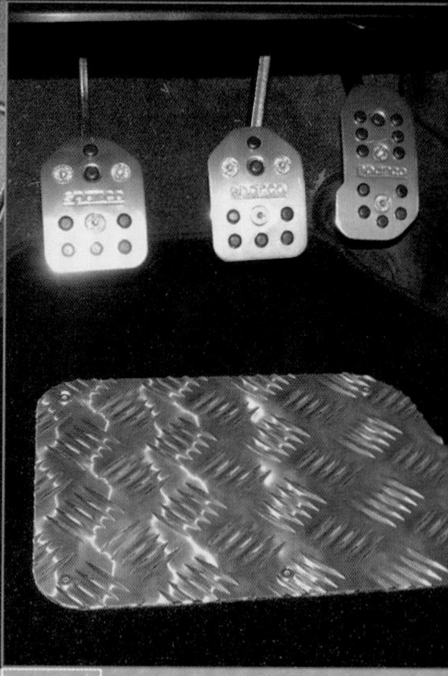

Ripping out the old carpets is actually quite a major undertaking - first, the seats have to come out (you might be fitting new ones anyway), but the carpets and underfelt fit right up under the dashboard, and under all the sill trims and centre console, etc. Carpet acts as sound-deadening, and is a useful thing to hide wiring under, too, so don't be in too great a hurry to ditch it completely.

A popular halfway measure to a fully decked-out chequerplate interior, tailored footwell plates are available from some suppliers. Because they're a tailored fit, they should stay put, not slide up under your pedals.

Chequerplate is tough but flexible, fairly easy to cut and shape to fit, and it matches perfectly with the racing theme so often seen in the modified world.

01 The easy option is to buy mats with chequerplate inserts where your heels go. And here's one we fitted earlier, posing with our pedal set.

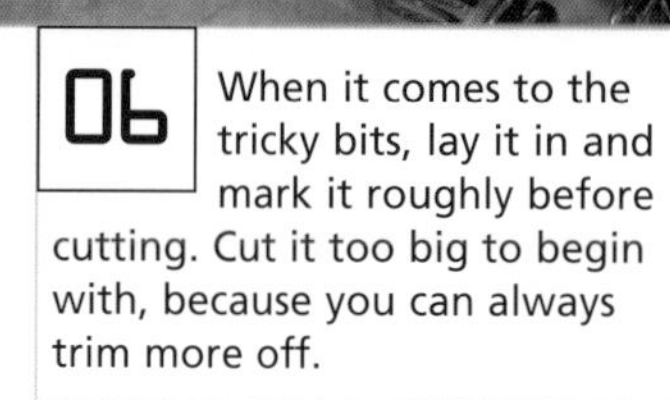

06 When it comes to the tricky bits, lay it in and mark it roughly before cutting. Cut it too big to begin with, because you can always trim more off.

07 This kick panel comes off on two clips, so you can tuck the chequer up behind and refit the panel over for a "perfect fit".

08 Now take the 'plate out and mount it on the board. Spray on plenty of spray adhesive.

02 The alternative to a fully-plated interior is to make up your own tailored mats. Start by trimming up a piece of card to fit the curvy bits . . .

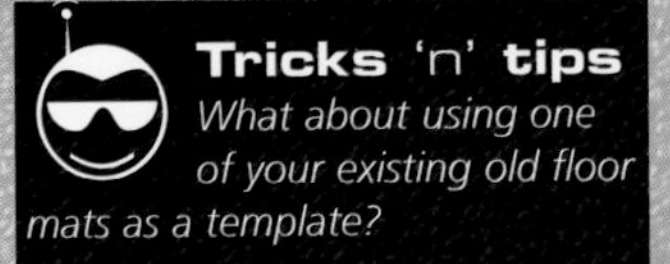

Tricks 'n' tips
What about using one of your existing old floor mats as a template?

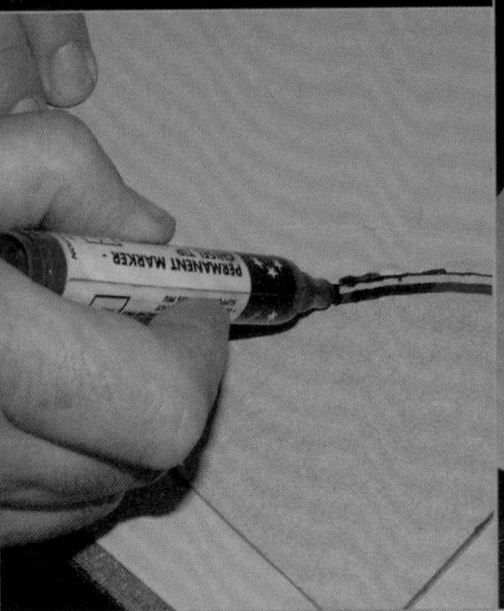

03 . . . then mark round onto some hardboard. The makers say not to fit their 'plate over carpets, because it'll flex too much and crack. This chequer is actually plastic look-alike, and it won't stand having your size 9s hoofing on it for long, so make up a solid-ish backing.

04 Cut the hardboard to shape then try it in place. You only need a board for the flat part of the floor (where your feet go) - the 'plate can go behind the pedals unsupported.

05 Mark the chequerplate up and trim it to shape.

09 Here's another use for your rims - use as a novelty paperweight while the glue dries!

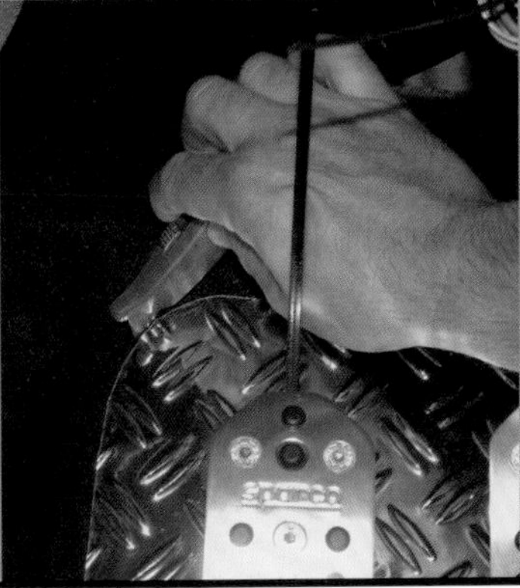

10 A bit more trimming with the mat in place, and you're nearly done.

11 On the driver's side, there's the throttle stop to deal with, on the floor under the pedal. Unscrew it from the floor, and mark round roughly where the hole in the 'plate needs to be.

12 Cut out the hole, and screw the stop back in to complete (no, the car won't go any faster without it - sorry).

Tricks 'n' tips
If you're completely replacing the carpet and felt with, say, chequerplate throughout, do this at a late stage, after the ICE install and any other electrical work's been done - that way, all the wiring can be neatly hidden underneath it.

Wheel cool

The steering wheel is one of the main points of contact between you and the car, it's sat right in front of you, and the standard ones are dull as a very dull thing. Thankfully sorting it out is simple.

Don't be tempted to fit too small a wheel if you've not got power steering. The Golf isn't exactly blessed with the lightest steering in the world, and a tiny-rimmed steering wheel will make manoeuvring very difficult.

Once you've shelled out for your wheel, it may be possible to fit it to your next car, too. When you buy a new wheel, you have to buy a boss (or mount) to go with it – the mounts are not pricey, so one wheel could be fitted to a different car for minimum cost.

A trick feature worth investigating is the detachable wheel/boss which we cover over the page.

Remove the old wheel as described earlier ("Removing stuff"), you're ready to kick off. Before doing anything, check that the horn contact is clean (scrub it with some emery paper until it's shiny) and

01 gently prise it out from the boss slightly.

06 . . . then the wheel itself.

07 Fit the wires to the rear of the horn button . . .

08 . . . then clip the button into the wheel.

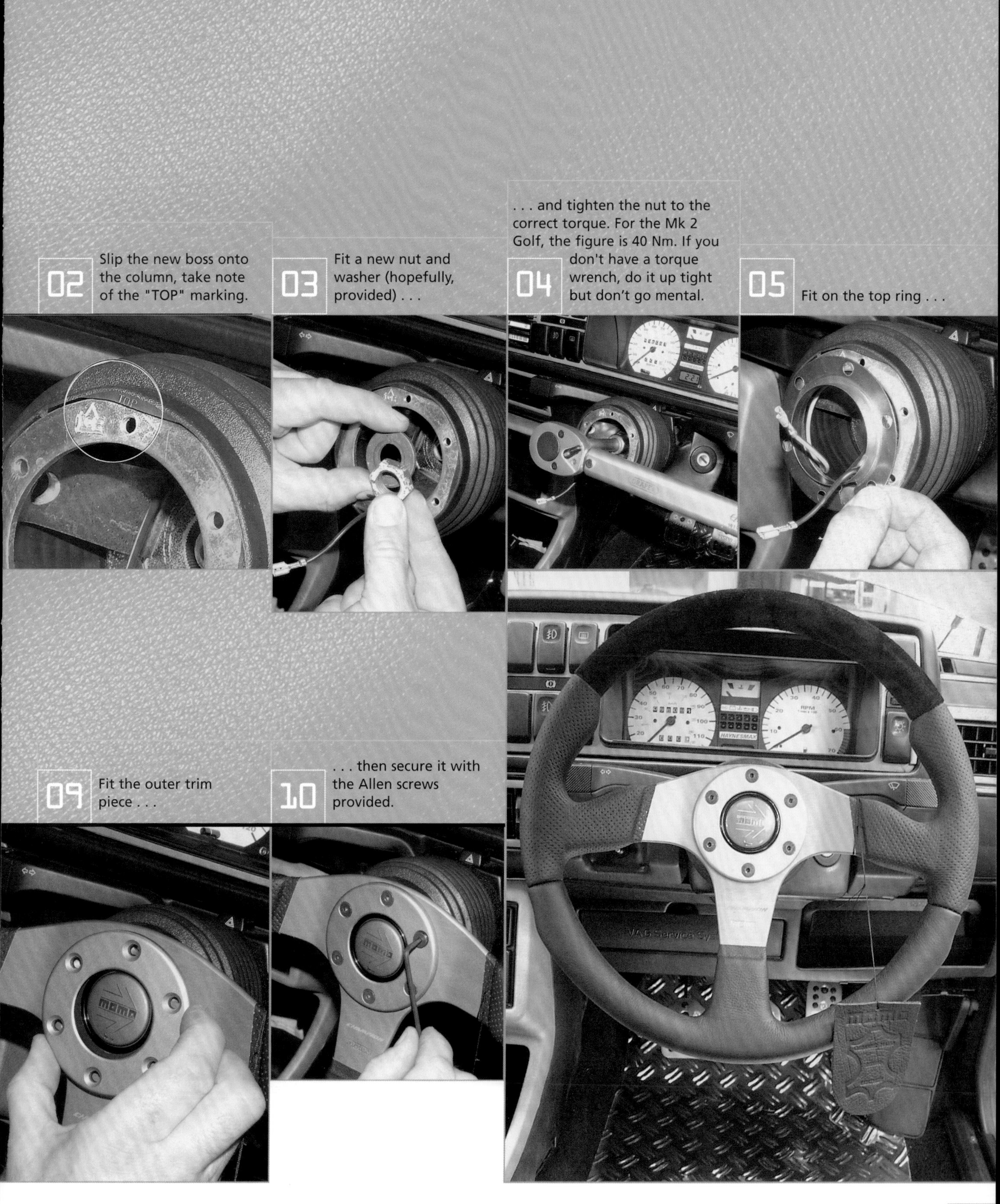

02 Slip the new boss onto the column, take note of the "TOP" marking.

03 Fit a new nut and washer (hopefully, provided) . . .

04 . . . and tighten the nut to the correct torque. For the Mk 2 Golf, the figure is 40 Nm. If you don't have a torque wrench, do it up tight but don't go mental.

05 Fit on the top ring . . .

09 Fit the outer trim piece . . .

10 . . . then secure it with the Allen screws provided.

Fitting a **wheel** with **snap-off** boss

This feature comes in handy when you park up and would rather the car was still there when you come back (something most people find a bonus). It's all very well having a steering wheel immobiliser or steering lock, but I doubt many thieves will be driving off in your car if the steering wheel's completely missing!

01 The first bit's the same as earlier - take off old wheel, check horn contact. Fit the boss (with the TOP mark at the top), and follow up with the new nut and washer combo. . .

02 . . . tighten the nut to the proper torque. It should be 40 Nm.

There are two anti-tamper plugs in the kit. You're meant to jam the heads into the Allen screws, then shear them off, stopping anyone unscrewing the snap-off boss and fitting their own wheel (to nick the car). After you fit the plugs, you'll have to drill them out to get the boss off again.

07 . . . then fit a nut and tighten up.

08 Fit the horn button to the snap-off boss front piece . . .

09 . . . then fit the boss to the wheel and tighten the Allen bolts.

10

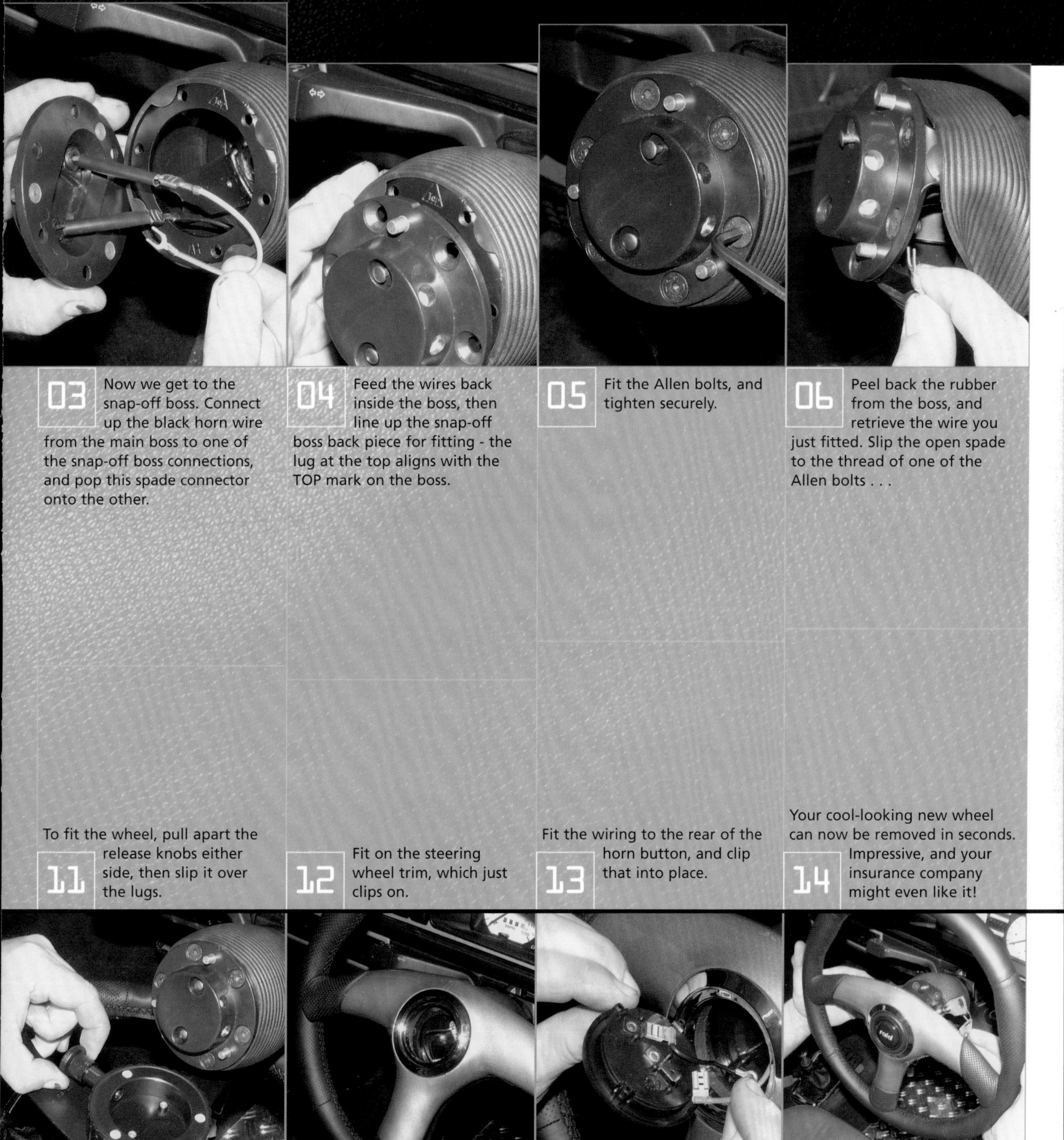

03 Now we get to the snap-off boss. Connect up the black horn wire from the main boss to one of the snap-off boss connections, and pop this spade connector onto the other.

04 Feed the wires back inside the boss, then line up the snap-off boss back piece for fitting - the lug at the top aligns with the TOP mark on the boss.

05 Fit the Allen bolts, and tighten securely.

06 Peel back the rubber from the boss, and retrieve the wire you just fitted. Slip the open spade to the thread of one of the Allen bolts . . .

11 To fit the wheel, pull apart the release knobs either side, then slip it over the lugs.

12 Fit on the steering wheel trim, which just clips on.

13 Fit the wiring to the rear of the horn button, and clip that into place.

14 Your cool-looking new wheel can now be removed in seconds. Impressive, and your insurance company might even like it!

Pedalling your Golf

Ally pedal extensions - a very cool race-style mod. They really look the part when combined with full chequerplate mats - available in several styles and (anodised) colours.

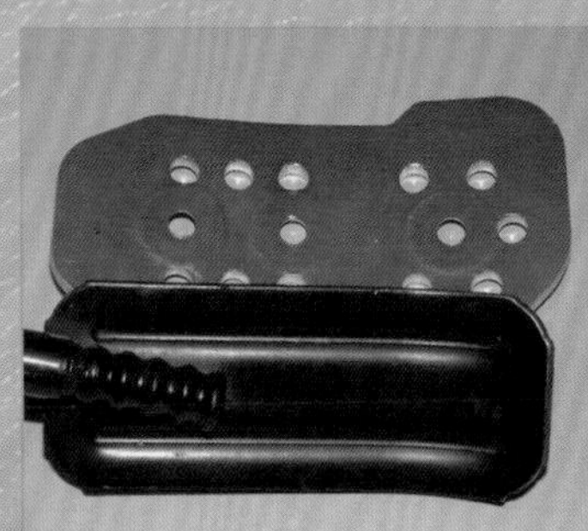

Achtung!
Check your insurance company's position regarding pedal extensions. A while ago there was a big fuss after a couple of cars with pedal extensions crashed . . .

01 Offer the pedal extensions up in place, and establish exactly where you'll be drilling through, to mount them. This is the throttle pedal, which we removed to show one problem. Check this very, very carefully, because it might not be as simple a job as you think... See "Bum notes".

02 Where necessary, prise off the old pedal rubbers.

03 Hold the extension firmly on the pedal, and drill through one hole only. Put a bit of wood behind the pedal, so you don't put a hole in something vital. Fit the bolt through the hole, secure tightly with the nut, then drill the next hole.

04 Before finally fitting the extensions, fit the rubber plugs to the holes provided, using a small screwdriver. The only pedal you can get away without rubbers is the throttle - you'll fail the MOT if your car has no clutch or brake pedal rubbers.

05 Fit your extension to the pedal, and fully tighten the nuts and bolts.

06 Check that all the pedals work properly. Press each one down as far as it'll go, and try combinations such as brake and clutch down together. We found that the nut on the back of the throttle pedal extension caught quite badly on the throttle stop, at full-throttle - could give you a fright! The throttle stop can be adjusted with a spanner, or it might need attention with a file. Sit back, and admire your handiwork. Just remember to check every so often that the nuts haven't come loose.

Bum Notes

01 On these extensions, using the intended mounting holes would have meant drilling through the pedal and the pedal stem, which isn't possible - the only one in the set which we could fit was for the throttle pedal, and then only using two of the three bolts. To use the countersunk holes, the extensions for the clutch and brake pedals would have to be offset to the left or right (you'll also have to make enough room to fit a nut to the bolt). If you're going to offset them, make sure you move them all the same way, or you'll mess up the pedal spacing, which could be dangerous .

02 For the clutch and brake pedals, we plugged the top mounting hole provided with one of the rubbers, and countersunk the holes either side of it . . .

03 . . . for drilling through into the pedal (so avoiding the pedal stem).

04 This meant we were two bolts short, but we sourced a pair locally.

First, make sure you can mount the tubes so you don't clout them with your feet every time you go for the clutch! Offer them in place first, and mark the holes. Removing the footwell trim is a matter of a few screws.

01

Neon lighting

Everyone knows that interior neons are a cool way to spice up an ICE install, but there's no reason why you can't fit them somewhere other than in the boot. . .

05

. . . crimped on a bullet with a wire running to our "neon" switch (a standard Golf foglight switch, from a scrapyard) . . .

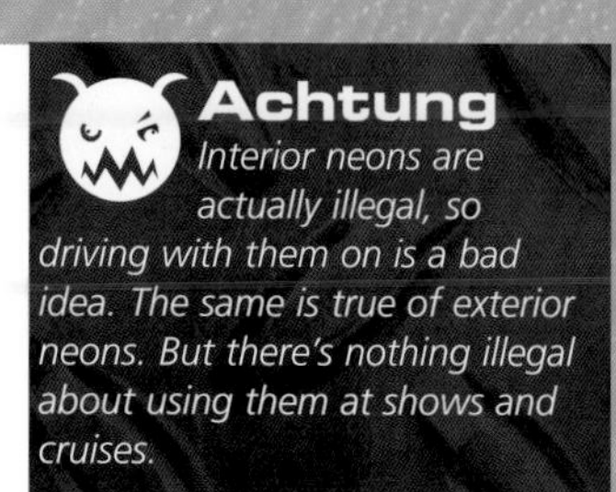

Achtung

Interior neons are actually illegal, so driving with them on is a bad idea. The same is true of exterior neons. But there's nothing illegal about using them at shows and cruises.

02 The neons we had are made to work off the cigar lighter socket, but they can be wired up more permanently, so chop off the plugs provided, and feed the wires behind the dash.

03 As neons only look any good at night, how about wiring them in so they only come on when the headlights are on? To do this take out main light switch, and use a test meter to find a wire which is live only when the lights are on.

04 On our Golf, we found a grey/red and a grey/black wire which fitted the bill, so we cut into one . . .

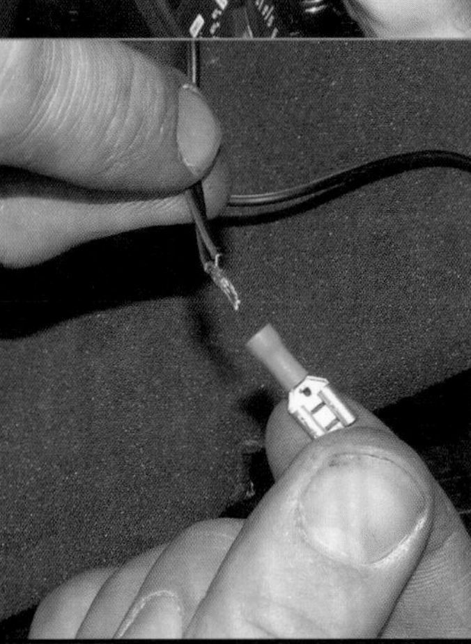

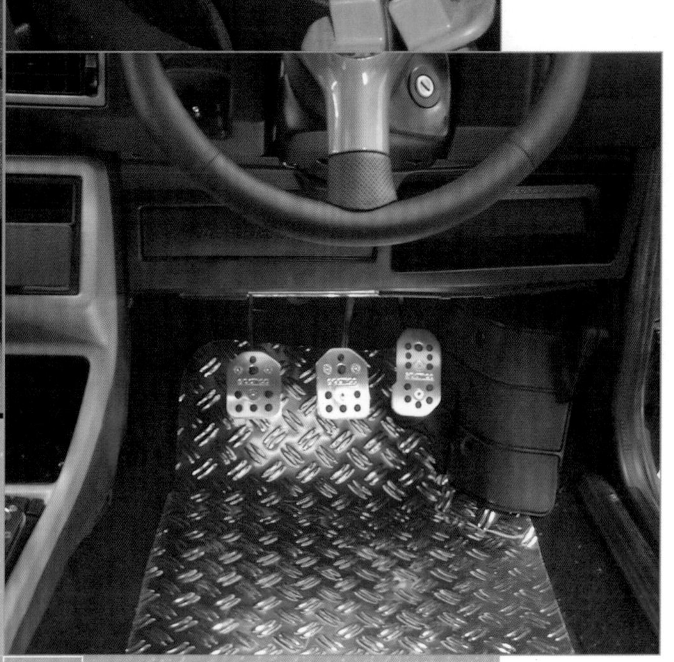

06 . . . and connected the live to the switch.

07 For the earth, join the two black wires from the neons to a spade connector, and plug them onto the earth block provided by VW, above the fusebox (photo in "Body styling", in the section on de-locking).

08 The final effect is pretty cool, though this photo only gives you some idea. Pedal extensions have never looked finer.

Are you **sitting** stylishly?

When fitting new seats, besides the seat itself, remember to price up the subframe to adapt it to the mounting points in your car. If you're going to fit harnesses too, make sure you only buy EC-approved ones, or an eagle-eyed MOT tester might make you take them out.

If you choose non-reclining seats, and have a 3-door Golf, make sure you get a subframe which tips. Unless that is you've already got rid of your rear seats! An alternative to replacement seats is to have your existing seats re-upholstered in your chosen colours/fabrics. If you've got a basic model, try sourcing GTI seats from a breakers. A secondhand GTI interior bought here will be a lot cheaper than buying new goodies, and you know it'll fit easily. Specialist breakers can supply something more upmarket in the shape of a leather interior from a Corrado.

01 Taking out the old chairs is surprisingly easy – one nut and bolt under the front of the seat is all you undo . . .

02 . . . then slide the seat backwards out of the floor runners, and - take it away!

03 Offer the seat frames into place first, to check for fit.

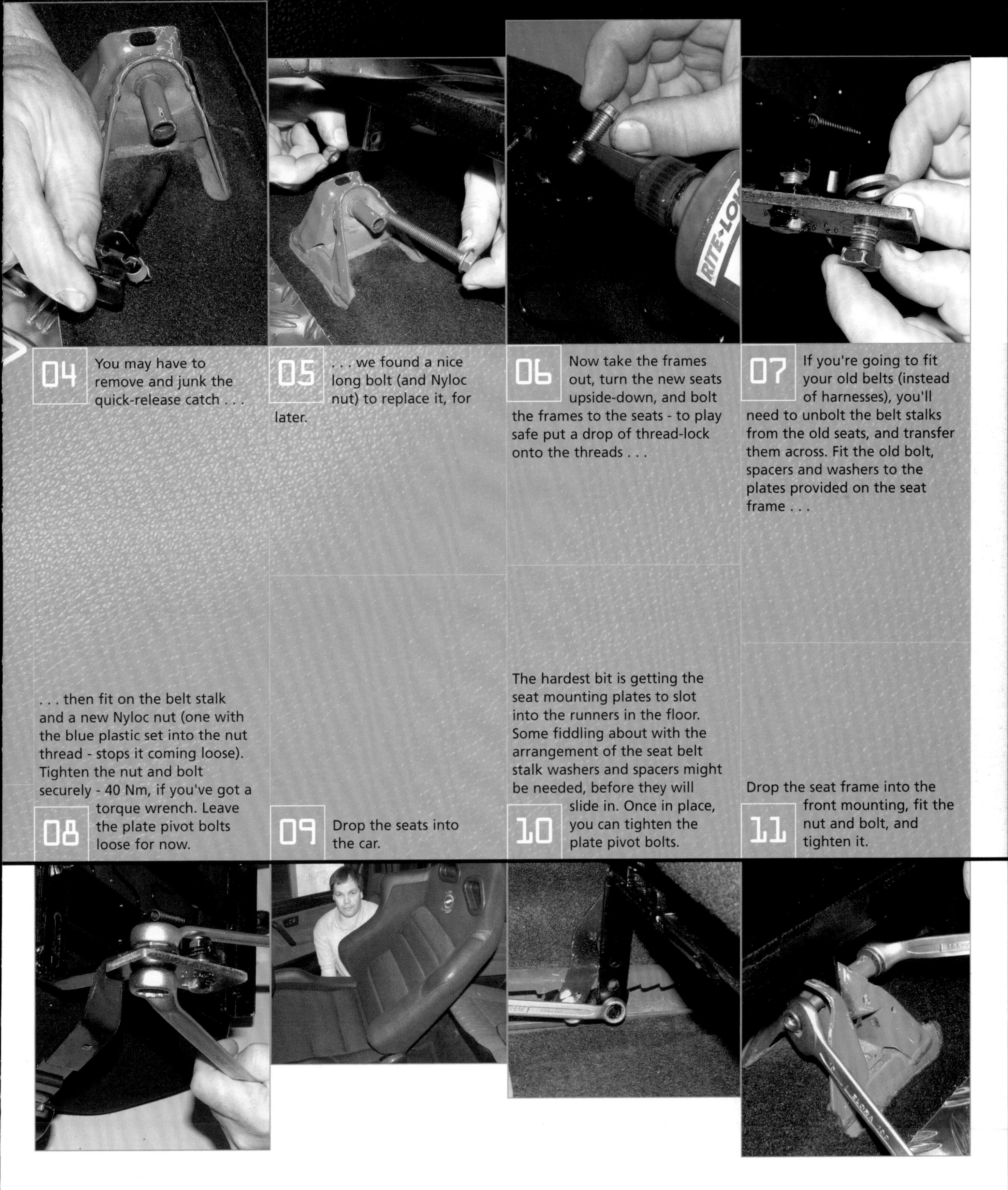

04 You may have to remove and junk the quick-release catch . . .

05 . . . we found a nice long bolt (and Nyloc nut) to replace it, for later.

06 Now take the frames out, turn the new seats upside-down, and bolt the frames to the seats - to play safe put a drop of thread-lock onto the threads . . .

07 If you're going to fit your old belts (instead of harnesses), you'll need to unbolt the belt stalks from the old seats, and transfer them across. Fit the old bolt, spacers and washers to the plates provided on the seat frame . . .

08 . . . then fit on the belt stalk and a new Nyloc nut (one with the blue plastic set into the nut thread - stops it coming loose). Tighten the nut and bolt securely - 40 Nm, if you've got a torque wrench. Leave the plate pivot bolts loose for now.

09 Drop the seats into the car.

10 The hardest bit is getting the seat mounting plates to slot into the runners in the floor. Some fiddling about with the arrangement of the seat belt stalk washers and spacers might be needed, before they will slide in. Once in place, you can tighten the plate pivot bolts.

11 Drop the seat frame into the front mounting, fit the nut and bolt, and tighten it.

Fitting **harnesses**

The most important thing with harnesses is what you mount them to. If you use the rear belt mounting points, and keep the rear seats, you may fail the MOT. If you have rear seats you legally have to have seatbelts. So if you don't want to risk it, you could mount the harnesses and the rear belt to the same fixings, or just take out the back seats. Removing the seats leaves the rear deck free for chequerplate, speakers, roll cages - whatever you like.

Never try making up your own seat belt/harness mounting points. Drilling your own holes and sticking bolts through is fine for mounting speakers and stuff, but it really isn't a clever idea to mess about with parts that are meant to save your life.

Tricks 'n' tips

In case you're thinking of fitting a longer bolt (which is a good idea), you'll soon find out that any old bolt won't do. Seat belt bolts usually have a different, finer-pitched thread than ordinary bolts. Don't force the wrong bolts in. Most car makers fit the same seat belt bolts, so either source some from a scrapyard, or go to a specialist nut 'n' bolt man.

Racing harness with rear seats

01 Check out the standard bolts, are they long enough to take both the old belts and the new straps, and still take a nut? Unbolt as before, then "assemble" all the bits onto the old bolt . . .

02 . . . and providing the old bolt's long enough, you can re-use it to pin the old and new stuff in together. Don't forget your torque wrench (40Nm).

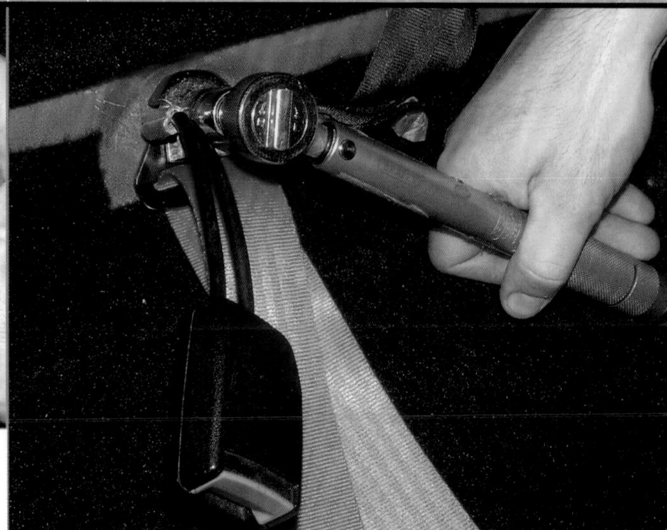

Racing harness no rear seats

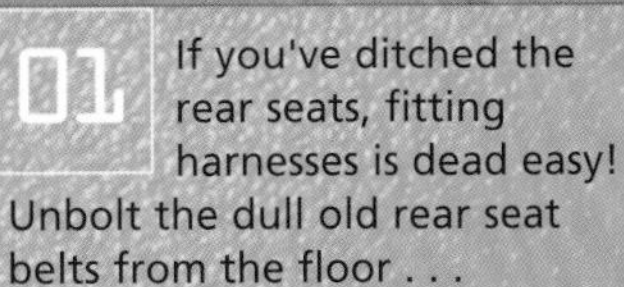

01 If you've ditched the rear seats, fitting harnesses is dead easy! Unbolt the dull old rear seat belts from the floor . . .

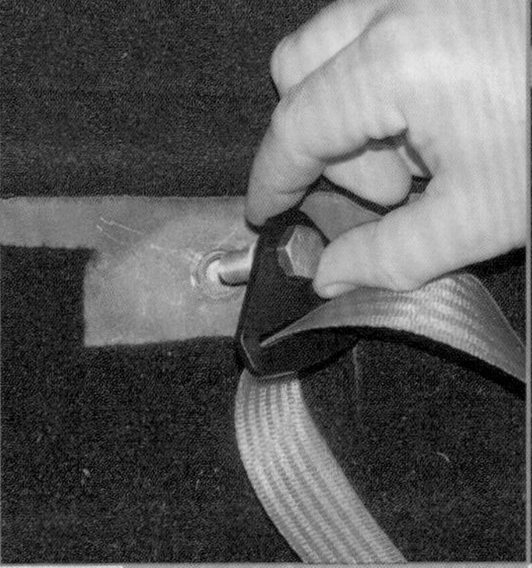

02 . . . and at the sides, hanging onto the bolts, washers and stuff . . .

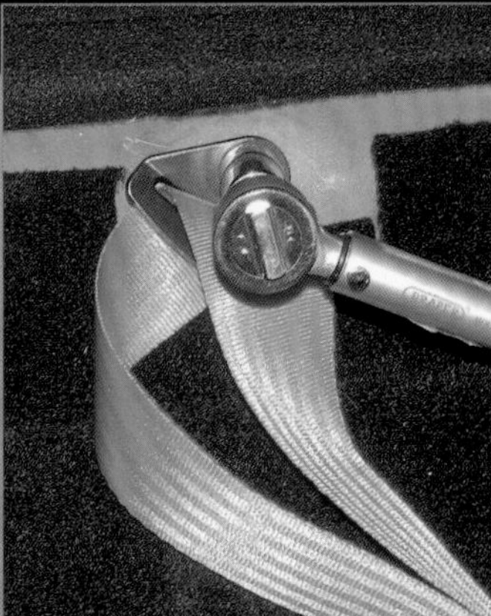

03 . . . and fit your new harnesses to the same holes, using the same bolts, then torque the bolts up to 40 Nm.

Racing harness and racing seats

01 Most race seats have mounting points provided for belts (either the old inertia reel stalks, or new harnesses). Don't go drilling any holes in the seat frames without checking with the seat company first. Drilling any holes of your own for mounting belts is a very bad idea...

02 And there you go! A Corbeau/Sparco combo!

03 Adjust the harnesses to hold you in comfortably and you're ready to roll.

Here's the finished head unit in place. It matches nicely with the silver dash trim, and the multi-coloured display looks really cool at night. Just the job.

ICE
Head unit

You might find with a ten-year-old car that someone had already been in the dash, and made a bit of a mess. Sorting it out just takes a bit of care and attention. Follow our guide and you shouldn't have any problems.

Also, when fitting anything like this to your car, read the instructions that come with the gear. We're giving you specific instructions that involve the car, rather than the stuff we're installing. If you're using another product brand or type, you need to know its individual requirements or you could end up doing something wrong. So, have a good read.

Tricks 'n' tips

Fitting an ISO connector to a car without one will mean a new head unit just plugs in.

01 The first job is to get the old player out of the dash. If you haven't got the correct removal tools, it may take a bit of fiddling.

02 If your car's wiring is in a mess like this it'll need sorting before you could go any further with things.

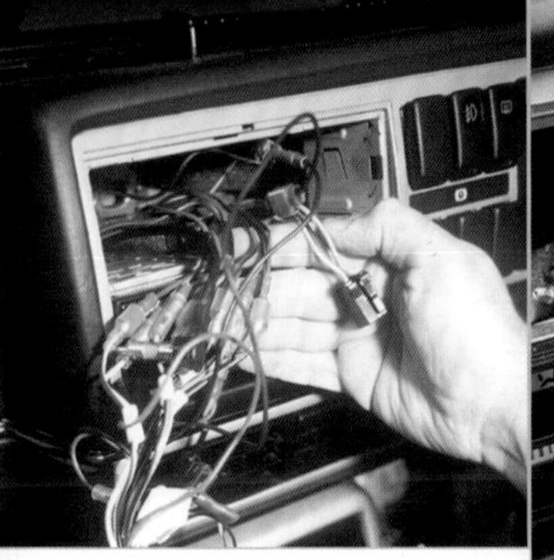

03 Remove all the non-standard additional wiring, including things like this Scotchlok. This type of connector has its uses, but in a car audio installation a decent joint is absolutely vital, so proper terminals or solder should be used instead.

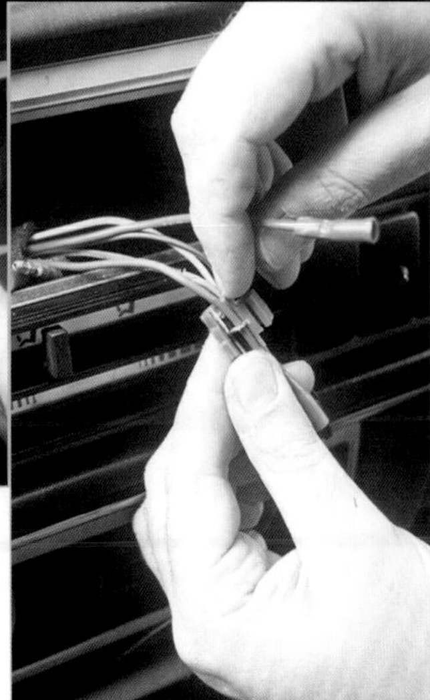

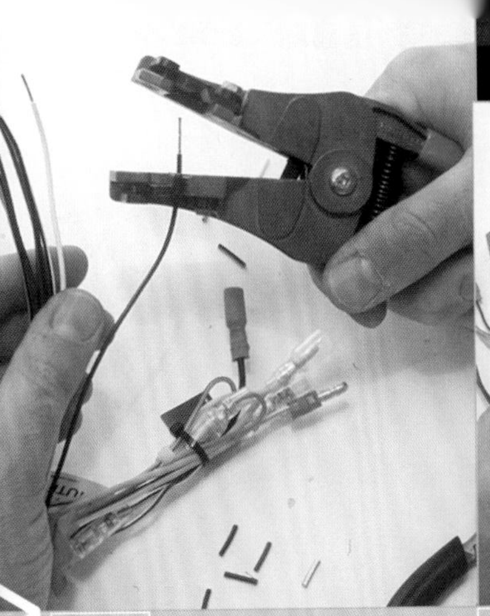

04 Here is the new Pioneer's wiring loom, minus the ISO plug that was fitted to it. This will join up to almost all new cars' wiring harnesses, but in our Golf's case, it was surplus to requirements. After cutting the plug off, and then stripping the speaker wires back, crimp matching bullet terminals onto the head unit's loom so that they join onto the loom in the Golf's dash. Preferably use wire strippers and ratchet crimping pliers to get good, solid connections between the wires and the terminals.

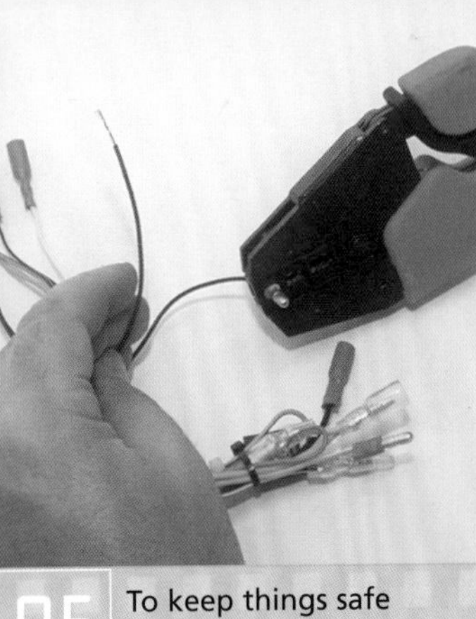

05 To keep things safe should the head unit ever need removing, always use the same method of termination. A positive feed of any kind - either a speaker feed or a 12-volt supply - is always given a female, or shrouded, terminal. The wire that plugs into it is given a corresponding male terminal, so that should the two ever be parted for any reason, the live end of the wire is covered by the shrouded female terminal.

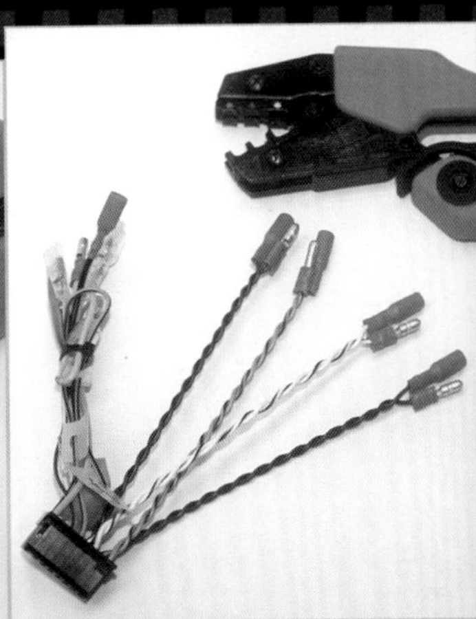

06 Once the terminations are made, tidy the loom up by twisting each pair of speaker output wires together, and by using cable ties to keep the power loom neat. The Golf has no switched live feed, so the permanent and switched feeds that go to the Pioneer set are joined together to allow constant operation.

07 Here you can see the Pioneer loom has been joined to the Golf loom. The head unit has been connected to the existing speaker wiring, even though we're using an amp for the new front speakers. The Pioneer will be powering the rear shelf speakers, and connecting the other wires keeps things neat.

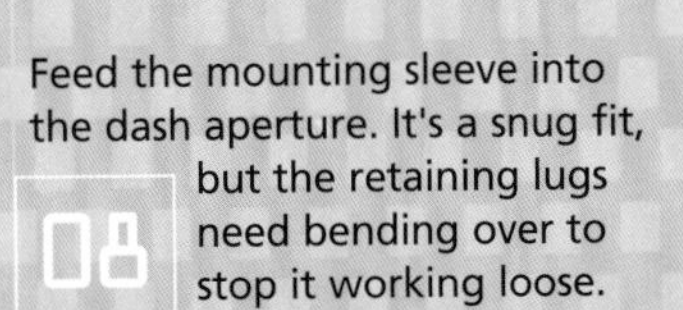

Feed the mounting sleeve into the dash aperture. It's a snug fit, but the retaining lugs need bending over to stop it working loose. **08**

The lugs can be bent over with a modified screwdriver, or anything that allows you to get to the right lug and bend it firmly into place. **09**

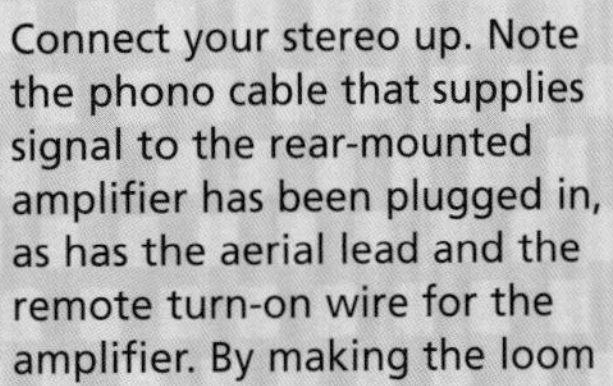

Connect your stereo up. Note the phono cable that supplies signal to the rear-mounted amplifier has been plugged in, as has the aerial lead and the remote turn-on wire for the amplifier. By making the loom neat on the bench, the job looks tidy and will be safe as well. **10**

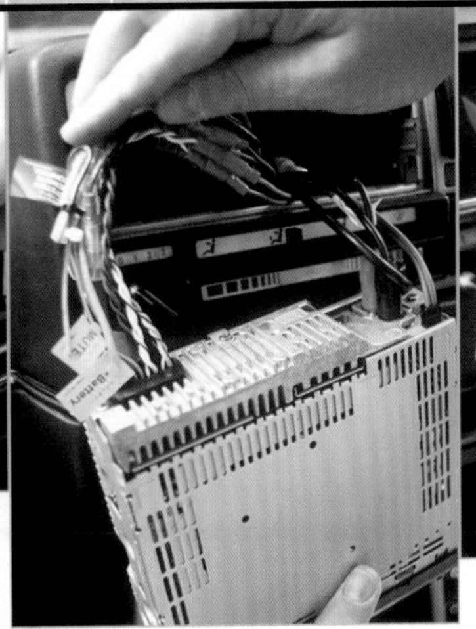

This rubber bung located into a bracket inside the dashboard, taking the weight of the set and allowing the CD damper mechanism to perform properly. It must be used otherwise the CD might skip over rough roads. When fitting the unit, never force it into place in case something is trapped behind it. Go gently and the set should just click in easily. **11**

Front Speakers

Getting good speakers into the front of a Golf isn't too bad, especially if you do what we did and use some door pockets from Audioscape. They look the part, are well made, and sound good too.

We used MTX component speakers for our Golf, meaning there is a six inch mid and a separate tweeter on each side of the car. They are fed from a passive crossover that sends highs to the tweeter and the rest of the signal to the mid-range, and they sound great.

It's a good idea to use the VW dash speaker position for the tweeter because they work well there, and they're hidden from prying eyes.

01 The tweeters are hidden under the dash grilles, which come off easily enough once you remove the hidden screw.

02 Then you need a shorty screwdriver to remove the original speaker, which leaves plenty of room for the new tweeter.

07 This is one of the two passive crossovers, and here it's been wired up with the outputs to the tweeter and the mid-range. The unit can hidden behind the dash when you've finished.

08 Cleaning the door skin prior to sound-deadening is a very important, if messy job. The door must be spotless otherwise the damping material won't stick properly and it won't work effectively.

09 Cut the sound-deadening (Dynamat Xtreme in this case) to size before removing the backing sheet and sticking in place. This Dynamat doesn't need heating up like other sound-deadening sheets, so you can apply it with a hardwood roller. Make sure it's rollered well onto the steel underneath, and pop any bubbles that form.

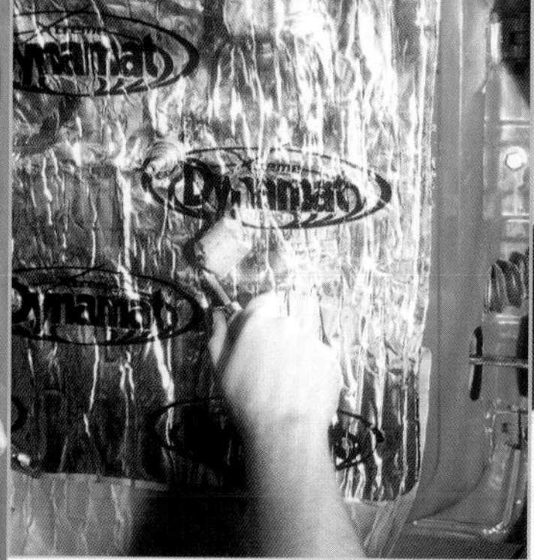

10 If you're fitting door pods like these, mark out where your speakers will go. Mask the edges so that they aren't damaged by the jigsaw when you cut out the mounting hole.

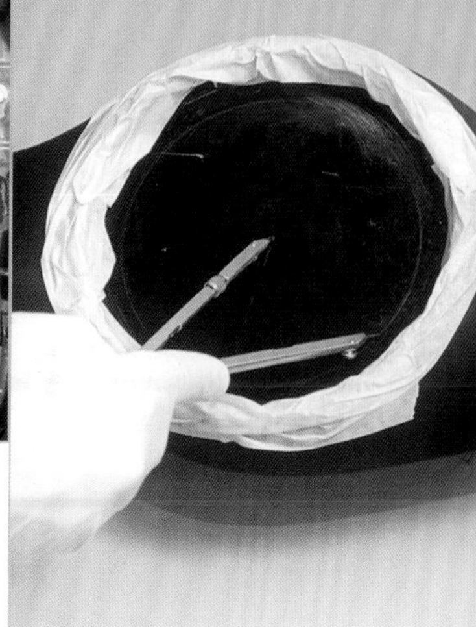

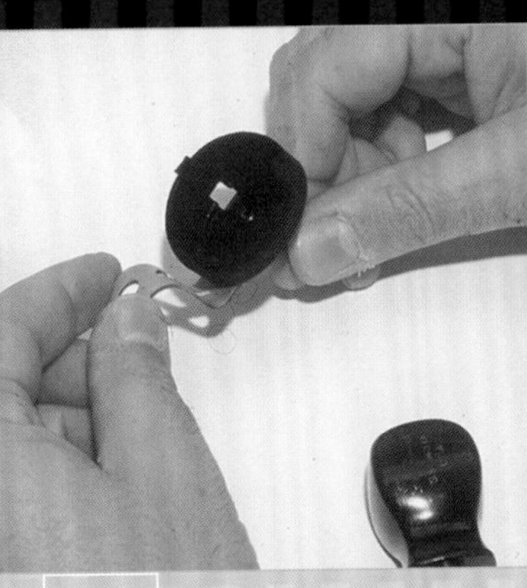

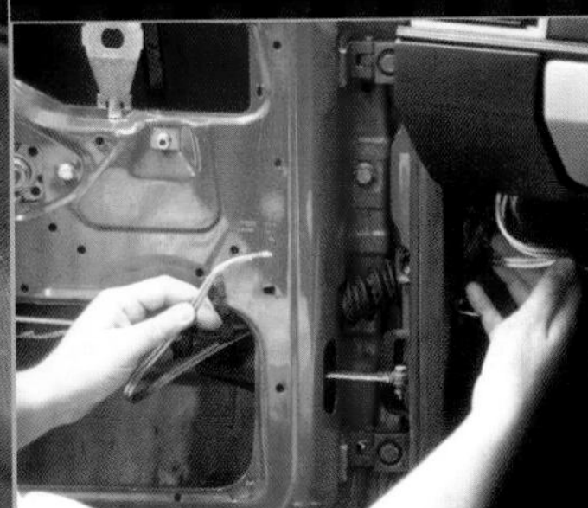

03 The tweeters are fitted onto small mountings made from the strip bracket that comes with most head units. By bending this into a flattened S-shape, it lowers the tweeter enough to sit it under the dashboard grille, and allows a little adjustment of where the tweeter is pointed.

04 After the tweeter mounting cup is screwed onto the bracket, the tweeter is clipped in place. Then it's fitted into the dash using one of the original speaker's screws. Drop the new wire into the dash where the crossover will be.

05 To get the mid-range speakers sorted, strip the Golf's door down. Once the hidden screws and fastenings are undone, carefully pull the panel away from the window channel, ready for the next bit.

06 While the door is stripped, run the speaker wire in through the rubber sleeves. You only need a piece of cable long enough to just go under the dash, where the crossover is going. If your Golf hasn't got the sleeves, you can buy them from VW dealers very cheaply. You must have this wire protection in place to save any problems later.

11 Once the hole is chopped out, try the speaker for size, and mark the screw holes using a pointed scribe. This is the easiest way to mark the hard glass fibre.

12 The next job is to remove the original door pocket along with its standard speaker.

13 Drill new holes to hold the door pod in place. Use at least six screws spread out round the panel to hold it firmly against the door card.

14 When the panel is firmly screwed on, and you've drilled the speaker screw holes, refit the supplied speaker wadding. If you leave it in while you drill the holes, you'll struggle to get the drill bit back out because the wadding will wrap around it.

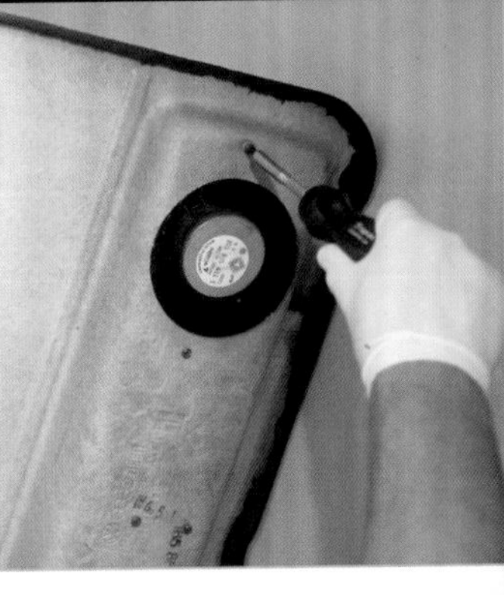

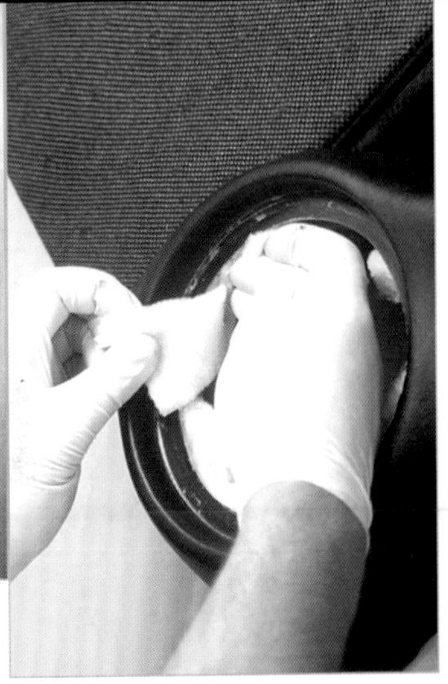

Rear speakers

ICE

Using the trim ring of the 6x9s, we decided on the position for the speakers on the shelf. This shelf looks exactly like a genuine Golf one once it's trimmed up, and you can't see the speakers, which helps keep thieves at bay.

01 Mark the screw holes, then drill them out.

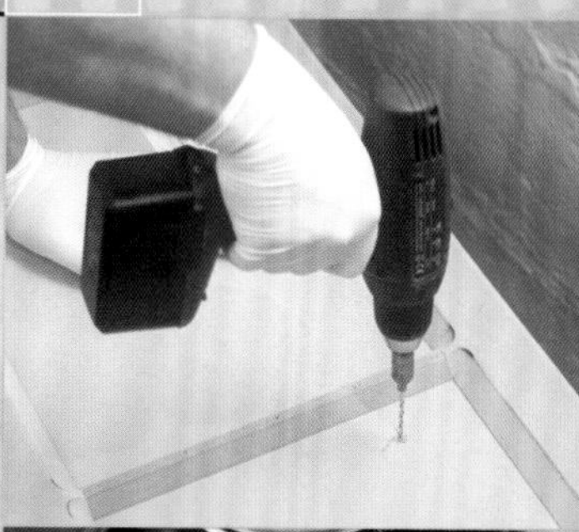

One way to get sounds in the back of your car is to fit an MDF shelf, and a pair of 6x9s.

There are a couple of things to beware of when using an MDF shelf, and the main one is the weight. so make sure you've got it well secured before you go throwing your car around. And be very careful when screwing the hinge blocks in place. You've only got one chance, so don't strip the wood out or you're in trouble.

Your shelf may come with strings to lift the shelf when you open the hatch. But as it's so heavy your tailgate struts may struggle to hold the weight.

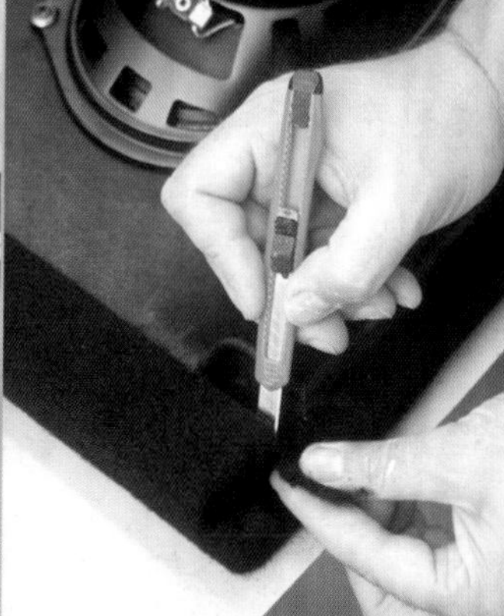

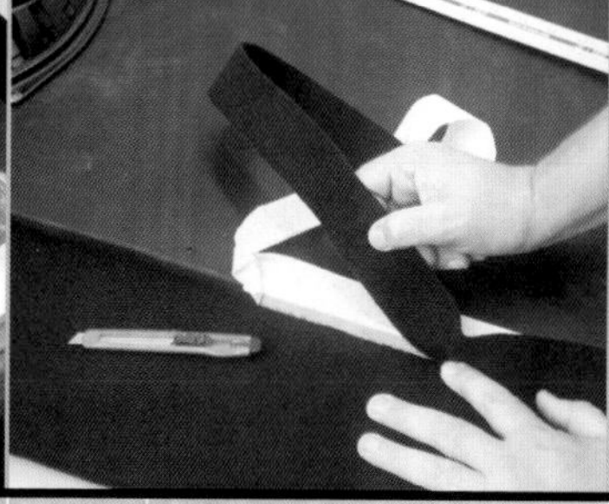

06 Spray glue on the shelf and the carpet, paying attention to not spraying it over the speaker areas. After the glue goes tacky, lower the shelf forward onto the carpet and flip over and smooth the two glued surfaces together.

07 Mask up the speakers to protect them against the glue, and then tape the shelf up to give a neat line where the carpet is to be trimmed. Spray the overlap and shelf . . .

08 . . . then fold the carpet onto the shelf. Begin to cut away the excess at the taped edge.

09 Carefully cut around the awkward areas to get a good finish.

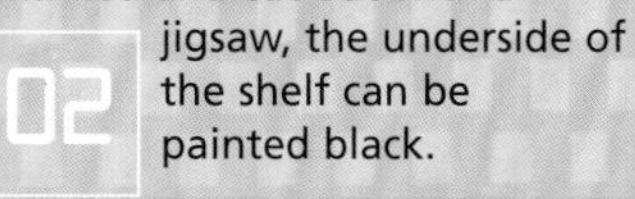

02 Once the speaker holes are marked and cut out with a jigsaw, the underside of the shelf can be painted black.

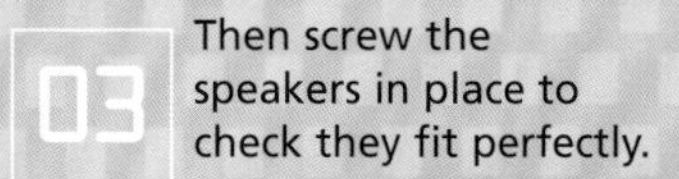

03 Then screw the speakers in place to check they fit perfectly.

04 Next staple the speaker cloth across the top of the speakers so that it stops the carpet trim from sagging later.

05 Size the carpet and cut to shape prior to gluing in place. Place the shelf on its side, on top of the upside-down carpet.

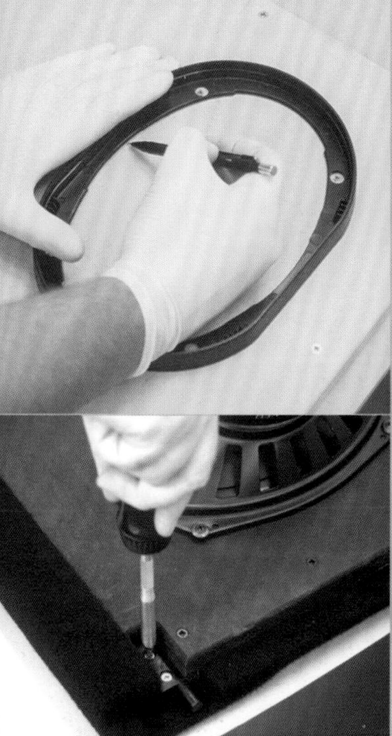

10 Once the carpet is stuck in place, the hinge pins are screwed onto the shelf. Be very careful here because the shelf isn't very thick where the screws go in and it's easy to strip the screw out to prevent mounting the hinge piece and then the shelf will be difficult to anchor in the car.

11 Solder the speaker wires in place to stop them coming off accidentally.

12 Use heatshrink to tidy the terminals after soldering, again working with red for positive and black for negative.

13 Tidy up the wiring using P clips to hold it at the edge of the shelf, and then fit a Neutrik (quick-release) connector on the cable end so that it plugs into the socket fitted on the amp rack.

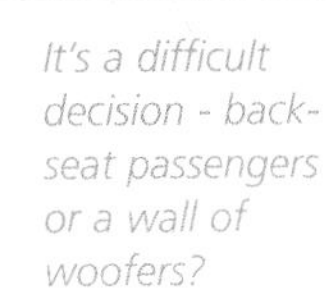

It's a difficult decision - back-seat passengers or a wall of woofers?

ICE

Sub woofer

If the boot on your car is a bit tatty, this is the time to sort it out. An install will never look good if the boot's a mess to begin with. So trim things up to look the part before you start on the music. Follow the steps and fit a new false boot floor and trim up the wheelarch and boot slam panel to make things look tidy. It only takes a bit of MDF and a roll of trunk-liner carpet, so if your car looks a bit worse for wear in the back, you know what to do, don't you?

01 The first job is to remove the boot carpet and spare wheel.

06 The ready-made sub box we fitted was first stuffed with wadding to help the speaker's performance.

07 The wiring may already be connected to the terminal cup on the box, so the ends just need stripping back . . .

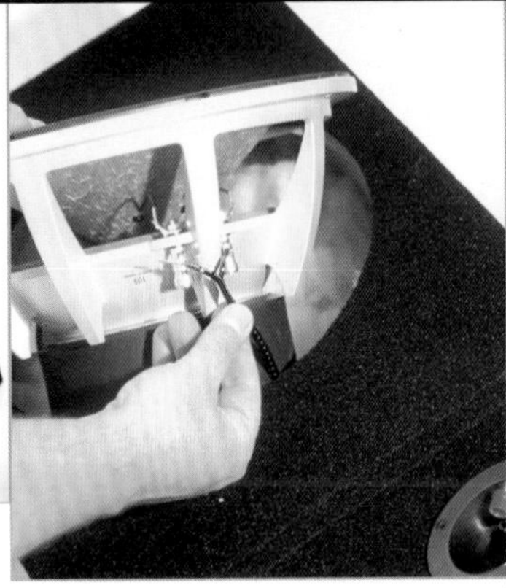

08 . . . and pushing into the sub's sprung-loaded terminals.

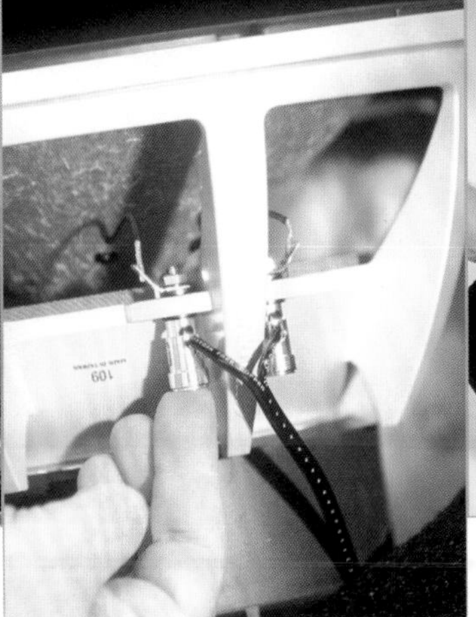

09 After carefully positioning the sub woofer to get it straight, the eight mounting holes are drilled with pilot holes, and the screws tightened steadily by hand to stop them being stripped out.

02 To get a flat boot floor you may have to bin the standard spare wheel and get a GTI space saver.

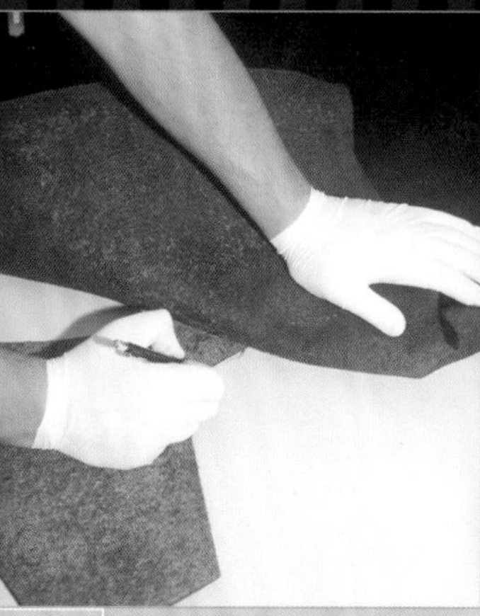

03 After using the boot carpet as a rough template to make an exact-sized cardboard one . . .

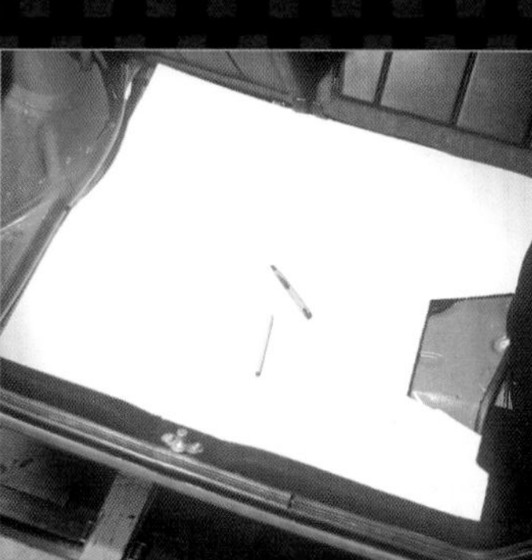

04 . . . cut a new floor from MDF.

05 The cardboard insert goes over the lump in the floor, and once it is covered with carpet, you can't tell that the floor isn't flat.

10 The wire from the amplifier is clamped under these screw terminals after it has been stripped back and covered with heatshrink. This neatens the cable ends and makes it more difficult to short out the wiring.

11 Finally screw down the box to the boot floor panel with L brackets. This is a vital job since the box and speaker weigh so much that they would be dangerous if they flew into the car in an accident.

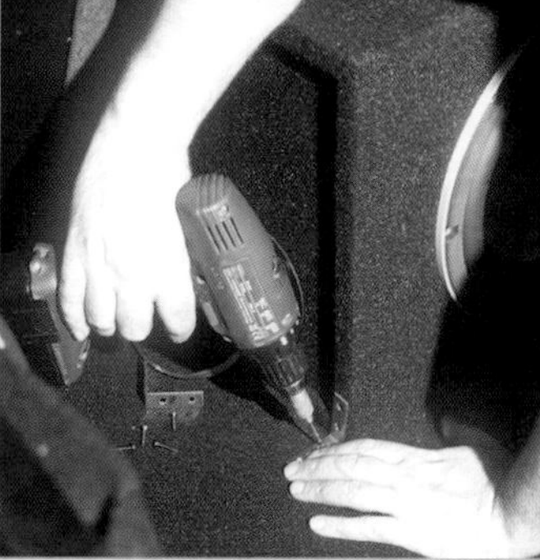

12 Here's the finished boot, with amp rack, floor and wheelarch trimmed up to match. Much better than standard, don't you agree?

Amp fitting

A quality car stereo system is nothing without an amplifier. Even if your head unit reckons it's got 4x50 watts of power, it won't sound anything like a decent amp of the same size.

For our Golf's system we used a four-channel Kicker amp to drive the front speakers and the sub woofer. We left the head unit to drive the rear speakers because they don't get that much use anyway.

Because the Golf was getting a pretty big sub box, we wanted to take up as little space as possible with the amp, so we went for a side-mounted rack to keep it out of the way. This left the maximum boot room, and in the unlikely event that the sub box was removed for carrying goodies, the amp won't be a problem.

01 After using a cardboard template to get the right size, cut an MDF panel for the amp to sit on. The slot at the back of the board is for an access flap so you can change the rear light bulbs without having to remove the rack.

Achtung!
MDF dust is nasty stuff to breathe in. Wear a mask when you're cutting, drilling or sanding it.

02 We are going to mount the Kicker amp at an angle to look nicer.

03 Once you figure where you're going to fit it, mark the wiring holes and drill them out.

04 These holes let the amp cables disappear behind the rack rather than trail over the boot floor.

05 This is the access flap being joined by a gaffa tape hinge. With the rack trimmed in trunk-liner carpet, you can hardly see the flap, and you can't see how big the wiring holes are.

06 This is the amp's earth wire. Screw it tightly to a point where the paint has been rubbed down to give a good earth, and then paint over any exposed metal to stop rust.

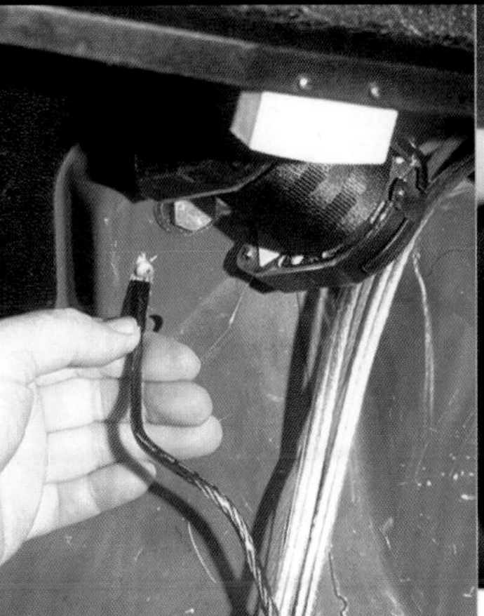

07 Pull the phono cables through the top of the rack, and the speaker and power wires through at the bottom. Screw the rack in place at the top on the shelf support, and at the bottom on two blocks screwed to the boot floor.

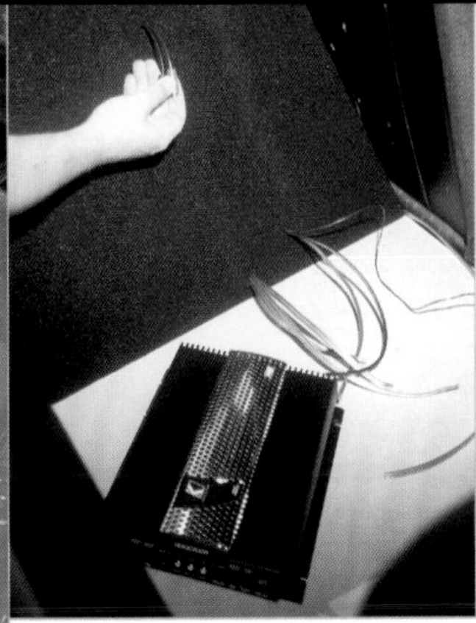

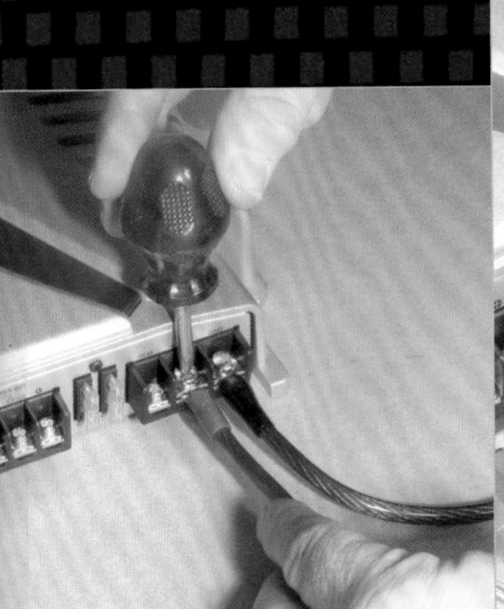

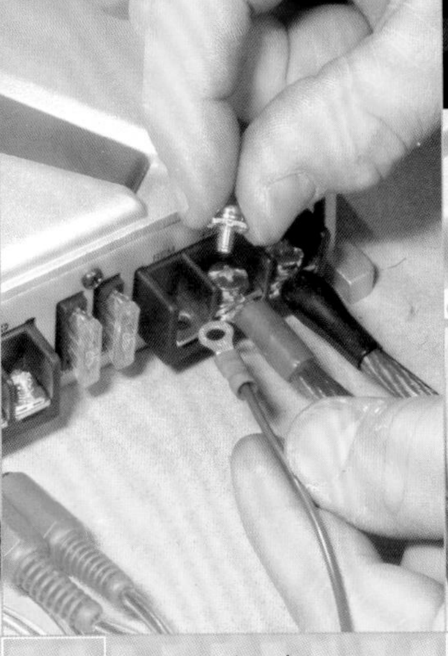

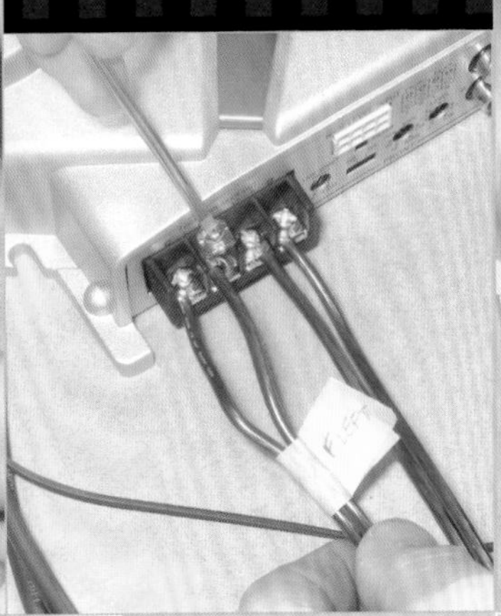

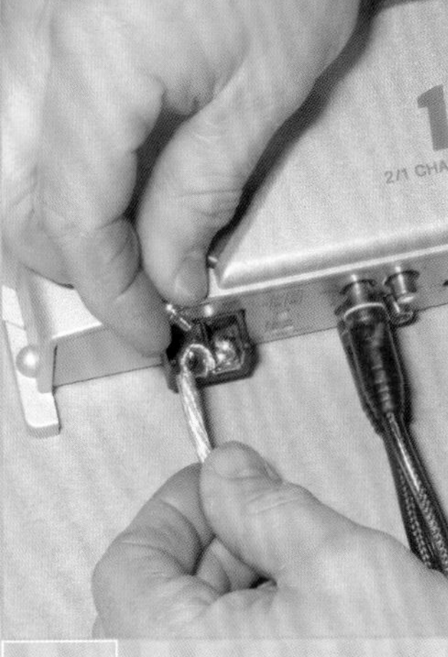

08 Time for some amp-wiring-up guidance. The earth, we did earlier. The all-important live supply is one amp connection you should really use a ring terminal on, rather than just stuffing a bare wire into the hole. And insulate any bare metal on the terminal - that live touches anything else, and the results won't be good.

09 Next up, it's the humble P-cont (remote) lead going on. This performs the vital function of carrying the 'switch-on' signal from your headset - without this, you won't hear much. The good news is, this is one time when size doesn't matter - it doesn't carry much current, so the wire can be as skinny as you like.

10 Read the amp's instruction book carefully when connecting any wires, or you might regret it, especially for bridged or tri-mode. Identify your speaker pos and neg/left and right wires with a piece of tape, and get them screwed on. As with the lives and earths, it's also vital there's no stray bits of wire left poking out.

11 It's not essential to use terminals on every amp connection. If you twist up the bared end of your wire first, then curl it like this so it wraps round the screw, you're sorted. Just make sure none of the bare wires can touch each other.

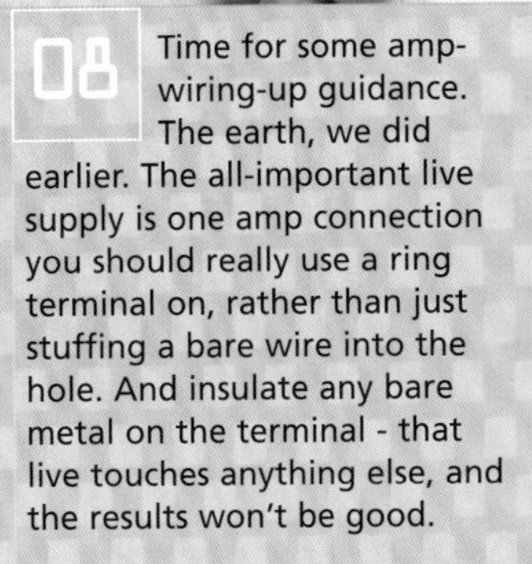

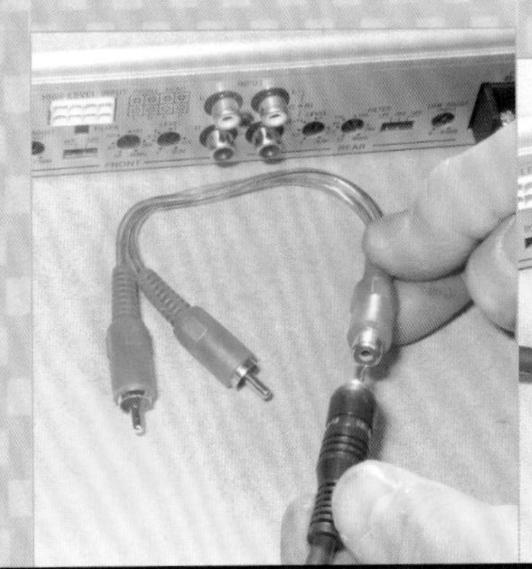

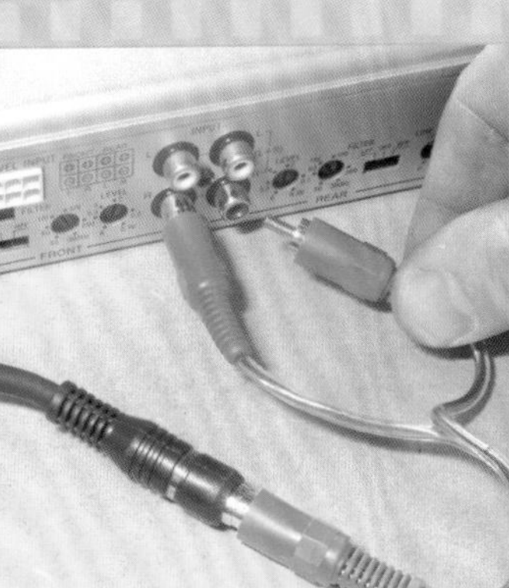

12 If you're using a four-channel amp to run front and rear speakers, you should really take a separate RCA lead from the front and rear outputs on your headset. There is a way of using just one RCA, however, by using adapter leads known as splitters (cunning, eh?). These plug into each end of the RCA lead, and double the number of outputs. Not all headsets offer two sets of RCA outputs (pre-outs), anyway.

13 Splitters aren't always clearly marked for left and right channels, so check what you're doing carefully - watch the red (right) and white (left) colour-coding, too. You can use splitters to run more than one amp from one RCA lead (though the 'gurus' say you shouldn't). But if the system ends up sounding fine, who cares?

14 A good tip is to leave the amps loose until after you've set them up - if you can, leave good access to the gain adjustment (volume) screws after final fitting, too. Starting at normal listening volume, with the amp gain turned down, put on a kicking track, then turn the gain up until the speakers just start to distort. Turn the gain down a tad from there, and you've a good basic setting. Amp gain and headset faders can now be tweaked to give a good balanced sound - or whatever tickles your lugholes.

15 Back to our Golf install, and the amp's in place - now the wires are going on. We'll have it kicking in no time.

Tricks 'n' tips

Very few systems work 100%, first time. If the amp LEDs don't light up, for instance, are they getting power? Are the P-cont/remote wires connected properly? If the sub doesn't kick, is the amp switch set to bridged or tri-mode, not stereo? Are the low-pass switches in the correct position? RTFM.

Wiring

If you don't wire up your car audio system correctly, you'll find yourself with all sorts of problems. Getting it right means decent music, no fire hazards, and no weird noises coming from the speakers. Getting it wrong can mean your car goes up in smoke.

When you're running the amplifier power wire, you must use a fuse near the battery, and you must use a grommet to protect the wire where it goes through the bulkhead. It's also a good idea to run the power lead well away from any vehicle looms to keep interference out of the system. At least the Golf Mk 2 doesn't have any airbags or seat belt tensioners to worry about.

The signal cable from head unit to amplifier needs running away from the car's wiring as well as the amplifier power cable so that it doesn't pick up any nasty noises. Speaker wire is the least affected by this, but it's still a good idea to keep it away from the car's looms just in case.

01 Crimping the terminal and fuseholder onto the power cable is a job for a large crimping tool. If you haven't got a suitable tool, you should be able to get a garage to nip them up for you.

Tricks 'n' tips

Don't forget that fantastic ICE makes a fantastic drain on the battery. You may need to fit an uprated battery, or even a secondary battery system. Ask your local ICE expert.

06 Moving inside, it's time to remove the seats, seatbelt, centre console and carpet to run the wire down the car. The seats are easy . . .

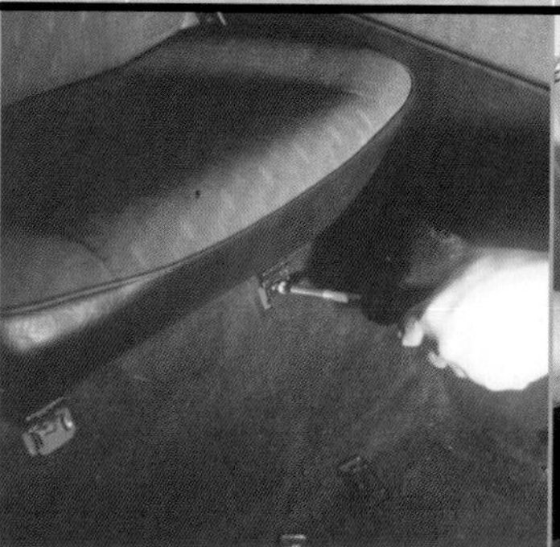

07 . . . and the sill rails come off once the screws are removed at each end.

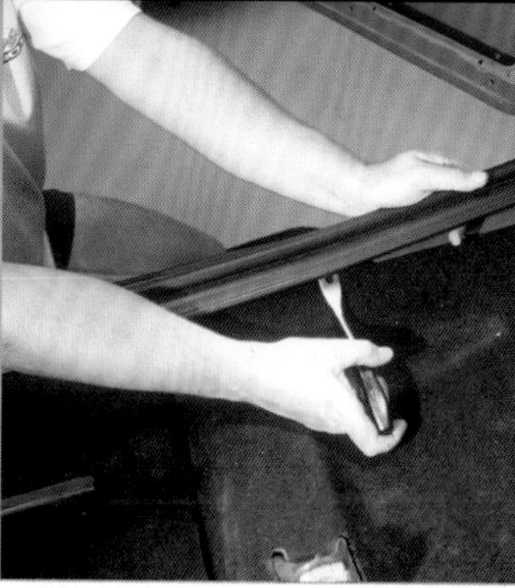

08 Be careful when taking the seatbelt off. Note the sequence of washers and spacers on the bolt so that it goes back together properly later.

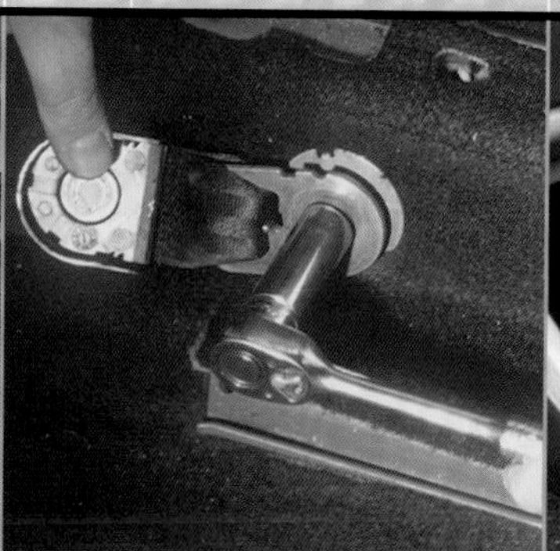

09 Once the gear lever gaiter panel has been prised up, the centre console's held by just one screw. Don't believe me?

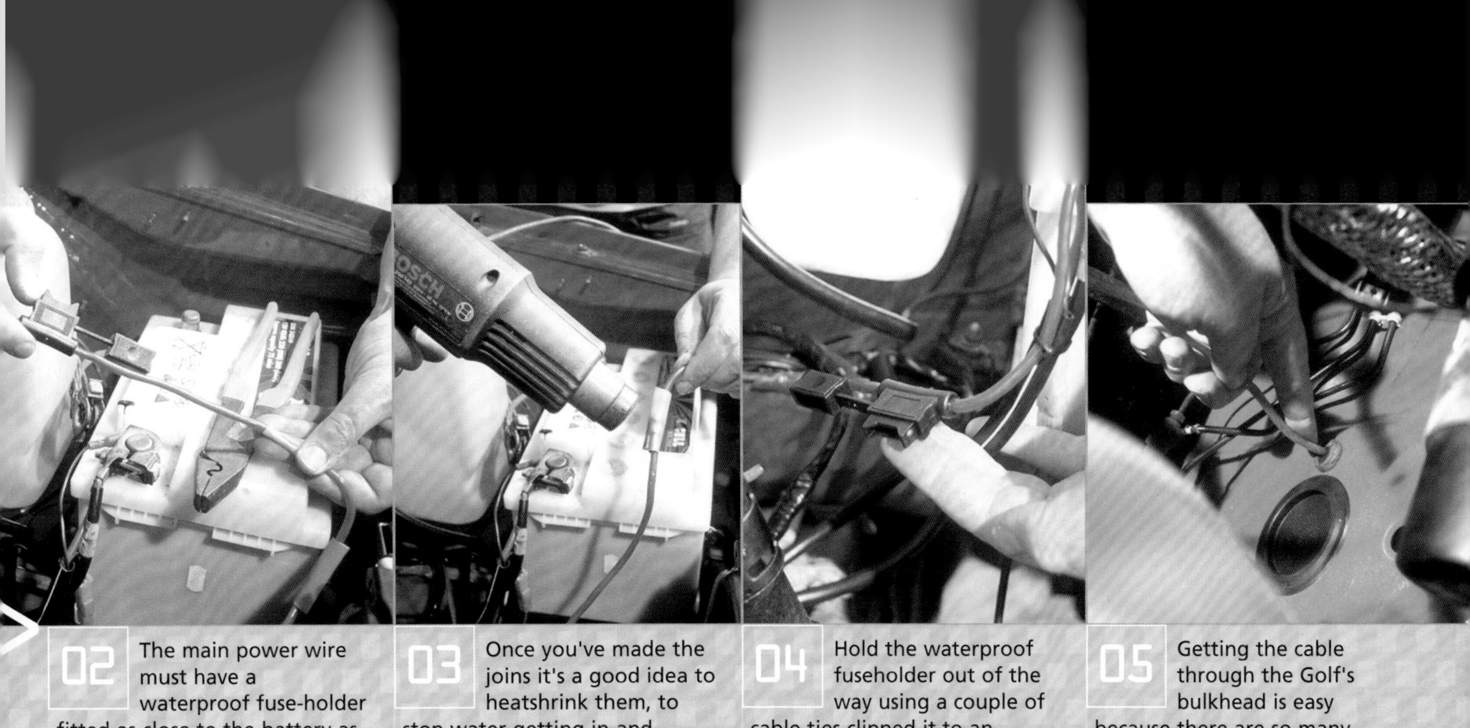

02 The main power wire must have a waterproof fuse-holder fitted as close to the battery as possible, as shown here.

03 Once you've made the joins it's a good idea to heatshrink them, to stop water getting in and corroding the joint.

04 Hold the waterproof fuseholder out of the way using a couple of cable ties clipped it to an existing VW cable. This looks neater, the fuse is still accessible, and it's safer too.

05 Getting the cable through the Golf's bulkhead is easy because there are so many grommeted holes already there. Simply remove a grommet, cut a small hole in it, and feed the power cable through the bulkhead before refitting the grommet into the hole. Do not put a cable through an unprotected hole. It will short out and cause problems later.

10 Well, here's the proof. You might need to wiggle it (just a little bit) to get it out.

11 Try to keep the power wire away from vehicle looms where possible. . .

12 . . . and away from other stereo cables.

13 Tape the wiring in place or use original clips if possible to keep things neat.

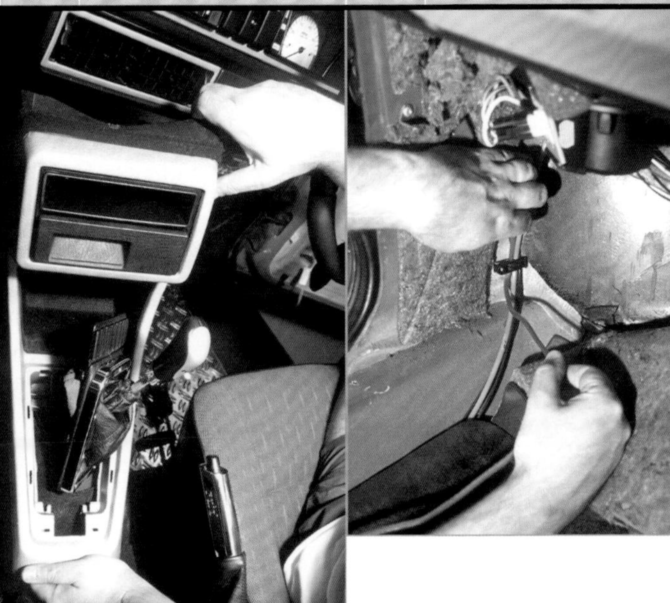

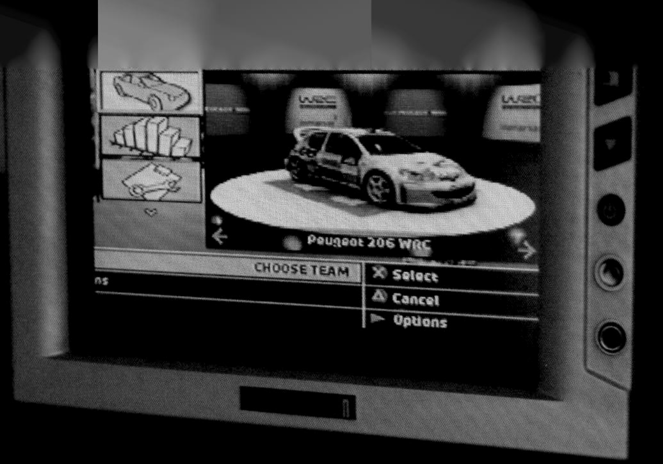

Playstation & screen

Bored of your CDs? Nothing on the radio? We have just the thing if you and a mate get bored, stuck in a 10-mile tailback on a bank holiday. Definitely a growing trend on the ICE scene, no top modded motor's complete these days without a games console, screen, DVD - where d'you stop? Just don't get caught playing it while you're moving, that's all.

Screen

01 The trickiest bit of all is deciding where it'll go - obviously, both front seat people have to see it, so somewhere central, but how high up? Try the screen and its bracket in place, and check it adjusts how you want it. Is it accessible from below/behind, for feeding-in the wires? This spot's looking good, but even with the headset out, drilling a hole's a bit tricky (the screen's too close).

02 On a Golf, the centre console's a land of opportunity when it comes to fitting a screen. If you can live without the centre cubbyhole and the ashtray, a screen fits here a treat . . .

03 . . . the only bummer is, you can't just unclip the unwanted plastic bits from the console – a touch with the hacksaw's the only way.

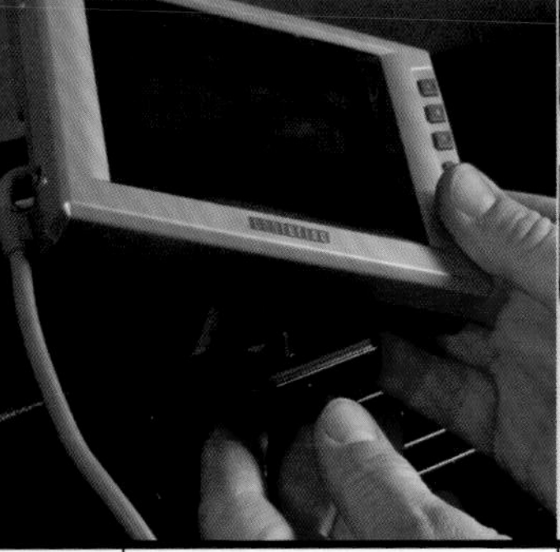

04 Now the screen can be mounted on, and the video lead plugged together. This Centurion screen's a budget model, but still has built-in speakers and even a headphone socket. Looks good, but it's not working yet - let's finish the job.

05 Our screen came with an all-in-one lead containing the three-part video feed from the PS2 (or DVD), and also the power supply/earth. We'll connect up the PS2 later - for now, we want power to our screen. They give you a cigar lighter plug, but this looks a bit pants - let's do it properly. Prise apart the halves of your plug, and you get wires - chop the end off . . .

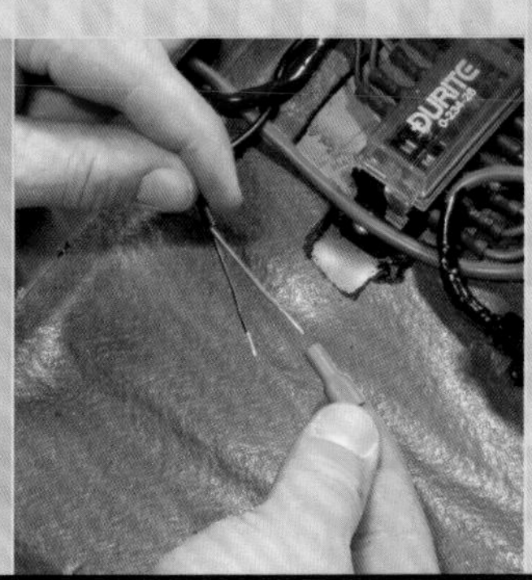

06 . . . strip the ends, and we have skinny red and black wires. The red's a live feed (you guessed it), which we're taking from the fusebox. The fusebox is a good spot to find an earth point for the black wire, too - or you can drill your own. The little green lights now tell us the screen's ready for input - let's give it some.

Playstation

01 To give power to your Playstation, you need an AC inverter - ours was about £50 from Comet. What this does is take your car's 12-volt DC electrics, and turns it into 240-volt AC, giving you a domestic three-pin socket in your car - how cool is that? As with our screen, our inverter came with a fag lighter plug, which we dismantled. This time, we took the live feed and earth from the same places as our amplifier (heavier leads).

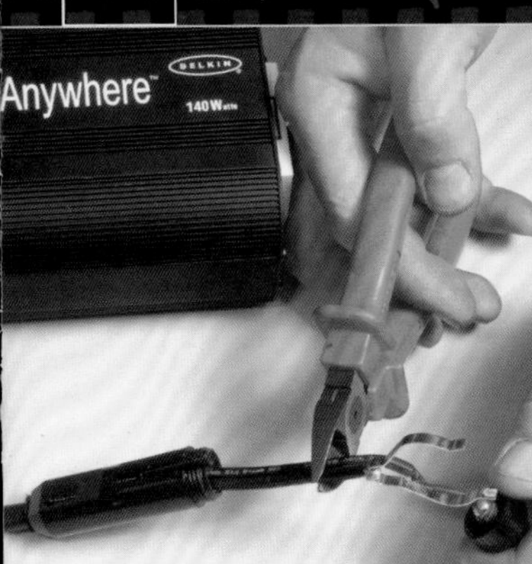

02 Our inverter had to be in the boot, to be near the PS2 itself - but we didn't want to make a feature of it. We struggled a bit for some kind of mounting bracket, but we managed to make one from a huge Jubilee clip . . .

03 . . . and there he is, wired-up and looking sweet. The Playstation now has power - what else do we need?

04 There's a whole bunch of wires to run down the car, so this is a good excuse to remove a seat or two and lift the carpets (if you want to do a neat job, that is). Besides the two controllers, there's the video/audio outputs to our screen to connect. Luckily, they're so well colour-coded, there's no danger of messing this up.

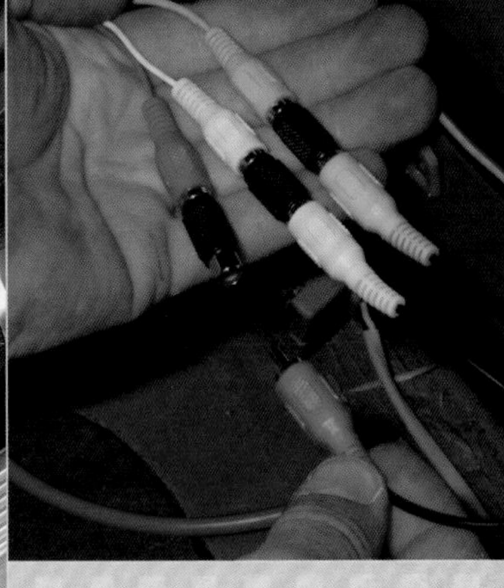

05 Just to ensure nothing goes wrong when those carpets go back down, tape up each connection. This stops them coming apart, and also stops the connectors earthing-out on the car floor.

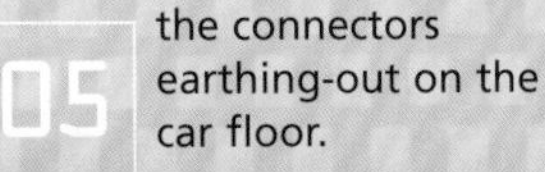

06 With power and video leads connected, and a screen that's ready to go, choose a suitable secure spot for the console, and its plug . . .

07 . . . and play. Our first-ever Playstation install, and it goes like a dream. Total cost, including screen, inverter and PS2 (with free game) - about £400. Now that's what we call a bargain - true in-car entertainment, and maximum respect.

12

Engines

Engines

Faster, faster!

We're not to going to tell you how to fit a VR6 into your Golf - that'd take a whole book on its own. If you're that serious, check out one of the many specialists around the country. What we tell you how to do is fit an air filter, tidy up your engine and generally sort what's already there. Always make sure your motor is sweet to start with, and get it tuned professionally after doing each job to get the most out of your mods.

Replacement engine

If your engine's past it, or you want a simpler route to more performance, how about an engine change? The trick is, of course, to make sure the "new" engine's better than the old one - some "recon" engines might actually be worse!

If your car's done a huge mileage, a newer lower-mileage motor will make a big difference. As long as the new engine's the same size as the old one, it won't affect the insurance - all you do is tell the DVLA, and they'll update the car's registration document.

Fitting a larger engine should be an easy enough upgrade, but this time, the insurance must be told, and it's likely they'll insist on a full engineer's report (these aren't especially expensive - look one up in the Yellow Pages). However, by the time you've fitted the new larger engine, your car is now officially "modified" and your premium is more than a standard larger-engined Golf would be!

Breathe easier

One of the simplest items to fit, the replacement air filter element, has been around for years. It has recently been overtaken in popularity by the induction kit (which is generally only available for fuel injection engines).

The idea of these items is to increase the flow of air into the engine, to help the engine to "breathe", but they can upset the air/fuel mixture and cause poor running. Having the car set-up afterwards by a rolling road is pretty much essential to make the mods actually work. On some fuel injection engines, feeding in extra air will "fool" the injection system into providing more fuel - ultimately, this will increase performance a bit, but will greatly increase fuel consumption and lead to an over-rich mixture, which could cause the car to fail the MOT. And don't even think about just taking out the air filter. The filter is there for a reason and you'll quickly damage the engine without one.

Once you've fitted your new filter or induction kit, even if you don't take the car to a rolling road for setting up, at least take it to a garage and have the emissions checked - any minor adjustments should ensure that the engine will still tick over okay, and should pass an MOT.

Other air filter-type mods

If you can't stretch to an induction kit, you could drill holes in the air filter box. But, don't try this on any Golf except the GTI (with the deep, square air filter box) or you might as well take the air filter out completely which is a no-no).

Only drill the air filter box below the level where the filter element sits, and don't drill on the engine-side of the box, just the bottom, front, back and the side nearest the wing. Making your airbox look like a Swiss cheese won't make the car faster, but it does give a throaty induction roar.

The same sort of effect can be gained by fitting a "power-pipe" between the air filter and the inlet manifold - this also has the welcome bonus of looking cool, too.

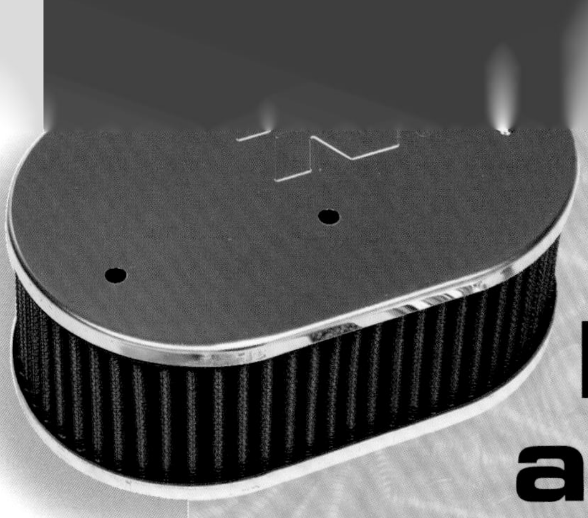

Bolt-on air filter

This is generally the only option available for carburettor-equipped engines. The standard air cleaner assembly is junked, and an air filter is bolted to the top of the carburettor instead.

There are usually two vacuum pipes running to the air cleaner housing, which must be disconnected (the pipe running to the base of the carb must be plugged). The vacuum pipes are used to improve fuel economy when the engine's cold, and to prevent carburettor icing in cold weather. Carburettor icing is a serious condition, where ice forms in or around the carb, but better filter manufacturers supply a kit to feed the warm air into the filter.

The old air filter will also have a larger-diameter crankcase breather hose (for sucking out oil fumes), which shouldn't be left disconnected, and should not be plugged. Some companies supply a kit to fit the pipe into the new filter, or can supply a separate "breather" which you fit onto the old pipe. If the breather pipe has to be left disconnected, make sure it can't get blocked, or kinked. Bear in mind that leaving it disconnected may lead to poor running and high emissions.

01 Remove the element, then disconnect the breather pipe from the air cleaner.

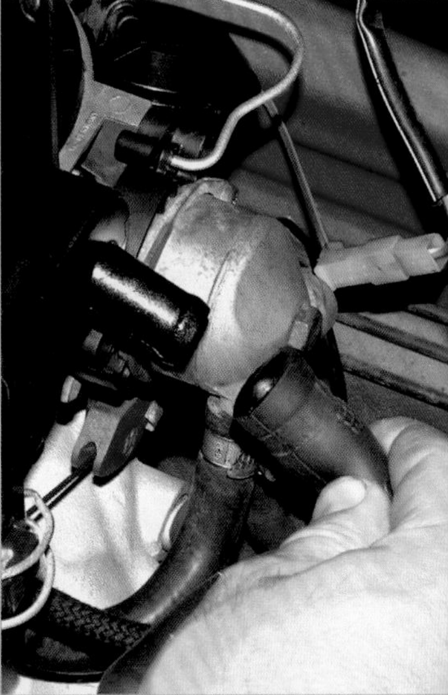

06 Ft the cork gasket over the top of the carb, then screw in the mounting studs.

07 The breather pipe which connects back to the rocker cover must not be left disconnected. K&N suggest drilling a hole in the filter base, to allow fitting a longer pipe (not supplied) into it. Offer the base into position first, to judge where the hole needs to be. Mark the hole on masking tape, and drill through.

08 Another option with the breather is to buy the separate filter which plugs into the end of the existing pipe. Our breather had to be oiled first . . .

Disconnect the two small vacuum pipes from the temperature switch on the side of the air cleaner. Note which one of the two pipes connects

02 back to the carburettor, as this will have to be blocked off later.

03 Pull the large air induction pipe from the inside of the front wing.

Check round the air filter to make sure there's nothing else

04 attached, then remove the air cleaner completely.

Find the small-bore vacuum pipe you disconnected earlier, which runs to the base of the

05 carb. Plug the open end of the pipe with a suitable bolt or screw.

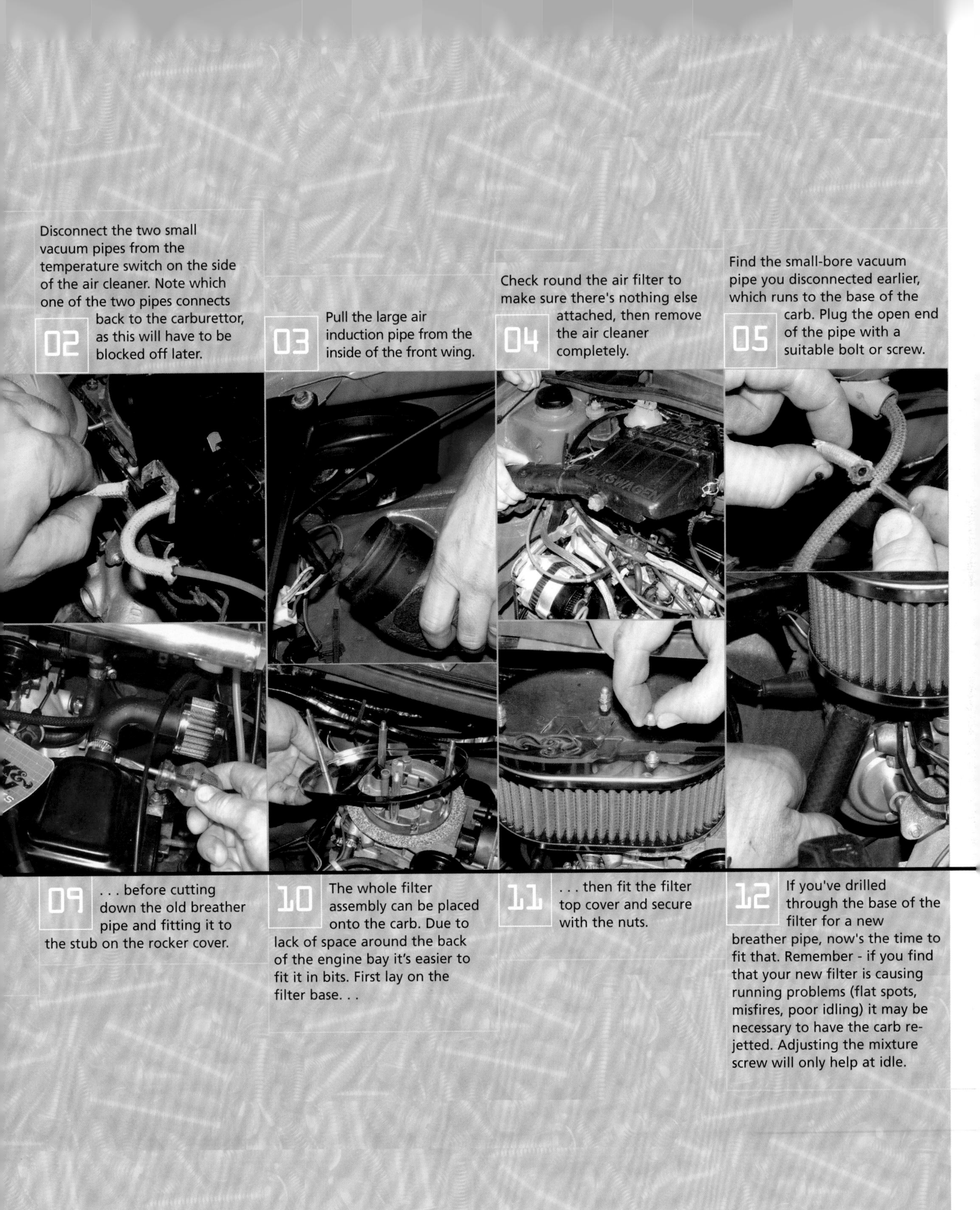

09 . . . before cutting down the old breather pipe and fitting it to the stub on the rocker cover.

10 The whole filter assembly can be placed onto the carb. Due to lack of space around the back of the engine bay it's easier to fit it in bits. First lay on the filter base. . .

11 . . . then fit the filter top cover and secure with the nuts.

12 If you've drilled through the base of the filter for a new breather pipe, now's the time to fit that. Remember - if you find that your new filter is causing running problems (flat spots, misfires, poor idling) it may be necessary to have the carb re-jetted. Adjusting the mixture screw will only help at idle.

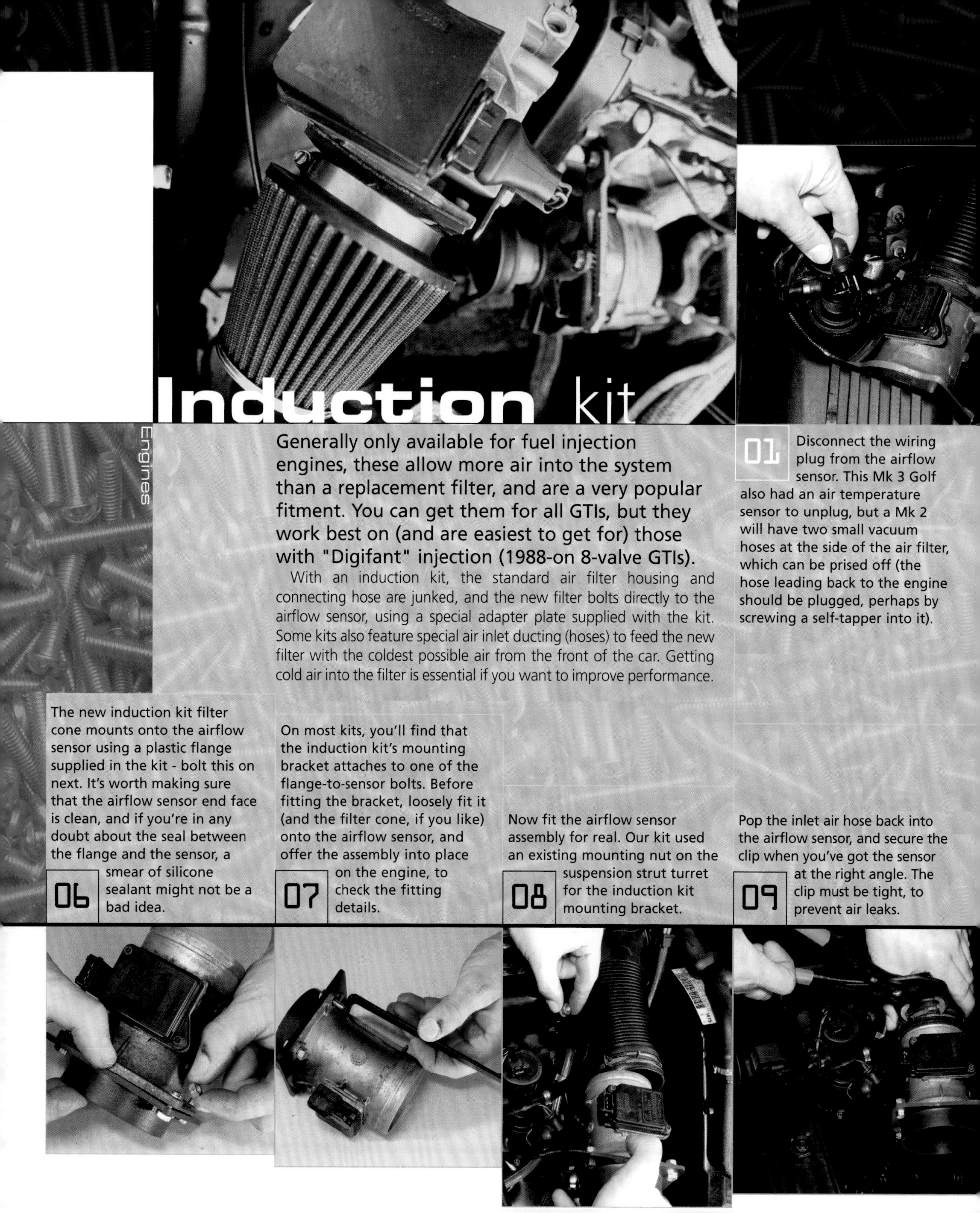

Induction kit

Engines

Generally only available for fuel injection engines, these allow more air into the system than a replacement filter, and are a very popular fitment. You can get them for all GTIs, but they work best on (and are easiest to get for) those with "Digifant" injection (1988-on 8-valve GTIs).

With an induction kit, the standard air filter housing and connecting hose are junked, and the new filter bolts directly to the airflow sensor, using a special adapter plate supplied with the kit. Some kits also feature special air inlet ducting (hoses) to feed the new filter with the coldest possible air from the front of the car. Getting cold air into the filter is essential if you want to improve performance.

01 Disconnect the wiring plug from the airflow sensor. This Mk 3 Golf also had an air temperature sensor to unplug, but a Mk 2 will have two small vacuum hoses at the side of the air filter, which can be prised off (the hose leading back to the engine should be plugged, perhaps by screwing a self-tapper into it).

06 The new induction kit filter cone mounts onto the airflow sensor using a plastic flange supplied in the kit - bolt this on next. It's worth making sure that the airflow sensor end face is clean, and if you're in any doubt about the seal between the flange and the sensor, a smear of silicone sealant might not be a bad idea.

07 On most kits, you'll find that the induction kit's mounting bracket attaches to one of the flange-to-sensor bolts. Before fitting the bracket, loosely fit it (and the filter cone, if you like) onto the airflow sensor, and offer the assembly into place on the engine, to check the fitting details.

08 Now fit the airflow sensor assembly for real. Our kit used an existing mounting nut on the suspension strut turret for the induction kit mounting bracket.

09 Pop the inlet air hose back into the airflow sensor, and secure the clip when you've got the sensor at the right angle. The clip must be tight, to prevent air leaks.

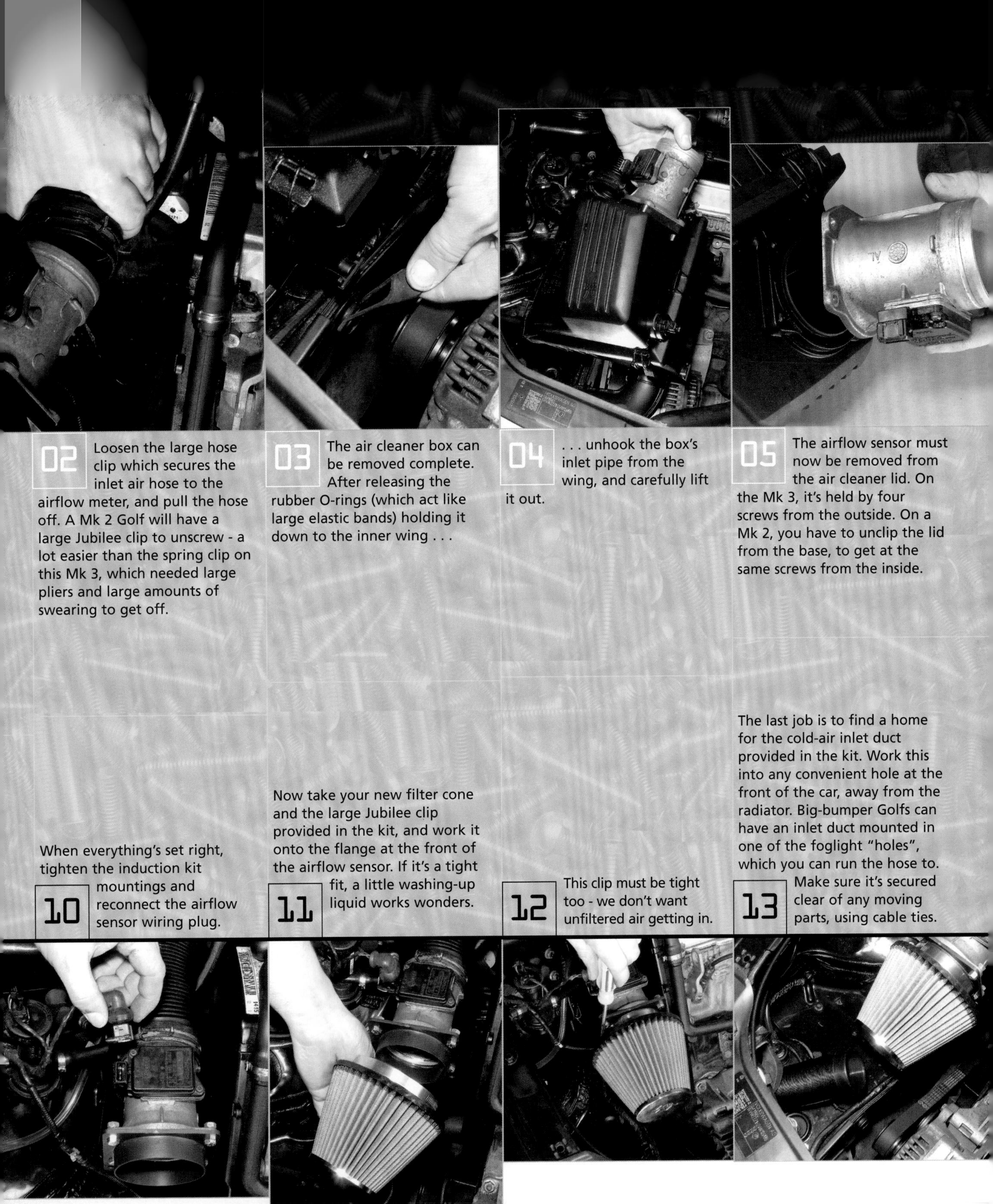

02 Loosen the large hose clip which secures the inlet air hose to the airflow meter, and pull the hose off. A Mk 2 Golf will have a large Jubilee clip to unscrew - a lot easier than the spring clip on this Mk 3, which needed large pliers and large amounts of swearing to get off.

03 The air cleaner box can be removed complete. After releasing the rubber O-rings (which act like large elastic bands) holding it down to the inner wing . . .

04 . . . unhook the box's inlet pipe from the wing, and carefully lift it out.

05 The airflow sensor must now be removed from the air cleaner lid. On the Mk 3, it's held by four screws from the outside. On a Mk 2, you have to unclip the lid from the base, to get at the same screws from the inside.

10 When everything's set right, tighten the induction kit mountings and reconnect the airflow sensor wiring plug.

11 Now take your new filter cone and the large Jubilee clip provided in the kit, and work it onto the flange at the front of the airflow sensor. If it's a tight fit, a little washing-up liquid works wonders.

12 This clip must be tight too - we don't want unfiltered air getting in.

13 The last job is to find a home for the cold-air inlet duct provided in the kit. Work this into any convenient hole at the front of the car, away from the radiator. Big-bumper Golfs can have an inlet duct mounted in one of the foglight "holes", which you can run the hose to. Make sure it's secured clear of any moving parts, using cable ties.

No quicker, **but it looks nice**

Of course, if you're embarrassed about how your engine looks, you could always claim your bonnet pull's knackered, and only open the bonnet while no-one else is around. But come on, even a boggo Golf's engine bay can be made to look well smart, with just a few simple mods.

First up - try cleaning the engine! How do you expect to emulate the show-stopping cars if your mechanicals are covered in grot? Get busy with the degreaser (Gunk's a good bet), then get the hosepipe out. You can take it down to the local jetwash if you like, but remember your mobile - if you get carried away with the high-power spray, you might find the car won't start afterwards!

When it's all dry (and running again), you can start. Get the polish to all the painted surfaces you reasonably can, and don't be afraid to unbolt a few of the simpler items to gain better access. Take off the rocker cover, and paint it to match your chosen scheme (heat-resistant paint is a must, really, such as brake caliper paint), set off with a funky oil filler cap. Or get a chrome rocker cover. The same spray you'd use for beautifying your Golf's interior plastic trim will also do wonders for things like rad hoses and other rubber items under the bonnet - but don't get any on the rubber drivebelts, or your Golf will squeal for mercy!

A strut brace is a nice underbonnet feature, especially when chromed, and bonnet lifter struts actually do something useful, besides looking cool. Braided hose covers, ally battery covers and bottles, mirror panels - all give the underbonnet a touch of glamour.

HT leads

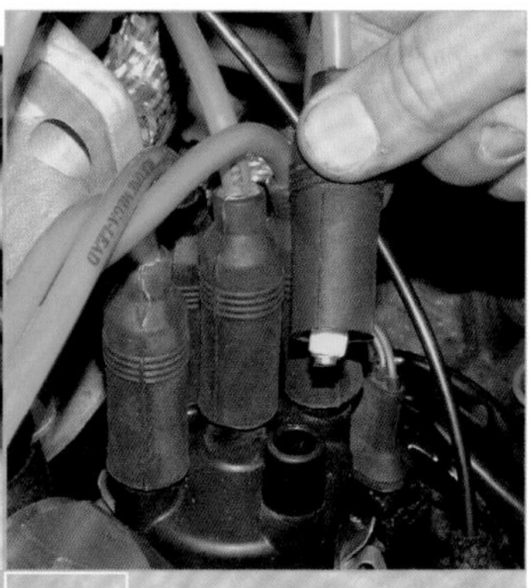

One word of warning about coloured HT leads and distributor caps - cheap ones really don't work, and could leave you stranded.

Ignition HT leads must be fitted in the right order - muck it up, and you'll have a Golf which won't start. If you really get it wrong, it's possible to cause an explosion inside the air filter! The trick here is to work step-by-step - never pull all the leads off at once, unless you've marked them first.

01 If you're changing the leads and distributor cap, fit the new leads first. Working on one lead at a time, pull the old lead off the spark plug, trace it through to the cap, and pull it off. Compare the lead with the new set, and pick the one closest in length. Fit the new lead to the cap, then route it through and fit to the spark plug.

02 When you've done all the plug leads, fit the new "king" lead to the ignition coil. Trace the lead from the connection in the centre of the cap up to the coil. In all cases, if the old leads are held in by clips or cable-ties, make sure the new leads are also tied up or clipped in tight (but without stretching them).

03 If you're changing the cap, remove the old one (held on by two spring clips or screws). Turn the caps over, and look underneath for notches in the rim, which locate in the distributor - turn the caps so that they are sitting the same way. One by one, transfer the HT leads from the old cap to the same position on the new one, fit the new cap and secure with the spring clips or screws.

Chrome battery cover

01 Not much to fitting one of these. Just one word of warning – don't leave out the packing piece inside the cover. Placing an unprotected metal cover directly across the metal battery terminals is a great way to have a serious fire - without the inner packing, that's just what you'll get.

02 There - now doesn't that look nice? Now you'll have to get an ally washer bottle to match.

Braiding hoses

Never fit hoses unless the engine's completely cold to start with - like first thing in the morning. The smell of burning flesh is never pleasant, especially when it's yours. Depending on which hoses you decide to treat, you could be removing ones containing hot coolant or fuel.

If you've got a GTI, and plan to braid your fuel lines, disconnect the hoses very carefully - have some rags wrapped around the pipes, so you don't spray high-pressure fuel everywhere.

01 First step is to remove your chosen hose. If supplies of braiding are limited, go for the hoses at the top of the engine first, then the ones underneath you can't see won't matter so much. If you're doing the cooling system hoses, drain the coolant and unscrew the Jubilee clips . . .

02 . . . or use pliers across the tangs of the sprung-type ones.

03 Unroll your braiding, then expand it to the right size using a suitable blunt object. Like a screwdriver handle.

Achtung!

If you're braiding coolant hoses, feel them first to make sure they're COLD. Have a bowl ready to catch the coolant in (antifreeze is poisonous despite its sweet smell, and will make a mess of your paintwork if you douse the engine bay and front wings with it!).

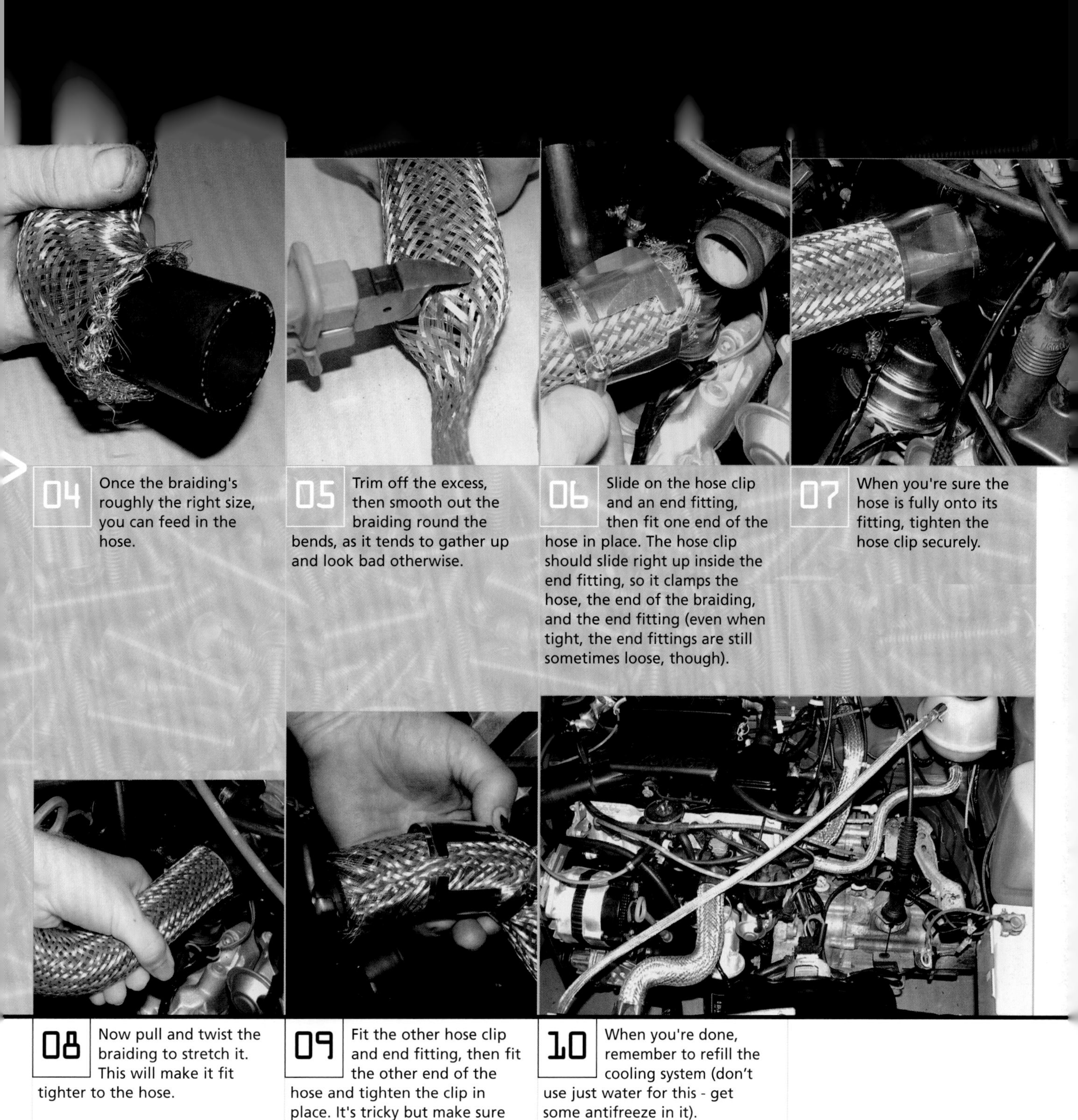

04 Once the braiding's roughly the right size, you can feed in the hose.

05 Trim off the excess, then smooth out the braiding round the bends, as it tends to gather up and look bad otherwise.

06 Slide on the hose clip and an end fitting, then fit one end of the hose in place. The hose clip should slide right up inside the end fitting, so it clamps the hose, the end of the braiding, and the end fitting (even when tight, the end fittings are still sometimes loose, though).

07 When you're sure the hose is fully onto its fitting, tighten the hose clip securely.

08 Now pull and twist the braiding to stretch it. This will make it fit tighter to the hose.

09 Fit the other hose clip and end fitting, then fit the other end of the hose and tighten the clip in place. It's tricky but make sure be sure the hose clip's in the right place on the stub, otherwise you'll have a leak!

10 When you're done, remember to refill the cooling system (don't use just water for this - get some antifreeze in it).

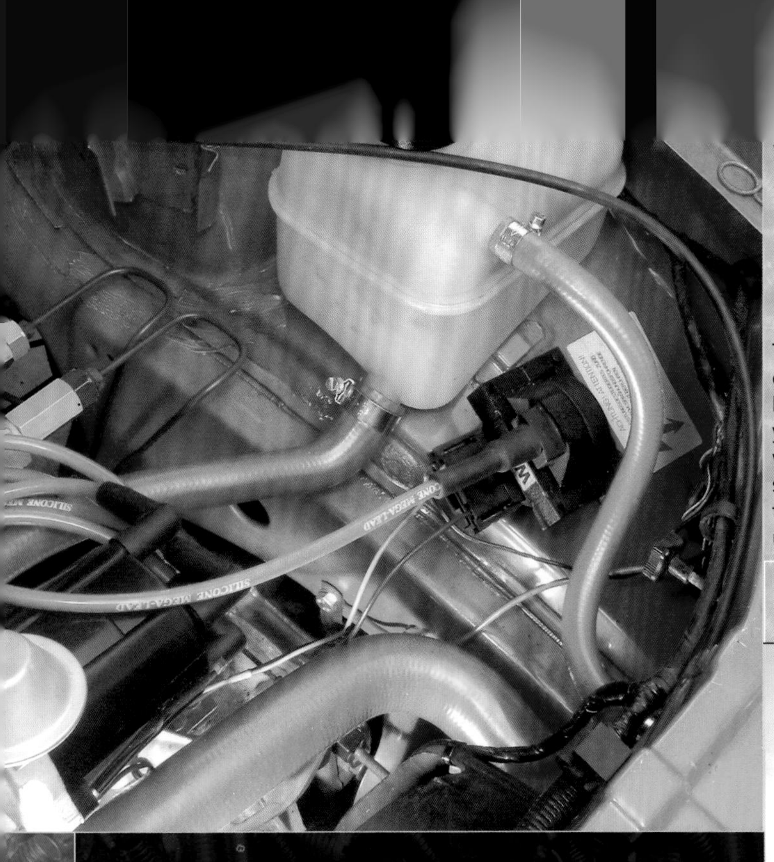

You's a hose

There are many ways to add detail and colour to otherwise boring components. Spraying your hoses is just one of those ways. Only apply paint that is suitable for engine bay use, as temperatures get very high under the hood. The good folk

01 from ABC Design supplied our Tube-It hose paint.

Choose the most visible hoses first, and be careful undoing the hose clips - there could be coolant or fuel in there. Don't even think about spraying the hoses in place - do you really want to colour-code the entire underbonnet area? Give the pipe a good clean to thoroughly degrease it - any oil

02 or silicone-slippery stuff, and the paint won't stick.

Achtung!

The engine must be completely cold before you start. Even if you've only done a quick lap, it would be dangerous to attempt doing anything with a remotely warm engine, as the fluids inside the pipe are often a lot hotter than they appear. Be warned!

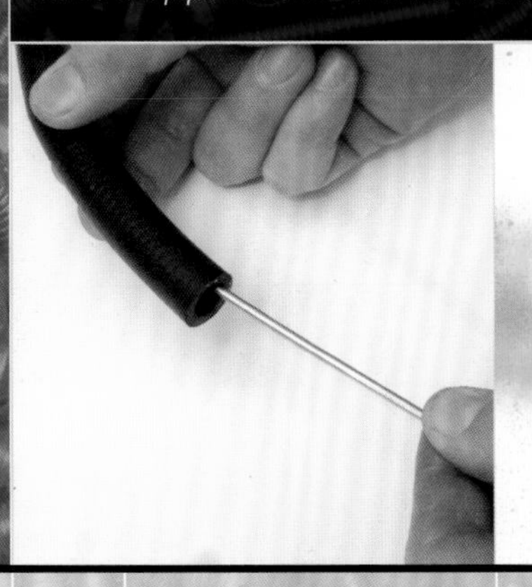

03 A preferred way of spraying, to ensure maximum coverage, is to hang the pipe from above. Use a stiff piece of wire inserted into the end of the hose (NOT poked through the hose) to hold onto.

04 Apply the paint in three or four light layers until pipe is evenly covered. You'll also have to wait a while (ideally, leave overnight) before that hose can go back on.

05 Given enough time to dry, this hose paint's really good stuff - doesn't crack or flake off. But we wouldn't advise going ballistic with the pressure washer, once the hose is back on - the paint might not be quite that good.

06 Tighten all hose clips securely - coolant leaks are not cool, and fuel leaks could be deadly. If you've lost any coolant, the system will need topping-up once you're done - you'll want a 50-50 mix of antifreeze and water, not just plain water.

Silicon **heaven**

Golf GTIs ('88-on 8Vs, all 16Vs and all Mk 3s) have an engine management system with a 'computer' at its heart, known as the ECU, or Electronic Control Unit. The ECU contains several computer chips, at least one of which has programmed onto it the preferred fuel/air mixture and ignition advance setting for any given engine speed or load - this information is known as a computer 'map', and the system refers to it constantly while the car's being driven. Obviously, with the current trend towards fuel economy and reducing harmful exhaust emissions, the values in this 'map' are set, well, conservatively, let's say (read 'boring'). With a little tweaking - like richening-up the mixture, say - the engine can be made to produce more power, or response will be improved, or both. At the expense of the environment. Oh well.

Companies like Superchips offer replacement computer chips which feature a computer map where driveability and performance are given priority over outright economy (although the company claims that, under certain conditions, even fuel economy can be better, with their products). While a chip like this does offer proven power gains on its own, it's obviously best to combine a chip with other enhancements, and to have the whole lot set up at the same time. By the time you've fitted an induction kit, four-branch manifold, big-bore pipe, and maybe even a fast-road cam, adding a chip is the icing on the cake - chipping an already-modified motor will liberate even more horses, or at least combine it with majorly-improved response. Volkswagen tuning specialists are best placed to advise you on the most effective tuning mods.

Another feature programmed into the ECU is a rev limiter, which cuts the ignition (or fuel) progressively when the pre-set rev limit is reached. Most replacement chips have the rev limiter reset higher, or removed altogether. Not totally sure this is a good thing - if the engine's not maintained properly (low oil level, cambelt changes neglected), removing the rev limiter and running beyond the red line would be a quick way to kill it. But a well-maintained engine with a rally cam fitted could rev off the clock, if the ECU would let it, so maybe not a bad thing after all...

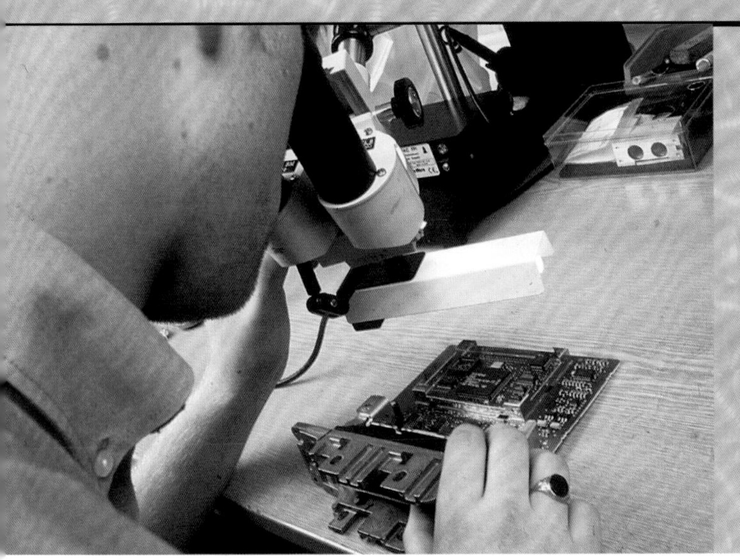

Now the bad news

Chipping is often thought of as an easy, 'no-tell' route to increased performance and driveability - after all, the ECU is well-buried inside the car, not on show, so who's gonna know? Needless to say, the insurance companies have been wise to this trick for a long time. A sure way to tell whether a 'performance' product does what it says on the tin is to see what it'll do to your premium - telling them you're fitting a chip will cost. Big-time. But, in the event of a claim, if they suspect your car's been 'chipped', rest assured, they will make efforts to find out, because if you haven't told them about it, it means they save on paying out. What's an insurance assessor's salary for one day, compared to the thousands you could be claiming in case of an accident or theft? Do it by all means, but at least be honest.

Fitting bonnet **lifters**

01 Once the lifters are fitted, you won't be able to adjust the bonnet fit. So make sure you're not going to need to move it, say for example if you fit a bonnet mounted "badboy" spoiler. Bonnet adjustment involves loosening off the two hinge bolts either side, and a lot of fiddling...

06 . . . then fit the bottom end of the strut (with a large washer, which we sprayed red to match) into the wing, and tighten up.

07 Back to the top, and the top fitting can be fed into the newly-drilled hole.

08 Now you can't see the end of the top fitting, so prise out this bung from the bonnet!

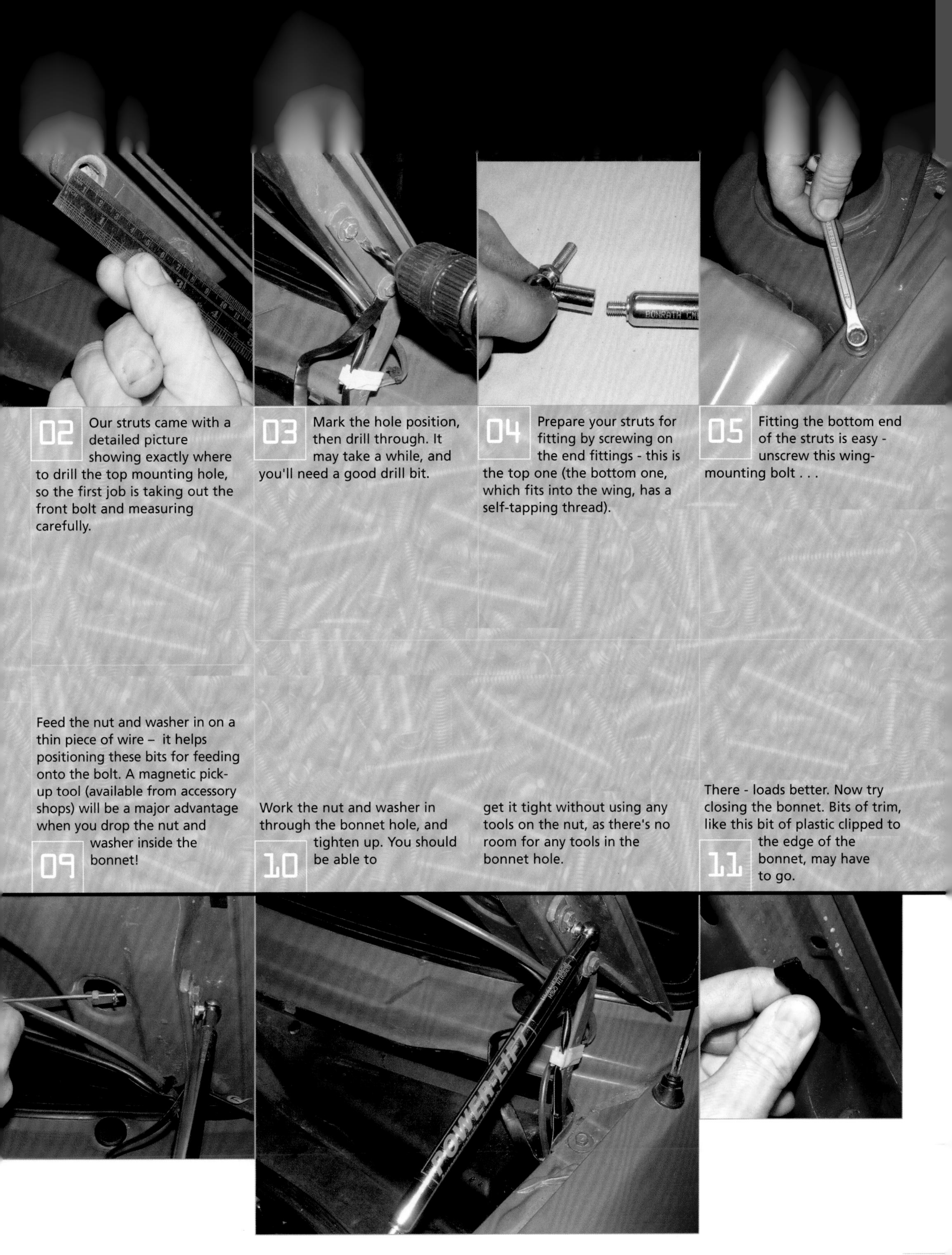

02 Our struts came with a detailed picture showing exactly where to drill the top mounting hole, so the first job is taking out the front bolt and measuring carefully.

03 Mark the hole position, then drill through. It may take a while, and you'll need a good drill bit.

04 Prepare your struts for fitting by screwing on the end fittings - this is the top one (the bottom one, which fits into the wing, has a self-tapping thread).

05 Fitting the bottom end of the struts is easy - unscrew this wing-mounting bolt . . .

09 Feed the nut and washer in on a thin piece of wire – it helps positioning these bits for feeding onto the bolt. A magnetic pick-up tool (available from accessory shops) will be a major advantage when you drop the nut and washer inside the bonnet!

10 Work the nut and washer in through the bonnet hole, and tighten up. You should be able to get it tight without using any tools on the nut, as there's no room for any tools in the bonnet hole.

11 There - loads better. Now try closing the bonnet. Bits of trim, like this bit of plastic clipped to the edge of the bonnet, may have to go.

Although not as effective as a full-uprated exhaust system, a back box alone will make a car sound and look nicer. Make sure you check when you're buying that it can be fitted to a standard system - you'll probably need something called a reducing sleeve for a decent fit, which is a cone-shaped section designed to bridge the difference between your small-diameter pipe and the larger-diameter silencer. Try to get a back box designed for your car, but if you go for a universal system measure your standard pipe as accurately as possible, or you'll have problems trying to get a decent seal between the old and new bits.

Fashion has entered the aftermarket exhaust scene, with different rear pipe designs going in and out of style. Everyone's done the upswept twin-pipe "DTM" style pipes, while an emerging trend is simply the "bigger the better" look.

If you've got a small-engined Golf, you might need to lightly modify your rear bodywork to accommodate a bigger rear pipe - Mk 2 models have an easily-removed panel fitted over a cut-out designed for a GTI twin-pipe box.

You will begin to see some useful power gains if you go for the complete performance exhaust system, rather than just the back box. Like the factory-fit system, the sports silencer will only work at its best if combined with the front pipe and, better still, the manifold it was designed for! Many aftermarket systems need careful fitting to stop them resonating or banging away underneath. A sports rear box alone shouldn't attract an increased insurance premium, but a full system could.

Some imported Golfs were fitted with a catalytic converter (or "cat"), and you're no doubt aware that the cat acts like a restrictor in the exhaust, inhibiting the gas flow and sapping some engine power (maybe 5 to 10%). Some companies market replacement systems which do away with the cat (a de-cat pipe), and these will have a useful effect. As all Mk 2 Golfs are pre-January 1993, you won't have to refit the cat when it's MOT time.

Fitting a back box

First we've got to lose some rusty bits. Loosen the rear wheel bolts, then jack up the whole back end of the car, and take off the wheels. Have a look in "Wheels & tyres" for more info on jacking up. The rear hubs must hang free for this, as the back section of the exhaust goes right up over the back suspension, and

01 you won't get it off, otherwise. Loosen off the clamp nuts . . .

02 . . . unhook the mounting rubbers . . .

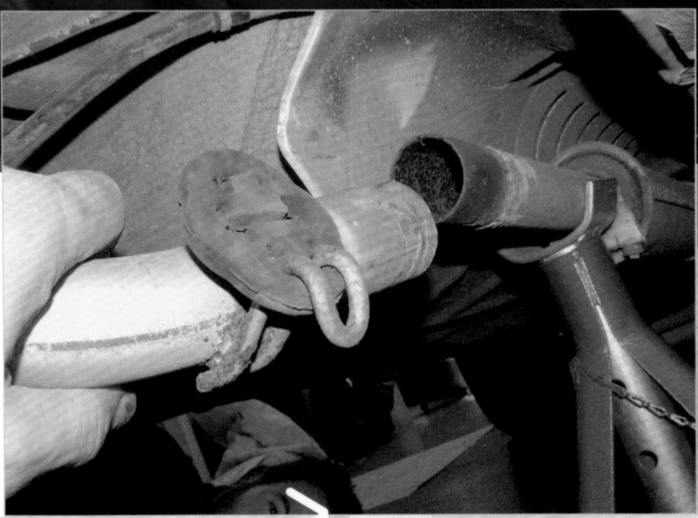

03 . . . and separate the pipes. There's a strong chance that they'll be well stuck together so you may have to resort to large hammers, chisels and plenty of swearing.

Achtung!
Don't be tempted to use a welding torch under the car. You're much too close to the petrol tank.

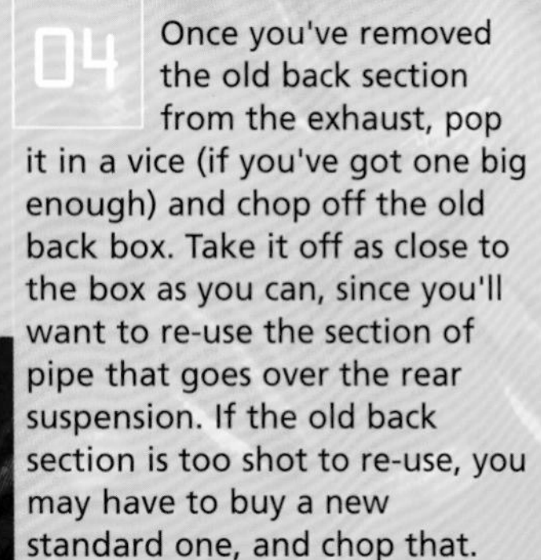

04 Once you've removed the old back section from the exhaust, pop it in a vice (if you've got one big enough) and chop off the old back box. Take it off as close to the box as you can, since you'll want to re-use the section of pipe that goes over the rear suspension. If the old back section is too shot to re-use, you may have to buy a new standard one, and chop that.

05 Our new back box required an extra section of pipe bought from a local motor factor. Refit the freshly-cut pipe back over the rear suspension, and slip it onto the centre section loosely.

06 Now we took off the pipe once more, and welded on the new bit we bought. You may have to get a garage to weld the pipes, using a MIG welder, or in this case with oxy.

07 If your Golf was a non GTI to start with, you'll probably have to chop away part of the rear valance - mark yourself a cut line . . .

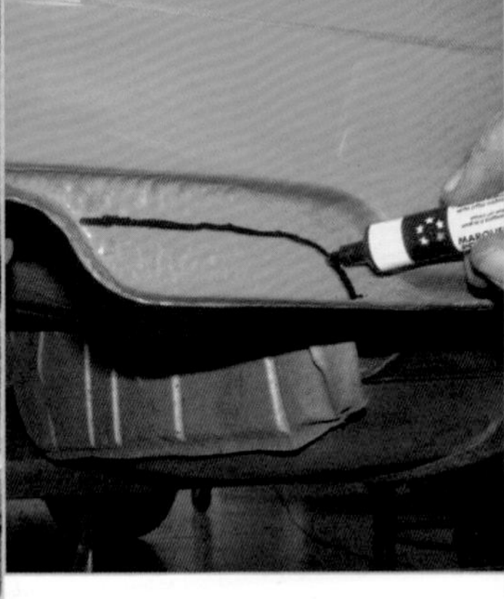

08 . . . then get busy with the hacksaw . . .

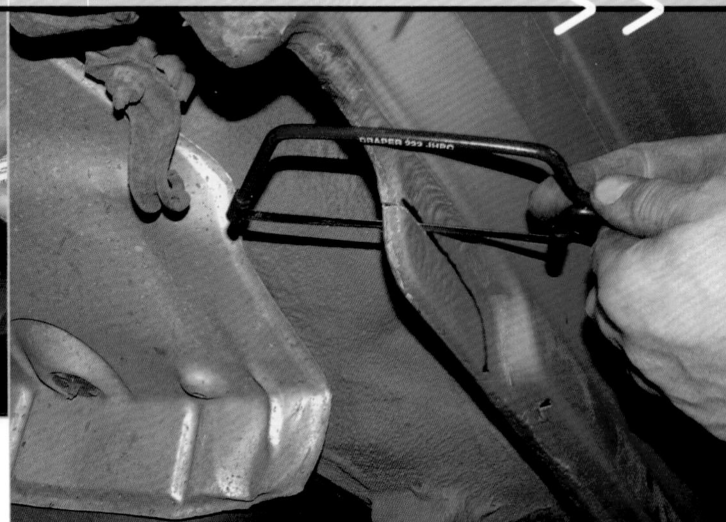

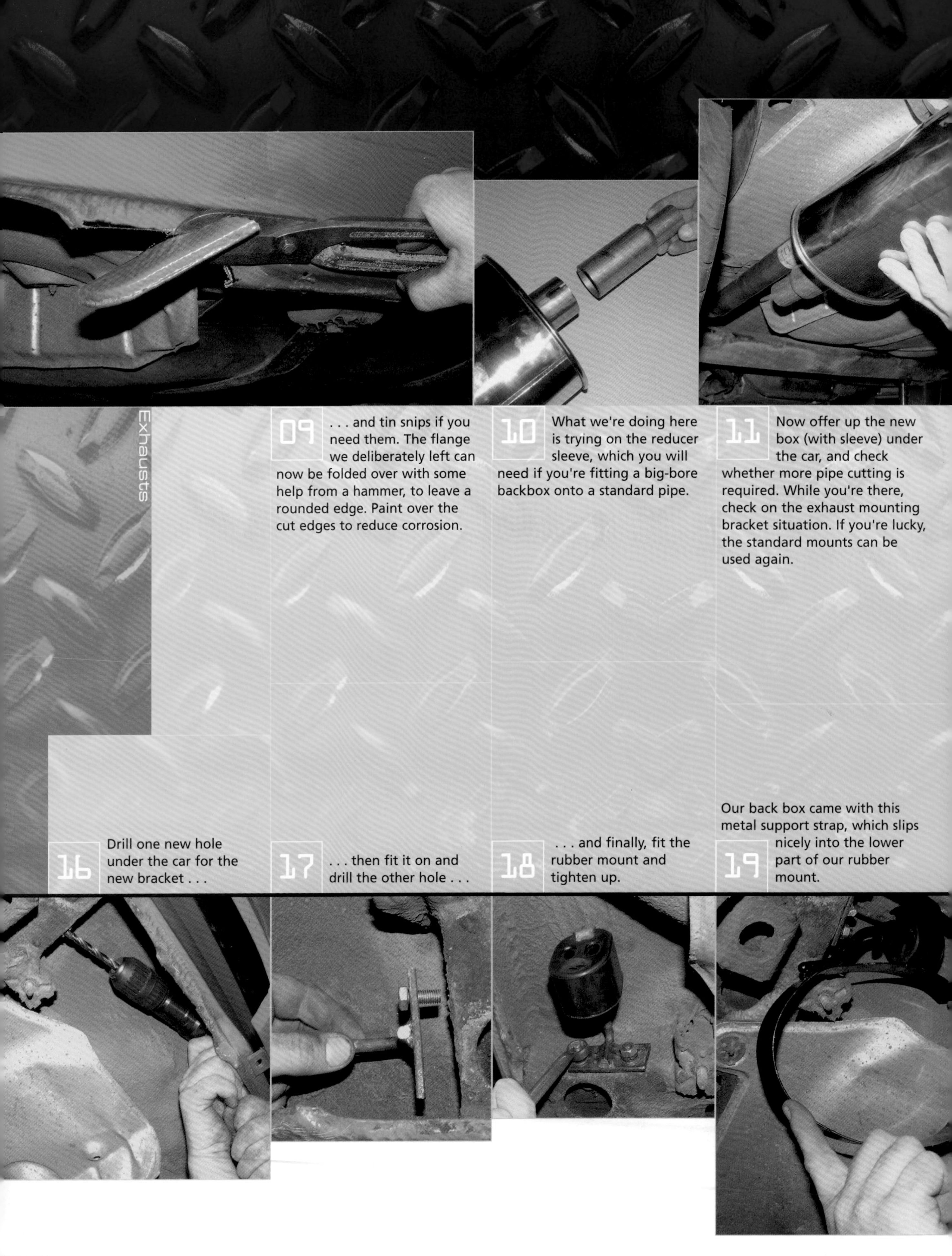

09 . . . and tin snips if you need them. The flange we deliberately left can now be folded over with some help from a hammer, to leave a rounded edge. Paint over the cut edges to reduce corrosion.

10 What we're doing here is trying on the reducer sleeve, which you will need if you're fitting a big-bore backbox onto a standard pipe.

11 Now offer up the new box (with sleeve) under the car, and check whether more pipe cutting is required. While you're there, check on the exhaust mounting bracket situation. If you're lucky, the standard mounts can be used again.

16 Drill one new hole under the car for the new bracket . . .

17 . . . then fit it on and drill the other hole . . .

18 . . . and finally, fit the rubber mount and tighten up.

19 Our back box came with this metal support strap, which slips nicely into the lower part of our rubber mount.

12 If not, take the pipe off again for more length adjustments. Finally, cut two slots in the end of the pipe (where it fits onto the reducing sleeve) to give the exhaust clamp something to do - you won't crush an uncut piece of pipe without risking the joint blowing.

13 If you find your mounting bracket is unuseable unbolt it, and scrap it.

14 You could go to a scrapyard and source the bits from another car's exhaust brackets. We welded a small piece of plate and a hanger from a Ford and . . .

15 . . . came up with this hanger.

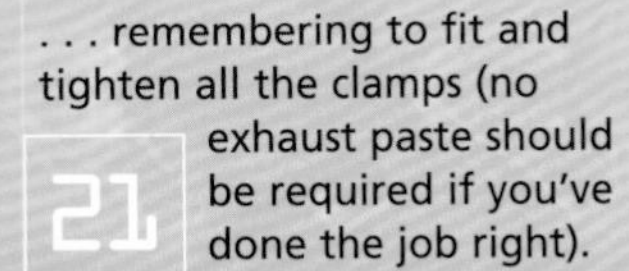

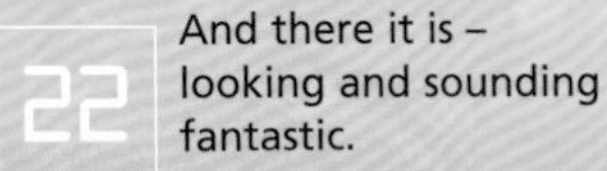

20 And at last! It's on with the box . . .

21 . . . remembering to fit and tighten all the clamps (no exhaust paste should be required if you've done the job right).

22 And there it is – looking and sounding fantastic.

14 Safety and tools

Reference

Safety

We all know that working on your car can be dangerous - and we're not talking about the danger of losing your street cred by fitting naff alloys or furry dice! Okay, so you'd be hard-pushed to injure yourself fitting some cool floor mats or a tax disc holder, but tackle more-serious mods, and you could be treading dangerous ground. Let's be honest - we have to put this safety section in to cover ourselves, but now it's in, it would be nice if you read it...

Burning/scalding

The only way you'll really burn yourself is if your car's just been running - avoid this, and you won't get burned. Easy, eh? Otherwise, you risk burns from any hot parts of the engine (and especially the exhaust - if you've got one, the cat runs very hot), or from spilling hot coolant if you undo the radiator hoses or filler cap, as you might when you're braiding hoses.

Fire

Sadly, there's several ways your car could catch fire, when you think about it. You've got a big tank full of fuel (and other flammable liquids about, like brake fluid), together with electrics - some of which run to very high voltages. If you smoke too, this could be even worse for your health than you thought.

a Liquid fuel is flammable. Fuel vapour can explode - don't smoke, or create any kind of spark, if there's fuel vapour (fuel smell) about.

b Letting fuel spill onto a hot engine is dangerous, but brake fluid spills go up even more readily. Respect is due with brake fluid, which also attacks paintwork and plastics - wash off with water.

c Fires can also be started by careless modding involving the electrical system. It's possible to overload (and overheat) existing wiring by tapping off too many times for new live feeds. Not insulating bare wires or connections can lead to short-circuits, and the sparks or overheated wiring which results can start a fire. Always investigate any newly-wired-in kit which stops working, or which keeps blowing fuses - those wires could already be smouldering...

Crushing

Having your car land on top of you is no laughing matter, and it's a nasty accident waiting to happen if you risk using dodgy old jacks, bricks, and other means of lifting/supporting your car. Please don't.

Your standard vehicle jack is for emergency roadside use only - a proper trolley jack and a set of axle stands won't break the overdraft, and might save broken bones. Don't buy a cheap trolley jack, and don't expect a well-used secondhand one to be perfect, either - when the hydraulic seals start to fail, a trolley jack will drop very fast; this is why you should always have decent stands in place under the car as well.

Steering, suspension & brakes

Screwing up any one of these on your car, through badly-fitted mods, could land you and others in hospital or worse. Nuff said? It's always worth getting a mate, or a friendly garage, to check over what you've just fitted (or even what you've just had fitted, in some cases - not all "pro" fitters are perfect!). Pay attention to tightening vital nuts and bolts properly - buy or borrow a torque wrench.

To be absolutely sure, take your newly-modded machine to a friendly MOT tester (if there is such a thing) - this man's your ultimate authority on safety, after all. Even if he's normally a pain once a year, he could save your life. Think it over.

Even properly-fitted mods can radically alter the car's handling - and not always for the better. Take a few days getting used to how the car feels before showing off.

Wheels

Don't take liberties fitting wheels. Make sure the wheels have the right stud/bolt hole pattern for your car, and that the wheel nuts/bolts are doing their job. Bolts which are too long might catch on your brakes (especially rear drums) - too short, and, well, the wheels are just waiting to fall off. Not nice. Also pay attention to the bolt heads or wheel nuts - some are supposed to have large tapered washers fitted, to locate properly in the wheel. If the nuts/bolts "pull through" the wheel when tightened, the wheel's gonna fall off, isn't it?

Asbestos

Only likely to be a major worry when working on, or near, your brakes. That black dust that gets all over your alloys comes from your brake pads, and it may contain asbestos. Breathing in asbestos dust can lead to a disease called asbestosis (inflammation of the lungs - very nasty indeed), so try not to inhale brake dust when you're changing your pads or discs.

Airbags

Unless you run into something at high speed, the only time an airbag will enter your life is when you change your steering wheel for something more sexy, and have to disable the airbag in the process. Pay attention to all the precautionary advice given in our text, and you'll have no problems.

One more thing - don't tap into the airbag wiring to run any extra electrical kit. Any mods to the airbag circuit could set it off unexpectedly.

Exhaust gases

Even on cars with cats, exhaust fumes are still potentially lethal. Don't work in an unventilated garage with the engine running. When fitting new exhaust bits, be sure that there's no gas leakage from the joints. When modifying in the tailgate area, note that exhaust gas can get sucked into the car through badly-fitting tailgate seals/joints (or even through your rear arches, if they've been trimmed so much there's holes into the car).

Tools

In writing this book, we've assumed you already have a selection of basic tools - screwdrivers, socket set, spanners, hammer, sharp knife, power drill. Any unusual extra tools you might need are mentioned in the relevant text. Torx and Allen screws are often found on trim panels, so a set of keys of each type is a wise purchase.

From a safety angle, always buy the best tools you can afford - or if you must use cheap ones, remember that they can break under stress or unusual usage (and we've all got the busted screwdrivers to prove it!).

DO Wear goggles when using power tools.

DO Keep loose clothing/long hair away from moving engine parts.

DO Take off watches and jewellery when working on electrics.

DO Keep the work area tidy - stops accidents and losing parts.

DON'T Rush a job, or take stupid short-cuts.

DON'T Use the wrong tools for the job, or ones which don't fit.

DON'T Let kids or pets play around your car when you're working.

DON'T Work entirely alone under a car that's been jacked up.

Legal modding? No such thing!!

The harsh & painful truth

The minute you start down the road to a modified motor, you stand a good chance of being in trouble with the Man. It seems like there's almost nothing worthwhile you can do to your car, without breaking some sort of law. So the answer's not to do it at all, then? Well, no, but let's keep it real.

There's this bunch of vehicle-related regulations called Construction & Use. It's a huge set of books, used by the car manufacturers and the Department of Transport among others, and it sets out in black and white all the legal issues that could land you in trouble. It's the ultimate authority for modifying, in theory. But few people (and even fewer policemen) know all of it inside-out, and it's forever being updated and revised, so it's not often enforced to the letter at the roadside - just in court. Despite the existence of C & U, in trying to put together any guide to the law and modifying, it quickly becomes clear that almost everything's a "grey area", with no-one prepared to go on record and say what is okay to modify and what's not. Well, brilliant. So if there's no fixed rules (in the real world), how are you meant to live by them? In the circumstances, all we can promise to do is help to make sense of nonsense...

Avoiding roadside interviews

Why do some people get pulled all the time, and others hardly ever? It's often all about attitude. We'd all like to be free to drive around "in yer face", windows down, system full up, loud exhaust bellowing, sparks striking, tyres squealing - but - nothing is a bigger "come-on" to the boys in blue than "irresponsible" driving like this. Rest assured, if your motor's anywhere near fully sorted, the coppers will find something they can nick you for, when they pull you over - it's a dead cert. Trying not to wind them up too much before this happens (and certainly not once you're stopped) will make for an easier life. There's showing off, and then there's taking the pee. Save it for the next cruise.

The worst thing from your point of view is that, once you've been stopped, it's down to that particular copper's judgement as to whether your car's illegal. If he/she's having a bad day anyway, smart-mouthing-off isn't gonna help your case at all. If you can persuade him/her that you're at least taking on board what's being said, you might be let off with a warning. If it goes further, you'll be reported for an offence - while this doesn't mean you'll end up being prosecuted for it, it ain't good. Some defects (like worn tyres) will result in a so-called "seven-day wonder", which usually means you have to fix whatever's deemed wrong, maybe get the car inspected, and present yourself with the proof at a police station, inside seven days, or face prosecution.

If you can manage to drive reasonably sensibly when the law's about, and can ideally show that you've tried to keep your car legal when you get questioned, you stand a much better chance of enjoying your relationship with your modded beast. This guide is intended to help you steer clear of the more obvious things you could get pulled for. By reading it, you might even be able to have an informed, well-mannered discussion about things legal with the next officer of the law you meet at the side of the road. As in: "Oh really, officer? I was not aware of that. Thank you for pointing it out." Just don't argue with them, that's all...

Documents

The first thing you'll be asked to produce. If you're driving around without tax, MOT or insurance, we might as well stop now, as you won't be doing much more driving of anything after just one pull.

Okay, so you don't normally carry all your car-related documents with you - for safety, you've got them stashed carefully at home, haven't you? But carrying photocopies of your licence, MOT and insurance certificate is a good idea. While they're not legally-binding absolute proof, producing these in a roadside check might mean you don't have to produce the real things at a copshop later in the week. Shows a certain responsibility, and confidence in your own legality on the road, too. In some parts of the country, it's even said to be a good idea to carry copies of any receipts for your stereo gear - if there's any suspicion about it being stolen (surely not), some coppers have been known to confiscate it (or the car it's in) on the spot!

Number plates

One of the simplest mods, and one of the easiest to spot (and prove) if you're a copper. Nowadays, any changes made to the standard approved character font (such as italics or fancy type), spacing, or size of the plate constitutes an offence. Remember too that if you've moved the rear plate from its original spot (like from the tailgate recess, during smoothing) it still has to be properly lit at night. You're unlikely to even buy an illegal plate now, as the companies making them are also liable for prosecution if you get stopped. It's all just something else to blame on speed cameras - plates have to be easy for them to shoot, and modding yours suggests you're trying to escape a speeding conviction (well, who isn't?).

Getting pulled for an illegal plate is for suckers - you're making it too easy for them. While this offence only entails a small fine and confiscation of the plates, you're drawing unwelcome police attention to the rest of your car. Not smart. At all.

Sunstrips and tints

The sunstrip is now an essential item for any modded motor, but telling Mr Plod you had to fit one is no defence if you've gone a bit too far. The sunstrip should not be so low down the screen that it interferes with your ability to see out. Is this obvious? Apparently not. As a guide, if the strip's so low your wiper(s) touch it, it's too low. Don't try fitting short wiper blades to get round this - the police aren't as stupid as that, and you could get done for wipers that don't clear a sufficient area of the screen. Push it so far, and no further!

Window tinting is a trickier area. It seems you can have up to a 25% tint on a windscreen, and up to 30% on all other glass - but how do you measure this? Er. And what do you do if your glass is tinted to start with? Er, probably nothing. Of course you can buy window film in various "darknesses", from not-very-dark to "ambulance-black", but being able to buy it does not make it legal for road use (most companies cover themselves by saying "for show use only"). Go for just a light smoke on the side and rear glass, and you'd have to be unlucky to get done for it. If you must fit really dark tints, you're safest doing the rear side windows only.

Some forces now have a light meter to test light transmission through glass at the roadside - fail this, and it's a big on-the-spot fine.

Single wiper conversion

Not usually a problem, and certainly not worth a pull on its own, but combine a big sunstrip with a short wiper blade, and you're just asking for trouble. Insufficient view of the road ahead. There's also the question of whether it's legal to have the arm parking vertically, in the centre of the screen, as it obscures your vision. Probably not legal, then - even if it looks cool. Unfortunately, the Man doesn't do cool.

Lights

Lights of all kinds have to be one of the single biggest problem areas in modifying, and the police are depressingly well-informed. Most people make light mods a priority, whether it's Morette conversions for headlights or Lexus-style rear clusters. If they fit alright, and work, what's the problem?

First off, don't bother with any lights which aren't fully UK-legal - it's just too much hassle. Being "E-marked" only makes them legal in Europe, and most of our Euro-chums drive on the right. One of our project cars ended up with left-hand-drive rear clusters, and as a result, had no rear reflectors and a rear foglight on the wrong side (should be on the right). Getting stopped for not having rear reflectors would be a bit harsh, but why risk it, even to save a few quid?

Once you've had any headlight mods done (other than light brows) always have the beam alignment checked - it's part of the MOT, after all. The same applies to any front fogs or spots you've fitted (the various points of law involved here are too many to mention - light colour, height, spacing, operation with main/dipped headlights - ask at an MOT centre before fitting, and have them checked out after fitting).

If Plod's really having a bad day, he might even question the legality of your new blue headlight bulbs - are they too powerful? Keeping the bulb packaging in the glovebox might be a neat solution here (60/55W max).

Many modders favour spraying rear light clusters to make them look trick, as opposed to replacing them - but there's trouble in store here, too. One of the greyest of grey areas is - how much light tinting is too much? The much-talked-about but not-often-seen "common sense" comes into play here. Making your lights so dim that they're reduced to a feeble red/orange glow is pretty dim itself. If you're spraying, only use proper light-tinting spray, and not too many coats of that. Colour-coding lights with ordinary spray paint is best left to a pro sprayer or bodyshop (it can be done by mixing lots of lacquer with not much paint, for instance). Tinted lights are actually more of a problem in daylight than at night, so check yours while the sun's out.

Lastly, two words about neons. Oh, dear. It seems that neons of all kinds have now been deemed illegal for road use (and that's

interior ones as well as exteriors, which have pretty much always been a no-no). If you fit neons inside, make sure you rig in a switch so you can easily turn them off when the law arrives - or don't drive around with them on (save it for when you're parked up). Distracts other road users, apparently.

ICE

Jungle massive, or massive public nuisance? The two sides of the ICE argument in a nutshell. If you've been around the modding scene for any length of time, you'll already know stories of people who've been done for playing car stereos too loud. Seems some local authorities now have by-laws concerning "music audible from outside a vehicle", and hefty fines if you're caught. Even where this isn't the case, and assuming a dB meter isn't on hand to prove the offence of "excessive noise", the police can still prosecute for "disturbing the peace" - on the basis of one officer's judgement of the noise level. If a case is proved, you could lose your gear. Whoops. Seems we're back to "do it - but don't over-do it" again. If you really want to demo your system, pick somewhere a bit less public (like a quiet trading estate, after dark) or go for safety in numbers (at a cruise).

Big alloys/tyres

One of the first things to go on any lad's car, sexy alloys are right at the heart of car modifying. So what'll interest the law?

Well, the first thing every copper's going to wonder is - are the wheels nicked? He'd need a good reason to accuse you, but this is another instance where having copies of receipts might prove useful.

Otherwise, the wheels mustn't rub on, or stick out from, the arches - either of these will prove to be a problem if you get stopped. And you don't need to drive a modded motor to get done for having bald tyres...

Lowered suspension

Of course you have to lower your car, to have any hope of street cred. But did you know it's actually an offence to cause damage to the road surface, if your car's so low (or your mates so lardy) that it grounds out? Apparently so! Never mind what damage it might be doing to your exhaust, or the brake/fuel lines under the car - you can actually get done for risking damage to the road. Well, great. What's the answer? Once you've lowered the car, load it up with your biggest mates, and test it over roads you normally use - or else find a route into town that avoids all speed bumps. If you've got coilovers, you'll have an easier time tuning out the scraping noises.

Remember that your new big-bore exhaust or backbox must be hung up well enough that it doesn't hit the deck, even if you haven't absolutely slammed your car on the floor. At night, leaving a trail of sparks behind is a bit of a giveaway...

Exhausts

One of the easiest-to-fit performance upgrades, and another essential item if you want to be taken seriously on the street. Unless your chosen pipe/system is just too damn loud, you'd be very unlucky to get stopped for it, but if you will draw attention this way, you could be kicking yourself later.

For instance - have you in fact fitted a home-made straight-through pipe, to a car which used to have a "cat"? By drawing Plod's attention with that extra-loud system, he could then ask you to get the car's emissions tested - worse, you could get pulled for a "random" roadside emissions check. Fail this (and you surely will), and you could be right in the brown stuff. Even if you re-convert the car back to stock for the MOT, you'll be illegal on the road (and therefore without insurance) whenever your loud pipe's on. Still sound like fun, or would you be happier with just a back box?

It's also worth mentioning that your tailpipe mustn't stick out beyond the very back of the car, or in any other way which might be dangerous to pedestrians. Come on - you were a ped once!

Bodykits

We've all seen Novas and Corsas with Combat kits, and Dimma kits on Peugeots - the popular ones for the UK market have all passed the relevant tests, and are fully-approved for use on the specific vehicles they're intended for. As long as you haven't messed up fitting a standard kit, you should be fine, legally-speaking. The trouble starts when you do your own little mods and tweaks, such as bodging on that huge whale-tail spoiler or front air dam/splitter - it can be argued in some cases that these aren't appropriate on safety grounds, and you can get prosecuted. If any bodywork is fitted so it obscured your lights, or so badly attached that a strong breeze might blow it off, you can see their point. At least there's no such thing as Style Police. Not yet, anyway.

Seats and harnesses

Have to meet the UK safety standards, and must be securely bolted in. That's about it. It should be possible to fasten and release any seat belt or harness with one hand. Given that seat belts are pretty important safety features, it's understandable then that the police don't like to see flimsy alloy rear strut braces used as seat harness mounting points. Any other signs of bodging will also spell trouble. It's unlikely they'd bother with a full safety inspection at the roadside, but they could insist on a full MOT test/engineer's report inside 7 days. It's your life.

While we're on the subject of crash safety, the police also don't like to see sub boxes and amps just lying on the carpet, where the back seat used to be - if it's not anchored down, where are these items gonna end up, in a big shunt? Embedded in you, possibly?

Other mods

We'll never cover everything else here, and the law's always changing anyway, so we're fighting a losing battle in a book like this, but here goes with some other legalistic points we've noted on the way:

a It's illegal to remove side repeaters from front wings, unless they're "replaced" with Merc-style side repeater mirrors. Nice.

b All except the most prehistoric cars must have at least one rear foglight. If there's only one, it must be fitted on the right. We've never heard of anyone getting stopped for it, but you must also have a pair of rear reflectors. If your rear clusters ain't got 'em, can you get trendy ones? Er, no.

c Fuel filler caps have to be fitted so there's no danger of fuel spillage, or of excess fumes leaking from the top of the filler neck. This means using an appropriate petrol-resistant sealer (should be supplied in the kit). Oh, and not bodging the job in general seems a good idea. Unlikely to attract a pull, though.

d Front doors have to retain a manual means of opening from outside, even if they've been de-locked for remote locking. This means you can't take off the front door handles, usually. It seems that rear door handles can be removed if you like.

e Tailgates have to have some means of opening, even if it's only from inside, once the lock/handle's been removed. We think it's another safety thing - means of escape in a crash, and all that.

f You have to have at least one exterior mirror, and it must be capable of being adjusted somehow.

g If you fit new fog and spotlights, they actually have to work. No-one fits new lights just for show (or do they?), but if they stop working later when a fuse blows, relay packs up, or the wiring connectors rust up, you'd better fix 'em or remove 'em.

h Pedal extensions must have rubbers fitted on the brake and clutch pedals, and must be spaced sufficiently so there's no chance of hitting two pedals at once. This last bit sounds obvious, but lots of extension sets out there are so hard to fit that achieving this can be rather difficult. Don't get caught out.

i On cars with airbags, if you fit a sports wheel and disconnect the airbag in the process, the airbag warning light will be on permanently. Apart from being annoying, this is also illegal.

j Pace-car strobe lights (or any other flashing lights, apart from indicators) are illegal for road use. Of course.

k Anything else we didn't think of - is probably illegal too. Sorry.

Any questions? Try the MOT Helpline (0845 6005977). Yes, really.

Thanks to Andrew Dare of the Vehicle Inspectorate, Exeter, for his help in steering us through this minefield!

Thanks to:

We gratefully acknowledge all the help and advice offered from the following suppliers, without whom, etc, etc. Many of those credited below went way beyond the call of duty to help us produce this book - you know who you are. Cheers, guys! Roll the credits...

ABC Design Autostyling Ltd
www.abcdesignltd.com

Alpine
01908 611556

Audioscape
01473 327510

Auto Acoustics
01932 849211

Autoleads
01420 476767

Automobile Sportique
0707 457 0725

BBG
0208 863 9117

Brown & Geeson Distribution Ltd (Momo)
01268 764411

C & R Enterprises
0115 978 5740

Corbeau Seats Ltd
01424 854499

CT Autoparts
08000 283 284

Demon Tweeks
01978 663000

Eurostyling (Folia tec)
0208 987 5519

Gamepath Ltd
01908 317707

German Car Company
01702 530440

Halfords
08457 626 625

K & N Filters
01925 636950

LA & RW Piper
(upholstery and re-trimming)
01963 441431

Larkspeed
08707 440101

Mécatechnic
www.mecatechnic.com

Path Group
01844 219000

Performance Parts Direct
01252 517272

Performance Products Ltd
01244 321300

Pioneer GB Ltd
01753 789700

R & A Design
01472 811711

Rage Products
01462 851956

RAID
01664 823792

Red Dot Racing Ltd
020 8888 2354

Richbrook
0208 543 7111

Ripspeed at Halfords
0845 609 1259

Savage, Trillogy
01280 822865

Sony
01932 816532

SPAX
01869 244771

Toyo Tyres
01933 411144

Venom Motorsport
01254 814444

Wolfrace Wheels
01621 859020

A special thankyou to:
Brodie Baxter
Kim Baxter
Neil Birkitt of *Volkswagen Driver* magazine (photos)
Andy Butler (ICE words)
Zoë Harrison (ICE pics)
Jon Hill (cover shots)
Ellen and Alan Larkin
Stewart Smith

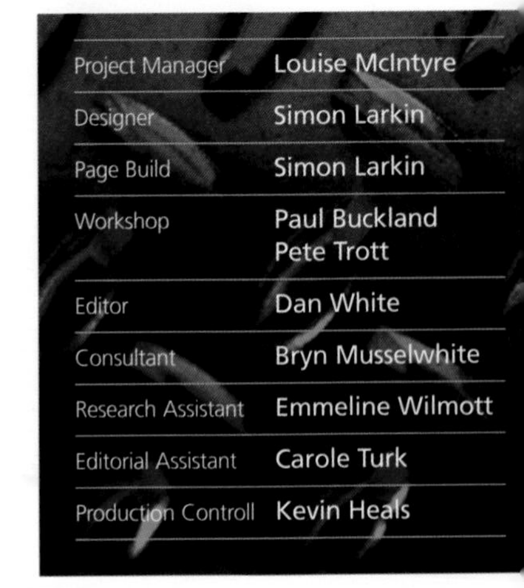

Project Manager	Louise McIntyre
Designer	Simon Larkin
Page Build	Simon Larkin
Workshop	Paul Buckland Pete Trott
Editor	Dan White
Consultant	Bryn Musselwhite
Research Assistant	Emmeline Wilmott
Editorial Assistant	Carole Turk
Production Controll	Kevin Heals

Would you call an electrician to change a lightbulb?

Haynes

So why take your car to a garage for the simplest bulb replacement or service?

With a **Haynes manual** telling and showing you everything you need to know **for less than the cost of 30 minutes of a garage mechanic's time*, what have you got to lose?** Haynes manuals are available from all good car accessory retailers and bookshops. For further information or to find your nearest stockist, call **01963 442030** or visit **www.haynes.co.uk**

Full listing over page ▶

*Average garage labour rate now **£40** per hour. Source: **Retail Motor Industries Federation**

Haynes Car Manuals

Alfa Romeo Alfasud/Sprint (74 - 88 0292
Alfa Romeo Alfetta (73 - 87 0531
Audi 80, 90 (79 - Oct 86 & Coupe (81 - Nov 88 0605
Audi 80, 90 (Oct 86 - 90 & Coupe (Nov 88 - 90) 1491
Audi 100 (Oct 82 - 90 & 200 (Feb 84 - Oct 89) 0907
Audi 100 & A6 Petrol & Diesel (May 91 - May 97) 3504
Audi A4 (95 - Feb 00 3575
Austin A35 & A40 (56 - 67) * 0118
Austin Allegro 1100, 1300, 1.0, 1.1 & 1.3 (73 - 82) * 0164
Austin/MG/Rover Maestro 1.3 & 1.6 (83 - 95) 0922
Austin/MG Metro (80 - May 90) 0718
Austin/Rover Montego 1.3 & 1.6 (84 - 94) 1066
Austin/MG/Rover Montego 2.0 (84 - 95) 1067
Mini (59 - 69) 0527
Mini (69 - 01) 0646
Austin/Rover 2.0 litre Diesel Engine (86 - 93) 1857
Austin Healey 100/6 & 3000 (56 - 68) * 0049
Bedford CF (69 - 87) 0163
Bedford/Vauxhall Rascal & Suzuki Supercarry (86 - Oct 94) 3015
BMW 316, 320 & 320i (4-cyl) (75 - Feb 83) 0276
BMW 320, 320i, 323i & 325i (6-cyl) (Oct 77 - Sept 87) 0815
BMW 3-Series (Apr 91 - 96) 3210
BMW 3- & 5-Series (sohc) (81 - 91) 1948
BMW 520i & 525e (Oct 81 - June 88) 1560
BMW 1500, 1502, 1600, 1602, 2000 & 2002 (59 - 77) * 0240
Chrysler PT Cruiser (00 - 03) 4058
Citroën 2CV, Ami & Dyane (67 - 90) 0196
Citroën AX Petrol & Diesel (87 - 97) 3014
Citroën BX (83 - 94) A to L 0908
Citroën C15 Van Petrol & Diesel (89 - Oct 98) 3509
Citroën CX (75 - 88) 0528
Citroën Saxo Petrol & Diesel (96 - 01) 3506
Citroën Visa (79 - 88) 0620
Citroën Xantia Petrol & Diesel (93 - 98) 3082
Citroën XM Petrol & Diesel (89 - 00) 3451
Citroën Xsara Petrol & Diesel (97 - Sept 00) 3751
Citroën Xsara Picasso Petrol & Diesel (00 - 02) 3944
Citroën ZX Diesel (91 - 98) 1922
Citroën ZX Petrol (91 - 98) 1881
Citroën 1.7 & 1.9 litre Diesel Engine (84 - 96) 1379
Fiat 126 (73 - 87) * 0305
Fiat 500 (57 - 73) 0090
Fiat Bravo & Brava (95 - 00) 3572
Fiat Cinquecento (93 - 98) 3501
Fiat Panda (81 - 95) 0793
Fiat Punto Petrol & Diesel (94 - Oct 99) 3251
Fiat Regata (84 - 88) 1167
Fiat Tipo (88 - 91) 1625
Fiat Uno (83 - 95) 0923
Fiat X1/9 (74 - 89) 0273
Ford Anglia (59 - 68) * 0001
Ford Capri II (& III) 1.6 & 2.0 (74 - 87) 0283
Ford Capri II (& III) 2.8 & 3.0 (74 - 87) 1309
Ford Cortina Mk III 1300 & 1600 (70 - 76) * 0070
Ford Cortina Mk IV (& V) 1.6 & 2.0 (76 - 83) * 0343
Ford Cortina Mk IV (& V) 2.3 V6 (77 - 83) * 0426
Ford Escort Mk I 1100 & 1300 (68 - 74) * 0171
Ford Escort Mk I Mexico, RS 1600 & RS 2000 (70 - 74) * 0139
Ford Escort Mk II Mexico, RS 1800 & RS 2000 (75 - 80) * 0735
Ford Escort (75 - Aug 80) * 0280
Ford Escort (Sept 80 - Sept 90) 0686
Ford Escort & Orion (Sept 90 - 00) 1737
Ford Fiesta (76 - Aug 83) 0334
Ford Fiesta (Aug 83 - Feb 89) 1030
Ford Fiesta (Feb 89 - Oct 95) 1595
Ford Fiesta (Oct 95 - 01) 3397
Ford Focus (98 - 01) 3759
Ford Galaxy Petrol & Diesel (95 - Aug 00) 3984
Ford Granada (Sept 77 - Feb 85) 0481
Ford Granada & Scorpio (Mar 85 - 94) 1245
Ford Ka (96 - 02) 3570
Ford Mondeo Petrol (93 - 99) 1923
Ford Mondeo Diesel (93 - 96) 3465
Ford Orion (83 - Sept 90) 1009
Ford Sierra 4 cyl. (82 - 93) 0903
Ford Sierra V6 (82 - 91) 0904
Ford Transit Petrol (Mk 2) (78 - Jan 86) 0719
Ford Transit Petrol (Mk 3) (Feb 86 - 89) 1468
Ford Transit Diesel (Feb 86 - 99) 3019
Ford 1.6 & 1.8 litre Diesel Engine (84 - 96) 1172
Ford 2.1, 2.3 & 2.5 litre Diesel Engine (77 - 90) 1606
Freight Rover Sherpa (74 - 87) 0463
Hillman Avenger (70 - 82) 0037
Hillman Imp (63 - 76) * 0022
Honda Accord (76 - Feb 84) 0351
Honda Civic (Feb 84 - Oct 87) 1226
Honda Civic (Nov 91 - 96) 3199
Hyundai Pony (85 - 94) 3398
Jaguar E Type (61 - 72) 0140
Jaguar MkI & II, 240 & 340 (55 - 69) * 0098
Jaguar XJ6, XJ & Sovereign; Daimler Sovereign (68 - Oct 86) 0242
Jaguar XJ6 & Sovereign (Oct 86 - Sept 94) 3261
Jaguar XJ12, XJS & Sovereign; Daimler Double Six (72 - 88) 0478
Jeep Cherokee Petrol (93 - 96)

Lada 1200, 1300, 1500 & 1600 (74 - 91) 0413
Lada Samara (87 - 91) 1610
Land Rover 90, 110 & Defender Diesel (83 - 95) 3017
Land Rover Discovery Petrol & Diesel (89 - 98) 3016
Land Rover Freelander (97 - 02) 3929
Land Rover Series IIA & III Diesel (58 - 85) 0529
Land Rover Series II, IIA & III Petrol (58 - 85) 0314
Mazda 323 (Mar 81 - Oct 89) 1608
Mazda 323 (Oct 89 - 98) 3455
Mazda 626 (May 83 - Sept 87) 0929
Mazda B-1600, B-1800 & B-2000 Pick-up (72 - 88) 0267
Mazda RX-7 (79 - 85) * 0460
Mercedes-Benz 190, 190E & 190D Petrol & Diesel (83 - 93) 3450
Mercedes-Benz 200, 240, 300 Diesel (Oct 76 - 85) 1114
Mercedes-Benz 250 & 280 (68 - 72) 0346
Mercedes-Benz 250 & 280 (123 Series) (Oct 76 - 84) 0677
Mercedes-Benz 124 Series (85 - Aug 93) 3253
Mercedes-Benz C-Class Petrol & Diesel (93 - Aug 00) 3511
MGA (55 - 62) * 0475
MGB (62 - 80) 0111
MG Midget & AH Sprite (58 - 80) 0265
Mitsubishi Shogun & L200 Pick-Ups (83 - 94) 1944
Morris Ital 1.3 (80 - 84) 0705
Morris Minor 1000 (56 - 71) 0024
Nissan Bluebird (May 84 - Mar 86) 1223
Nissan Bluebird (Mar 86 - 90) 1473
Nissan Cherry (Sept 82 - 86) 1031
Nissan Micra (83 - Jan 93) 0931
Nissan Micra (93 - 99) 3254
Nissan Primera (90 - Aug 99) 1851
Nissan Stanza (82 - 86) 0824
Nissan Sunny (May 82 - Oct 86) 0895
Nissan Sunny (Oct 86 - Mar 91) 1378
Nissan Sunny (Apr 91 - 95) 3219
Opel Ascona & Manta (B Series) (Sept 75 - 88) 0316
Opel Kadett (Nov 79 - Oct 84) 0634
Opel Rekord (Feb 78 - Oct 86) 0543
Peugeot 106 Petrol & Diesel (91 - 02) 1882
Peugeot 205 Petrol (83 - 97) 0932
Peugeot 206 Petrol and Diesel (98 - 01) 3757
Peugeot 305 (78 - 89)* 0538
Peugeot 306 Petrol & Diesel (93 - 99) 3073
Peugeot 309 (86 - 93) 1266
Peugeot 405 Petrol (88 - 97) 1559
Peugeot 405 Diesel (88 - 97) 3198
Peugeot 406 Petrol & Diesel (96 - 97) 3394
Peugeot 406 Petrol & Diesel (99 - 02) 3982
Peugeot 505 (79 - 89) 0762
Peugeot 1.7/1.8 & 1.9 litre Diesel Engine (82 - 96) 0950
Peugeot 2.0, 2.1, 2.3 & 2.5 litre Diesel Engines (74 - 90) 1607
Porsche 911 (65 - 85) 0264
Porsche 924 & 924 Turbo (76 - 85) 0397
Proton (89 - 97) 3255
Range Rover V8 (70 - Oct 92) 0606
Reliant Robin & Kitten (73 - 83) 0436
Renault 4 (61 - 86) * 0072
Renault 5 (Feb 85 - 96) 1219
Renault 9 & 11 (82 - 89) 0822
Renault 18 (79 - 86) 0598
Renault 19 Petrol (89 - 94) 1646
Renault 19 Diesel (89 - 96) 1946
Renault 21 (86 - 94) 1397
Renault 25 (84 - 92) 1228
Renault Clio Petrol (91 - May 98) 1853
Renault Clio Diesel (91 - June 96) 3031
Renault Clio Petrol & Diesel (May 98 - May 01) 3906
Renault Espace Petrol & Diesel (85 - 96) 3197
Renault Fuego (80 - 86) * 0764
Renault Laguna Petrol & Diesel (94 - 00) 3252
Renault Mégane & Scénic Petrol & Diesel (96 - 98) 3395
Renault Mégane & Scénic Petrol & Diesel (Apr 99 - 02) 3916
Rover 213 & 216 (84 - 89) 1116
Rover 214 & 414 (89 - 96) 1689
Rover 216 & 416 (89 - 96) 1830
Rover 211, 214, 216, 218 & 220 Petrol & Diesel (Dec 95 - 98) 3399
Rover 414, 416 & 420 Petrol & Diesel (May 95 - 98) 3453
Rover 618, 620 & 623 (93 - 97) 3257
Rover 820, 825 & 827 (86 - 95) 1380
Rover 3500 (76 - 87) 0365
Rover Metro, 111 & 114 (May 90 - 98) 1711
Saab 95 & 96 (66 - 76) * 0198
Saab 99 (69 - 79) * 0247
Saab 90, 99 & 900 (79 - Oct 93) 0765
Saab 900 (Oct 93 - 98) 3512
Saab 9000 (4-cyl) (85 - 98) 1686
Seat Ibiza & Cordoba Petrol & Diesel (Oct 93 - Oct 99) 3571
Seat Ibiza & Malaga (85 - 92) 1609
Skoda Estelle (77 - 89) 0604
Skoda Favorit (89 - 96) 1801
Skoda Felicia Petrol & Diesel (95 - 01) 3505
Subaru 1600 & 1800 (Nov 79 - 90)

Sunbeam Alpine, Rapier & H120 (67 - 76) * 0051
Suzuki Supercarry & Bedford/Vauxhall Rascal (86 - Oct 94) 3015
Suzuki SJ Series, Samurai & Vitara (4-cyl) (82 - 97) 1942
Talbot Alpine, Solara, Minx & Rapier (75 - 86) 0337
Talbot Horizon (78 - 86) 0473
Talbot Samba (82 - 86) 0823
Toyota Carina E (May 92 - 97) 3256
Toyota Corolla (Sept 83 - Sept 87) 1024
Toyota Corolla (80 - 85) 0683
Toyota Corolla (Sept 87 - Aug 92) 1683
Toyota Corolla (Aug 92 - 97) 3259
Toyota Hi-Ace & Hi-Lux (69 - Oct 83) 0304
Triumph Acclaim (81 - 84) * 0792
Triumph GT6 & Vitesse (62 - 74) * 0112
Triumph Herald (59 - 71) * 0010
Triumph Spitfire (62 - 81) 0113
Triumph Stag (70 - 78) 0441
Triumph TR2, TR3, TR3A, TR4 & TR4A (52 - 67) * 0028
Triumph TR5 & 6 (67 - 75) * 0031
Triumph TR7 (75 - 82) * 0322
Vauxhall Astra (80 - Oct 84) 0635
Vauxhall Astra & Belmont (Oct 84 - Oct 91) 1136
Vauxhall Astra (Oct 91 - Feb 98) 1832
Vauxhall/Opel Astra & Zafira Diesel (Feb 98 - Sept 00) 3797
Vauxhall/Opel Astra & Zafira Petrol (Feb 98 - Sept 00) 3758
Vauxhall/Opel Calibra (90 - 98) 3502
Vauxhall Carlton (Oct 78 - Oct 86) 0480
Vauxhall Carlton & Senator (Nov 86 - 94) 1469
Vauxhall Cavalier 1300 (77 - July 81) * 0461
Vauxhall Cavalier 1600, 1900 & 2000 (75 - July 81) 0315
Vauxhall Cavalier (81 - Oct 88) 0812
Vauxhall Cavalier (Oct 88 - 95) 1570
Vauxhall Chevette (75 - 84) 0285
Vauxhall Corsa (Mar 93 - 97) 1985
Vauxhall/Opel Corsa (Apr 97 - Oct 00) 3921
Vauxhall/Opel Frontera Petrol & Diesel (91 - Sept 98) 3454
Vauxhall Nova (83 - 93) 0909
Vauxhall/Opel Omega (94 - 99) 3510
Vauxhall Vectra Petrol & Diesel (95 - 98) 3396
Vauxhall/Opel Vectra (Mar 99 - May 02) 3930
Vauxhall/Opel 1.5, 1.6 & 1.7 litre Diesel Engine (82 - 96) 1222
Volkswagen 411 & 412 (68 - 75) * 0091
Volkswagen Beetle 1200 (54 - 77) 0036
Volkswagen Beetle 1300 & 1500 (65 - 75) 0039
Volkswagen Beetle 1302 & 1302S (70 - 72) 0110
Volkswagen Beetle 1303, 1303S & GT (72 - 75) 0159
Volkswagen Beetle Petrol & Diesel (Apr 99 - 01) 3798
Volkswagen Golf & Bora Petrol & Diesel (April 98 - 00) 3727
Volkswagen Golf & Jetta Mk 1 1.1 & 1.3 (74 - 84) 0716
Volkswagen Golf, Jetta & Scirocco Mk 1 1.5, 1.6 & 1.8 (74 - 84) 0726
Volkswagen Golf & Jetta Mk 1 Diesel (78 - 84) 0451
Volkswagen Golf & Jetta Mk 2 (Mar 84 - Feb 92) 1081
Volkswagen Golf & Vento Petrol & Diesel (Feb 92 - 96) 3097
Volkswagen LT vans & light trucks (76 - 87) 0637
Volkswagen Passat & Santana (Sept 81 - May 88) 0814
Volkswagen Passat Petrol & Diesel (May 88 - 96) 3498
Volkswagen Passat 4-cyl Petrol & Diesel (Dec 96 - Nov 00) 3917
Volkswagen Polo & Derby (76 - Jan 82) 0335
Volkswagen Polo (82 - Oct 90) 0813
Volkswagen Polo (Nov 90 - Aug 94) 3245
Volkswagen Polo Hatchback Petrol & Diesel (94 - 99) 3500
Volkswagen Scirocco (82 - 90) 1224
Volkswagen Transporter 1600 (68 - 79) 0082
Volkswagen Transporter 1700, 1800 & 2000 (72 - 79) 0226
Volkswagen Transporter (air-cooled) (79 - 82) 0638
Volkswagen Transporter (water-cooled) (82 - 90) 3452
Volkswagen Type 3 (63 - 73) * 0084
Volvo 120 & 130 Series (& P1800) (61 - 73) * 97010
Volvo 142, 144 & 145 (66 - 74) 0129
Volvo 240 Series (74 - 93) 0270
Volvo 262, 264 & 260/265 (75 - 85) * 0400
Volvo 340, 343, 345 & 360 (76 - 91) 0715
Volvo 440, 460 & 480 (87 - 97) 1691
Volvo 740 & 760 (82 - 91) 1258
Volvo 850 (92 - 96) 3260
Volvo 940 (90 - 96) 3249
Volvo S40 & V40 (96 - 99) 3569
Volvo S70, V70 & C70 (96 - 99) 3573

* = Classic Reprints

Haynes Manuals

Haynes Car Service and Repair Manuals are available from car accessory retailers.
For further information or to find your nearest stockist, call **01963 442030** or visit **www.haynes.co.uk**